Praying with Saint Luke's Gospel

Daily Reflections on the Gospel of Saint Luke

Edited by Father Peter John Cameron, O.P.

MAGNIFICAT®

Publisher: **Pierre-Marie Dumont**
Editor-in-Chief: **Peter John Cameron**, O.P.
Senior Editor: **Romanus Cessario**, O.P.
Managing Editor: **Catherine Kolpak**
Editorial Assistant: **Andrew Matt**
Administrative Assistant: **Nora Macagnone**
Senior Managing Editor: **Frédérique Chatain**
Editorial Coordinator & Permissions: **Diaga Seck-Rauch**
Iconography: **Isabelle Mascaras**
Cover Design: **Solange Bosdevesy**
Translator: **Janet Chevrier**
Proofreaders: **Andrew Matt, et al.**
Production: **Sabine Marioni**

Contributors: **Father Timothy Bellamah**, O.P., **Douglas Bushman,**
Father Gary C. Caster, Father John Dominic Corbett, O.P.,
Father Lawrence Donohoo, Anthony Esolen, J. David Franks,
Father Michael Gaudoin-Parker, Father Anthony Giambrone, O.P.,
Frances Hogan, Father William Joensen, Heather King,
Father Joseph T. Lienhard, S.J., **Monsignor Gregory E. S. Malovetz,**
Father Francis Martin, Regis Martin, Father Fidelis Moscinski, C.F.R.,
Father Vincent Nagle, F.S.C.B., **Father George Rutler,**
Father Richard G. Smith, Father James M. Sullivan, O.P.,
Father Albert Trudel, O.P., **Father Richard Veras,**
Father Emmerich Vogt, O.P.

Cover: *Saint Luke*, Valentin de Boulogne (1591-1632), Versailles and Trianon Castles, Versailles, France. © RMN-GP (Château de Versailles) / Daniel Arnaudet / Jean Schormans.

Edition number: MGN 12005

ISBN: 978-1-936260-41-6

Foreword

Father Peter John Cameron, O.P.

A t the center of the Gospel of Luke stands arguably the world's most famous parable: the parable of the prodigal son—a parable told only by the Evangelist Saint Luke. Perhaps the most shocking thing about this progressively shocking parable is that, upon welcoming his wayward son home, the father commands his servants, "Quickly bring the finest robe and put it on him" (Lk 15:22). Not only does the father receive the boy back with unconditional compassion, but he elevates him, investing him with a dignity and authority identical to his own. A servant busy about his duties on the estate glancing quickly might mistake the prodigal for the master.

Christ's clothing

The significance of the prodigal's "finest robe" appears when viewed against the role Christ's clothes play in Luke. After the birth of Jesus, the Blessed Virgin Mary "wrapped him in swaddling clothes" (Lk 2:7). When the angel of the Lord appeared to the shepherds and announced, "Today in the city of David a savior has been born for you who is Messiah and Lord," he also provides the shepherds with a sign by which to recognize Jesus when they go to see him: "This will be a sign for you: you will find an infant wrapped in swaddling clothes" (Lk 2:11-12).

What gives the hemorrhaging woman the chutzpah to draw close to Christ so as to "steal" a healing is that he is wearing a cloak trimmed with fringe easy anonymously to touch (Lk 8:44). What emblazons the event of the Transfiguration on the minds of the disciples who witnessed it is the fact that Jesus' "clothing became dazzling white" (Lk 9:29)—a foreshadowing of the glory that will array the risen Lord. How startling it must have been for those same disciples if they managed to glimpse their captured Master as he went from Herod's court to Pontius

Pilate. For after Herod and his soldiers treated Jesus "contemptuously and mocked him," they clothed him "in resplendent garb" (Lk 23:11)—garb alarmingly alike that of the transfigured Christ.

What fills Peter with expectant amazement on Easter morning as he stoops down to peer into Christ's empty tomb is that he "saw the burial cloths alone" (Lk 24:12). What hope just the clothing of Jesus Christ generates!

The need for salvation

The Evangelist Luke likes to reference clothing in order to "expose" our need for salvation. For example, what strikes us as especially appalling and terrifying about the possessed Gerasene man who lived among the tombstones is that "for a long time he had not worn clothes" (Lk 8:27). Conversely, Saint Luke pinpoints the distinctive decadence of the rich man oblivious to the beggar Lazarus by this detail: he "dressed in purple garments and fine linen" (Lk 16:19). Our Lord reveals us to ourselves—and our temptation to let anxiety dominate our lives—with the observation that "not even Solomon in all his splendor was dressed" like the glorious wild flowers. And "if God so clothes the grass in the field that grows today and is thrown into the oven tomorrow, will he not much more provide for you?" (Lk 12:27-28).

Similarly, Jesus rails against the scribes "who like to go around in long robes" (Lk 20:46). Maybe this is why, when Jesus summons the Twelve and sends them out with authority over all demons and to cure diseases, he includes the specific instruction, "Take nothing for the journey, neither walking stick, nor sack, nor food, nor money, and let no one take a second tunic" (Lk 9:3). The Twelve are not like the self-adoring scribes or the self-absorbed rich man; their simple, spare dress—for which they have no spare—demonstrates their reliance on the One they preach.

The counsel inscribed by Saint Luke finds confirmation in the letters of Saint Paul. Gospel holiness entails a definite divesting: "You have taken off the old self with its practices" (Col 3:9).

This is not a merely mystical endeavor; it assumes concrete, flesh-and-blood form. For instance, "whoever has two cloaks should share with the person who has none" (Lk 3:11). Also, "from the person who takes your cloak, do not withhold even your tunic" (Lk 6:29). Christian disciples acknowledge their need for a Redeemer like the people "spreading their cloaks on the road" (Lk 19:36) to welcome Christ's victorious entry into Jerusalem. What we do with our clothing reveals the disposition of our heart toward Christ.

However, this stripping of our old behaviors does not leave us naked like the Gerasene demoniac. As God's chosen ones, we put on "heartfelt compassion, kindness, humility, gentleness, and patience" (Col 3:12). "For all of you who were baptized into Christ have clothed yourselves with Christ" (Gal 3:27)—attire that far outstrips the resplendence of the rich man, Solomon, or the scribes.

Our experience reminds us how much we resemble the man who fell victim to robbers as he went down from Jerusalem to Jericho: "They stripped and beat him and went off leaving him half-dead" (Lk 10:30). They beat him *after* they stripped him so as not to stain with blood the clothing they were robbing. Whatever puts us in the state of being half-dead—worldly persecution...our problems, fears, and sufferings...the cruelty or inconsiderateness of others...our own sins—only makes us languish all the more for the Good Samaritan (another parable narrated uniquely by Luke). In our woundedness we wait for him, "for he has clothed me with a robe of salvation,/ and wrapped me in a mantle of justice" (Is 61:10).

Clothed with the finest robe

Getting back to the prodigal son: there is something particularly despicable about him. In demanding his inheritance and departing, he treats his father as if he were already dead and he in effect disowns his family. By choosing to do his squandering in a distant land, he turns his back on his ethnicity, his people. And by hiring himself out to feed pigs, he spurns his religion.

All the same, when the prodigal son at last appears on the horizon, the father rushes to get him robed. The superabundance of the father's love may call to mind the Old Testament story of Joseph whose father Jacob loved him so much of all his sons that he made for him a long robe (Gn 37:3). The two fathers have something else in common: when the son gets separated from the father—Joseph through the exile brought on by his brothers' betrayal, and the prodigal through his self-exile brought on by betraying his own heart—the father lives for the day of their reunion.

The point is this: no matter how lost we may get because of our own selfishness and defiance and rebellion toward God… no matter how awful the ruin we bring upon ourselves through self-indulgence and our insistence on doing things our way… no matter how wasted, squalid, and squandered the sum of our life may seem, the Father waits with an aching heart to clothe us with the finest robe. That robe, says Saint Augustine, is the dignity which Adam lost.

No wonder, then, that our risen Savior's final words in the Gospel of Luke before he ascends into heaven are these: "I am sending the promise of my Father upon you.… Stay in the city until you are clothed with power from on high" (Lk 24:49). Clothe me, Lord, with the Father's own love so that I may be filled with his compassion and tenderness and forgiveness toward others. May my life overflow with mercy. Clothed with his love, let me leave behind whatever does not matter. Free me from my guilt, my shame, my regrets. May I be always vigilant, keeping watch for those snared in their sins, those trapped in their hurts, those desperate for somewhere to turn. May I rush to them with the promise of hope, a new beginning. Help me be the one to make others feel so loved that they never want to leave you again.

INTRODUCTION
Doctor Luke

Frances Hogan

Dear Doctor Luke—as many refer to the author of this favorite Gospel—is a very skilled writer. He knows how to get his readers to picture the scenes he describes in their own heads so clearly that each one feels a part of the mystery being unfolded. Who, for example, has not been to Bethlehem with Mary and Joseph on the night Jesus is born? Do we not join the shepherds in their glorious amazement at the wonder of "God-with-us"? Are we not "a fly on the wall," so to speak, when Simeon gives his terrible prophecy to Jesus' teenage Mother? Do we not feel deeply for her when her dreadful future is foretold? Have we not walked with Jesus through all the scenes of the Gospel as part of the crowd? Yes, we have been there! Luke writes his Gospel on our hearts where it cannot be erased.

Luke paints a most wonderful picture of Jesus as "The Man." Matthew portrays him as the "King of the Jews." Mark portrays him as "God's holy servant," and John portrays his divinity. Luke's Gospel can be summarized as "Behold the Man!" Everything that God ever intended in creating humans is seen in Jesus. We only have to look to him to see what *human* means, and to see what a complete masculine person could be like.

Prayer, Compassion, and Action

First, Luke portrays Jesus as a man of prayer. His wholeness is such that he is in communion with both God and man. He does not hide his prayer life. His disciples are aware of his "rising before dawn to pray" as they travel with him. He "prays all night" before great occasions. His last week on earth is saturated in prayer. The way Jesus prays is different from what the disciples knew before meeting him. He does not say prayers. He is in communion with God. He is even transfigured and spiritualized on Mount Tabor. This is so different that the disciples ask him to teach them how to pray this new way. Jesus responds by teaching them how to become true sons of God.

Second, Luke shows Jesus as a man full of compassion—so unlike the portrayal of men today, especially in the media. Everyone is welcome. Children feel free in his presence. He is available and approachable. He will enter into your sorrows and remove the cause of your tears. This is a different world from the macho, cold, hard, even cruel image of the male today. Let us join him in one of these moments of compassion.

In chapter 7 Jesus bumps into a funeral procession leaving the town of Nain. He discovers that the broken-hearted mother is a widow, and that this is her only son. He walks over to join the group. "Do not weep," he says, knowing that the widow loses everything when she loses the only person who can keep her alive. Let's join them. In a short while Jesus knows that he himself will be on the bier, and his own broken-hearted mother will be the widow. Luke wants you to see this, because when he tells the woman not to weep, he is also speaking with his disciples and the future Church in mind. For they too will be the "widow" having "lost" everything. Both now and then Jesus will amaze everyone by a silent resurrection when everything will be restored to the relevant widow. Thus Luke says to us: "Go deeper, and you will find treasure hidden in the text. It is there for you to pick up."

Jesus is not usually pictured as a campaign organizer, nor as a powerful leader, so let's have a look. In chapter 9, Jesus sends out six pairs of disciples to evangelize for him. Once they have successfully completed the first trip, he then sends out thirty-eight more pairs of evangelizers in the following chapter. That's a blitz campaign in such a small place! He does not allow people to be "camp followers." No! He turns them all into missionaries. Nor does he take any excuses from the weak or the fearful (9:57-62). Instead he tells them that it is such a privilege to be part of the founding of the kingdom of God that that is the only consideration (10:21-24).

As the new Messianic leader, Jesus is afraid of no one. He challenges the leadership of the Sanhedrin, the scribes and Pharisees who are the scholars and Scripture teachers of Israel. He tells them what things are like *on the inside*, facts which are known only to God (11:37–12:12). They, in turn, challenge him in chapter 20 on his interpretation of Scripture. This is vigorous, manly debate about truth. He eventually takes strong action to clear out the temple in 19:45-46.

Holy Rogues

Let us now touch some of the themes in Luke's Gospel, for there are many. One of my favorites is Luke's apology for rogues! Only someone with a great sense of humor would tell us that the prodigal son, who wastes his property and his life, is somehow "better" than his dependable older brother (see chapter 15)! As a Gentile, Luke takes the courage to say that the tax collector in chapter 18, who is despised for robbing his own people in the service of a foreign power, could get closer to God than one of their own religious leaders! Oops! That turns everything on its head! But my favorite is the so-called "good" Samaritan in chapter 10. The "goodies" in the story are those on their way to the temple of Jerusalem to worship God. The Samaritan is a despised heretic, as far as those "goodies" are concerned. He is worthless. Then we find the Son of God identifying himself with the despised Samaritan against the others! God was on the side of the "bad" one, because "God is love" (1 Jn 4:8). Luke wants to say that things are not what they seem in life. Look deeper.

Gender Balance

As the only Gentile to write a Gospel, Luke answers a problem that is very real today. This is the question of gender balance in society, and in the Church. His writings illustrate Saint Paul's teaching that "there is neither Jew nor Greek...there is not male and female; for you are all one in Christ Jesus" (Gal 3:28). I will illustrate this gender balance. If the angel Gabriel reveals good news to a wealthy priest, he will announce even greater news to a poor girl in chapter 1. If Simeon, an old man, recognizes the Christ in Mary's Newborn, then an old woman, Anna, will sing his praises and proclaim him to everyone in chapter 2. If Jesus heals the son of a widow in chapter 7, you will find him healing the daughter of Jairus in chapter 8. In chapter 13 we find Jesus healing a crippled woman on the sabbath, and in chapter 14 he heals a crippled man on the sabbath also. I will leave it to you to look for the gender balance in the parables. Lastly, Jesus shocks his society by openly having men and women disciples, a thing unheard of!

I cannot finish before looking at one of Luke's own favorite themes—that of riches versus poverty. This is obviously a real concern in the early Church, and Luke sides with Jesus, who never owns anything except his own soul. He devotes chapter 16 to this subject, but prepares us in advance. With the parable of the rich farmer in chapter 12, Luke deals with the problem of hoarding riches—which is considered "normal" in our society. The shortness and fragility of life are emphasized and the fact that you leave the earth poorer than you came into it. You even have to leave the body behind! The anxiety, trouble, and frustration that riches bring is illustrated in 16:1-13.

Luke's answer to all this is trust in divine providence, which takes care of all creatures, all of the time (12:22-32). In fact, Luke goes even further and tells us to give our wealth away (12:33-34)! This is the opposite of our banking system, which is based on usury.

Nevertheless, Luke is telling us a great truth: "Whatever you want, give it away." To discover God's incredible generosity to us, all we have to do is what he does. Reach out to others who are in need. For example, if we want forgiveness, then give it to others! If you want understanding from others, just give some to those who need it. If you want money to cover your needs, then give alms. Nothing can be simpler!

When you have finished reading the reflections in this book, go to Luke himself, and allow the Word of God to take you on an exciting journey of meeting God and getting to know him personally.

An Invitation to Saint Luke's Gospel
Labor of Love: Birth of Joy

Andrew Matt

"The head's just too big. We're looking at a possible C-section here," announces the doctor.

After twenty-nine hours of labor, this isn't the kind of news a mother in the delivery room wants to hear. "Oh no, please, not a C-section," my wife pleads. A few seconds pass, and then she makes an announcement of her own: "I'm sorry, but I'm going to have to pray now. HAIL MARY, FULL OF GRACE…"

Martha is beyond exhausted. But somehow she's kept on going, pushing and breathing. Hour after hour. I don't know how she's done it. I've been by her side almost the whole time. However, like the Apostles in Gethsemane, I cave midway and take a nap. Yet Martha braves on—focused, fearless, giving everything she's got.

Both of us are now praying out loud together. Suddenly we're told that our baby's head has been fitted with a soft suction cup: the last resort before a Caesarian section.

"BLESSED IS THE FRUIT OF YOUR WOOOOOOMB…" Martha croons.

With a last mighty push, aided by some added suction, out pops Samuel, slippery as a seal pup and glistening with life.

The next thing I know, I'm cutting the umbilical cord. Then I look up and behold the most beautiful sight in the world. My wife's face is flushed with fatigue, yet she's beaming like a young girl. Our hungry newborn has latched on right away and is nursing in her arms. I look Martha in the eyes, and her smile radiates a joy that fills the entire room.

"I'm the luckiest person on the planet," she says. "Look how gorgeous he is."

Luke's Joy: Childbirth and Women

Saint Luke, "the beloved physician" (Col 4:14), writes his radiant Gospel as if he's standing in the birthing room after having just delivered a baby. He's so elated that he doesn't even take his scrubs off—he starts composing on the spot, in the warm afterglow of birth. On every page of his Gospel,

Luke the obstetrician reveals his reverence for childbirth and motherhood. His narrative abounds with references to birth and maternal tenderness (thanks to Luke we have the Birth and Infancy Narratives of Jesus and John the Baptist, as well as Mary's *Magnificat*). His affection and admiration for women is palpable (Luke introduces us to thirteen women not mentioned elsewhere in the Gospels). And his account overflows with joy not only at the birth of Jesus and John, but at the ongoing birth of new life that Christ's Passion, Death, and Resurrection bestows upon the world (variations of the word "joy" occur more often in Luke than in John, and more than in Matthew and Mark combined).

In what follows, we will reflect briefly on four passages unique to Luke's Gospel, in which the Evangelist displays his art of spiritual obstetrics most poignantly. We will see how Jesus' love for man is so profound that he is stirred to the very depths of his divine *splanchna* or "womb."

Zechariah's *Benedictus*

Not surprisingly, Luke uses the word *splanchna* (one of three Greek terms for "womb") in a wider variety of contexts than the other Evangelists. First, right after the birth of John the Baptist, Zechariah sings of "the tender [*splanchna*] mercy of our God" (1:78). Here Luke hearkens back to the rich, physiological language of the Old Testament, in which the Hebrew term *rachamim* (from *rechem*: womb) is used over and over again—in the Psalms, Isaiah, Hosea—to describe God's merciful love. As Blessed John Paul II notes, "Zechariah speaks of the 'tender mercy of our God,'…namely, *rachamim* (Latin translation: *viscera misericordiae*), which identifies God's mercy with a mother's love."

Jesus and the Widow of Nain

Early in his public ministry, Jesus encounters a funeral procession. A weeping widow is about to bury her only son. With no one to support her now, the widow has effectively become an orphan. "When the Lord saw her, he was moved with pity [*esplanchnisthe*]" (7:13). "Moved with pity" is a pale reflection of the gut-wrenching reaction conveyed by Luke's verb (with its root *splanchna*). The widow's plight so overwhelms Jesus that he trembles with compassion. Identified here for the first time as "Lord," what Jesus does next reveals that the Defender of orphans and widows (Ex 21:21-22; Ps 68:6) has stepped forth from the pages of the Old Testament to help a bereft widow. *Rachamim* aquiver, he touches the bier and brings the dead boy back to life. Then, in a gesture that restores life to the widow, "Jesus gave him to his mother" (7:15). Fresh from the womb of Mercy, both mother and son are born anew.

The Good Samaritan

Jesus now transfers his own merciful "womb" into the protagonist of one of his greatest parables. "But a Samaritan traveler who came upon [the half-dead man] was moved with compassion [*esplanchnisthe*] at the sight" (10:33). Just as Jesus saw the "half-dead" widow and was shaken to the core, so the sight of the man left for dead on the road sends pangs of sorrow surging through the Samaritan's *splanchna*. Unlike Jesus, however, the Samaritan does not work a great miracle. Or does he? What we see is that he lavishes the afflicted man with immediate, personal, hands-on care. In essence, the Samaritan's *insides go out* and take flesh in acts of mercy that nourish and give birth to new life. Jesus says, "Go and do likewise" (10:37). Which is another way of saying: "Go work miracles of love—become the Eucharist for your neighbor."

The Prodigal Son's Father

In his most famous and unforgettable parable of mercy, Jesus reveals the paternal "womb" of his infinite forgiveness. After having prepared his confession, the prodigal son returns home to beg his father's forgiveness. "While he was still a long way off, his father caught sight of him, and was filled with compassion [*esplanchnisthe*]" (15:20). Here we see the father's *splanchna* standing on tiptoe, aching, and then sprinting forth: "He ran to his son, embraced him and kissed him." By letting himself be loved, the son receives the grace of new life. "Now," exclaims the father, "we must celebrate and rejoice" (15:32).

All of Luke's joy is summed up in the willingness to be born anew within the wide-wombed embrace of God's mercy. Let us radiate the joy of Luke's Gospel by giving birth to mercy and forgiveness with our lives.

Listening to Someone's Story

Father Gary C. Caster

Since many have undertaken to compile a narrative of the events that have been fulfilled among us, just as those who were eyewitnesses from the beginning and ministers of the word have handed them down to us, I too have decided, after investigating everything accurately anew, to write it down in an orderly sequence for you, most excellent Theophilus, so that you may realize the certainty of the teachings you have received. (Lk 1:1-4)

This narrative describing "the events that have been fulfilled" tells the story of Jesus' life. Saint Luke wants Theophilus to know that the teachings he has received are not the result of sophisticated ideas or academic theories, but are grounded in actual historical events. His investigation into "all that has been handed down by the eyewitnesses" aims at securing for Theophilus, and each of us, our identity as Christians.

Working at a college campus has reinforced for me the importance of storytelling. In fact, each Sunday evening students gather to listen to one of their peers describe the people, places, and experiences that have shaped that student's life. This is one of the most well-attended gatherings on campus, for it is the simplest way for students to get to know each other better. And although our lives are not simply the result of the experiences that have shaped them, the "narrative of events" we share with one another nonetheless places our lives within the certainty of what's real, because we can relate to dates and times, people and places, and we all appreciate a good story.

Saint Luke's "orderly sequence" of events is a written example of our campus' Story Time. His narrative establishes the facts of Christianity for Theophilus in order to ensure that his understanding does not drift off into all sorts of innovations or abstractions. Saint Luke wants Jesus to be truly known because Christianity is always an encounter with the Man at the center of the Gospel.

As a "minister of the word," Saint Luke takes great care with what's been handed on, so that Jesus can accurately "tell his own story." Listening to what Jesus shares with us in the Gospel of Luke will enhance our understanding of the man whose life we follow, and shed light upon the teachings that flow from Jesus' life.

Heavenly Father, help me open my life's story to the power of your Word, so that the events that marked his time on earth might shape the events that mark my own.

Longing for Life

Father Gary C. Caster

In the days of Herod, King of Judea, there was a priest named Zechariah of the priestly division of Abijah; his wife was from the daughters of Aaron, and her name was Elizabeth. Both were righteous in the eyes of God, observing all the commandments and ordinances of the Lord blamelessly. But they had no child, because Elizabeth was barren and both were advanced in years.
(Lk 1:5-7)

The story of Christianity begins "in the days of Herod, King of Judea," and unfolds within the parameters of the relationship of a childless couple. The noble heritage of this priest "of the division of Abijah" and "daughter of Aaron" situates them within the narrative of the people of Israel, who also longed for the birth of a child that would redeem and restore them.

Being "without child" is a cause of great suffering for many couples. Being "advanced in years" only adds to the pain that's felt when the desire for children remains unfulfilled. I know of many married couples who understand the situation Elizabeth and Zechariah faced. These couples are truly exemplary to me because they have chosen to direct their pain in many positive ways. For example, they are typically the first to respond to the needs of others, and they try as best as they can to nurture those around them. One woman I know keeps her trunk filled with simple gifts for children of all ages so that she always has something on hand that might brighten a child's day.

Every human heart contains a prayer not yet answered and a desire yet to be fulfilled. Like Zechariah and Elizabeth, we will experience in our spiritual lives periods of emptiness, times in which the words of our prayers and our acts of worship seem barren or sterile. We will experience what it's like to move forward in the practice of our devotions without any sense of God's presence. At such times we can draw back from others and the world by retreating into our pain, or we can, "by observing all the commandments," keep our spiritual "trunk" filled with spiritual gifts that can brighten another person's day.

As the story of Christianity unfolds, Zechariah and Elizabeth teach us how to live through these periods of emptiness and longing even when they last for an extended period of time.

Gracious Father, grant that I remain faithful to you even when I am feeling empty and you seem far away. Help me keep my life ever open to your saving love.

The First Visitation

Father Gary C. Caster

Once when [Zechariah] was serving as priest in his division's turn before God, according to the practice of the priestly service, he was chosen by lot to enter the sanctuary of the Lord to burn incense. Then, when the whole assembly of the people was praying outside at the hour of the incense offering, the angel of the Lord appeared to him, standing at the right of the altar of incense. (Lk 1:8-11)

As a child I enjoyed watching the smoke from the incense shift and swirl before the monstrance during Eucharistic adoration, especially when it was my "turn before God" to be a server. The different shapes would often influence my conversation with God as I knelt while "the whole assembly of the people was praying."

Today, "serving as a priest" affords me ample opportunities to watch the smoke rise before the Blessed Sacrament as I whisper the names of those for whom I promise prayers. I often think of this scene and what it must have been like for Zechariah, when in the midst of his accustomed tasks he experienced something so unexpected. His angelic visitation brings to mind how true it's been for me that my most profound experiences of God's presence have happened when I am busy with things that are routine and familiar. This is precisely what Saint Luke wants us to understand about Christianity. It is the story of God's presence entering into and filling up what's ordinary and expected in the most extraordinary and unexpected ways.

Although this surely wasn't the first time Zechariah entered "the sanctuary of the Lord," it was his first encounter with an angel. We learn from this that God's love and concern is something decidedly personal. Through this first New Testament "visitation" we see God taking the initiative to penetrate the distinctive circumstances of Zechariah's life in a crucial way, one that is equally connected to the prayers of the assembly gathered outside.

While the "hour" and way in which God "visits" each of us may be altogether different, it's never for us alone. The angel of the Lord comes for the people at prayer as much as he comes to Zechariah. God's initiative on behalf of any one of us is always undertaken for all of us.

Heavenly Father, help me to recognize your presence in my life, especially in my daily tasks, so as to serve you better in the sanctuary of the world.

Troubled by God's Plan

Father Gary C. Caster

Zechariah was troubled by what he saw, and fear came upon him. But the angel said to him, "Do not be afraid, Zechariah, because your prayer has been heard. Your wife Elizabeth will bear you a son, and you shall name him John. And you will have joy and gladness, and many will rejoice at his birth, for he will be great in the sight of [the] Lord." (Lk 1:12-15a)

"Zechariah was troubled by what he saw." Of course he was! His prayer was simply that he and Elizabeth would have a child. God's response to his petition went well beyond what Zechariah was expecting. The presence and the words of the angel instantly call into question everything Zechariah had previously thought about himself, his wife, and of course, God. As a priest, Zechariah knows that more is happening here than the heralding of a son. The words of the angel make this clear, for John "will be great in the sight of the Lord," and "many will rejoice at his birth."

The ways God chooses to answer our prayers can be unsettling. Sometimes a simple request for greater patience can lead one into a situation in which patience is in greater demand. Sometimes we really are "troubled" by God's response to our prayers, even when he answers them.

Being truly open to God's assistance may even mean moving to places we never thought we'd live, serving in ways we never imagined we were capable, and learning things about ourselves, others, and the world that we never before considered. That has certainly been true in my life. I once told the bishop who later ordained me, "Over my dead body would I ever be a priest for the Diocese of Peoria!"

The astonishment and uncertainty that mark this angelic encounter serve as the foundation upon which Saint Luke's story of Christianity will continue to be told. From the beginning, God's response to the human condition has been absolutely astonishing and wholly unimaginable; and so it remains. There is no reason we should ever be afraid, for God truly hears our prayers. Although we may be amazed at the boldness of God's plan as it unfolds in our lives, accepting it is the way toward possessing the same "joy and gladness" Zechariah and Elizabeth will experience at the birth of their son.

Almighty Father, calm my troubles and ease my fears, help me to be always open to your plan for my life so that I can experience the joy and gladness of your limitless love.

17

God Provides a Personal Trainer

Father Gary C. Caster

"[John] will drink neither wine nor strong drink. He will be filled with the holy Spirit even from his mother's womb, and he will turn many of the children of Israel to the Lord their God. He will go before him in the spirit and power of Elijah to turn the hearts of fathers toward children and the disobedient to the understanding of the righteous, to prepare a people fit for the Lord." (Lk 1:15b-17)

The troubling presence of the angel is now magnified by the description of Zechariah's son. The portrait portrays a figure of biblical significance because John will "drink neither wine nor strong drink" and "be filled with the holy Spirit even from his mother's womb." Zechariah knows very well that the life of the child to be born is more than just an answer to his and Elizabeth's prayers.

The words of the angel, therefore, draw attention to the great sensitivity by which God introduces his plan to turn "the hearts of fathers" toward their children. Rather than take the disobedient by surprise, God chooses instead to prepare his people by making them spiritually fit. John will serve the Lord as a kind of "personal trainer" by helping his people "turn to the Lord their God," a movement that is not always easy. John will go before the Lord instructing the children of Israel about how to get ready for God's coming.

This "turn," sometimes called repentance or conversion, is a life-long endeavor. Fortunately, God continues to provide men and women who serve as "personal trainers" to help strengthen our understanding of righteousness. Whether they are part of the great community of saints or are contemporary members of Christ's Body, their assistance is a perfect reminder that God's sensitivity to our condition and his providential care never diminishes.

Personally, I'm glad I don't have to figure out for myself how to build up my life in order to follow Christ. My own list of personal trainers is quite long, and I am deeply grateful for each one of them. I have been fortunate that God has led me to people whose lives exude the same spirit and power as the life of John, people whose instruction both challenges and encourages me to exercise my spirit so I can continue running toward the Father without growing weary.

Almighty Father, help me be attentive to the people you place in my life, sent to help me grow in righteousness so that I may be fit to enter into your presence.

The Need for Quiet
Father Gary C. Caster

Then Zechariah said to the angel, "How shall I know this? For I am an old man, and my wife is advanced in years." And the angel said to him in reply, "I am Gabriel, who stand before God. I was sent to speak to you and to announce to you this good news. But now you will be speechless and unable to talk until the day these things take place, because you did not believe my words, which will be fulfilled at their proper time." (Lk 1:18-20)

Whether in church or at school, in a library, classroom, or movie theater, we have all heard, and many of us have said, "Shhh." This isn't always meant as a rebuke to a group or an individual. Often it is a simple reminder that there is a right time and a right place for conversation. A simple reminder to be "speechless" can enhance our experience of worship, learning, and entertainment.

The angel Gabriel was sent to speak to "an old man" who happens to be a priest. Thus Zechariah should have been familiar with the ways of God. Even if the initial encounter was troubling, the "good news" announced by Gabriel should not have been. Of all people, Zechariah should have known all things are possible with God. So, until "the day these things take place," Gabriel is simply saying "Shhh." Quieting Zechariah will give him plenty of time to think about everything the angel has said.

There are many moments in our lives when it would have been better to "bite our tongues," when our guardian angels should have whispered "Shhh" in our ears. Silence is a necessary part of our life in the spirit, which we learn here at the beginning of Saint Luke's Gospel.

Although Gabriel's words may come across as a punishment, not being able to talk actually transforms Zechariah. Because of his silence, Zechariah's presence becomes a grace for the people with whom he shares his life. His condition is a daily reminder that "he had seen a vision in the sanctuary."

Being freed from having to explain over and over again what took place also allows Zechariah to reflect upon his encounter with Gabriel without the intrusion of other voices. While Zechariah grows into a deeper awareness of and appreciation for everything that took place as the incense burned before God, he becomes more and more a constant reminder that God is up to something.

Loving Father, let me welcome the silences you impose as opportunities to grow in my acceptance that your plans for me will always be fulfilled at their proper time.

No Time Limit on Prayer

Father Gary C. Caster

Meanwhile the people were waiting for Zechariah and were amazed that he stayed so long in the sanctuary. But when he came out, he was unable to speak to them, and they realized that he had seen a vision in the sanctuary. He was gesturing to them but remained mute. Then, when his days of ministry were completed, he went home. (Lk 1:21-23)

The people waiting outside seem to have placed some sort of time limit on prayer and worship. Zechariah's delay might begin as a curiosity, but it ends with genuine wonder. When he emerges "unable to speak to them," the people realize that something extraordinary has taken place in the sanctuary of the Lord.

Zechariah's predicament now also becomes a gift for those awaiting his return. More than just a sign that a vision has taken place, it is an invitation for them to enter into the same quiet reflection into which Zechariah has been plunged as he completes the days of ministry and awaits the birth of his son. Perhaps his gestures are meant to convey this invitation rather than explain what had just taken place. Regardless, what's clear is that everyone present has been drawn into the actions of God as announced by the angel.

The description and details of extraordinary events are meant to do the same. As a boy, I spent one entire summer in my backyard waiting for Mary to appear (she never came). Reading about the experience of the children of Fatima changed the way I thought about God's care for us and how he continues to lavish his love upon us. It also deepened my devotion to the Mother of Jesus. Since that summer I have never once questioned God's love for and belief in me.

Apparitions of our Lady, miraculous healings, and locutions and visions approved by the Church should move within our hearts a deeper appreciation for the many ways God speaks to us. Extraordinary spiritual events should propel us toward the sanctuary of the Lord and prayer, invigorate our participation in the sacraments, and open our minds to Scripture and the teachings of Christ so that we can complete whatever work the Lord has asked of us until our days are completed and we return to our true home.

Eternal Father, help me draw closer to you through all the means provided by the Church. May I immerse and secure my life ever more within the continuing signs of your abiding love.

Retreating in Seclusion
Father Gary C. Caster

After this time [Zechariah's] wife Elizabeth conceived, and she went into seclusion for five months, saying, "So has the Lord done for me at a time when he has seen fit to take away my disgrace before others." (Lk 1:24-25)

The events in the sanctuary of the Lord accompany Zechariah to the sanctuary of his home. The conception of his child shines new light upon the bond that exists between husband and wife, revealing conjugal love as an integral part of God's plan. The story of Christianity unfolds as a drama that is intimately bound up with the concrete joys and suffering of married life.

The sorrow and "disgrace" Elizabeth has carried could only be taken away by God. Through the words of an angel and the righteousness of this couple we learn that God wants to remove from our lives whatever obstacles may prevent us from properly seeing him, ourselves, others, and the whole of creation. For this reason God has given us the sacrament of confession, so that our lives might perpetually be filled with the extraordinary gift of his presence. Disgrace is not meant to define our lives; God's love for us is.

With the conception of the child John, Elizabeth correctly perceives that something extraordinary is happening, something more than just an answer to her frequently spoken prayer. She goes into seclusion, not to escape God's plan, but in order to preserve and reflect upon the amazing events that are taking place.

Elizabeth's decision to "go on retreat" shows how important such time is in our lives as Christians. It is important that we regularly make time to be alone and undistracted, retreating in order to meditate upon all that God has done for us by removing the "disgrace" of sin. In quiet solitude, Elizabeth will be able to appreciate God more fully and to understand how the life of her son is entwined with the life of God. God has given her the gift of being a mother. In turn Elizabeth, through her seclusion, is giving God the gift of herself. Taking time to be alone with God allows each of us the opportunity to do the same.

Heavenly Father, in Christ you have removed the disgrace of original sin. Help me to see more clearly how your providential plan of love touches all aspects of my life.

Highly Favored

Father Gary C. Caster

In the sixth month, the angel Gabriel was sent from God to a town of Galilee called Nazareth, to a virgin betrothed to a man named Joseph, of the house of David, and the virgin's name was Mary. And coming to her, he said, "Hail, favored one! The Lord is with you." But she was greatly troubled at what was said and pondered what sort of greeting this might be. (Lk 1:26-29)

The way in which Saint Luke records the angel Gabriel's next announcement shows once more the personal nature of what has begun to unfold. In one sentence we are told the name of the town, the name of the betrothed, and the name of the Virgin. These simple, yet important details assert the intentionality with which God is acting. Gabriel is sent to Nazareth and nowhere else because God's plan centers upon a particular young woman living there, Mary. The careful construction of the record of this event establishes at the very beginning that there is nothing random in God's providential care for us. By attentively presenting the facts, Saint Luke effectively shows us that Christianity could not have happened any other way.

And yet we also learn from the way Saint Luke describes the encounter that this young woman betrothed "to Joseph of the house of David" was not anticipating a visitation by an angel. His greeting would certainly be troubling to someone who had never thought of herself as "favored" by God. Pondering Gabriel's words indicates that Mary had no prior thoughts about holding a unique place before God. Simply put, Mary didn't think of herself as special or privileged, and certainly not in a position to be addressed in this fashion by God's messenger.

At the initial moment of this encounter we already glimpse what Christ wants to show each of us. We are all special and unique before God! At times it has been difficult for me to accept that God believes in me, especially when I haven't believed in myself, or been able to recognize what God sees in me. Yet I know that this truth has been spoken to me by Christ. I also know that Mary is always ready to help us accept that Gabriel's announcement of favor is actually a profession of God's love, a love intended for each one of us.

Heavenly Father, you show the depth of your love in the personal care you have for all your children. Help me to accept your love for me so that I in turn can help others accept your love for them.

An Ideal Companion

Father Gary C. Caster

Then the angel said to [Mary], "Do not be afraid, Mary, for you have found favor with God. Behold, you will conceive in your womb and bear a son, and you shall name him Jesus. He will be great and will be called Son of the Most High, and the Lord God will give him the throne of David his father, and he will rule over the house of Jacob forever, and of his kingdom there will be no end." (Lk 1:30-33)

The angel Gabriel is able to comfort Mary because he knows that through her deep faith and abiding trust she "has found favor with God." Gabriel is therefore careful to clothe his announcement in the language and history exclusive to her people and to her situation. Mary's betrothal to Joseph is subtly incorporated into the announcement of God's plan because with her people, Mary has been awaiting the restoration of David's throne. With great care, Gabriel relates the conception of "the child in her womb" with the hopes of David's descendants, and deliberately shifts the attention away from Mary to that of her Son, Jesus. Gabriel does so in order to reassure Mary that she will continue to live her life as she always has, at the service of God.

In our desire to serve God, the things we do often draw undue attention upon us. After nineteen years, I think of this every time I celebrate Mass or whenever I lead a parish mission. It truly can be frightening to find ourselves in positions we never wanted or sought out. Doing the work of God often puts us in situations that challenge our comfort level. When Blessed Teresa of Calcutta told me to come every Wednesday night and care for people with HIV/AIDS, my first response was, "I can't." Fortunately she wouldn't take no for an answer. The three years I had the privilege of serving changed my Christian life.

More than anyone else, Mary knows what this is like. So, at the beginning of Saint Luke's narrative, she is introduced to us as an ideal companion and fitting confidante. Because Mary knows what it's like to serve God in the most unimaginable way, she can calm our own fears about giving to God whatever he asks of us. Like a good mother, she repeatedly centers our attention, gently reminding us that we serve "the Son of the Most High."

Merciful Father, let me never be afraid to serve you. With Mary at my side, let me accept that everything you ask of me is always at the service of your Son and hers.

How Can This Be?

Father Gary C. Caster

But Mary said to the angel, "How can this be, since I have no relations with a man?" And the angel said to her in reply, "The holy Spirit will come upon you, and the power of the Most High will overshadow you. Therefore the child to be born will be called holy, the Son of God. And behold, Elizabeth, your relative, has also conceived a son in her old age, and this is the sixth month for her who was called barren; for nothing will be impossible for God." (Lk 1:34-37)

With her simple question Mary demonstrates an uncommon humility and a tremendous depth of spirit. It seems impossible to her that a child of Adam and Eve, a woman born into a world disordered by sin, could find favor with God. She speaks from the human side of the divide between God and those created in his image and likeness. She sees herself in solidarity with the human condition, not above or outside of it. Why indeed would God address himself to a finite, limited creature, especially one who has had "no relations with a man"?

Mary's words are also a plea. She is asking the angel to help her understand how she is to live under the weight of the way in which God's favor will be expressed in her life.

Sensing this, the angel Gabriel not only responds to her plea but also provides someone to whom Mary can turn. The Holy Spirit will enable Mary to bear the overwhelming reality of God's presence in the person of his Son, while with Elizabeth she will be able to share the incomprehensibility of God's love as it has been expressed in each of their lives.

God making use of our lives for the unfolding of his plan remains a burden we simply cannot carry on our own. "How can this be?" is for many of us a regular part of our interior conversation with the Lord. We often find ourselves struggling to comprehend how we could possibly live up to what God asks of us.

Like Mary, we have need of finding a suitable means for expressing both our questions and our gratitude. Because we could never alone carry the burden of being loved by God or the humility with which God's love has been expressed, Jesus has given us to each other as members of his Body. It is also the reason he has given to his Body the woman that is his Mother.

Loving Father, through the power of the Holy Spirit you have overshadowed my life so that it can bear and reflect the truth of your infinite love. Help me to accept the weight of your love, a task that is easy and a burden that is light.

Identity in Vocation

Father Gary C. Caster

Mary said, "Behold, I am the handmaid of the Lord.
May it be done to me according to your word."
Then the angel departed from her. (Lk 1:38)

Instead of retreating from the angel's words, Mary expresses a new self-awareness: "I am the handmaid of the Lord." She does not speak resigned or defeated; she speaks with the confidence that comes from believing that all things truly are possible with God. She speaks as someone who has recognized in the words of the angel the fulfillment of everything for which her heart has yearned: to please the Lord.

Through the message of the angel Gabriel, Mary also comes to recognize that by this invitation God is not merely asking her to do something, but to become someone. It isn't simply a womb that God needs, but rather the totality of her being. The free gift of Mary's feminine humanity will give flesh and blood to all that God longs to do and everything he yearns to say to the human family. Through the angel Gabriel, God has asked that Mary be wedded to his generative paternity, and by her answer we know that Mary has discovered her identity within the uniqueness and privilege of this implausible vocation.

God's call is always an invitation to discover ourselves anew, to see ourselves from the divine perspective. Our vocation is an invitation to give our own flesh and blood so that the unimaginable possibilities of God can continue to be made manifest in the world.

On the day I was ordained, the Church promised me nothing. It was I who promised the Church that I would open the whole of myself to God, physically, emotionally, and spiritually. The "yes" I spoke to God and the promises I made to the Church didn't end that day. They continue to be the means by which I experience the full, rich, and abundant life that is Christ's promise. Our willingness to say with Mary, "May it be done to me according to your word," is the only way of satisfying the deepest yearning of our hearts.

Loving Father, the message of your angel changed for ever the life of the Virgin Mary. Help me open my life more fully to your Word, her Son, so that I may be changed into the person you have always known me to be.

God Brings People Together

Father Gary C. Caster

During those days Mary set out and traveled to the hill country in haste to a town of Judah, where she entered the house of Zechariah and greeted Elizabeth. When Elizabeth heard Mary's greeting, the infant leaped in her womb, and Elizabeth, filled with the holy Spirit, cried out in a loud voice and said, "Most blessed are you among women, and blessed is the fruit of your womb." (Lk 1:39-42)

Elizabeth's words give Mary an opportunity to celebrate the great works of God that have taken place in each of their lives. Elizabeth's words aren't meant to distance Mary from other women, but rather to highlight the incredible way in which God has chosen to redeem and restore his people. Elizabeth's words are a celebration of God's creative initiative.

The joy of the child in Elizabeth's womb also indicates that this is more than a family reunion. These two cousins have certainly spent time together before, but now they face one another with a deep sense of wonder and of awe. They stand transparent before one another, perfect mirrors for the divine action that now determines their place in the world. Elizabeth's words provide an opening for Mary to share what's burning inside her heart. It's as if Elizabeth is saying to her cousin, "I know what's going on; it's all right."

We all need a company of friends with whom we feel free to share the ways in which God is manifesting his love and his presence in our lives. When asked by young people what difference being a follower of Christ makes, one of the first things I say is, "the people he places in my life." Only by saying "yes" to God and leaving my home for a state in which I had never lived and knew nobody, was God able to fill my life with friends of his Son, men and women of such exuberant faith and honest humanity. This company of friends is the reason I tell people that I have the best life of anyone I know.

Mary's haste to see Elizabeth challenges any notion that God's privileges set people apart. What God has undertaken in Mary is not for her alone. God's actions always bring people together, to be filled with the Holy Spirit and to experience true joy.

Eternal Father, let me stand transparent before others so that they may see the works you are accomplishing in me and be confident of your works in their lives.

Christian Community

Father Gary C. Caster

"And how does this happen to me, that the mother of my Lord should come to me? For at the moment the sound of your greeting reached my ears, the infant in my womb leaped for joy. Blessed are you who believed that what was spoken to you by the Lord would be fulfilled." (Lk 1:43-45)

Mary's greeting touches the very depths of wonder that eclipse all that has taken place in the house of her cousin. Elizabeth's bold pronouncement at the sound of Mary's greeting issues from an ever increasing sense of amazement concerning the works of God. "How does it happen" that she should find herself with child? "How does it happen that the mother of [her] Lord" should come to her? There is no doubt in Elizabeth's mind that through the explicit action of God, her life now has an entirely new horizon.

Elizabeth's inspired words are a soothing balm for Mary. Referring to her as "the mother of my Lord" is meant to be reassuring, as is the reference to the joy of "the infant in my womb." Elizabeth wants Mary to know that because she believed everything the Lord said, both their lives have been set in a new and decisive direction. Elizabeth's words allow Mary to gather together the thoughts and emotions stirred up by the encounter with the angel, and give them voice.

The meeting of these two women is an icon of Christian community, a window into what it means to have been brought together by the Son of the Most High. The joy they share is a gift of the Spirit that unites them in a bond that transcends their family relationship. Their lives now become an incarnate sign of God's desire to prepare a people fit for him.

There is no greater joy for me than traveling around the country and encountering people with whom I can share openly and without restraint the ways in which God daily punctuates my life with signs of his presence. The Christian community is for me a genuine experience of what Saint Luke is celebrating in this encounter. Like Mary and Elizabeth, I have met many people who generate for me the freedom that lets me be myself with God as I serve his people.

Almighty Father, help me to believe everything you have spoken through your Word and through his Body, the Church, so that I may be filled with the joy of the Holy Spirit.

The Greatest Work of God

Father Fidelis Moscinski, C.F.R.

And Mary said: "My soul proclaims the greatness of the Lord;/ my spirit rejoices in God my savior./ For he has looked upon his handmaid's lowliness;/ behold, from now on will all ages call me blessed./ The Mighty One has done great things for me,/ and holy is his name." (Lk 1:46-49)

D o we realize that in this great hymn of praise, the *Magnificat*, Mary speaks not only of herself but of us as well? She prophesies that "from now on will all ages call me blessed." She foresees that throughout the centuries Christians, saints and sinners alike, will declare her "blessed." Every time we pray the Hail Mary her prophecy is fulfilled.

When we repeat Elizabeth's words, "Blessed are you among women, and blessed is the fruit of your womb," we are recognizing "the great things" that God has done for her. God has created her sinless; he has chosen her to be the Mother of the Savior and of the Church; and he has glorified her body and soul in heaven.

Our praise of the *Blessed* Virgin Mary does not terminate with her but with God himself. For example, if we enter an art museum and there behold a stunning and beautiful work of art, a painting or sculpture, our praise ultimately goes to the artist who created it and not to the object itself. In the same way, our veneration for the Blessed Virgin Mary, for all her graces and privileges, is simply another way of loving and honoring God himself.

In fact, we ourselves receive a blessing when we call Mary "blessed." She shares of her fullness of grace with each of us in her Son Jesus. And just as one who appreciates a great work of art in some mysterious way enters into the mind and heart of the artist through his work, so too in our proclamation of Mary's blessedness we enter into the riches of God's love for us, the treasures of his heart.

Mary's song is our song. Her joy is our joy because we know that God desires to do great things for us as well. Holy is his name.

Father of all blessings, I marvel at the wonders of grace you have bestowed upon the Blessed Virgin Mary; may I unite my praise with hers and receive a share in the bounty of your riches.

Throne Reversal

Father Fidelis Moscinski, C.F.R.

"His mercy is from age to age/ to those who fear him./ He has shown might with his arm,/ dispersed the arrogant of mind and heart./ He has thrown down the rulers from their thrones/ but lifted up the lowly." (Lk 1:50-52)

Who are these people? Who are "the arrogant of mind and heart" that God has dispersed and thrown down from their thrones? And who are the "lowly" and "those who fear him" whom he has lifted up?

An incident from the life of Saint Francis of Assisi can help answer this question. One time the saint was traveling with a companion, and they stopped at a church to pray. The brother who was with Francis saw in a vision among the many thrones in heaven one that was more honorable than the rest, ornamented with precious stones, and radiant with all glory. He wondered whose throne it might be. Then he heard a voice saying to him: "This throne belonged to one of the fallen angels, but now it is reserved for the humble Francis."

Later, this brother asked Francis: "What, Father, is your opinion of yourself?" He answered, "It seems to me that I am the greatest of sinners, for if God had treated any criminal with such great mercy, he would have been ten times more spiritual than I." The brother then perceived that humility will raise Francis to the throne which was lost through pride.

God has thrown down and dispersed the arrogant angels who rebelled against him; and God has exalted the humble and lowly. And among all the saints the *most* humble and the *highest* exalted is Mary—the handmaid of the Lord who submits entirely to his holy will.

This Queen of heaven and earth reveals to us a surprising and paradoxical truth about ourselves: the more we humble ourselves in the presence of God, the higher his condescending love will raise us up. But if we succumb to the illusion of pride in the arrogance of our hearts, we share the fate of those who are cast down.

All-powerful Father, in Mary and all your saints I see your merciful love lifting up the lowly; today I ask you to cast out any arrogance in my heart and fill it with an abiding humility.

29

Hungry for Love

Father Fidelis Moscinski, C.F.R.

"The hungry he has filled with good things;/ the rich he has sent away empty./ He has helped Israel his servant,/ remembering his mercy,/ according to his promise to our fathers,/ to Abraham and to his descendants forever." Mary remained with [Elizabeth] about three months and then returned to her home. (Lk 1:53-56)

Every day we experience moments of hunger. Perhaps a slight grumbling in the stomach and a glance at some advertisement of our favorite food leads to a mouth-watering trip to the fridge. We satisfy our hunger and go on with life.

But while we are conscious of physical hunger, do we not instinctively know that our deepest hunger is not physical but spiritual? We all hunger for love: every human person needs to encounter a deep, sustaining, life-giving love in order to be truly happy. For most of us this occurs in the heart of the family from the time of our childhood. But sadly, some people are deprived of this love in varying degrees. The most tragic cases are babies in some foreign orphanages who are severely neglected and never experience the physical and emotional warmth of parental love.

The neuroscience journalist Maia Szalavitz co-authored a book entitled *Born for Love: Why Empathy Is Essential—and Endangered.* She has written of the plight of these love-starved children. "Basically, they die from lack of love. When an infant falls below the threshold of physical affection needed to stimulate the production of growth hormone and the immune system, his body starts shutting down." Science confirms what we already know: we all need love in order to live.

The Blessed Virgin Mary proclaims to us today: "The hungry he has filled with good things." She herself experienced the deepest satisfaction of her hunger for love when incarnate Love himself—Jesus Christ—was conceived in her womb. God satisfies the hunger of the human heart by giving us his Son. At the Last Supper and now in every Catholic Mass Jesus gives himself to us as the Bread of Life. He fills us with the gift of divine love and invites us to share that love with others as Mary did with Elizabeth.

Most loving Father, help me to open my heart to receive again today the gift of your Son Jesus who satisfies my hunger for love and renews me with your divine life.

The Gift Which Renews Hope

Father Fidelis Moscinski, C.F.R.

When the time arrived for Elizabeth to have her child she gave birth to a son. Her neighbors and relatives heard that the Lord had shown his great mercy toward her, and they rejoiced with her. (Lk 1:57-58)

The birth of a child, even in difficult circumstances, is very often an occasion of joy, wonder, and thanksgiving. We marvel that a new, unique, and precious life has come into our world. The cooing, caresses, and smiles which the little bundle elicits from even the stodgiest adult points to a sublime truth: every child is a gift from God.

Elizabeth, her neighbors, and relatives all see in the birth of John a sign of God's mercy and goodness. This little child is welcomed as a true gift from the Lord and a special cause for hope. God is faithful to his promises and prepares the way for our salvation.

The life-changing hope and joy which the birth of a child could bring was recently dramatized in a movie called *Children of Men*, based on a book by P. D. James. It tells of a stark future in which humanity has been afflicted for many years by a plague of infertility. There are no more children. Hopes have vanished, despair sets in, and man's life is filled with fear, poverty, and violence. But in the midst of this childless world a woman inexplicably becomes pregnant and gives birth. It is a sign of hope: perhaps a cure for the global sterility can now be found. All of a sudden this one, small, weak child becomes the focus of humanity's hopes. The child's very presence stops a raging battle and inspires great acts of self-sacrifice.

The births of John and Jesus were not only occasions of profound joy but also history-changing events. Through the gifts of these children God was restoring hope to mankind. The joy of Elizabeth and her relatives is ours as well. We are challenged today to see in each and every newborn child not a burden to be avoided or a product to be manipulated but rather a priceless treasure and generous gift from God who brings joy and hope to all.

Life-giving Father, you have created and blessed each of us in your Son, Jesus; bestow upon us your Spirit that we may always rejoice in your gift of life and trust in your goodness and mercy.

What's in a Name?

Father Fidelis Moscinski, C.F.R.

When [Elizabeth's neighbors and relatives] came on the eighth day to circumcise the child, they were going to call him Zechariah after his father, but his mother said in reply, "No. He will be called John." But they answered her, "There is no one among your relatives who has this name." (Lk 1:59-61)

It is always interesting to read each year the lists of the most popular names given to newborn babies. Some names are new, many are quite traditional. In 2010 the top names were: Jacob, Ethan, Michael, and Isabella, Sophia, and Emma. The choice of names for children is always a favorite topic of conversation in families, and it was no different for Elizabeth and Zechariah.

When it came time to name their newborn child, the family put forward some traditional names, such as Zach Jr. Good enough for the father, good enough for the son. But Elizabeth recognized that in her son God was doing something new. An old name would simply not be appropriate. Filled with the Holy Spirit, Elizabeth was able to transcend human custom ("There is no one among your relatives who has this name") and perceive in her child a *new* grace, a *new* visitation of God. In fact, the name "John" means "God is gracious."

John's name pointed to a new presence and action of God in the world. John himself would point out "the Lamb of God, who takes away the sin of the world" (Jn 1:29). He identified for all of us the source of new life, the One who could lift us out of our sinful past and give us a new life of grace.

But we need the Holy Spirit, as Elizabeth did, to sense this new possibility of grace offered to us by Jesus. We need his help to accept it and live within it each day. Our difficulty is that we often resist change; we cling to the old ways of acting and thinking precisely when God is asking us to move forward into a new and deeper life with him. Today we cast aside the comforts of conformity and recognize with Elizabeth God's desire to re-create us anew in his eternal love.

Gracious Father, you are always at work in my life, inviting me to begin again as a loving disciple of Jesus. Help me to embrace with gratitude the gift of new life you offer me today.

Speak, and Be Not Silent!

Father Fidelis Moscinski, C.F.R.

So [Elizabeth's neighbors and relatives] made signs, asking his father what he wished him to be called. He asked for a tablet and wrote, "John is his name," and all were amazed. Immediately his mouth was opened, his tongue freed, and he spoke blessing God. Then fear came upon all their neighbors, and all these matters were discussed throughout the hill country of Judea. (Lk 1:62-65)

Zechariah was afflicted with an unusual case of muteness during the pregnancy of his wife Elizabeth. This muteness was a consequence of his questioning, even doubting, the angel Gabriel's message announcing the conception of John, his son. But when Zechariah manifested his faith, he was delivered of his paralysis of speech, "his mouth was opened, his tongue freed, and he spoke blessing God." Both his nine-month muteness and his sudden recovery of speech were dramatic signs noticed by many.

It is a curious phenomenon of today that many people choose to protest publicly some perceived injustice by placing duct tape over their mouths. They intend others to see this action as a sign of opposition to something or that their voices are being silenced. Although this kind of protest ranges across the political spectrum it certainly catches our attention. Why would someone willingly silence himself in this way? Speech is so much a part of our human identity and behavior that its loss signals to us that something is terribly wrong.

Zechariah's muteness indicated a lack of faith; the muteness of protesters could indicate a lack of justice. But there is also another very common muteness in the world today, not as dramatic perhaps, but far more serious: silence about God himself. In the midst of so much incessant talk in our society, how much do we hear—or speak ourselves—about God? The One who gives us the very gift of speech often appears curiously absent from so many conversations—at work, at home, in the media.

It was God who opened Zechariah's mouth and it was about God that Zechariah spoke. The father of the "voice of the bridegroom" testified—as his son was later to do also—to the "word of God." How often do I use the precious gift of speech to witness to the blessings of God in my life?

Father of the Eternal Word, you created me with the power of speech in order to testify to your greatness and love; free my tongue to proclaim your blessings to others today.

Have You Received the Spirit?

Father Fidelis Moscinski, C.F.R.

All who heard these things took them to heart, saying, "What, then, will this child be?" For surely the hand of the Lord was with him. Then Zechariah his father, filled with the holy Spirit, prophesied, saying: "Blessed be the Lord, the God of Israel,/ for he has visited and brought redemption to his people." (Lk 1:66-68)

In the first couple of chapters of Saint Luke's Gospel we continually come across characters he describes as "filled with the holy Spirit." Mary is told by Gabriel that "the holy Spirit will come upon you," Elizabeth and John receive this same holy Spirit at the Visitation (1:41), Simeon has the holy Spirit upon him (2:25), and now we read that Zechariah also is "filled with the holy Spirit."

What does this mean, and who or what is this Holy Spirit? "Spirit" is obviously something immaterial, without a body. It can penetrate and take hold of something physical. We commonly speak of a person or group as possessing a certain spirit. "That man has a spirit of gentleness" or "that team has a real spirit of unity." Spirit is intangible yet real, personal but shared with others. Spirit seems to influence our thoughts and actions, even giving us capacities we did not have before.

"The Holy Spirit" is of course God's Spirit, the Third Person of the Most Holy Trinity along with the Father and the Son. We receive him into ourselves at baptism which makes us sons and daughters of God and sharers in his divine life. This Spirit of truth and love enlightens our minds and empowers our wills so that we can both know and love God. He is personally present to us and at the same time dwells within the entire Church.

To be filled with this Holy Spirit, as were Mary, Elizabeth, and Zechariah, simply means to receive fully that for which we were created. A glass is made to be filled with water, a balloon is made to be filled with air, a candle is made to burn a flame. Water, wind, and fire: all images of the Holy Spirit who seeks to penetrate our souls, transform our lives, and bring to perfection our capacities to know and love for ever Father, Son, and Holy Spirit.

Heavenly Father, you have visited your people and brought them redemption through your Son; fill me now with your Holy Spirit that I may become the person you created me to be.

When a Plan Comes Together

Father Fidelis Moscinski, C.F.R.

"He has raised up a horn for our salvation/ within the house of David his servant,/ even as he promised through the mouth of his holy prophets from of old:/ salvation from our enemies and from the hand of all who hate us,/ to show mercy to our fathers/ and to be mindful of his holy covenant." (Lk 1:69-72)

Intelligent people make plans. The businessman plans how to make money; the politician plans how to get re-elected; the mother plans how to care for and feed her children. We all make plans, great and small, in order to achieve our goals. And those plans which are well made and well executed are successful.

I was recently explaining to one of my brothers how to play chess. I said, "It's not enough simply to know how the pieces move, you need to have *a plan*: you need to know what you want to accomplish and precisely how you are going to do it." Without some kind of a plan whether in life or in chess we flounder, stumble, and fail.

What about God? Does he have a plan, and if so, what is it? His plan is called divine providence: the mysterious workings of his knowledge and will creating all things and directing them to their proper goal, including you and me. At the center of God's plan is our salvation in Jesus Christ. The inspired words of Zechariah describe this amazing plan. He speaks of God remembering his "holy covenant"—the sacred bond he made with the house, that is, the dynasty of King David. From within this dynastic family God raises up a "horn"—a biblical symbol of strength. This is Jesus, "the son of David" (Mt 1:1), the one who was "promised through the mouths of his holy prophets." God's ultimate purpose is to show the depths of his love for us in the life, death, and Resurrection of Jesus—the perfect fulfillment of his plan.

Nothing in the universe escapes God's loving plan. Every detail of our lives has been foreseen by him. All that he desires of us is that we cooperate with him, submit all *our* plans to him, and allow him to fulfill what he has promised: salvation from our enemies and eternal peace in his kingdom.

Almighty Father, I stand in wonder at your mysterious and loving plan to save me in Jesus, your Son; today I surrender all my plans to you as I pray, "Your will be done."

There You Are!

Father Fidelis Moscinski, C.F.R.

"And [to be mindful of] the oath he swore to Abraham our father,/ and to grant us that, rescued from the hand of enemies,/ without fear we might worship him in holiness and righteousness/ before him all our days." (Lk 1:73-75)

Zechariah prophesies that God will "grant us that…we might worship him in holiness and righteousness." As a Jewish priest he was quite familiar with the worship of God in the temple: the ancient prayers, the reverential solemnity, and the continual sacrifices offered in the presence of a holy God.

We too are familiar with the regular worship of God every Sunday during holy Mass. What is that experience like for us? I imagine it varies. Sometimes it could be quite peaceful and recollected; sometimes we may feel anxious or worried as we insistently present our petitions to God hoping that he will hear us; and at other times it may be just a struggle to fight off distractions or boredom.

But reflecting on the experience of worship in this way is unfortunately quite misguided because the worship of almighty God is not really about us after all. It's about him—giving God the adoration and honor which is his due.

I came across a quote recently that expresses two very different attitudes a person can have: "Some people walk into a room and say, 'Here I am!' Other people walk into a room and say, 'Ah, there you are!'" When we enter our church or begin a time of private prayer, do we say to God, "Here I am!" or "There you are!" Is our worship fundamentally self-focused or God-focused?

It might help if we recall that the very act of worshiping is itself a gift from God. Zechariah tells us that God *grants to us* that we might worship him. He gives us his Spirit which makes us pray, "Abba, Father!" In fact, God saves us through worship because in humbly acknowledging him as our Creator and Savior, our Lord and Master, we are freed from the sin of self-centeredness and the temptation to make an idol of anything in this world.

Holy and everlasting Father, you draw me to yourself, the source of all holiness and righteousness; may I worship you in spirit and truth now and always.

Like Father, Like Son

Father Fidelis Moscinski, C.F.R.

"And you, child, will be called prophet of the Most High,/ for you will go before the Lord to prepare his ways,/ to give his people knowledge of salvation/ through the forgiveness of their sins,/ because of the tender mercy of our God/ by which the daybreak from on high will visit us/ to shine on those who sit in darkness and death's shadow,/ to guide our feet into the path of peace."
(Lk 1:76-79)

William Shakespeare once wrote, "It is a wise father that knows his own child."

Zechariah, having just become a father, speaks to his newborn son, John: "You, my child, will be called a prophet of the Most High." He knows by divine revelation his son's prophetic identity and mission. And although John is only eight days old and cannot understand these words, yet Zechariah affirms his son's value and purpose in this world. This is the task of every father with his child. John will grow up secure in the knowledge of who he is in God's eyes and what he must do: prepare the way of the Lord and give his people knowledge of salvation.

A very unique and special relationship exists between fathers and sons. The son receives from his father his sense of self, a view of the world, and instruction on how he ought to live. And the father sees in his son the image of himself and a precious gift entrusted to his life-long care. Theirs is a bond willed by God and intended for the good of both.

A little story illustrates this. One night a father overheard his son pray: "Dear God, make me the kind of man my daddy is." Later that night, the father prayed, "Dear God, make me the kind of man my son wants me to be."

This sacred bond between a father and a son is lived out supremely in the eternal communion between God the Father and his Son, Jesus Christ. At the solemn moment of Jesus' baptism, his Father declares to him his identity and his tender love: "You are my beloved Son; with you I am well pleased" (Lk 3:22). And Jesus knows his mission, for he has come "to give my life as a ransom for many" (Mt 20:28).

What about us? We receive our deepest identity and our most exalted vocation from God our Father: to live as his own beloved sons and daughters.

Eternal Father, you have made me your adopted child by the grace of your Son; grant that I may be faithful to this precious gift and always pleasing to you.

What Grows in the Desert

Father Fidelis Moscinski, C.F.R.

*The child grew and became strong in spirit, and he was
in the desert until the day of his manifestation to Israel.*
(Lk 1:80)

Doesn't it seem a little strange that Saint Luke describes the child John growing and becoming strong "in the desert"? This is not the usual place we associate with growth, life, and bounty. It's certainly not a place to raise children. Rather, the desert is often perceived as a place of barrenness, extreme heat, and mortal danger.

Perhaps John only entered the desert as an adult. But the Scriptures seem to suggest the reality of spiritual growth in the context of deprivation, even isolation. Is such a thing possible? Yes, if we understand that spiritual progress always requires a return to the Word of God and a desire to be continually nourished by him. This happens only if we first turn away from the distracting words and worldly voices which clamor for our attention. Only in the silence of the desert can the seed of God's Word bear fruit in us.

Consider the life of a famous hermit of the Egyptian desert. Arsenius was a man of the world and a tutor of the emperor's sons. While he was still living in the palace, he prayed to God: "Lord, lead me in the way of salvation." And a voice said to him, "Arsenius, flee from men and you will be saved." Then, having withdrawn to the desert, he made the same prayer again and he heard: "Arsenius, flee, be silent, pray always, for these are the source of sinlessness."

John the Baptist fled from men, was silent, and encountered God's Word in the desert. That Word then took deep root in him, grew and bore much fruit until he himself became a "voice of one crying out in the desert:/ 'Prepare the way of the Lord'" (Lk 3:4).

God wants us also to grow and become strong in the Spirit. So he leads us into the "desert"—a place of interior silence, a place of prayer, where we can hear, embrace, and live by his abundant Word.

*Father of the incarnate Word, Jesus Christ, help me to be still and
know that you are my God; help me to be silent and ever more
open to receiving your life-giving Word into my soul.*

The Lord in History

Father Richard G. Smith

In those days a decree went out from Caesar Augustus that the whole world should be enrolled. This was the first enrollment, when Quirinius was governor of Syria. So all went to be enrolled, each to his own town. And Joseph too went up from Galilee from the town of Nazareth to Judea, to the city of David that is called Bethlehem, because he was of the house and family of David. (Lk 2:1-4)

Considering his role in the life of Jesus, Pontius Pilate gets considerable attention in the Nicene Creed that Catholics recite together at Mass each week: "He [Jesus] was crucified under Pontius Pilate, he suffered death and was buried." The only other human person mentioned by name in the Creed is the Virgin Mary. There is, of course, no comparing the two! Pilate gets a mention not because of his character, or lack thereof, but because he is a real man who lived in a real place and played a role in human history. Placing the death of Jesus in the context of the governorship of Pontius Pilate underscores the truth that Jesus' death and Resurrection are not part of a disembodied cosmic myth, standing over and against human history, but events that happen within human history.

Likewise, Saint Luke is careful to include the names of two Roman leaders, Caesar Augustus and Quirinius, in his recounting of the birth of Jesus. At the beginning of his Gospel, Saint Luke assures Theophilus, to whom he addresses his words, that he has made a careful examination of what had previously been handed down regarding Jesus' life so that he could relate it anew and in an orderly fashion. Saint Luke envisions his task as Evangelist as something like that of an historian (though *more* than an historian as well) because the incarnation happens in history. He mentions these specific two men for the same reason we mention Pilate in the Creed—as a way of placing the life of Jesus in the context of living human history. Jesus wasn't born just *anywhere* or at *any* time; the Word was incarnate in a *real* place, Bethlehem, in a *real* time, during the reign of Caesar Augustus and the governorship of Quirinius. Likewise, Jesus is present and active in our own time not as an idea or a movement, but in real places, in real human hearts and life.

Almighty Father, you guide the whole of human history as you guide the whole of my life. May I be open to the ways you call me to be your servant in my own time and place in history.

Christ Awakened

Father Richard G. Smith

[Joseph went] to be enrolled with Mary, his betrothed, who was with child. While they were there, the time came for her to have her child, and she gave birth to her firstborn son. She wrapped him in swaddling clothes and laid him in a manger, because there was no room for them in the inn. (Lk 2:5-7)

With a few simple words, Saint Luke captures the imagination: "she wrapped him in swaddling clothes and laid him in a manger." That simple and human image has inspired some of the greatest masterpieces of art and music ever created. Art, in turn, owes much to the poor man from Assisi who helped shape the Christian imagination for many centuries. The tradition of the Christmas crèche seems to have begun in the small hill-town of Greccio in central Italy. There, on Christmas Eve in 1223, Saint Francis organized the first Christmas crèche as a sort of living tableau depicting the birth of the Savior. Saint Francis' first biographer, Thomas of Celano, describes how the saint stood before the scene filled with awe and wonder at the beauty of Jesus' humble birth. He also relates that, according to the testimony of an eyewitness, as Francis approached the lifeless doll representing the infant Jesus it suddenly came to life.

Saint Francis' biographer found the miracle to be fitting, since Christ had formerly been "given over to oblivion" in the hearts of many of the townspeople until the artistry of Saint Francis brought Christ back to life in them. The phrase "given over to oblivion" is so strong that we might wonder if it's an exaggeration. On the other hand, we also know that the daily, often hectic routines of life and our own anxieties and struggles can threaten to overwhelm our hearts so that there's little room for Jesus. While it might be going too far to say we've given Jesus over to oblivion in our hearts, perhaps we find ourselves needing our sense of his presence to be stirred in us. Saint Luke and Saint Francis both understood well that the scenes of Jesus' life, presented in all their simplicity and beauty, have the power to awaken the human heart and soul when we allow them to capture our imagination.

Loving Father, as I read and pray with the Sacred Scriptures, the gift of your very Word, may my love for you be stirred and renewed, that I may enthusiastically embrace the life in Christ to which I have been called.

Causa Nostrae Laetitiae

Father Richard G. Smith

Now there were shepherds in that region living in the fields and keeping the night watch over their flock. The angel of the Lord appeared to them and the glory of the Lord shone around them, and they were struck with great fear. The angel said to them, "Do not be afraid; for behold, I proclaim to you good news of great joy that will be for all the people." (Lk 2:8-10)

On the grounds of Saint Joseph's Seminary in Dunwoodie, Yonkers, New York, a small statue of our Lady holds her infant Son. From an artistic point of view, nothing about the statue is uniquely outstanding, and it is very similar to the tens of thousands of other statues of Mary and the infant Jesus in Catholic churches and shrines around the world. Yet, this particular statue has been well loved by seminarians for many years. I think it is the title at the base of the statue that makes it so beautiful and so treasured: *Causa Nostrae Laetitiae*, Latin for "Cause of Our Joy."

Although this Marian title is included in the Litany of Loreto, it is not a title we hear very often. The image of Mary holding out her Son in the statue makes clear that it is Jesus himself who is our "Joy." When Mary gives her "yes" to bearing Jesus, she becomes the *cause* of our Joy. The angels proclaim "good news of *great joy*" to the shepherds, and this is not a throwaway phrase on Saint Luke's part. That joyful proclamation is, in fact, the very heart of our Christian faith—God is with us, near to us, loving us, redeeming us. Jesus comes, not to add to our burdens in life, but to set us free to receive the fullness of life! And so, before all else, the Christian message is one of great joy! In coming to know Jesus, we come to know true and lasting joy. In his masterful homilies, Pope Benedict often says that joy is *the* defining characteristic of a Christian disciple. In our own time, this is an especially important dimension of our faith to appreciate: there is no stronger human witness to Jesus Christ and his Gospel than the joyful life of self-giving love embraced by his disciples!

Gracious Father, as I embrace Jesus, my Joy, anew each day, may my very life become a witness to the life and peace and joy he alone brings.

Infinity Dwindled to Infancy

Father Richard G. Smith

"For today in the city of David a savior has been born for you who is Messiah and Lord. And this will be a sign for you: you will find an infant wrapped in swaddling clothes and lying in a manger." And suddenly there was a multitude of the heavenly host with the angel, praising God and saying: "Glory to God in the highest/ and on earth peace to those on whom his favor rests." (Lk 2:11-14)

In the Gospels, Jesus often laments the desire of the crowds for great signs as proof of his divinity. While they are asking for large, dramatic signs of God's presence and action in the world and in their lives, they miss the sign of that presence and action—Jesus himself. Human nature is remarkably consistent. Even today, people are willing to spend great amounts of time, energy, and money traveling to places where dramatic signs of the divine allegedly take place—even if it's only a tree stump resembling Jesus' face somewhere in New Jersey! But we can miss the subtle, often more powerful, signs of God's love and presence in our daily lives.

In one of his finest poems, "The Blessed Virgin Compared to the Air We Breathe", Father Gerard Manley Hopkins writes that our Lady "Gave God's infinity/ Dwindled to infancy/ Welcome in womb and breast,/ Birth, milk, and all the rest." The sign given to the shepherds that night in Bethlehem was an ordinary newborn child being cared for by his Mother—our great and mighty God "Dwindled to infancy." There's not much of a "wow" factor in that sign. In fact, it is apparent only to those who look with eyes of faith and eyes of love. The simple and open hearts of these shepherds were able to perceive what many others did not.

The great sign of Jesus' continuing presence and action among us is the Church's sacraments, above all the Eucharist. In the Eucharist, Jesus remains, in a sense, "Dwindled to infancy" as a gentle, quiet presence among his people. Because the Eucharist can appear so ordinary, we can miss the awesome love that is revealed and shared there. Like the shepherds, we need simple and open hearts in order to perceive Jesus' presence—and we don't need to go very far at all, or spend a lot of money, to find him.

Eternal Father, open my eyes and my heart to the quiet, subtle ways you choose to act in the world and in my life; help me to perceive Jesus, your Son, especially in the gift of the Eucharist.

42

The Christmas Trees of New York City

Father Richard G. Smith

When the angels went away from them to heaven, the shepherds said to one another, "Let us go, then, to Bethlehem to see this thing that has taken place, which the Lord has made known to us." So they went in haste and found Mary and Joseph, and the infant lying in the manger. When they saw this, they made known the message that had been told them about this child.

(Lk 2:15-17)

Most tourists visiting New York City in December find their way to the famous Christmas tree in Rockefeller Center. Unfortunately, far fewer will discover a less famous, though even more beautiful, tree a few blocks north of Rockefeller Center at the Metropolitan Museum of Art. Actually, the tree itself is not particularly noteworthy—it is the seventeeth-century crèche from Naples, Italy, which surrounds the tree that makes it worth a visit. There we see all the usual characters: dozens of angels, the shepherds and sheep, the wise men, the donkey and ox, Mary and Joseph.

What makes the crèche so unusual, though, are all the other scenes around it—vignettes of everyday life in seventeenth-century Naples. Among the many scenes, we see a man walking a dog, a little boy dragging his mother somewhere, a woman baking bread in the kitchen, a man sleeping by the water fountain, even a young man flirting with a young woman. There is something beautifully human and real about these representations. And while they are all very beautiful, ultimately they are just scenes of simple people in their ordinary, everyday lives. That is what is so wonderful about the crèche: if any one of those ordinary people living their ordinary lives were to just turn the corner (around the tree), they would find the wondrous scene of the newly born Jesus surrounded by Mary, Joseph, and the dozens of angels. The newborn Jesus is so close to any one of them, that they could walk up and touch him. And that's the point of the crèche. God is that close.

In Saint Luke's telling, the birth of Jesus is revealed first of all to ordinary people, people like you and me, in the midst of their work who only need turn the corner to discover the God who wants no distance between us and himself.

Kind Father, you have made known to me the gift of Jesus, who is present to me each day; help me to recognize his presence and respond to his love.

43

The Gospel Terrifies Me

Father Richard G. Smith

All who heard it were amazed by what had been told them by the shepherds. And Mary kept all these things, reflecting on them in her heart. Then the shepherds returned, glorifying and praising God for all they had heard and seen, just as it had been told to them. (Lk 2:18-20)

In his most influential theological text, the German theologian Rudolf Otto uses a Latin phrase, *mysterium tremendum et fascinans* ("fearful and fascinating mystery") to describe the human person's experience of the "Holy." Our experience of God is at once beautiful and terrifying. The appearances of God (and even of angels) in the Old Testament are often accompanied by the phrase, "Do not be afraid!" precisely because an encounter with the divine can be terrifying. Even the shepherds themselves need an assurance that they ought not be afraid when the multitude of angels initially appear to them. But, as the shepherds depart from the manger they are filled with a sense of the *mysterium fascinans* of their encounter with the Christ child. They have met Jesus, and nothing in their lives will be the same—and so there is a joy to their encounter with God. The joy in their hearts overflows into full-throated praise of God. The sense of *mysterium tremendum* will no doubt come later.

Saint Luke tells us that the shepherds make known the Good News they have received—in other words, they spread the Gospel. In one of his sermons, Saint Augustine says, "The Gospel terrifies me." He realizes that to whom much has been given, much is expected. As a preacher of the Gospel, Saint Augustine realizes that he must live what he preaches. The Gospel calls for an undivided heart given over to the Lord and a life lived according to the pattern of Jesus' own life. In our encounter with Jesus, we are invited to enter a life-giving and life-changing friendship; our response to that friendship is a confident love and trust in Jesus, allowing him to guide our hearts. That is a high calling, and it is a terrifying calling, but it is also a beautiful calling.

Heavenly Father, may your perfect love cast out all fear from my heart so that the good work you have begun in me be brought to completion in Christ.

Name above All Names
Father Richard G. Smith

When eight days were completed for his circumcision, he was named Jesus, the name given him by the angel before he was conceived in the womb. When the days were completed for their purification according to the law of Moses, [Joseph and Mary] took him up to Jerusalem to present him to the Lord, just as it is written in the law of the Lord, "Every male that opens the womb shall be consecrated to the Lord," and to offer the sacrifice of "a pair of turtledoves or two young pigeons." (Lk 2:21-24a)

S aint Luke records the fact so simply: "he was named Jesus." The sound of the name of someone we love, or even the written appearance of that name, can be beautiful to us. On the dedication page for one of his books of poetry, the American author Raymond Carver dedicates his work to his wife by writing her name four times—as though he enjoyed simply spelling out her name. One of the great signs of the intimacy between God and the people of Israel in the Old Testament is God's revelation of the divine name to God's people. God invites the people of Israel into a covenantal relationship in which they could call upon the very name of God in their prayer. Traditional Hebrew piety forbade the actual pronunciation of the divine name and, when the name was written, it was abbreviated to its four consonants as YHWH and pronounced *Adonai*, so that God's name would never be blasphemed or casually mentioned.

Some scholars suggest that early Christians carried over reverence for the divine name by abbreviating "Jesus" as "IHS" (the first three letters of his name in Greek) in their art and biblical manuscripts. The abbreviated name of Jesus is reminiscent of the four letter abbreviation of the divine name in the Old Testament and is further evidence that Christians believed in Jesus' divinity from the very beginning. Of course, traditional Christian piety places no restrictions on reverently pronouncing the name "Jesus." For those of us who have chosen to spend our lives with Jesus, his name is both beautiful and powerful. The North American martyr Saint Isaac Jogues kept a private journal in the months before his brutal martyrdom. At the end of one entry, Jogues writes the name "Jesus" three times—like Raymond Carver, he seems to take comfort and joy in simply writing and looking at the name of the One he loved.

Loving Father, I give you thanks and praise for revealing yourself to me in the human face and name of Jesus. May Jesus your Son be a continual source of comfort and joy in my life.

Embracing Jesus

Father Richard G. Smith

Now there was a man in Jerusalem whose name was Simeon.
This man was righteous and devout, awaiting the consolation of
Israel, and the holy Spirit was upon him. It had been revealed
to him by the holy Spirit that he should not see death before he
had seen the Messiah of the Lord. He came in the Spirit into
the temple; and when the parents brought in the child Jesus to
perform the custom of the law in regard to him, he took him
into his arms and blessed God. (Lk 2:25-28)

Simeon "took him into his arms"—there is perhaps no more tender and human scene in all of Scripture than this. A man who had grown old while patiently waiting for God to fulfill his promises embraces a tiny newborn infant, who is God incarnate. The old man Simeon embraces the New Man, Jesus. It is impossible to remain unmoved! The great theologian and preacher, Origen of Alexandria, seems himself to have been moved by the scene. In a homily on this text, he urges his congregation to embrace the child Jesus, just as Simeon has embraced him. The homily is one of the first instances of Christian devotion to the Christ child, and Origen is emphatically *concrete* in his words to the congregation. He tells them that if they want to hold Jesus they, too, ought to embrace him with their own hands. Christian discipleship is nothing less than our embracing Jesus Christ, the incarnate Word of God, who has already embraced us. As Pope Benedict repeats over and again in his homilies, to be a Christian is to enter into an intensely personal friendship with Jesus.

Origen teaches us that the Christian embrace of Jesus is not an abstraction that occurs in our imagination. We embrace Jesus in concrete ways, *with our own hands*: we truly embrace him in our service of others, most especially the poor; we embrace him in our spouses, children, parents, siblings, and friends; and, above all else we embrace him in the sacraments, especially the Eucharist. When Origen preached on this scene from Saint Luke's Gospel, his congregation was preparing to share in the Eucharist and so his words take on a special Eucharistic significance—the tender, human experience of Simeon who embraces the infant Jesus is, in fact, the experience of every Christian who is privileged to come to Jesus in the Eucharist.

Eternal Father, thank you for the continuing gift of the incarnation of your beloved Son Jesus; guide my thoughts and actions each day so that I, like Simeon, may embrace Jesus anew.

Compline

Father Richard G. Smith

[Simeon said,] "Now, Master, you may let your servant go/ in peace, according to your word,/ for my eyes have seen your salvation,/ which you prepared in sight of all the peoples,/ a light for revelation to the Gentiles,/ and glory for your people Israel." (Lk 2:29-32)

The building in which I attended college seminary was built as a monastery for Visitation nuns. It was in the chapel of that building, where the sisters had gathered in choir for decades to chant the divine office, that I was introduced to the daily celebration of the office. Several times a week we seminarians would come together at 9 PM in the darkened chapel to pray the final office of the day known as compline. The central prayer of compline does not change from day to day or with the liturgical year, as do the other parts. This prayer is often called by its first two words in Latin: the *Nunc Dimittis*. It is the prayer that Simeon prays as he leaves the temple after meeting Jesus. The office of compline is a favorite among many priests and religious, especially when it is prayed in common. There is something about gathering to praise God in the quiet stillness of a dark chapel, voicing psalms and prayers that are often known by heart so that a book is often not required, that opens and expands the human heart.

As a college seminarian, I was very aware that the prayer of Simeon had been sung in that chapel by religious sisters long before I was born and, in fact, had echoed and reechoed on the lips of Christians as a night prayer for centuries upon centuries. The prayer of Simeon becomes *our* prayer as we, with Simeon, acknowledge that we have *seen* the Messiah with our own eyes and have *embraced* him with our own hands. There is a peace that comes from our knowing Jesus—our hearts are no longer restless and searching—it is a grateful peace expressed in the prayer of an old man that will once again be voiced by the praying Body of Christ all over the world tonight.

Good and faithful Father, I am grateful to stand in the midst of your Church, joining the praise and thanksgiving of your people that has continued through the centuries. May the words of these prayers continue to guide and shape my heart.

The Suffering of Love
Father Richard G. Smith

The child's father and mother were amazed at what was said about him; and Simeon blessed them and said to Mary his mother, "Behold, this child is destined for the fall and rise of many in Israel, and to be a sign that will be contradicted (and you yourself a sword will pierce) so that the thoughts of many hearts may be revealed." (Lk 2:33-35)

In one of his homilies, Origen of Alexandria uses the suggestive phrase "the suffering of love." He means that loving another person will, at one time or another, require a measure of suffering by the one who loves. We willingly sacrifice our own comfort for the people we love, we give of ourselves without thinking of the cost and, above all, we share in the pain of someone we love when he or she suffers. In fact, we often wish we could actually take on the physical suffering of someone we love, so that he or she would not have to experience such pain. In all of our important relationships in life, we bear the suffering of love. When we are with someone for the "long haul" we are willing to do things we never thought we'd have the strength to do and endure things we thought we'd never be able to endure, simply because we love the other person.

Simeon's comment to Mary—it is an aside, really—that a sword will pierce her own heart because of the beautiful child she holds, must have startled her. Who wants to hear something like that about a newborn son? On the other hand, in her heart, Mary must have already known that she would bear the suffering of love for Jesus. Mary cast her lot entirely with her Son. She loved him in the way only a mother can love and followed him with all her heart. Mary is the first disciple, the greatest disciple, and so we ought to expect our Christian discipleship to resemble hers. We should not, then, be surprised when we experience a certain amount of discomfort and even pain on account of our faith in Jesus. It is all part of the "suffering of love" we willingly bear for the One who loves us beyond all measure.

Loving Father, your Son Jesus is the Pearl of great price in my life; may I always bear the suffering of love with joy and patience as a Christian disciple.

Reborn, Not Born

Father Richard G. Smith

There was also a prophetess, Anna, the daughter of Phanuel, of the tribe of Asher. She was advanced in years, having lived seven years with her husband after her marriage, and then as a widow until she was eighty-four. She never left the temple, but worshiped night and day with fasting and prayer. And coming forward at that very time, she gave thanks to God and spoke about the child to all who were awaiting the redemption of Jerusalem. (Lk 2:36-38)

I like the prophetess Anna because she feels like someone I know. Anna reminds me of the people God has used in my life to bring me the gift of Christian faith. Anna is a quiet, hidden presence in this scene. She could not have had an easy life, being widowed at a young age in a society that made women legally and socially dependent upon men. Despite whatever difficulties she may have experienced in life, she remains faithful to the Lord— daily seeking his face through prayer and acts of fasting and penance. She must have been a familiar person in the temple, and the title "prophetess" indicates she was respected as a friend of God. She comes forward only at the very end of the scene in the temple, her mouth filled with praise and thanks, ready to share her discovery of the Savior with the world.

Recently, a young man approached me after Sunday Mass asking to become a Catholic. I asked him his religion, and he responded that he was simply "Christian"; in fact, he had been born a Christian. Of course, it doesn't work that way: Christians are made, not born—or better, Christians are *reborn* in baptism. That is to say, to be a Christian is a *gift*, a gift that God offers us through other people. Often enough, it is the quiet, faithful, authentic discipleship of a Christian that makes Christianity appealing to us in the first place.

Those people who are the instruments of God's grace in our lives frequently resemble Anna: people like our mothers and fathers, our grandparents and siblings, our parish priests and teachers whose presence in our lives is sometimes taken for granted. Like Anna, they are ready to share their discovery of the Savior with us. Like Anna, they are familiar people to us, friends of God, content to remain in the background and a constant gentle presence in our lives.

Loving Father, I thank you for the gift of life, for the gift of new life in Christ you have shared with me in baptism. I thank you also for the Christian men and women you have brought into my life as witnesses to the Good News of Jesus Christ.

The Silence of the Gospels

Father Richard G. Smith

When [Joseph and Mary] had fulfilled all the prescriptions of the law of the Lord, they returned to Galilee, to their own town of Nazareth. The child grew and became strong, filled with wisdom; and the favor of God was upon him.

(Lk 2:39-40)

Except for the brief story about Jesus in the temple when he was twelve years old, this is as much as any of the Gospels tell us about the life of Jesus from his early childhood to young adulthood. Naturally, we are curious about those years, which make up the major part of Jesus' life on earth, and we would like to know more. But this is all we have in God's Word—silence. Anything other than silence about these years of Jesus' life is conjecture, not revelation. Silence can make us very uncomfortable, and often we try to fill our lives with noise to avoid complete silence. What we perceive to be silent gaps in Scripture, especially as they relate to Jesus' life, can also make us uncomfortable. We can rush to fill that silence with imagined details.

For several years as a young priest, I felt a strong attraction to make a weeklong silent retreat at a hermitage I had discovered nearby. At the same time, the thought of a week alone in a secluded cabin without music, television, or a computer and with nothing to read but the Scriptures made me anxious. Truthfully, I was afraid of the silence and what I might discover in that silence, and so I put off the retreat for a long time. I finally got past my fear and anxiety and went on the retreat. What I found in the silence was awesome. I came to a knowledge of God and an experience of God's love for me that was far deeper than my previous encounters with the Lord.

Perhaps the silence of Scripture when it comes to details like the early life of Jesus are not gaps we ought to try and fill with fanciful details. Rather, they are opportunities for us to rest in and spend time with what God *does* reveal to us about Jesus in the Gospels.

Gracious Father, the pace of life I keep can be, at times, an excuse for not making room for you in my life; free me from the fears and anxieties of life, that I may be more ready simply to rest in your love and listen to your Word.

Heaven's Ceiling

Father Richard G. Smith

*Each year [Jesus'] parents went to Jerusalem for the feast of
Passover, and when he was twelve years old, they went up
according to festival custom. After they had completed its days,
as they were returning, the boy Jesus remained behind in
Jerusalem, but his parents did not know it. (Lk 2:41-43)*

Here is a small window into the life of Jesus during his
childhood. Saint Luke recounts that it was the yearly custom of Mary and Joseph to bring Jesus to Jerusalem for
the celebration of the Passover. Like all good parents, they wished
to pass on what they most valued to their child. By taking Jesus to
Jerusalem for the Passover each year, they were not only passing
on their own faith in the one true God of Israel but at the same
time shaping Jesus' religious imagination and identity as a Jew. Although these verses are the briefest introduction to the story that
follows, they illustrate the diligence of Mary and Joseph in Jesus'
religious upbringing.

Parents play a powerful role in shaping the religious imagination
and identity of their children. When I was a child, the word "heaven"
immediately brought about a clear image of a dark wooden ceiling
with heavy beams going across it. From the time I was seven, my
family attended Mass in our suburban parish school's gymnasium
since there was no church building. Years later, as a young adult, I
returned for the first time to the parish church in the Bronx where
I had spent my first six years. That church's ceiling was the same
one I had always imagined in heaven—obviously, at some point
very early in my childhood, my parents had taught me that church
is where God is to be found or that church is "God's house" and
the image remained well into adulthood. In much more profound
ways, what I was taught and what I saw as a child has continued
to shape my understanding not simply of heaven, but of God himself! Whether our own childhood is a gift or an obstacle toward
coming to know the living God, Mary and Joseph show us the
awesome power and responsibility we have in the faith lives of our
children.

*Heavenly Father, thank you for the gift of my faith and for those
who have shared their Christian faith with me; may the influence
I have in the lives of others, especially of children, always serve to
bring them to a deeper knowledge and love of you.*

Lost, Then Found

Father Richard G. Smith

Thinking that [Jesus] was in the caravan, [his parents] journeyed for a day and looked for him among their relatives and acquaintances, but not finding him, they returned to Jerusalem to look for him. After three days they found him in the temple, sitting in the midst of the teachers, listening to them and asking them questions, and all who heard him were astounded at his understanding and his answers. (Lk 2:44-47)

Several years ago a controversial anti-smoking ad was filmed in Australia depicting a young child crying in a train station after losing his mother. The commercial's narrator exhorts smokers to stop smoking for the sake of their children, who would be left all alone at the death of a parent. The controversy arose because the four-year-old actor was actually allowed to lose sight of his mother for a moment during filming, and the intense distress that resulted was genuine. The ad remains available on the Internet and is heartbreaking to watch. Perhaps seeing a child in distress over being lost touches a primal fear in all of us—the fear of being lost, the fear of being alone in the world.

Later in his Gospel, Saint Luke relates several of Jesus' parables of being lost and then found. The culmination of those stories is that of the so-called prodigal son. When the father celebrates the son's return at the end of the story, he exclaims that his son was dead and is now alive, lost and now found! Being away from the father, being lost, is likened to death—and, perhaps, even *worse* than death. In this scene, it is Jesus who seems to wander off, but Mary and Joseph who are in distress. We would expect Jesus, as the lost one, to be filled with terror. But he is not. Jesus is with his Father, in the Father's house. Naturally, Mary and Joseph are filled with the terror any parent would feel having lost a child in a large city.

But this may also be another of the "lost and found" Gospel scenes so important to Saint Luke. Mary and Joseph are the ones who lose sight of Jesus, they are the ones who are lost. Only when they are with Jesus again—we might even say only when they are "found"—does their terror subside and their peace return.

Almighty Father, you are my life, and to be with you is the fullness of joy and peace and life; in your loving care for me, I am never truly alone. Help me to live in the certainty of your love and presence each new day.

Great Anxiety and Gradual Understanding

Father Richard G. Smith

When his parents saw [Jesus], they were astonished, and his mother said to him, "Son, why have you done this to us? Your father and I have been looking for you with great anxiety." And he said to them, "Why were you looking for me? Did you not know that I must be in my Father's house?" But they did not understand what he said to them. (Lk 2:48-50)

Jesus seems harsh here—or, at the very least, insensitive to the "great anxiety" of Mary and Joseph who, after three days, must have feared the worst for him. Once a child in a class I was teaching expressed surprise that Mary didn't smack Jesus for what the child saw as Jesus' fresh response! Of course, that is the response of neither Mary nor Joseph. Saint Luke tells us "they did not understand." When we love another person we want to understand him or her, and there is pain when we don't understand. On a human level, no one was closer to Jesus than Mary and Joseph. Mary is the first and perfect disciple of Jesus. And yet, things were not always completely clear for her or for her husband. This is one of those times, and there were most certainly others, when they simply had to trust that Jesus knew what he was about, even if they did not.

The experience of Mary and Joseph is also the experience of the Twelve and of the other disciples of Jesus in the Gospels. More often than not, at least before the Resurrection, they, too, do not understand Jesus. But they don't walk away from him; they remain with him and trust him even if they themselves don't have all the answers. Only gradually do they come to understand Jesus. Only gradually do they perceive how Jesus acts in their lives.

We often don't understand, either. When we are filled with "great anxiety" over the real pains and struggles of life, and when Jesus appears to be insensitive or slow acting when it comes to responding to that anxiety, it is tempting just to walk away. But the fullness of life, the answer to our questions and struggles, comes only from trusting in Jesus who gradually opens and expands our hearts so that we can understand.

Almighty and eternal Father, though I may not always understand you or how you act in my life, I am confident in your love, knowing that even now you are making all things work together for the good in my life.

Shelter of the Word

Father Richard G. Smith

[Jesus] went down with [his parents] and came to Nazareth, and was obedient to them; and his mother kept all these things in her heart. And Jesus advanced [in] wisdom and age and favor before God and man. (Lk 2:51-52)

There is an ancient and persistent Christian tradition that Saint Luke was not only a physician, but an artist. Indeed, there are several icons of our Lady attributed to him, and he is sometimes called the first icon writer, or painter. Reading his Gospel, it is clear how such a tradition would arise. Saint Luke paints beautiful pictures with his words, so much so that many of the most loved and frequently depicted themes of Western art are derived from his Gospel. Whatever modern art history might determine about the paintings attributed to him, there is no denying Saint Luke has the heart of a poet. Having recounted the story of Jesus' birth from the Annunciation to the finding in the temple, Saint Luke writes that Mary "kept all these things in her heart." It is a poetic and beautiful way to describe Mary's contemplation of her Son. More than anyone else, Mary looked upon her Son with eyes of love, and treasured all her experiences with him, even those that might have been painful or confusing to her initially.

In the woods of western New Jersey, there's a small community, or laura, of the Hermits of Jesus of the Heart of Jesus who live an intensely contemplative life. A title they invoke for our Lady is "Shelter of the Word." Mary does not shelter the Word for nine months only—as Saint Luke teaches us, she continually shelters and contemplates the Word in her heart. For the hermits, Mary is the model Christian contemplative. They understand their vocation in the Church to be similar "shelters of the Word," holding the Word in their hearts and treasuring all their experiences with him, even those that might be painful or confusing. The lives of such contemplatives become something of an icon for all of us Christians. We, too, are to become shelters of the Word, at all times holding and treasuring the Word in our hearts.

Loving Father, may I become more and more like Mary, holding and contemplating your Word in my heart, that I, too, may become a true shelter of the Word of God.

The Presence We Are Called to Be

Monsignor Gregory E. S. Malovetz

In the fifteenth year of the reign of Tiberius Caesar, when Pontius Pilate was governor of Judea, and Herod was tetrarch of Galilee, and his brother Philip tetrarch of the region of Ituraea and Trachonitis, and Lysanias was tetrarch of Abilene, during the high priesthood of Annas and Caiaphas, the word of God came to John the son of Zechariah in the desert.
(Lk 3:1-2)

On the Sunday after Thanksgiving I had to attend an event an hour away from my home. I also needed to be back that evening for an event at my parish. Under normal circumstances it would be no easy feat to get back in time, but with holiday traffic I was pushing my luck.

Nearing my destination, I noticed how nice the area was. No time for sightseeing, I thought, and continued on my way. I arrived at the first event, but my eye was always on the clock. When the time came, I got in my car and began to drive, believing I had beat the odds. Once more I noticed how pretty the area was, deciding I should come back when I had time. Soon time was not on my side. I was stuck in traffic. Sitting in the car I began to look around me and witnessed something I might have missed if I hadn't had to stop. There were over a hundred young people raking people's leaves and putting them in bags. Up and down every block, yellow shirts everywhere. When the traffic speed resumed, I actually slowed down to see what the shirts said. More than a hundred yellow shirts with the words: THE CHURCH OF GOD.

Sometimes in life it seems that the loudest voices are the pessimists, the angry politicians, or the news team giving us celebrity news that is not news. The world is filled with Caesars and Herods, Pilates and Philips who care about the bottom line, but not about people. At times the world can seem like a desert without hope. Our response is often to speed ahead and try to avoid as much of it as possible.

But then something forces us to slow down. And we have to look around us. If we are willing to look with the eyes of faith, we will see the presence of God everywhere.

Gracious Father, send me your Spirit, that I may be a sign of your presence to all.

A Voice That Speaks the Promise

Monsignor Gregory E. S. Malovetz

[John] went throughout [the] whole region of the Jordan, proclaiming a baptism of repentance for the forgiveness of sins, as it is written in the book of the words of the prophet Isaiah: "A voice of one crying out in the desert:/ 'Prepare the way of the Lord,/ make straight his paths./ Every valley shall be filled/ and every mountain and hill shall be made low./ The winding roads shall be made straight,/ and the rough ways made smooth,/ and all flesh shall see the salvation of God.'" (Lk 3:3-6)

The waitress cleared our plates, and offered us coffee as we came to the end of our meal. Like so many other lunches we shared, Ed and I spent the time catching up and sharing the latest news. Ed was a priest ordained before I was born and had served as a military chaplain during the Vietnam War. I remember that afternoon, stirring my coffee, when I asked what was the hardest part of being an Army chaplain. Ed rarely spoke about those days, so he looked far off for quite some time. He said many parents of soldiers who were killed would write him, wanting to know something about their son's time in Vietnam, and even his last days. Because there were so many soldiers, Ed could not have known each personally. Yet he still wrote the parents, acknowledging their sorrow, speaking tenderly of their son, and offering the promise that God was with him in those last terrible moments. Ed looked down for a moment, and then at me. *They needed to hear that God had not forgotten them.*

When John the Baptist looked at the world, he saw the challenges and struggles people faced. Life was not a smooth, easy road, but one with many twists and unexpected detours. John realized that people needed to hear Good News. They needed to know that God was coming to heal, to forgive, and to create a new beginning. John embraced the work of a prophet: to let his voice announce to others that God had not forgotten them.

My friend Ed died this year after a lifetime of letting his voice be used to comfort and assure people that God was very near. In a time when no Internet or cell phones existed, he used a letter to carry a message of hope. The challenge of our present time, with so much technology available, is whether our voice will do the same.

Gracious Father, send me your Spirit, that my voice and my life will announce to others that you are near.

The Risk of Discipleship

Monsignor Gregory E. S. Malovetz

[John] said to the crowds who came out to be baptized by him, "You brood of vipers! Who warned you to flee from the coming wrath? Produce good fruits as evidence of your repentance; and do not begin to say to yourselves, 'We have Abraham as our father,' for I tell you, God can raise up children to Abraham from these stones. Even now the ax lies at the root of the trees. Therefore every tree that does not produce good fruit will be cut down and thrown into the fire." (Lk 3:7-9)

It arrived on a large flatbed truck. Landscapers brought the necessary machinery and equipment. I watched as they lifted a thirty-foot October Glory maple with a three-ton ball, and then planted it in a friend's front yard. While moving the tree from the truck and then lowering it into the ground was fascinating to watch, it was what happened next that amazed me. The large branches had been carefully and intricately tied together to protect the tree during transport. Once the tree was in place, workers climbed the tree with cat-like movements. They seemed to dance through the tree knowing which tree limbs to use in their climb. The workers carefully cut the ropes, freeing the tree and unfurling the branches until the green leaves filled the entire space.

The image of a tree is frequently used as a sign of discipleship in the New Testament. As a healthy tree is green and bears fruit, so the true disciple is one whose life is vibrant, life-giving, and visible to the world. John the Baptist offers, however, a stern warning. Appearances are only appearances. Confronting a crowd that was going through the motions, he tells them that a life of faith comes not from what you do, but from who you are.

We often think of discipleship in terms of what we do. My mind goes back to those workers swinging through the tree. It is an image of people who take risks, who work together, and who free the branches so that there will be beauty. Our discipleship is found in the risks we take, the willingness to work together, and using our lives to free others.

After a brutal winter the tree in my friend's yard was brown with no leaves. It clearly had not made it and would be replaced. But in our life nothing can replace the opportunity we are given each day to take the risk of discipleship.

Gracious Father, send me your Spirit, so that I may take the risk each day to free others with your love.

The Gestures of Life

Monsignor Gregory E. S. Malovetz

And the crowds asked [John], "What then should we do?"
He said to them in reply, "Whoever has two cloaks should share
with the person who has none. And whoever has food
should do likewise." (Lk 3:10-11)

The sign could not be any larger or clearer: Eight Items or Fewer. As I stand in the line with my two items, I realize the man in front of me has placed at least twenty items on the conveyor belt. I think nothing of it until I feel his eyes looking at me with my two items. Realizing he is over the limit, the man becomes apologetic and tries to make amends by letting me go ahead of him. I tell him that is not necessary. Besides, I point out, the cashier has already started ringing up his order. I see that this pains him even more, so I kiddingly add, "Unless you want to pay for my stuff." His response was serious: "I would be happy to do that." I didn't let him, but was touched by his genuine gesture of kindness.

The repentance John the Baptist preached was not about feeling sorry for doing something wrong. As Jesus would later reveal, repentance has little to do with feeling guilty or remorseful. It has everything to do with embracing a bigger vision. Everything we have been given is a gift from God. We are truly repentant when we admit that we have not always lived that vision.

The crowds' question, "What should we do?" is ours too. We live in a world where there is an unfair distribution of goods. Perhaps if we put the things we own on a conveyor belt, we might realize we are over the limit when others have so little. But the answer to "What should we do?" may not be holding a garage sale or bringing boxes of stuff to a homeless shelter. It is first the looking around and noticing. Who stands with me and who have I failed to notice? It is realizing there is someone who needs to be clothed and fed by my genuine gesture of kindness.

Gracious Father, send me your Spirit, that I may be gracious, generous, and kind.

A Bigger Dream

Monsignor Gregory E. S. Malovetz

*Even tax collectors came to be baptized and they said to [John],
"Teacher, what should we do?" He answered them, "Stop
collecting more than what is prescribed." Soldiers also asked
him, "And what is it that we should do?" He told them, "Do not
practice extortion, do not falsely accuse anyone, and be satisfied
with your wages." Now the people were filled with expectation,
and all were asking in their hearts whether John might be
the Messiah. (Lk 3:12-15)*

The party following the Easter Vigil was a great celebration of new beginnings. At one point I found myself talking with the four-year-old son of a man received into the Church that night. I asked the boy what would be happening the next day. His answer was two words: "Easter Bunny." I inquired whether he thought the Easter Bunny would be stopping by my house. His answer was a matter of fact, "No way." When I asked him why not, the explanation was another two words, "No kids." I told him that this made me a little sad and it seemed a bit unfair. He replied, "Well, he's not going to come. But at least you can dream."

We can read John the Baptist's answer to the tax collectors and soldiers and hear it as a list of things not to do. Tax collectors and soldiers had bad reputations in first-century Palestine, and many of their practices did not help their image. John, however, wants to do more than just change bad behavior. He wants them to have a different view of their place in the world. As God's children they didn't have to leave their jobs. They just had to dream a bigger dream. Even as soldiers and tax collectors they could be signs of God's loving presence in the world. This is why the people's hearts were filled with expectation. Unlike other religious leaders, he was telling them that with God's love a new beginning was possible.

We may not be the kind of people who extort, cheat, or accuse others falsely. Yet each of us knows a place in our life where we are petty, jealous, selfish, or unkind. We are aware of those moments when we said the thoughtless thing or looked the other way. Many times we insist it is too hard to change, or that we can't. In those moments two words are the answer: *Dream big.*

Gracious Father, send me your Spirit, that I may be changed, and become more like your Son.

Seeing the Good News

Monsignor Gregory E. S. Malovetz

John answered them all, saying, "I am baptizing you with water, but one mightier than I is coming. I am not worthy to loosen the thongs of his sandals. He will baptize you with the holy Spirit and fire. His winnowing fan is in his hand to clear his threshing floor and to gather the wheat into his barn, but the chaff he will burn with unquenchable fire." Exhorting them in many other ways, he preached good news to the people. (Lk 3:16-18)

Their eyes move from the clock to the door and then to the volunteer sitting at the information desk. This ritual continues for several hours. The family paces the surgical waiting room. When the orthopedic surgeon finally enters the room, he is still in scrubs. He looks over the room and, spotting the family, goes to them. The doctor explains that the surgery was a success, provides them with details, and informs them it will be several hours before they can see their loved one. As they pepper him with questions, the surgeon reaches into the pocket of his white lab coat. Pulling out his cell phone, he begins to make a call. On the other end is his physician's assistant who is in the recovery room with the patient. Both have cell phones that enable you not only to talk but see someone in real time. The family delights not only in hearing the good news about their loved one. They are thrilled actually to see and hear him.

One day I asked the surgeon why he makes this call after every surgery. He explained, "I can tell them their family member is all right. But there's nothing like seeing for themselves."

John the Baptist exhorted the people in many ways to believe the Good News. Exhort means to console, encourage, or persuade someone earnestly. John used words and images to preach God's coming and the power of God's love. But what consoled, encouraged, and persuaded people were John's passion, commitment, and confidence that God was with him.

Our world today may be different from John's world. But the human spirit is the same. People come to faith not through doctrine or poetic words. It is through our passion, commitment, and confidence that God is with us. The challenge each day is to find new ways to reveal the Good News. It may be as close as the cell phone in our pocket.

Gracious Father, send me your Spirit, that I may find new ways to live your Good News.

Where You're Meant to Be

Monsignor Gregory E. S. Malovetz

Now Herod the tetrarch, who had been censured by [John] because of Herodias, his brother's wife, and because of all the evil deeds Herod had committed, added still another to these by [also] putting John in prison. (Lk 3:19-20)

It is 5 AM. Two days have passed since Hurricane Irene hit, leaving me without electricity and water. That is, unless you count the three feet of water in my basement. Restless, I get in my car and drive through the streets. I come upon an open convenience store and stop for a much needed cup of coffee. A man outside is drinking coffee and smoking a cigarette. As I approach the store, I encounter a woman who is agitated and talking quickly. She needs to get to work, but every road she has tried is blocked. I make several suggestions that apparently she has already tried. Looking up and down the road, she says, "I got to be there and I don't know how I'm going to do it." The man standing near us sips his coffee, takes a drag off his cigarette, and says, "Well, if you can't get there, then maybe that's not where you're supposed to be."

John the Baptist had a large group of enemies. It is no wonder that he winds up in prison. Cut off from the world, prison must have been a dark and depressing place for him. Yet we never hear him complain. Like all the prophets before him, John knows God is with him in this darkness. This is where he is supposed to be.

As we travel the road of life, we will encounter storms. Some may flood our basement; others flood our heart with depression, disappointment, or anger. We may feel like we are in prison. We may want to blame God or others or ourselves. That too is part of the journey.

The promise of faith is that God is in the storm. In those moments we may experience grace in a way we never thought possible. Understandably, we may want to be somewhere else. We come into God's light when we are able to say, "Well, this is the place I'm supposed to be."

Gracious Father, send me your Spirit, that I may know your presence wherever I am.

A Truth to Remember

Monsignor Gregory E. S. Malovetz

After all the people had been baptized and Jesus also had been baptized and was praying, heaven was opened and the holy Spirit descended upon him in bodily form like a dove. And a voice came from heaven, "You are my beloved Son; with you I am well pleased." (Lk 3:21-22)

The afternoon sun was brilliant against the blue Charleston sky. The news crew was ready, as the reporter looked up and then directly into the camera. A few people from the neighborhood gathered, pointing to the large crane and the task it was about to begin.

Touring the South Carolina city with three friends, we stumbled upon this scene in front of Charleston's cathedral. A renovation included a new tower, and on this afternoon when most of the city was unaware, workers were affixing a huge gold cross on the top. The workers were dwarfed by the massive stone, yet with steady movements guided it into place. For one brief moment, a few people were united as they stood under a golden cross. And then everyone left and continued the rest of the day.

Luke offers the image of Jesus being baptized in the river with others. It is an image that we will see many times in his Gospel. Luke tells of Jesus standing with the poor, the marginalized, the sick and suffering. In living this way, Jesus shows us what the discipleship of the baptized looks like.

I think about that group standing with Jesus in the water. Did they actually see the dove and hear the voice? How did that moment change them? Baptism is an event most of us don't remember. What matters is not that we remember an event, but remember what it means. We are all the beloved sons and daughters of God. Too many things in life cause us to forget this truth. Our mission is to live in such a way that we help each other remember.

My mind wanders back to that lovely day with my friends in Charleston. It was a surprising, wonderful, and inspiring moment. Later that year, one of these friends would die, a sorrow we continue to carry. But the memory of that moment, like the memory of baptism, is one of love.

Gracious Father, send me your Spirit, that I may be comforted and sustained by the memory of love.

What's in a Name

Monsignor Gregory E. S. Malovetz

*When Jesus began his ministry he was about thirty years of age.
He was the son, as was thought, of Joseph, the son of Heli,
the son of Matthat, the son of Levi, the son of Melchi, the son of
Jannai, the son of Joseph, the son of Mattathias, the son of Amos,
the son of Nahum, the son of Esli, the son of Naggai, [...]*
(Lk 3:23-25)

I look through the list of names, pressing my reading glasses closer to my face. I have been sitting at the computer for several hours. I am tired and it is late, but I am compelled to continue. The handwritten census is in unusual cursive; it is hard to determine if the letters are an o, a, e, or i. My interest in family genealogy has grown in the past months, a passion I share with my sister. It is both frustrating and fascinating. As I move through this ancient form of record keeping, my phone sounds that I have received an instant message from my sister. "I found them." The three-word message is like a discovery of a treasure.

A genealogy traces a family lineage and history. Its purpose is to go back, one generation after another, to help discover those who came before us. It helps us understand how their lives and choices shape who we are today.

With today's passage, we begin five days of reflecting on the genealogy of Jesus in Luke's Gospel. At first glance, some names may seem unusual while others are familiar. The truth is that this genealogy is not accurate or completely historical. For most of today's names there is no other biblical reference than today's passage. We can be confused and despair, wondering what is the point.

The word genealogy comes from the two Greek words for "generations" and "knowledge." Luke is not as interested in providing a family tree as he is in giving us the knowledge that Jesus, who is God's Son, shares our human life. Every human person, in every generation, is brother or sister to him.

Some people can trace their roots back several centuries. Others can only go back two generations. What about our spiritual genealogy? It may be a family member, a friend, or a person you hardly knew who brought you to faith. To whom are you grateful for having found Christ?

Gracious Father, send me your Spirit, that I will always be grateful to those who have brought me to your Son.

Finding the Answer

Monsignor Gregory E. S. Malovetz

[T]he son of Maath, the son of Mattathias, the son of Semein,
the son of Josech, the son of Joda, the son of Joanan,
the son of Rhesa, the son of Zerubbabel, the son of Shealtiel,
the son of Neri, the son of Melchi, the son of Addi,
the son of Cosam, the son of Elmadam, the son of Er, [...]
(Lk 3:26-28)

Someone saw him waiting for the bus to New York City. There was nothing unusual about that. But when he didn't return, family members began to wonder and worry. This relative of mine had fallen on tough times. Two failed marriages and financial struggles were just two of his many problems. At his home it was discovered he had left behind every form of identification. It seemed as though he was leaving behind every part of his old life, and moving to create a new identity. He got on that bus over forty years ago. Despite countless searches over the years he was never found.

Did you notice the name Er? Unlike others on the list, he actually has a story in Genesis. We are told he was wicked. What happens to him, to his wife Tamar, his brother, and his father is so salacious that you may be shocked this story is in the Bible. You may wonder, what was Luke thinking including Er?

Luke's Gospel is filled with stories about Jesus with people others did not like. Some of these people had made terrible choices. Others were victims of society's cruel judgment. Jesus spends time with them. He eats with them and listens to their story. What we learn is that despite our opinions, every human life matters to God. There is no person so lost or confused who could not be healed by the grace of God.

We may not have an uncle who disappeared or a family member whose life embarrasses us. But we have a family member who tries our patience or we don't understand. We can spend time analyzing, judging, wishing they were different, and insisting we are right. Or we could ask, what is God teaching me about myself through this person. Uncomfortable and hard to do? You bet. In searching for that answer we find what it means to belong to the family of Jesus.

Gracious Father, send me your Spirit, that I may listen to what you are telling me through the people in my life.

The Excitement of Faith

Monsignor Gregory E. S. Malovetz

[T]he son of Joshua, the son of Eliezer, the son of Jorim, the son of Matthat, the son of Levi, the son of Simeon, the son of Judah, the son of Joseph, the son of Jonam, the son of Eliakim, the son of Melea, the son of Menna, the son of Mattatha, the son of Nathan, the son of David, [...] (Lk 3:29-31)

The orchestra is in place. The curtain will soon go up. I am with my sister waiting to see a Broadway musical starring the actor Daniel Radcliffe. You can feel the excited anticipation in the theater, especially among young people who know this actor from his movies. From my seat, I see a woman seated in one of the side balconies. She is smiling and clapping and jumping up and down in her seat. Through most of the performance she maintains this action. From her seat, she can see Radcliffe before most of the audience does. This puts her in a frenzy that my sister notices. My sister nudges me saying, "Now that is some kind of excited. I think she will fall out of the balcony once he appears."

I admit it. This is the third of five days reflecting on a list of uninteresting and uninspiring names. There is no fear I will fall out of my chair in excitement at the mention of Jonam, Melea, or Mattatha. A writer uninspired.

My attention, however, kept coming to Nathan, a son David had with Bathsheba. It intrigued me that his son shared the same name as the prophet who condemned David's relationship with Bathsheba. The prophet Nathan didn't simply judge David. Nathan had a passion that David and others live as the kind of people God wanted them to be. Nathan must also have had a passion to be joyful, for it says in Chronicles that he was involved in the music in the temple.

What is it in life that excites us? Are we passionate about discovering what kind of person God wants us to be, or are we content to coast through life? I believe that is the challenge for today. We can join a list of names no one knows or recognizes. Or we can live in such a way that others will notice us, and be excited by the faith they see us living.

Gracious Father, send me your Spirit, that my faith may be energized today.

To Be a Nahshon

Monsignor Gregory E. S. Malovetz

[T]he son of Jesse, the son of Obed, the son of Boaz,
the son of Sala, the son of Nahshon, the son of Amminadab,
the son of Admin, the son of Arni, the son of Hezron,
the son of Perez, the son of Judah, the son of Jacob,
the son of Isaac, the son of Abraham, the son of Terah,
the son of Nahor, [...] (Lk 3:32-34)

The boat moves gently through the water. Once we pass the "no wake zone" the speed is increased and we are flying through the bay. They move from the front of the boat to the back, and to the front again. The speed and the water excite them as the wind blows through their hair. We arrive at a sandbar, and as the anchor is dropped, they are anxious to get in the water. They nearly knock us over as they dive like Olympic champions off the stern.

My friend's two golden retrievers have the attention of everyone as they swim toward the sandbar. Like synchronized swimmers, they return the toy thrown for them to fetch. As many times as I have witnessed these dogs in water up to their necks, I will usually hear someone say, "Look at those cool dogs."

According to Jewish midrash, the Red Sea did not immediately part when the Israelites arrived there. As the Israelites panicked and cried in despair, it was Nahshon who entered the water. It was when the water was up to his nose that the waters parted. Through the centuries the Yiddish expression "to be a Nahshon" means one who takes the initiative, often in a dramatic way.

Through the waters of baptism, God takes a dramatic initiative, calling us to be his children. We know that baptism calls us to a life of discipleship. The word "discipleship" may be used so often that it no longer has the power to energize and challenge us. Perhaps we might think of baptism as a daily call *to be a Nahshon*. Every generation has produced individuals who champion the cause of peace, justice, and the dignity of every human person. People see them as more than "cool." They are seen as the ones who are anxious to get in the water of life. What waters might get parted, what life might get saved, because with faith you dived in?

Gracious Father, give me your Spirit, that I may take the initiative each day to reveal your saving grace.

The Life That Is Noticed

Monsignor Gregory E. S. Malovetz

[T]he son of Serug, the son of Reu, the son of Peleg, the son of Eber, the son of Shelah, the son of Cainan, the son of Arphaxad, the son of Shem, the son of Noah, the son of Lamech, the son of Methuselah, the son of Enoch, the son of Jared, the son of Mahalaleel, the son of Cainan, the son of Enos, the son of Seth, the son of Adam, the son of God. (Lk 3:35-38)

She lived in the same house her entire adult life; first with her husband and then as a widow for nearly forty years. As her life unfolded, motherhood was not to be part of it. My great-aunt Mae, a perpetual sidekick to her siblings' families, was a second mother and grandmother to three generations. She was funny and warm. Aunt Mae worked in a plastics factory, baked delicious cookies, drove a green car, and every Sunday visited my grandmother and played gin rummy. To the world, her life might not have been noticed. But to those of us who loved her, we noticed and believed God did too.

Little is told about Enoch in Genesis. But his claim to fame is more than being the great-grandfather of Noah. There must have been something about him that God noticed. In one short verse we are told that "Enoch walked with God" (Gn 5:24). To walk with someone is to be going in the same direction. The image is of a person who was headed in the same direction as God. The tradition is that, like Elijah the prophet, Enoch did not die but was taken up to heaven.

Walking with God. Going in the same direction. We could spend a lifetime reflecting on those two statements. Each day is an opportunity to look at our life and consider whether the choices I made came from walking with God. Or do my choices suggest I am walking in another direction.

We are fortunate when we meet people we know are walking with God. They often shape the direction of our lives. My Aunt Mae was one of those people who shaped us with love and laughter. In doing so, she showed us God.

With this final reflection on Luke's genealogy, we see that the lineage ends with God. For the believer, in life and in death, it always does.

Gracious Father, send me your Spirit, that I may always walk with you.

Led into Temptation

Father John Dominic Corbett, O.P.

Filled with the holy Spirit, Jesus returned from the Jordan and was led by the Spirit into the desert for forty days, to be tempted by the devil. He ate nothing during those days, and when they were over he was hungry. (Lk 4:1-2)

Our Mother the Church has a long memory. She has had long experience of people who think that they are smarter than the devil and stronger than the devil and are capable of defeating the devil. Their track record is not good, and the history of the Church is littered with the scandals brought about by those who thought that the admonition to avoid occasions of sin didn't apply to them. The Catholic Church has one basic strategy for dealing with evil when it presents itself for our embrace. It goes something like this: "Run like hell!" It's not for nothing that the Lord's Prayer ends with the petition "Lead us not into temptation, but deliver us from the evil one."

So this particular reading presents us with a problem. Why did Jesus ignore this advice? It seems that he went into the desert precisely to encounter temptation. Why do this? The Gospel tells us that Jesus "was led by the Spirit into the desert." So it was a matter of obedience and not a matter of ego or a need to try his spiritual strength.

But why was he sent? There are two possibilities. The first would be that Jesus went to be tested on our behalf. There is a mysterious solidarity between him and us, and so the victories that he wins he doesn't win for himself alone. We went with him into the desert and with him we emerge victorious.

The other possibility is that Jesus went to the desert in order to have his sense of his own mission purified. He had been baptized by John in the Jordan and had heard the words "This is my beloved Son." What could that mean to Jesus as he began his ministry? Satan was on hand to offer false suggestions and thereby to provide Jesus with the occasion to learn to be the Son through obedience. That lesson would lead him to the cross.

Father, help us to be humble enough to avoid occasions of sin and wise enough to learn from our trials what it means to be your children.

If You Are the Son

Father John Dominic Corbett, O.P.

The devil said to [Jesus], "If you are the Son of God,
command this stone to become bread." Jesus answered him,
"It is written, 'One does not live by bread alone.'"
(Lk 4:3-4)

Most of us have had the experience of thinking about what we should do, and then having an idea come to us as though it were purely our own, and then recognizing it as having originated elsewhere. "Oh, that's Dad talking" or "That's Mom's voice." Recognizing whose voice is speaking can make all the difference.

Could Jesus have had an experience like that? In the desert he could have been thinking, "I am the Son of God. What am I going to do about this?" This is the point where Satan might have suggested, "If you are the Son of God command this stone to become bread," and this is the point at which Jesus would have immediately recognized the voice as the voice of the evil one.

Why this suggestion? The Lord rained down bread from heaven in order to teach his people as well as feed them. He wanted them to learn that he was their father and that, although he might lead them into some hard times and strange places, they could always trust him with their lives. The bread that came was food from a father who they must trust and rely on. A father cares for his child and the Lord cares for his people.

The heart of Satan's suggestion is that Jesus as God's Son need not and should not rely on his Father. The prerogative of divine Sonship is the use of divine powers for one's own convenience and not with reference to his Father's plan. Jesus is to command and not to ask. He is in charge and need not trust in his Father's providence.

Jesus refuses this and says, "One does not live by bread alone but by every word that comes from God's mouth." We feed on the truth of God's Word when we see that he is our Father and cares for all our needs.

Father, help us to know that we can trust your promises to us,
and to rely on them so deeply that they become the very food of
our soul.

The Power and the Glory

Father John Dominic Corbett, O.P.

Then [the devil] took [Jesus] up and showed him all the kingdoms of the world in a single instant. The devil said to him, "I shall give to you all this power and their glory; for it has been handed over to me, and I may give it to whomever I wish. All this will be yours, if you worship me." Jesus said to him in reply, "It is written: 'You shall worship the Lord, your God,/ and him alone shall you serve.'" (Lk 4:5-8)

There are kingdoms and kingdoms. We think first of all of political and military realms. And so Satan treated our Lord to a vision of himself as a sort of Caesar or Napoleon or President of the USA (without Congress or the Supreme Court impeding his will).

But there are other kinds of kingdoms. He saw all of them. Think what that must mean. In an instant, he owned the silken luxuries of Persia. He could run and strive in the Olympics with effortless perfection. In the same instant, he was choirmaster in Vienna and created soaring melodies that made the compositions of Mozart seem like "Three Blind Mice." He grasped the intellectual glories of ancient Greece piercing the mysteries of change and form as well as the relativities of time and space that captivate our own time. He knew what could and could not change in man without man ceasing to be man. He could be secure in his possession of authority over the tree of the knowledge of good and evil.

All this was on offer. Who could resist such an offer? Only Jesus himself. Of course the offer was a delusion and a snare, and our Lord could not have been fooled even for that instant. What was offered was comprehensive human mastery of the human being, and Jesus already knew this from the inside. What was offered was already his by right.

Jesus embraced the fullness of human life including its glories. He is sensible of them but he is not impressed by them. He is not dazzled. They are beneath him evoking his compassion, not above him evoking his desire. There is only one who commands him and evokes worship.

The devil presents himself as worthy of worship. Satan presents himself as Success, but Jesus knew then as now that success, as a word, is powerless to name the mystery of his Father. Success is not one of the names of God.

Father, teach us to see that the mystery of your love is not adequately communicated in sheer mastery. Help us to see that in worshiping you we are not worshiping success.

Testing God

Father John Dominic Corbett, O.P.

Then [the devil] led [Jesus] to Jerusalem, made him stand on the parapet of the temple, and said to him, "If you are the Son of God, throw yourself down from here, for it is written: 'He will command his angels concerning you,/ to guard you,' and: 'With their hands they will support you,/ lest you dash your foot against a stone.'" Jesus said to him in reply, "It also says, 'You shall not put the Lord, your God, to the test.'" (Lk 4:9-12)

We know that God often writes straight with crooked lines, but we are surprised to find that Satan does so as well. Not that he means to. He would never willingly shed light on God's promises in the Psalms, and yet here he does so despite his worst efforts.

He wanted to provoke Jesus into putting his Father on trial. There would only be two reasons for doing that. The first would be because Jesus really did doubt his Father's power or goodness. The second would be to try to make his Father do his bidding rather than the reverse. If Jesus acted out of either of those reasons, then Jesus would have proven not that he was God's Son but that he wasn't.

Satan's choice of Scripture was unwittingly prophetic. "With their hands they will support you, lest you dash your foot against a stone." This is exactly what happened in the garden of Gethsemane. An angel was sent there at the precise moment when Jesus was at most risk of "dashing his foot against a stone." Being tripped up by a stone is Scripture's way of talking about being scandalized—that is, being led to sin by rejecting God's plan. Luke's Gospel is unique in that it tells us of an angel strengthening Jesus and keeping him firm in his resolve to drink the cup that his Father has given him—the cup of his Passion. The angels did support Jesus in the garden. They did this lest he "dash his foot against a stone"; lest he be "scandalized," and turn away from Calvary. God's protection was not from the cross but from deviating from the path that led to the cross.

We often ask for protection in our prayers. Do we ever ask for the angels to strengthen us lest we stumble away from the grace conveyed only in submission to the saving will of God for us?

Father, teach us to see in faith that your protection and providence is always effective for those who call on you.

The Elan of the Spirit

Father John Dominic Corbett, O.P.

*When the devil had finished every temptation, he departed from
[Jesus] for a time. Jesus returned to Galilee in the power of the
Spirit, and news of him spread throughout the whole region.
He taught in their synagogues and was praised by all.*
(Lk 4:13-15)

We have all known those blessed with charisma. Charisma seems to be associated with leadership. It also has to do with the capacity to communicate. A charismatic military leader seems able to communicate his courage, confidence, as well as his plans to his platoon. A charismatic political leader is able to communicate his vision of a renewed society, and to do so in such a manner that when his followers act on his behalf they seem to act as one. A charismatic teacher is able to sweep her students into the adventures of her own penetrating and creative mind. This is a gift and it cannot be taught.

Saint Luke's Gospel tells us that Jesus returned to Galilee in the power of the Spirit. Returning in the power of the Spirit surely means that Jesus returned laden not only with the experience of his Father's direct rule over his life as the Christ, but also in the charisma of the Spirit, that is, in the capacity to communicate to others the actual experience of God intervening to save his people.

News of him spread. How could it not? If charisma is the capacity to communicate, then the ultimate charisma would be not only to have the gift of communicating oneself, but also of ensuring that the others who have been swept up into what you have seen would themselves be able to share with still others the substance of what they have seen in faith. Indeed this very gift has been woven into the DNA of the Church, not by a succession of charismatic personalities, but by the presence of the Spirit who, using word and sacrament, even today breathes the breath of God into our souls. The more we actually believe this and cooperate with the Spirit's action, the more news of him will spread.

*Father, help us to be open to the joy of hearing the Gospel as news
and to the privilege of announcing it to our brothers and sisters.*

Target Audience

Father John Dominic Corbett, O.P.

[Jesus] came to Nazareth, where he had grown up, and went according to his custom into the synagogue on the sabbath day. He stood up to read and was handed a scroll of the prophet Isaiah. He unrolled the scroll and found the passage where it was written: "The Spirit of the Lord is upon me,/ because he has anointed me/ to bring glad tidings to the poor./ He has sent me to proclaim liberty to captives/ and recovery of sight to the blind,/ to let the oppressed go free,/ and to proclaim a year acceptable to the Lord." (Lk 4:16-19)

A long time ago Saturday Night Live's Garret Morris did a very funny if somewhat insensitive skit about communication. The setting was a TV news studio. An announcer began in a normal voice: "And now the news for the hearing impaired." Garret Morris seated in the background followed up in a bellowing voice with "AND NOW THE NEWS FOR THE HEARING IMPAIRED," as though shouting in a microphone would make any difference.

Communication is, of course, a two way street. It does no good at all to have all of the arts and methods of communication if the target audience is incapable of receiving the message. Shouting does not help the deaf. Visual aids do not help the blind.

This suggests two possible takes on today's Gospel passage. One interpretation would be that if God is truly to save us, he must not only act on us from the outside, bringing power to bear that we do not of ourselves possess. God must also create within us a principle of response. A healing act can only occur in a body already alive. Even God cannot heal a corpse.

But this is no cause for despair. If we are not only exteriorly burdened but inwardly blighted, we need not lose heart. God can supply even the interior principle of response in us so that we can be actively engaged in our own salvation.

There is another, nearly opposite, way of interpreting this passage. Here we would take poverty, blindness, imprisonment, not as obstacles to hearing the Gospel, but as preconditions. Only when a human being has lost everything can he be brought at last to throw himself on the generosity and love of God. In God, might and powerlessness, riches and poverty are the same. Only the poor can know this by heart, so only they can respond to the invitation to the kingdom.

Father, please heal from within our incapacity to respond to you and show us the mystery of your poverty so that we might grow rich in your grace.

Fulfilled in Your Hearing

Father John Dominic Corbett, O.P.

Rolling up the scroll, [Jesus] handed it back to the attendant and sat down, and the eyes of all in the synagogue looked intently at him. He said to them, "Today this scripture passage is fulfilled in your hearing." And all spoke highly of him and were amazed at the gracious words that came from his mouth.

(Lk 4:20-22a)

Psychologists distinguish between short-term and long-term memory. Both are essential, of course. We could not function without being able to recall what we did and said in the very recent past. But the loss of long-term memory would be even more devastating. For it is in our long-term memories that we have access to who we are. Our name, our family, our foundational relationships are all located there.

As with individuals, nations and peoples also have long-term memories. Israel had a very long-term memory consisting in the foundational gracious acts of God in which God called this people to be his own. This fidelity of God was tested to the limit. It found expression in chastisement as well as in consolation.

When Jesus came to the synagogue that day and read that prophecy from Isaiah, he awakened everyone's long-term memory. He awakened memories of many prophets foretelling disaster and oppression and blindness as the penalty for obstinate sin. He awakened long-term memories of exile and loss, as well as the promise of the prophet about a day of jubilee in which all debts to God would be forgiven and all of the blessed promises of God fulfilled.

Jesus announced that this day had now come. "Today this Scripture passage is fulfilled in your hearing." He also implied that it was fulfilled through his own person. It must have been astounding. It must have been nearly impossible to believe. It must have seemed much too good to be true. All were amazed, though in different ways. Some were dazzled into belief because they so badly wanted it to be true. Others were amazed that anyone would dare claim to settle fifteen hundred years of longing in one afternoon. Could all of the promises of God be made good in one person? That was the issue then. It is still the issue now.

Father, do not let the long seasons of waiting for you blind us to the moments when you visit us with the offer to make us anew.

Ushers

Father John Dominic Corbett, o.p.

[Those in the synagogue] also asked, "Isn't this the son of Joseph?" [Jesus] said to them, "Surely you will quote me this proverb, 'Physician, cure yourself,' and say, 'Do here in your native place the things that we heard were done in Capernaum.'" And he said, "Amen, I say to you, no prophet is accepted in his own native place." (Lk 4:22b-24)

Not everyone was impressed. As the magnitude of Jesus' claim registered in the synagogue, he faced a rising tide of skepticism, suspicion, and incredulity. Only an ongoing parade of wonders would suffice to overcome the mind's habit of clinging for dear life to the familiar and the routine. We can just hear the conversation in the back room of the synagogue where the ushers are exercising their timeless privileges of smoking, counting the collection, and (best of all) skipping the sermon.

"Isn't this the carpenter's son?"

"Yes, that's right."

"Joseph, hmm, now there was a good man. Never had much to say, you know, but what little he said always made sense. Always liked him."

"Honest, too! Why didn't this son of his follow him in the family business?"

"Do we really need another rabbi? We already pay the one we have in this village too much, if you ask me."

"He sure has a lot to say (unlike his dad)! What is he saying?" (Pause) "So the kingdom of God is coming, is it? Well, we've heard that before."

"We need to repent? Well, I dare say that's true, but I also say we don't need to hear this from the likes of him."

"If he's going to go on as though he were someone special, shouldn't he, you know, prove it? I heard rumors the other day about him curing a blind man. If he wants me to drop everything to get ready for God's great day, then I want to see him cure somebody too, right here, right now!"

And so we insist that we are in charge. God will not be permitted into our world except by our leave, on our schedule, according to our expectations. It's a wonder God manages to get through at all.

Father, save us! Save us from our arrogance in presuming to dictate to you the hour and manner of our visitation.

Selective Healing

Father John Dominic Corbett, O.P.

*"Indeed, I tell you, there were many widows in Israel in the days
of Elijah when the sky was closed for three and a half years and
a severe famine spread over the entire land. It was to none of
these that Elijah was sent, but only to a widow in Zarephath in
the land of Sidon. Again, there were many lepers in Israel during
the time of Elisha the prophet; yet not one of them was cleansed,
but only Naaman the Syrian." (Lk 4:25-27)*

Who has first claim on your love? Is it your nearest and
dearest? That seems most natural even if some people
think that such favoritism seems contrary to justice.
Does God have favorites? Does he have a people who, so to
speak, have first dibs on his love and attention? The whole Bible
teaches that this is true. Although God created everything and
every people, yet there is one people that is, as Deuteronomy puts
it, "peculiarly his own." These he teaches, guides, rewards, rebukes,
and punishes in a way unknown to any other people. These are his
own, the apple of his eye.

So when Jesus pointed out that God skipped his own widows
during the time of Elijah in order to take care of a pagan widow,
it really got their attention. Why would God do that? Naaman the
leper was another puzzling case. He was a general of an army of
God's enemies. Why would God let the limbs of his own people
wither while blessing this ignorant pagan?

Why indeed? It may have something to do with jealousy. Perhaps healing these pagans and thus marking them out for special
favor was God's way of making Israel jealous and thereby reminding Israel of its unique privilege of worshiping the only true God.

It may also have been about God showing his true colors. While
it is true that Israel was chosen by God, it was chosen by God so
that all the other nations might be chosen as well. The whole sweep
of God's mighty hand, which began with Egyptians tumbling into
the Red Sea, would continue and not rest until it scooped up the
whole human race as his chosen abode and bride.

We have been specifically chosen and named by God in our
baptism. This is a supernatural privilege of the highest order. Can
we be glad that this isn't just about us?

*Father, help us to see that you do not love us any the less because
you love and have saved the whole world.*

Casting Jesus Out

Father John Dominic Corbett, O.P.

When the people in the synagogue heard this, they were all filled with fury. They rose up, drove [Jesus] out of the town, and led him to the brow of the hill on which their town had been built, to hurl him down headlong. But he passed through the midst of them and went away. (Lk 4:28-30)

Fury is the reaction we have when something noxious to us has obstinately lodged itself in our world. Fury makes us want to attack it, dislodge it, and blast it far away so it can never enter our world again. Fury is not reserved for terrible or dangerous things. Foolish opinions, a car stalled in the middle of a busy highway, an endless faucet drip, a colleague who will not let us hear the last of a mistake that we made, all can inspire fury, provided that they refuse to relinquish their hold on our lives. It's true that this reaction is usually suppressed by reason, often forcibly and with difficulty.

Fury is not limited to things that are truly noxious. It can be inspired by what is truly good, provided that the good is perceived as evil and that the good stubbornly makes its claim and refuses to relinquish its hold.

When Jesus spoke in the synagogue "they were filled with fury." Furthermore "they rose up," which suggests that they had felt themselves weighed down by Jesus' words. His teaching had all of the weight of authority, which simply could not be dispelled. His very presence was a claim, and acknowledging that claim required profound change of mind and heart and personal allegiance. The claim would not be withdrawn and therefore had to be removed.

And so in a fury they moved to cast Jesus out of their world.

They needn't have worried. Jesus who is weighty with the glory of God is also as light as air, and he moved from their grasp and went his way.

Sometimes we feel the pressure of truth bearing in upon us, and this can evoke fury and rebellion as well as a sense that, however distasteful, the grace of truth will never leave us. But we need to take care lest Jesus, having offered us the grace of truth in a moment of crisis, finally pass us by.

Father, help us to be grateful for the persistence of your patient offer of grace. Let us never allow Jesus to pass us by.

Just between Us

Father John Dominic Corbett, O.P.

Jesus then went down to Capernaum, a town of Galilee. He taught them on the sabbath, and they were astonished at his teaching because he spoke with authority. In the synagogue there was a man with the spirit of an unclean demon, and he cried out in a loud voice, "Ha! What have you to do with us, Jesus of Nazareth? Have you come to destroy us? I know who you are— the Holy One of God!" (Lk 4:31-34)

It has become a date movie cliché by now. "You had me at hello." The formula indicates that sometimes the essential features of a relationship reveal themselves very quickly—even from the first instant of the first meeting.

The Bible's way of talking about this is a formula question. "What have you to do with us?" has the same meaning as the question "Are you with us or our enemies?" that Joshua asked the angel captain of the Lord of Hosts on the eve of the battle of Jericho. It is the same question that Jesus asked his mother at the wedding feast of Cana: "What is there between us? My hour has not yet come."

These questions are about relationships within the context of the plan of God for his people's salvation. The demons know that they have a relationship with Jesus Christ. They know because they have chosen to obstruct God's plan in any way that they can, and they know that Jesus is the one who brings that plan to fulfillment. So they know from the beginning that their work is to try to destroy his.

That work is holiness. Jesus is the Holy One of God. He is the One whose humanity belongs to God so totally that it finds its termination not in a human but in a divine person. Jesus in his holiness belongs to God and wills that every human being belong to God through him. So the demon wills that every human person be unholy, unclean, that is, severed from him. "What is there between us?" is a declaration of perpetual warfare waged in the soul of each person.

What of us? When was the last time in prayer we asked the Lord, "What is there between us?" in hopes of understanding and embracing the truth that is our own vocation? When was the last time we dared consider the implications of our share in the universal call to holiness?

Father, transform our prayer into a truthful search for your plan in our lives. May we be holy as you are holy.

No Harm Done

Father John Dominic Corbett, O.P.

Jesus rebuked [the demon] and said, "Be quiet! Come out of him!" Then the demon threw the man down in front of them and came out of him without doing him any harm. They were all amazed and said to one another, "What is there about his word? For with authority and power he commands the unclean spirits, and they come out." And news of him spread everywhere in the surrounding region. (Lk 4:35-37)

Cancer is a terrible disease partly because the only way to cure it is to attack it in such a way that the whole body seems to be under attack. The price of survival can be a form of mutilation.

Moral and spiritual evil often works in the same way. It entwines. It attacks by slow insinuation, gradual infiltration, invited and accepted co-dependence. It very rarely attacks in such a way as to leave the lines of demarcation clear. It does not attack in such a way as to make disengagement cost-free or straightforward. Indeed, the damage feared from a break can be so great that one submits to the continuing presence of evil, rather than risk the ripping and the tearing and exposure and perhaps emptiness that would accompany a real fight.

So the man who accepts a small bribe on one occasion must accept and perhaps offer another larger one at the next occasion or risk exposure. The man who lies to his wife about his whereabouts during a business trip will need a good memory and considerable powers of invention if he is to preserve his secret. In a short time he is buried alive under a mound of lies, and the consequences of truthful confession might well be the end of his marriage. And so he lies again.

Jesus comes with the power of God to destroy the power of evil. A mark of the perfection of this power is its capacity to free the one in its grip without destroying the one in its grip. The Gospel tells us that the demon, obeying the word of Christ, threw the man to the ground indeed, but "without doing him any harm."

We may at times find ourselves trapped in moral evil and fearful of the price of freedom. Let us never fear to beg Christ to cast out our demons, not without consequence or price indeed, "but without doing us any harm."

Father, help us to know that whatever price we must pay for our freedom in you is providentially designed for our healing and not our harm.

Group Intervention

Father John Dominic Corbett, O.P.

After [Jesus] left the synagogue, he entered the house of Simon. Simon's mother-in-law was afflicted with a severe fever, and they interceded with him about her. He stood over her, rebuked the fever, and it left her. She got up immediately and waited on them. (Lk 4:38-39)

The Gospels sometimes need to tell the same story twice because telling it once and in only one way leaves something very important out.

The story about Peter's mother-in-law is like that. Saint Matthew tells the story and he particularly mentions that she got up after her cure and waited on *him*. This highlights the fact that the relationship that the disciple has with Jesus is irreducibly personal. All of our faith, all of our love, all of our service, is specifically directed to him and through him to his Father. It is the same with him. He does not heal us, forgive us, save us en masse. He knows each one of his sheep by name.

Saint Luke's account of the same miracle would never deny what was just said, but it does highlight a different truth. He highlights the truth that the healing and saving power of Jesus is accessible through the group of disciples that believe in him.

Notice how this works. Jesus comes in the front door and right away the disciples tell Jesus about her. It's not as though Jesus didn't already know that she was sick or that he couldn't have gone into her room right away and cured her. But Peter and the others needed and wanted to tell him, maybe not just about her fever but about her. They all knew her, and each one may have wanted to contribute his own story. Taken together, their testimony about her was full of the reasons Jesus should cure her and therefore full of love. This is powerful intercession indeed, and the Gospel leaves us no doubt that it was effective.

Notice also that when she is raised up she waits on *them*. Looking around the room she sees as many reasons to thank God as she sees people standing around her. And so she serves him in them and them in him. In this interchange of love Christ was and is found.

Father, we praise you for those people you have given us to serve. May we find you in them and may they find you in us.

Bad Press

Father John Dominic Corbett, O.P.

At sunset, all who had people sick with various diseases brought
them to [Jesus]. He laid his hands on each of them and cured
them. And demons also came out from many, shouting, "You
are the Son of God." But he rebuked them and did not allow
them to speak because they knew that he was the Messiah.
(Lk 4:40-41)

I n the world of politics, cable news coverage is 24/7. For a politician working in this environment, there is no such thing as
all good news all the time. Since cable news thrives on conflict, the news will interpret any politician's actions in the light that
is calculated to generate as much conflict and controversy as is
possible. For this reason, when events take an unfavorable turn,
politicians are advised to get out ahead of the story, to anticipate
coverage, and to spare no effort to feed the media their own spin.
It's a deeply manipulative art. We call it damage control.

The demons are involved in their own spin and damage control operations here. Jesus has arrived in power, and is making
his Father's kingdom present through his preaching, teaching, and
miracles. There is no way that the demons can prevent this.

Nevertheless, they can try to derail it. They do this by mixing
truth in lies and lies in truth. The truth is in the words that they
speak even as they are being expelled. "You are the Son of God!"
They try to take control of the truth by shouting the truth.

The lie is in the manner in which they proclaim it. They sen-
sationalize. They triumph. They gloat. They preen. They chortle.
They strut. They are his press agents and they are in the magic
circle. They *know*. Their manner of speech turned the very truth
of the Gospel into a lie.

But Jesus silenced them both in the short and long run. In the
short run, his sheer authority and power as God's Son was more
than sufficient to reduce them to silence. In the long run, his way
as the Suffering Servant, brought to the memory of the Church by
the action of the Holy Spirit, for ever discredits witnesses to Christ
who chortle, preen, and strut.

Father, help us to be true witnesses to your Son, not only by the
words we say but also in the way in which we say them.

Mission Statement

Father John Dominic Corbett, O.P.

At daybreak, Jesus left and went to a deserted place. The crowds went looking for him, and when they came to him, they tried to prevent him from leaving them. But he said to them, "To the other towns also I must proclaim the good news of the kingdom of God, because for this purpose I have been sent." And he was preaching in the synagogues of Judea. (Lk 4:42-44)

Jesus came on a mission. It is true that he could not be pinned down to any one place. No one place could claim his undivided presence or attention. For all of that, he did not wander because each place that he worked in was a place that he had been sent to. He was on the move.

He is still on the move. He is still being sent. Of course, things are different since his Resurrection. As the risen Savior, Christ is present in the whole of his creation. That makes it hard to see how he could be sent anywhere if he is already everywhere. Even though Jesus as the Son of God is present in every place and every time, he is still "sent" when he comes to be present in a new way. This new way is in the minds that perceive him anew in a deepened faith and in the heart that awakens in a new way to his love. This doesn't happen by our initiative or because we happen to start thinking about him but because our minds and wills become the place he visits. And he still visits because he is still being sent by his Father. Anytime we grow in love, when we grow in faith, when our minds and hearts seem to understand him a little better, we should pause in reverence. Jesus of Nazareth is passing by.

He comes to us on mission in every Mass. Part of his mission is to send us on mission as well. We see this in the last words addressed by the priest to the congregation: *Ite, missa est*—"Go, you are sent." We are sent into the world from the Mass. We are sent to bring his presence into that world wherever we go. This will happen with greater frequency and power the more sensitive we become to the Word he gives us breathing forth love.

Father, teach us to recognize those moments when your Word visits us. Help us learn what you wish to teach.

Crowded Out

Father Albert Trudel, O.P.

While the crowd was pressing in on Jesus and listening to the word of God, he was standing by the Lake of Gennesaret. He saw two boats there alongside the lake; the fishermen had disembarked and were washing their nets. Getting into one of the boats, the one belonging to Simon, he asked him to put out a short distance from the shore. Then he sat down and taught the crowds from the boat. (Lk 5:1-3)

In the early morning, when the waters of the lake where my family vacationed were still, even whispers carried to shore from the boats of the fishermen some distance away. The placid surface of the water brought the sound of voices clearly to the shore, and this may provide another reason, beyond overcrowding, for Jesus' decision to make Simon Peter's boat his pulpit that day as he addresses the crowd. As the eager crowd presses along the shore, Jesus' voice reflects off the water, providing some natural amplification for them.

Psalm 29 echoes in the background: "The voice of the LORD is over the waters;/ the God of glory thunders,/ the LORD, over the mighty waters./ The voice of the LORD is power;/ the voice of the LORD is splendor" (vv. 3-4). The crowd hears not the mighty voice which "splinters the cedars of Lebanon" in the psalm, but the gentle voice of the Lord, resounding over the waters, awing them, attracting them, with an invitation to new life. Jesus fishes for their hearts in the gentle waters of Lake Gennesaret, and he fishes for our hearts, not with a fisherman's deceptive lure, hook, or net, but with the truth that satisfies hearts, heard resounding off the surfaces of our day, in the quieted mind of one in prayer.

Quieted in prayer, perhaps the day's events take on a new character within us, seen from the perspective of grace. An argument with a co-worker, the help received from others over an unintentional clumsy mistake, the sympathy we offer at a friend's loss, all of these may communicate something of Jesus' incarnate Word of Truth hidden in our daily fleshly existence. Suddenly, after tuning out the dissonance of our busy lives, Christ's voice comes clear across the lake of these events, beckoning us in the unlooked-for charity we receive, the unexpected patience we manifest, the hidden cross we bear.

Heavenly Father, quiet our hearts and minds that we might hear your voice resounding in the ordinary encounters of our lives.

Into the Deep

Father Albert Trudel, O.P.

After [Jesus] had finished speaking, he said to Simon, "Put out into deep water and lower your nets for a catch." Simon said in reply, "Master, we have worked hard all night and have caught nothing, but at your command I will lower the nets." When they had done this, they caught a great number of fish and their nets were tearing. They signaled to their partners in the other boat to come to help them. They came and filled both boats so that they were in danger of sinking. (Lk 5:4-7)

The place where confessions took place at World Youth Day 2002 was called "Duc in Altum Park," borrowing from the Lord's command to "put out into deep water," and Blessed John Paul II's Apostolic Letter, *Novo millenio ineunte*, which commented on this verse. From sunrise to sunset, priests heard a constant stream of confessions from the youth in the bright sun, close by the waters of a lake. Here the Church's fishermen pulled into Peter's boat, the Church, a rich and varied catch of youth who desired to live a more genuine Christian life. Some may have scoffed before the event at the size of the space, deeming its expectations prodigal and unrealistic, but like Peter's expectations, they were proven spectacularly wrong. The challenge to "put out into the deep" defies our worldly expectations, and asks us to trust in grace's efficacy beyond the hopes shaped by previous disappointment.

My expectations from life, founded in what I think achievable through my own efforts, never aspire to the heights possible in an encounter with Jesus. His superabundance meets my emptiness and thirst with a plenitude that overwhelms me. Christ's fullness opens my horizon to an openness unrestricted by the past, to an unexpectedness that transforms my cross, my job, my annoying sibling, my family crisis from so much empty mesh into nets tearing with the weight of riches. Burdens and challenges become opportunities for grace to work.

Jesus' challenge to put out into deep water directs our gaze forward to possibilities beyond our strength because, in encountering Jesus, in trusting his Word, we no longer live by our own strength, but by his. In creation, God the Father, Son, and Holy Spirit drew something out of nothing; in the Gospel, Jesus provides a catch where none existed; in our lives, he fills our emptiness and makes us his witnesses.

Almighty Father, grant us confidence that your Son has changed and will change our emptiness into abundance.

Weak at the Knees

Father Albert Trudel, O.P.

When Simon Peter saw this, he fell at the knees of Jesus and said, "Depart from me, Lord, for I am a sinful man." For astonishment at the catch of fish they had made seized him and all those with him, and likewise James and John, the sons of Zebedee, who were partners of Simon. Jesus said to Simon, "Do not be afraid; from now on you will be catching men." When they brought their boats to the shore, they left everything and followed him. (Lk 5:8-11)

There are few times I have ever felt "weak at the knees." Most of these have been moments of sheer joy, rather than amazement, but I imagine the physical experience is the same: overcome with strong emotion, I could barely summon the energy to remain standing. While this may be the case with Peter, he falls not only on his own knees but also at Jesus' knees, an ancient posture of pleading for mercy. In ancient Greek epic poems, one character embraces the knees of someone in authority in order to beg for mercy. The gesture puts the one begging at a complete disadvantage. Defenseless, he surrenders to the judgment of the one standing over him.

What makes Peter's amazement curious is where it leads: the fisherman pulls in an astounding catch, captured through another's power. That amazement might lead, in a shallower person, to greed for more; in Peter, it leads to an awareness of unworthiness. Peter's cry here foreshadows his declaration of faith later (Lk 9:20), since he calls Jesus by the name "Lord" (*Kyrie*), a title usually reserved for the divinity. His experience as a fisherman informs him that only a divine power could produce such a catch after his failed efforts the night before, and even this hint of Jesus' identity drives him down, kneeling, humbling himself before Jesus' knees.

When we humble ourselves in the Lord's presence, we may make the same acknowledgment of unworthiness, saying, in more words than Peter's, "Why, O Lord, do you allow this sinful person to remain here in your presence?" Yet the Lord tells us, as he did to Peter, that we need not make ourselves perfect (even if we *could* do so) before we present ourselves to him, but rather, by grace he desires to make us his own eloquent witnesses. He wills us for himself through love, not through our self-made worthiness.

Merciful Father, help us acknowledge that you have chosen us, not because we have perfected ourselves in your sight, but because of your merciful love. May we always find our worthiness in the love your Son has for us.

Extending a Hand

Father Albert Trudel, O.P.

*Now there was a man full of leprosy in one of the towns where
[Jesus] was; and when he saw Jesus, he fell prostrate, pleaded
with him, and said, "Lord, if you wish, you can make me clean."
Jesus stretched out his hand, touched him, and said, "I do will
it. Be made clean." And the leprosy left him immediately. Then
he ordered him not to tell anyone, but "Go, show yourself to the
priest and offer for your cleansing what Moses prescribed;
that will be proof for them." (Lk 5:12-14)*

A priest once told me of his encounter with Blessed John
Paul II: when their conversation was interrupted by an
aide, the pope gently kept his hand on the forearm of the
priest, as if to say, "I have not forgotten you, and I am still present
to you." Video footage of the pope during his World Youth Day
encounters with people confirmed his frequent use of the power
of human touch to bridge divides, to reassure, console, communicate, and strengthen, as he held the hand or touched the face of
so many of those who came before him. Often those who received
his attention were overwhelmed with emotion, not just because of
his celebrity, but because his touch transmitted his wholehearted
presence to them in their need.

We need only look to Jesus' encounter with the unnamed leper to
see the inspiration for the pope's practice. Jesus could have healed
the leper with a word of command, as he did the centurion's servant (Mt 8:13), the Canaanite woman's daughter (Mt 15:28), or the
ten lepers (Lk 17:12). If he had done so, he would have kept the law:
anyone who touched a leper would be considered unclean and an
outcast. As Jesus' touch cleanses the leper from his physical disease,
it also restores his human dignity through this simple expression of
human contact, so necessary for any person. Jesus' healing touch
restores this man, who was once dead to his community, to the life
of human contact, to work, and to common worship.

Jesus' consoling touch extends to us, particularly in the sacraments of the Eucharist and reconciliation, but also in the love
enfleshed by those who extend Christ's touch to us, allowing the
grace they have received to overflow into our lives. We, in turn, set
free from our sin, can, by extending a hand, speaking a word of
encouragement, or acting selflessly, extend Christ's healing touch,
which renders all things clean.

*Forgiving and healing Father, help us to acknowledge your power
to save us, and to extend the hand of your selfless love so that
many may be set free.*

Days Like This

Father Albert Trudel, o.p.

*The report about [Jesus] spread all the more, and great crowds
assembled to listen to him and to be cured of their ailments,
but he would withdraw to deserted places to pray.*
(Lk 5:15-16)

The day began with minor crisis upon crisis, as the visiting
priest assigned to take the funeral Mass, caught in traffic,
ran late; the holy water, necessary for the funeral rite, was
missing; I had another funeral to attend, and a school Mass to say
in the early afternoon. I locked the parish safe by accident, leaving
necessary things inside, and I had no combination. Do I step into
the situation, and say the funeral Mass? Do I wait? How would
I get the safe open? Deadlines and expectations grew larger in my
head, weighed in scales already freighted with anxiety. I rushed
about like a madman wondering what should happen next.

Jesus certainly had days like this, judging from these two verses.
Great crowds, mentioned again just a few verses later and elsewhere in the Gospel (Lk 5:19; 8:45), accompany Jesus, pressing in
on him. Yet he finds "deserted places to pray" nevertheless. Once
again, Jesus shows us the way out of the morass of competing
obligations and responsibilities, not through constant frenetic
activity, but by maintaining the vital link to the Father in prayer.
The expectations of a crowd waiting to listen to him, or to be healed
by him, do not distract him from what he knows is necessary for
his mission. Union with the Father in prayer provides the source
of Jesus' strength and, in his human nature, he recognizes the need
to depart to a deserted place, as he heals the sick and preaches to
the great crowds.

We may well ask where those deserted places in our own lives
lie. While evident needs may press upon us, Jesus invites us to
withdraw into the interiority of the human heart that provides
a refuge even in the midst of distracting noise. There, we know
Christ accompanies us. The awareness of Christ's presence in that
deserted place refreshes us.

*Benevolent and life-giving Father, help us see you as the source
of our strength, and to turn to you, like Jesus, in the stress and
frantic moments of life. Help us meet you and your Son in the
deserted places of our hearts.*

Paralysis

Father Albert Trudel, O.P.

One day as Jesus was teaching, Pharisees and teachers of the law were sitting there who had come from every village of Galilee and Judea and Jerusalem, and the power of the Lord was with him for healing. And some men brought on a stretcher a man who was paralyzed; they were trying to bring him in and set [him] in his presence. But not finding a way to bring him in because of the crowd, they went up on the roof and lowered him on the stretcher through the tiles into the middle in front of Jesus. (Lk 5:17-19)

There are certain ways I like things done: the way my socks are arranged, or the way my clothing is folded, or the way the coffee is made in the morning. As I get older, I find myself less flexible, a little more intransigent when I see others doing things another way. In more important matters of life, this can lead to a kind of paralysis of my own choosing: locked in my own way of doing things, I find it difficult to act when the situation might demand it. In light of this sense of moral paralysis, we may ask, "Who is the real paralytic in this passage?"

Unwilling to attend to the needs of the paralytic, the Pharisees and teachers remain "sitting there," passively obstructing the way, calling to mind the Lord's rebuke later in the Gospel: "You impose on people burdens hard to carry, but you yourselves do not lift one finger to touch them" (Lk 11:46). Perhaps their unwillingness to make way for the paralytic stems from the tendency in Jesus' day to relate illness with sinfulness (see, for example, the disciples' question about the blind man in Jn 9:2). The Pharisees passively obstruct not only the paralytic's way. Their passive unwillingness to move in their hearts and thoughts also prevents them from seeing Jesus as he is.

The persistence and activity of the man's friends, as they lower him in front of Jesus, contrasts with the Pharisees' inaction. The friends have so identified the paralytic's good with their own that they perform this risky maneuver, finding a new way forward: they overcome the obstacle of shared inaction by means of shared and extraordinary action. Their love, manifest in deeds, conveys someone else into the presence of Christ. How might we see ourselves, not as passive obstacles, but active instruments of God's love, carrying and lowering those whom we love into his presence?

Loving and merciful Father, grant us the selflessness and compassion of your Son, that by our acts we might bear others into your presence.

Saved Together

Father Albert Trudel, O.P.

*When [Jesus] saw their faith, he said, "As for you, your sins
are forgiven." Then the scribes and Pharisees began to ask
themselves, "Who is this who speaks blasphemies? Who but God
alone can forgive sins?" Jesus knew their thoughts and said to
them in reply, "What are you thinking in your hearts?"*
(Lk 5:20-22)

If you have ever watched a well-orchestrated construction
project come together, you have seen the power of human
community at work. I recall watching something as simple as
the landscaping project in the courtyard of my seminary, and seeing
how different elements—the digging and leveling, the pouring of
the concrete, the laying of the brick, the planting of trees—all came
together through the efforts of different hands in an amazingly
short time confirmed that sense of common achievement.

Jesus "sees" the faith of all those around him, just as he "knows"
the thoughts of the scribes and Pharisees. In both cases, these hidden, interior dispositions provoke Jesus' respective responses. The
faith, not of the paralytic alone, but of all those assisting him, provokes Jesus' statement of forgiveness, but the Pharisees' unbelief
provokes a rebuke. The interior dispositions of these two different
groups become instrumental in the offer of grace, or its refusal,
and in this sense they have much to teach us about salvation within the community of faith, the Church. None of us is saved alone;
the community of faith plays an essential role in our salvation.

Those helping the paralytic become instruments, not only in his
physical healing, but also in his spiritual healing, the forgiveness
of his sins. They share in his hope, founded on faith, that Jesus
can heal, and so they move into action, uniting their efforts with
the paralytic's intention. Jesus looks on them with an eye to their
whole offering, not just their physical effort, but the spiritual as
well, and he responds to the whole work, to the whole body. Our
salvation comes, not through our individual works and prayers,
but through the grace given to the community of faith, lived
out faithfully in the midst of one another. Our faith, lived well,
becomes instrumental in the salvation of others.

*Father of the Church, grant us the grace so to act with and in your
grace that we might bring many into your Son's presence, in the
communion of the faithful.*

Absolver of Bonds

Father Albert Trudel, o.p.

[Jesus said,] "Which is easier, to say, 'Your sins are forgiven,' or to say, 'Rise and walk'? But that you may know that the Son of Man has authority on earth to forgive sins"—he said to the man who was paralyzed, "I say to you, rise, pick up your stretcher, and go home." He stood up immediately before them, picked up what he had been lying on, and went home, glorifying God. Then astonishment seized them all and they glorified God, and, struck with awe, they said, "We have seen incredible things today." (Lk 5:23-26)

Since the tragedy of 9/11, I look at firefighters with awe, particularly when I remember the television footage of firemen climbing the Twin Towers, all the while knowing the deadly peril that awaited them. The courage and integrity of those men, not only as a matter of words, but of action, never ceases to amaze me, mainly because the distance between saying something and doing it can often be rather long these days. We stand amazed, like the crowd, when actions not only meet, but exceed our usual expectations.

The proof Jesus provides for his ability to forgive sins, and of his divinity, involves not just amazement of this kind, but also a certain amount of irony. He performs a miracle that, on the face of it, seems more difficult than saying "Your sins are forgiven." When we look at the case more closely, could we not say that the spiritual wounds of sin represent the graver illness, and so the miracle of spiritual healing represents the more difficult miracle? Jesus knows us, however, and he knows that while we cannot see forgiveness, we *can* see physical healing of this magnitude. The manifestation of his power to heal our bodies gives us a visual image of his power to heal our souls, to set us free, like the paralytic, from what binds us, so that we might stand and walk in strength.

Through our mistrust of Jesus' words, or perhaps through our own defeated self-confidence, we can enter a spiritual paralysis of sorts, thinking that the healing of our moral lives depends solely upon our own efforts and self-discipline. In the healing of the paralytic, Jesus shows us not only his power to release us from the bonds of vicious habits, but that his grace is necessary for our release. The one who can heal bodily ills can likewise heal our souls.

Merciful Father, give me the grace to trust in your Only Begotten Son's power to release me from my bonds and to inspire me to act in charity.

A Transforming Gaze

Father Albert Trudel, O.P.

After this [Jesus] went out and saw a tax collector named Levi sitting at the customs post. He said to him, "Follow me." And leaving everything behind, he got up and followed him. Then Levi gave a great banquet for him in his house, and a large crowd of tax collectors and others were at table with them.
(Lk 5:27-29)

I had just asked my homeroom class for a volunteer to collect the daily class donation for the missions, and Heath, a tough student not unfamiliar with trouble, raised his hand. Immediately, critical misgivings gripped me: surely he volunteered, not out of the goodness of his heart, but so that he might pocket some of the proceeds. On the other hand, perhaps (like myself in my doubts) no one had ever shown him any degree of trust. Perhaps he needed someone to believe in him, to break the cycle of mistrust and demonstrate to him his worthiness.

Levi's encounter with Christ shows us the transformative power, not only of trust, but of the love that rests at the foundation of respect for another. Jesus takes notice of Levi, sitting at his tax booth, who is used to being spurned as the worst of sinners and a traitor to his people. Whether or not we understand the Gospel account as an abbreviated narrative of actual events makes no difference: this stranger's expressive and loving gaze, his attention, changes Levi. Levi's complete and total break with his former life, leaving everything behind for Jesus, makes sense from this perspective. Levi's response, so absolute and final, comes from a conviction born of an encounter with Jesus, whose transformative regard manifests Levi's dignity and "love-worthiness" as a person.

Jesus' regard for us, spoken in the Scriptures, manifest to us on the cross, and made present for us in the Eucharist, enables us to extend his gaze, his regard for others out into our world. In the end, I took a risk and accepted Heath's offer. Guess what? We raised the most for the missions that year, and (not simply through my intervention, but through the care and concern of many in the school) Heath became a different person.

Loving Father, you pour out your mercy upon us in your Son's selfless gift of himself to us. Grant us the grace to imitate that selflessness which transforms us and those around us.

The Ease of Labels

Father Albert Trudel, O.P.

The Pharisees and their scribes complained to [Jesus'] disciples, saying, "Why do you eat and drink with tax collectors and sinners?" Jesus said to them in reply, "Those who are healthy do not need a physician, but the sick do. I have not come to call the righteous to repentance but sinners."

(Lk 5:30-32)

A priest friend had invited me to his parish rectory for dinner, where his pastor, a monsignor who also worked in the bishop's office, welcomed me to their table. We had a good discussion, and at some point in the meal, in a slightly critical manner, I asked some questions about a letter the priests of the diocese had recently received from the bishop's office. The good monsignor quizzed me about my reaction to the letter, and took great interest in what I had to say. He then informed me that he himself had written the letter for the bishop. It was easy for me to speak about the letter as long as its author remained safely anonymous, but you can imagine my embarrassment when he gently identified himself.

The Pharisees and scribes do not identify persons with names, but with labels: Levi's friends become an anonymous collection of "tax collectors and sinners," which in turn makes it easier to think of them as a faceless group, not as individuals, or even as wounded souls, in need of healing. When we cease to look at the person, we fail to respond to them in their fullness as images and likenesses of God; we see instead only a truncated aspect of a whole that might otherwise compel us to respond.

Jesus sees his dinner companions with eyes wide open. He harbors no illusions about their virtue, but on the other hand, his appreciation of their humanity, and his love for them as persons, enables him to see their needs. He reaches out to them as the physician who restores their full humanity, just as he reaches into ours, and continues to restore us. We, in turn, can choose to notice only a label, or to extend to another the loving hand of our healing physician through the way we respond to him or her.

Father of the poor, open our eyes to see your image and likeness even in those we dislike; grant us the grace to offer them your healing presence in their need.

Fasting and Feasting

Father Albert Trudel, o.p.

And [the Pharisees and their scribes] said to [Jesus], "The disciples of John fast often and offer prayers, and the disciples of the Pharisees do the same; but yours eat and drink." Jesus answered them, "Can you make the wedding guests fast while the bridegroom is with them? But the days will come, and when the bridegroom is taken away from them, then they will fast in those days." (Lk 5:33-35)

Shakespeare's comedies all end in a marriage, or the promise of marriage, and we can see why. The joy of the wedding celebrates lives united, and the joy of that realized wholeness, its satisfaction, completes and harmonizes the awkward fragments in the search for happiness that provoked laughter throughout the rest of the play. We feel the same joy at a wedding in which the couple truly "complete" one another, in which their selfless love for one another, celebrated in the sacrament, bonds the couple in a wonderful whole.

Jesus' references to himself as a bridegroom and the Church as his bride inspired Saint Paul, and consequently the Church, to see in sacramental marriage a rich metaphor for the selfless love of Jesus for his Church. The extended hymn to the Easter candle at the Easter Vigil proclaims that, in the Resurrection, "things of heaven are wed to those of earth, and divine to the human." Christ completes us by restoring the lost innocence of Adam and Eve, by restoring our communion with the heavenly Father.

The metaphor of marriage, and its accompanying sense of feasting, helps us make sense of Christian fasting as well. Just as lovers, divided from one another, will make sacrifices to manifest the depth and fidelity of their love, so our love for the Lord, in his relative "absence" from us, draws us to sacrifices that remind us of our reliance on him. While we wait for Christ's second coming, we fast from food or from vices to remind ourselves that Christ alone satisfies us; we spend time before the Blessed Sacrament as we yearn for Christ's presence among us in glory. The Pharisees and scribes see fasting as a rigorous discipline that proves one's righteousness; Christ invites us to sacrifice as an act of expectant love that acknowledges Christ alone as our source of true fulfillment.

Father of our Lord Jesus Christ, grant us the grace to love your Son with our whole lives, and to find in him the source and summit of our joy.

93

Something Old, Something New

Father Albert Trudel, O.P.

And [Jesus] also told [the Pharisees and their scribes] a parable. "No one tears a piece from a new cloak to patch an old one. Otherwise, he will tear the new and the piece from it will not match the old cloak. Likewise, no one pours new wine into old wineskins. Otherwise, the new wine will burst the skins, and it will be spilled, and the skins will be ruined. Rather, new wine must be poured into fresh wineskins. [And] no one who has been drinking old wine desires new, for he says, 'The old is good.'" (Lk 5:36-39)

Looking through old department store catalogues offers an education in the variety of human tastes and how culture shapes them. How could we dare to have worn those colors, those materials, or that cut? How could certain household products ever have interested us? On the other hand, we might also note how little some things have changed: general features of formal wear and business suits (at least, outside of the anomalous period of the 1960s) usually change very little. We might even engage in nostalgia for the excellence of something no longer available to us. Looking through the catalogue may confirm our usual cultural prejudice in favor of the "new," but it also can deepen our appreciation for the goodness of the "old."

Jesus carefully distinguishes between old and new in his parable, without emphasizing one to the disadvantage of the other. The old and new represent the old and new covenants, which in some respects are incompatible: for example, fasting in the new covenant shares many aspects with the older asceticism of the law, but its new rootedness in our longing for Christ distinguishes it significantly from the old practice. The old law, however, has much to teach us about the asceticism of a fast as a reliance on God for what we need. As a revelation of the one God, both covenants speak to us: the old preparing the way for the new and definitive revelation in Christ, and the new drawing on the tradition of the old.

While we do not practice the old law, we see it anew through the lens of Christ's revelation, and we freely draw on the truths it transmits to us about God's faithfulness to his chosen people. Our faith does not draw upon fads or fashions, but upon the truths God has communicated to us from age to age, and which renew us each day.

O God and Father, giver of grace to every age, grant that we may always search the Scriptures with your understanding, so that we might see your hand in every age, including our own.

The Lord of the Sabbath

Father Timothy Bellamah, O.P.

*While [Jesus] was going through a field of grain on a sabbath,
his disciples were picking the heads of grain, rubbing them in
their hands, and eating them. Some Pharisees said, "Why are
you doing what is unlawful on the sabbath?" Jesus said to them
in reply, "Have you not read what David did [...]? [How] he
went into the house of God, took the bread of offering, which
only the priests could lawfully eat, ate of it, and shared it with
his companions." Then he said to them, "The Son of Man is
lord of the sabbath." (Lk 6:1-5)*

Even the most industrious people, if they have any sense at all, know the importance of relaxation. Good rest is crucial for doing anything well, to say nothing of enjoying health and happiness. But there are many ways of seeking rest, not all of them salutary. It is not uncommon for people to be left more fatigued, more jaded, by their quest for recreation than by their work.

The sabbath is about much more than taking a break. It is a sacred day of peaceful gratitude recalling God's rest after the six days of creation. That God has commanded such a repose indicates that our wellbeing depends on it (Ex 16:26). Mere entertainment will not do. By accusing the Apostles of violating the sabbath by picking grain to satisfy their hunger, the Pharisees show a failure to understand it, supposing it to be little more than an obligation imposed for its own sake, rather than a divine gift given for our good.

By saying that he is the "lord of the sabbath," Jesus does nothing to diminish it. To the contrary, he gives it new meaning, revealing himself to be the Creator who was present at the first sabbath and showing this rest to consist in personal communion with him. Though Christians often suppose that their only respite must lie on the other side of the grave, Jesus invites us into his rest right now by the life of grace. As Saint Catherine of Siena put it: "All the way to heaven is heaven because Christ is the way." And yet, Jesus' lordship over the sabbath also directs our attention forward, to our eternal peace, where he will introduce us to the life he has enjoyed from all eternity with the Father and the Holy Spirit. By faith, we are free to enter that rest even now. As the Letter to the Hebrews tells us, "For we who believed enter into that rest."

Heavenly Father, help us to seek our rest only in you, so that our every work may happily find its completion in you.

The Power to Stand

Father Timothy Bellamah, O.P.

On another sabbath [Jesus] went into the synagogue and taught, and there was a man there whose right hand was withered. The scribes and the Pharisees watched him closely to see if he would cure on the sabbath so that they might discover a reason to accuse him. But he realized their intentions and said to the man with the withered hand, "Come up and stand before us." And he rose and stood there. (Lk 6:6-8)

Jesus would appear to have a dilemma on his hands. Standing in the temple on a sabbath, he is confronted by a man with a withered right hand whom he wants to help. But he sees some Pharisees watching and waiting for a chance to find him breaking the law. They don't much care whether or not the man is healed. Their concern is protecting their power. What would you do here? A painless course of action would be to speak to the man discreetly to arrange a meeting at some other time and place. That way he could be healed with no offense taken and no trouble started.

However tricky this situation may appear to us, to Jesus it presents no problem at all. Living in his Father's love, he doesn't need to be liked. He is therefore willing to dispense with good manners and even proper protocols when necessary to do his Father's will. Here it is necessary so that this anonymous man may have life more abundantly. Jesus can heal him later, elsewhere, but he does so on this sabbath day, in the temple, knowing well that he will incur the Pharisees' rage. Why? God alone knows the whole answer, but clearly he wants the man to rise and stand in the temple, in front of everyone. Even before Jesus restores the hand, he restores the man, as a full member of society, free to stand before everyone, free to worship God without fear. It is for this that God has created him, and it is for this that Jesus recreates him. The tragic effect of sin is alienation or separation—from communion with God, from the life of the Church, and from oneself. Far more wonderful than the restoration of physical health is Jesus' undoing of sin, as he tells those so stricken, "Come up and stand before us."

Dear Father, grant us the grace we need to stand in the communion of the saints and to serve you in drawing all people into the beatitude you have prepared for us.

The Power to Create and to Save

Father Timothy Bellamah, O.P.

Then Jesus said to [the scribes and Pharisees], "I ask you, is it lawful to do good on the sabbath rather than to do evil, to save life rather than to destroy it?" Looking around at them all, he then said to [the man with a withered hand], "Stretch out your hand." He did so and his hand was restored. But they became enraged and discussed together what they might do to Jesus.

(Lk 6:9-11)

"Question authority" say the bumper stickers. Here we find Jesus doing just that, asking the Pharisees about good and evil, life and death, and this because of their indifference to the man with the withered hand. Concerned with protecting their authority and power, they don't much care whether the man is healed, or not. Power of this kind is inimical to all that is good in the human spirit, crushing freedom, and thwarting the yearnings of the human heart, bringing death to anyone who gets in its way. Left to itself, human power is too often like that of the Pharisees, or of a dictator, proceeding from the muzzle of a gun, and blind to God's wisdom. Since the time of Adam, this way of grasping and exercising power has been normal for us; it's what the rulers of the Gentiles do. Hence the bad names of power and authority. On the cross, Jesus experiences this tragedy far more bitterly than any of us ever will.

Still, Jesus confronts the Pharisees, not as an anarchist, but as the revealer of another authority and another power. Involving no coercion, God's power is creative, operating within the human spirit, giving life and freedom. This wonder he also experiences personally in his Resurrection. By questioning the Pharisees, he sets forth a rule for the exercise of authority in the service of divine wisdom and of others. If human authority is to serve God, it must have the cross as its model, remaining uninterested in human power and directed to God's kingdom. Should we be wise enough to surrender to God's authority in Christ, we will come to understand Paul's words to the Corinthians, "So whoever is in Christ is a new creation: the old things have passed away; behold, new things have come" (2 Cor 5:17).

Heavenly Father, help us to recognize the wonders of your creative, liberating power in our lives and bringing to fulfillment the freedom Christ won for us on the cross.

The Lord of Trust

Father Timothy Bellamah, O.P.

In those days [Jesus] departed to the mountain to pray, and he spent the night in prayer to God. When day came, he called his disciples to himself, and from them he chose Twelve, whom he also named apostles: Simon, whom he named Peter, and his brother Andrew, James, John, Philip, Bartholomew, Matthew, Thomas, James the son of Alphaeus, Simon who was called a Zealot, and Judas the son of James, and Judas Iscariot, who became a traitor. (Lk 6:12-16)

Before the Apostles can entrust themselves to Jesus by responding to his call, he entrusts himself to them. Accepting the unique invitation Jesus has for each one of us demands that we trust him, but before we can even entertain the possibility, he has already entrusted himself to us. In accepting these twelve into his friendship, Jesus trusts them with his life, knowing full well that his trust can and will be violated. Anyone who has been betrayed by a friend knows some small part of the sorrow Peter, the other Apostles, and of course, Judas, cause Jesus. And yet, he asks us to share his life, not because we are perfect, but that we might come to share in his perfection.

Knowing our shortcomings, Jesus offers himself to us in friendship, not in a vain expectation that we will be perfectly faithful, but in the clear knowledge that we won't. Yet he does it anyway. Why? God alone understands completely, but one place to start looking for answers is his desire to have us trust him. He trusts us out of longing for our trust in him. His offer of saving truth, "wiser than human wisdom" (1 Cor 1:25), can be received only in trust, in faith in him; his offer of eternal life, which "eye has not seen" (1 Cor 2:9), can be received only in trust, in hope in him; his offer of mercy, "that he might have mercy upon all" (Rom 11:32), can be received only in trust, the trust that he will put away our sins rather than cast them in our faces.

The Lord has no better way, no other way, of eliciting our trust in him than by entrusting himself to us. Placing himself in our hands, he waits for us to place ourselves in his. His willingness to face the prospect of betrayal of his trust bespeaks his desire for ours.

Heavenly Father, grant us the grace to discover the love of your Son, who hands himself over to us, that we might hand ourselves over to him.

The Power That Comes forth from Him

Father Timothy Bellamah, O.P.

And [Jesus] came down with [the Twelve] and stood on a stretch of level ground. A great crowd of his disciples and a large number of the people from all Judea and Jerusalem and the coastal region of Tyre and Sidon came to hear him and to be healed of their diseases; and even those who were tormented by unclean spirits were cured. Everyone in the crowd sought to touch him because power came forth from him and healed them all. (Lk 6:17-19)

In our time people don't normally try to obtain a healing by touching someone else. We have other ways of trying to get well. The first recourse is often a trip to the medicine cabinet or the pharmacist. And if that doesn't work, there are always the less pleasant and more expensive alternatives of surgery and therapy. But even the wonders of modern medicine often fail to make people well. In such cases, it is not unusual for them to turn to God in prayer. Sometimes he grants those who ask in faith the healing they want, sometimes he doesn't, but he never sends them away empty-handed. People are capable of demanding a healing or a miracle from God as a precondition for believing in him and loving him, supposing, "If God gives me what I want, I will believe in him; if not, I won't." This amounts to an attempt to manipulate God, to make him conform to our will.

Authentic prayer proceeding from faith works the other way around, allowing our will to be conformed to God's by accepting his will for us. For this we need divine grace. God wants it for us infinitely more than we want it for ourselves, and he knows where our happiness lies better than we do. This is why he will not always grant us what we ask for. He "is able to accomplish far more than all we ask or imagine, by the power at work within us" (Eph 3:20). His will is better than ours.

Knowing that power comes forth from Jesus, everyone in the crowd seeks to touch him. They seek only to touch him, not to manipulate him. Whenever we receive a sacrament, Jesus Christ does what neither any doctor nor any medicine could ever do, touching our souls and pouring forth his grace, restoring us to a life beyond all our desiring.

Merciful Father, your will is for none other than our good. Grant us the grace to accept the healing you offer, far more wonderful than all we ask or imagine.

Being Rich in Poverty

Father Timothy Bellamah, O.P.

And raising his eyes toward his disciples [Jesus] said:
"Blessed are you who are poor,/ for the kingdom of God is
yours./ Blessed are you who are now hungry,/ for you will
be satisfied./ Blessed are you who are now weeping,/
for you will laugh." (Lk 6:20-21)

Even people who have never experienced it understand material poverty well enough to exhaust themselves in avoiding it. Who wants to do without sustenance or shelter, not to mention the other fine things in life? But the kind of poverty Jesus talks about is less obvious.

In his instruction on beatitude, our Lord teaches us something about ourselves and something about God. In saying that the poor are blessed, he reminds us that before God we are all poor. Neither our money, material possessions, achievements, nor anything else we may trust in can buy us anything from him. He owes us nothing. Some people live and die without realizing this. Others find out only at the ends of their lives when stripped of their health and confronted with the impending loss of all they hold dear. Then they finally come to realize that before God they are absolutely poor, that they are beggars. Hopefully, we learn sooner.

Confronted with poverty of this kind, we have two options. One of them is to rebel in anger because we cannot have ultimate happiness on our own terms, our way. The other is to turn to God rejoicing in our destitution, trusting in the mercy of him who raises up the lowly and fills the hungry with good things, knowing that those who trust in him cannot be put to shame. This is true poverty of spirit, the kind of deprivation that draws us into the life of God by making us trust in him for all good things.

In giving us this teaching, Jesus tells us something about our own poverty and about God's mercy. But he also tells us something about himself, the God-man, the eternal Son of the Father, who, being rich, became poor for our sake. In the Eucharist, all his riches are ours.

Bountiful Father, grant us the wisdom to rejoice in our poverty,
trusting only in the surpassing riches of your heavenly kingdom.

The Witness of the Saints

Father Timothy Bellamah, O.P.

"Blessed are you when people hate you,/ and when they exclude and insult you,/ and denounce your name as evil/ on account of the Son of Man./ Rejoice and leap for joy on that day! Behold, your reward will be great in heaven. For their ancestors treated the prophets in the same way." (Lk 6:22-23)

Being hated is a strange cause for rejoicing, but Jesus speaks these words to console his followers. Those who follow him should not be surprised by opposition and conflict. And yet, hardly a day goes by without reports of people laying down their lives for all kinds of causes, some more noble than others. Even terrorists do as much, thinking of themselves as victims of hatred and calling themselves "martyrs." We shouldn't be surprised, then, if Christians are sometimes spoken of as just another one of so many competing groups of extremists.

But anyone wondering about the difference between Christian martyrs and fanatics need look no further than Christ's own words and deeds. Terrorists lay down their lives out of hatred, while true martyrs, in the imitation of Christ, lay down theirs not because they hate, but because they love; not because they hate, but because they are hated. Elsewhere, Jesus tells his disciples that the world will hate them because they have hated him first (cf. Jn 15:18). The reasons for this are many, but one of the chief is the displeasure of correction—by their words and deeds the saints are a living re-proof to those who ignore God's law. Another is that those who hate, being spiritually dead, envy the saints, who are alive in God's grace, growing in goodness and true happiness. This is why our Lord's words are cause for rejoicing. Suffering hatred for his name is proof for us that we are sharers in his life. By these words Jesus gives us courage, and by his cross and Resurrection he gives us knowledge of such a life that we should be willing to die for it. This life we receive in the Eucharist, with the result we should be willing to die only for love of the one who has loved us and given himself for us (cf. Gal 2:20).

Loving Father, in the moments of tribulation, grant us the grace to lay down our lives only for love of you and your kingdom, that we may be living witness to your Son's surpassing love for all your children.

The Path of Love

Father Timothy Bellamah, O.P.

"But woe to you who are rich,/ for you have received your consolation./ But woe to you who are filled now,/ for you will be hungry./ Woe to you who laugh now,/ for you will grieve and weep./ Woe to you when all speak well of you,/ for their ancestors treated the false prophets in this way."
(Lk 6:24-26)

"Whoever dies with the most toys wins," or so they say. Left unsaid by the saying is what, exactly, is won. But to anyone supposing this to be true, Jesus says "woe," or, in other words, calamity, horror. Appalling to modern sensibilities, this warning provides a sobering account of our condition in this life. One way to understand it is to consider money and all the many toys it can buy calamitous, horrible. But that is not what Jesus says. After all, he is speaking of people, not things. Specifically, he speaks to and about those who seek their happiness in money, possessions, food, or anything other than God. However much they may appear to be winners, those satisfied by wealth are the worst of losers, because they have placed their confidence and hope in realities that can only disappoint. What is worse, by giving wealth priority to friendship with Christ, they have held him cheap. This is the true calamity, the true horror, of dying with nothing more than a pile of toys, because Christ will not be held cheap.

Sobering though it may be, Jesus' warning is remarkably consoling, because it teaches us something of what he offers us. If we should be prepared to sacrifice everything for our friendship with him, we realize the inestimable worth of the life he offers us and the price he has paid to win it for us. He cannot be held cheap, because he has not held us cheap. We will not go far trying to follow him with no more than lip service, failing to allow his ways to invade our ways, failing to allow his cross into our lives, failing to love. We have two paths before us then: the path of fear or selfishness, or the path of love. The choice is ours.

Father of mercy, your love for us surpasses all our understanding. Grant us the grace to respond to your love as true sons and daughters in your Son.

The Love That Conquers Hatred

Father Timothy Bellamah, O.P.

"But to you who hear I say, love your enemies, do good to those who hate you, bless those who curse you, pray for those who mistreat you. To the person who strikes you on one cheek, offer the other one as well, and from the person who takes your cloak, do not withhold even your tunic."

(Lk 6:27-29)

L oving one's enemies may seem a lot to expect of those of us who sometimes have trouble overlooking even petty offenses. If ignoring someone who cuts us off in traffic doesn't come easy, how could we ever befriend those who consider themselves our enemies? If friendship is sharing of life, as Aristotle describes it, befriending enemies would seem to be foolish. And yet, the message of the cross is foolishness to those who are perishing (cf. 1 Cor 1:18). On the cross, God's incarnate Wisdom prayed, "Father, forgive them, they know not what they do" (Lk 23:34). Jesus so desired to establish friendship with us that he "became flesh and made his dwelling among us" (Jn 1:14). He continues this life of friendship in the Eucharist, showing his extreme love for us; he offers us his bodily presence in the meantime between his Ascension and his return. In the truth of his Body and Blood he unites us intimately to himself, sharing his life with us. Forgiving the enmity we so often create, he invites us to live with him in friendship. And this he never ceases to do, putting to death that enmity we so often create, and always inviting us into closer friendship with him. As Saint Paul tells the Romans, "While we were enemies, we were reconciled to God through the death of his Son" (Rom 5:10).

Befriending one's enemies is a dangerous business. It cost Christ his life, and it has since cost countless martyrs theirs. We may never face such danger, but if we want to live with Christ in friendship we will have to love those who consider themselves our enemies, and even people who cut us off in traffic. If we can manage a prayer for them, we already live with them in charity. Sharing God's life with them, we ourselves partake of that same life.

Heavenly Father, as we live in the midst of strife, never allow us to be defeated by hatred. Enkindle our hearts with the fire of your love that we may be instruments of your peace.

The Mercy That Triumphs over Judgment

Father Timothy Bellamah, O.P.

"Give to everyone who asks of you, and from the one who takes what is yours do not demand it back. Do to others as you would have them do to you. For if you love those who love you, what credit is that to you? Even sinners love those who love them. And if you do good to those who do good to you, what credit is that to you? Even sinners do the same." (Lk 6:30-33)

One of the basic precepts medical students are encouraged to learn is "First, do no harm." This is a valuable reminder to doctors to consider whatever harm may result from their actions and to avoid procedures whose risks outweigh their prospective benefits. But people sometimes turn this principle into a justification for selfish behavior, with words such as "I never hurt anyone." By this standard, not doing evil suffices to make us good—as long as we don't hurt anyone by our actions, we can content ourselves with the assurance that we are beyond reproach.

By commanding us to give without expecting anything in return, our Lord gives us a lesson in God's justice and mercy, reminding us that all we are and have is his gift. A consequence of this lesson is that the freedom we hold so dear is vested with responsibility. We have been granted it so that we might become instruments of God's goodness. Doing no harm may suffice for staying out of trouble with the police, but it will not do for living as the sons and daughters God has created us to be. Divine justice requires that we do good to those to whom we owe nothing and from whom we stand to gain nothing, because this is how God has dealt with us. Owing us nothing and standing to gain nothing, he has given us life, and the precious gift of the new life of grace in his Son, risen from the dead. Our own sacrifices add nothing to God's happiness, so they cannot begin to compensate. All the same, in the economy of divine mercy, our works of charity for those unable to repay us become expressions of gratitude. By them we acknowledge our debt to God and fulfill the requirements of his justice, all the while becoming like his Son, whose "mercy triumphs over judgment" (Jas 2:13).

Merciful Father, breathe forth your Son's Spirit upon us, that with his gifts we may use our freedom to bring your peace into the world.

The Genuine Article

Father Timothy Bellamah, O.P.

"If you lend money to those from whom you expect repayment, what credit [is] that to you? Even sinners lend to sinners, and get back the same amount. But rather, love your enemies and do good to them, and lend expecting nothing back; then your reward will be great and you will be children of the Most High, for he himself is kind to the ungrateful and the wicked."
(Lk 6:34-35)

As he lists the many hardships he has faced while preaching the Gospel, Saint Paul tells the Corinthians of scourgings, beatings, and shipwrecks, and then mentions a less obvious danger—false brothers (cf. 2 Cor 11:25-26). The Church has always had its frauds, some easier to spot than others. By these hard teachings our Lord tells us how to spot the true Christian. Giving without expecting anything in return, loving and doing good to enemies, being merciful, refraining from judgment—these are the marks of the genuine article. Any impostor can dress up in distinctive clothing or flaunt external signs of piety, and any fool can love those who love in return, but only the children of the Most High can love an enemy or lend with no expectation of repayment. Such endeavors cannot be faked because they lie beyond the natural capacities of mere mortals, however talented they may be.

This arduous way of love presupposes God's grace. Only those who live in Christ, inspired by the Holy Spirit and crying out to the Father, can hope to live by it. Difficult though it may be, Jesus would not put forward this way of love were it not possible. It is he who makes it possible, and this he does by drawing us into the love he has shared with his Father from all eternity. And yet, he instructs us in it not merely because it is possible, but because it is crucial. It is the road to heaven. We would never dare to walk this arduous road, if not for the proof Christ gives us by his own life, death, and Resurrection. Instead, we would be tempted to withdraw in fear, either by disavowing this way of life, or by trying to fake it. Should we be brave enough to confide in him, we will find him making us into the genuine article.

Loving Father, pour forth your Spirit into our hearts that we may overcome the spirit of this world to enjoy the true freedom of your Son.

Freedom from Judgment

Father Timothy Bellamah, O.P.

"Be merciful, just as [also] your Father is merciful. Stop judging and you will not be judged. Stop condemning and you will not be condemned. Forgive and you will be forgiven. Give and gifts will be given to you; a good measure, packed together, shaken down, and overflowing, will be poured into your lap. For the measure with which you measure will in return be measured out to you." (Lk 6:36-38)

No mere legislator's mandate could be as liberating as our Lord's command to stop judging—it frees us from the fear of being judged by anyone other than God, whose mercy endures for ever. No policeman, elected official, cleric, angel, or saint in heaven can peer into our souls. God alone sees and judges them because he alone brings them into existence. But our Lord's instruction liberates us in another respect—it frees us from wasting our precious limited time and energy in this life gazing at and judging others. We have been given life for more worthwhile pursuits.

And yet, Saint Paul tells the Corinthians that the spiritual person judges all things (cf. 1 Cor 2:15). Few people, in fact, can get through a day without making many kinds of judgments. As soon as we have decided that the weather is nice or that a meal is good, we have arrived at a judgment. Of course, such judgments are about things, not people. Still, at times people must judge people. Policemen, judges, or prospective spouses, for example, must make judgments about others, and they do so legitimately provided they have good reason and refrain from pronouncing upon anyone else's status before God. Of course, human judgment is prone to error. If our judgments are to be just, they must proceed from the love of justice, rather than our biases, and they must be the fruit of wisdom, which is right judgment according to God's reasons.

This brings us to yet another way in which Jesus' instruction sets us free. Should we be wise enough to put to good use our conscience, that God-given capacity for judging our own actions, we will see ourselves as the beneficiaries of our Lord's surpassing mercy. This awareness should lead us to repentance and forgiveness of others, rather than to judgment and condemnation of them (cf. Rom 2:4). Then, we will share the only mercy that endures for ever.

Heavenly Father, help us to see the wonders of your mercy in our lives, so that we may become servants of that same mercy for all your people.

The Grace of Clear Vision

Father Timothy Bellamah, O.P.

And [Jesus] told [the people,] "[...] Why do you notice the splinter in your brother's eye, but do not perceive the wooden beam in your own? How can you say to your brother, 'Brother, let me remove that splinter in your eye,' when you do not even notice the wooden beam in your own eye? You hypocrite! Remove the wooden beam from your eye first; then you will see clearly to remove the splinter in your brother's eye."
(Lk 6:39-42)

Wise, prescient people are often called "farsighted" because they see things beyond the ken of others, especially the "shortsighted." And yet, sometimes we have the most trouble seeing what is closest to us. One of the harder lessons novice drivers must learn is that a car passing on the right just a few feet away is often much less easily seen than one several miles ahead. The blind spots behind such lapses are particularly vexing because they are themselves unseen and unknown. When people become nearsighted they usually know it, as they notice their increasing difficulty in discerning distant objects, such as road signs. But it's quite common for people to drive for years blithely unaware of such things as blind spots, until finding out about them the hard way.

By this parable Jesus tells us that our own failings darken our perceptions in much the same way, all the while remaining hidden. As a result, we arrive at faulty judgments of others, oblivious to the murkiness of our perceptions of them. Like the wooden beam in Jesus' parable, our faults lie too close to home to show up in our normal gaze and come to light only when we make a deliberate effort to unmask them. Should we go about this painful task alone, confident only in our abilities to help ourselves, we will soon end up in despair, confused and defeated by our shortcomings. We can go about this difficult business if we can catch some glimpse of the way God sees the world and us in it.

By his light Christ reveals us to ourselves, not to shame us, but that we might see ourselves, warts and all, as his creatures basking in his mercy. So enlightened, we will be equipped to see others in the same light, and help them along the way who has the name of Christ.

Heavenly Father, you know all things. Enlighten our minds so that we may see ourselves and others clearly by the light of your wisdom and so discern your saving action in our world.

The Fruitfulness of Grace

Father Timothy Bellamah, O.P.

"A good tree does not bear rotten fruit, nor does a rotten tree bear good fruit. For every tree is known by its own fruit. For people do not pick figs from thornbushes, nor do they gather grapes from brambles. A good person out of the store of goodness in his heart produces good, but an evil person out of a store of evil produces evil; for from the fullness of the heart the mouth speaks." (Lk 6:43-45)

It is easy enough to see how actions, good or bad, are like fruit, good or bad. The kind word or the helpful gesture from a friend or stranger is sweet and life-giving. Seeing the happy effect of our own kind word or deed offered to the friend or stranger at the right moment is also vivifying. Then again, the back-biting remark, the gratuitous insult, or the inconsiderate or mean gesture from someone else reeks and leaves a sour aftertaste. Still more acidic is the awareness of the effect on others of our own selfishness. But the core of Jesus' lesson is about the sources of good or bad fruits, the kinds of persons who act well or badly. However arbitrary or isolated our actions may seem to us, Jesus tells us that they proceed from our character, for better or for worse.

What is it, then, that makes us good or bad? The answer is illustrated for us early on in Luke's Gospel, in Mary's reply to the angel Gabriel: "Behold, I am the handmaid of the Lord. May it be done to me according to your word" (Lk 1:38). By her graced acceptance of God's will for her, she keeps her will in perfect conformity to his and becomes fruitful beyond all imagining. By surrendering her will to God's, Mary proclaims the fruitfulness of his creative, life-giving will, and she partakes of God's fruitfulness, bearing his Son. It is all too easy for us to suppose that our will is better than God's, that we are most likely to find happiness, freedom, and peace doing things our way, but a look at the world around us is enough to show the sterility and death of that option. Our conformity to God's will is a wonderful grace, given by the Fruit of Mary's womb, who chooses us and appoints us to go and bear fruit that will remain (cf. Jn 15:16).

Heavenly Father, in your will is our peace. Grant us the grace to accept your will for us that we may remain in your Son and bear everlasting fruit.

Words Stronger than Death

Father Timothy Bellamah, o.p.

"Why do you call me, 'Lord, Lord,' but not do what I command?
I will show you what someone is like who comes to me, listens to
my words, and acts on them. That one is like a person building
a house, who dug deeply and laid the foundation on rock [...].
But the one who listens and does not act is like a person
who built a house on the ground without a foundation.
When the river burst against it, it collapsed at once
and was completely destroyed." (Lk 6:46-49)

There is nothing unusual about news reports of houses destroyed by floods, fires, landslides, or earthquakes. But even the most sensationalistic accounts generally refrain from pointing the accusing finger at God. Most people realize that such events result from natural forces. That is why anyone building a house with no foundation next to a river could be called a fool. Were such a fool to blame God after seeing the house washed away in a flood, he could be called delusional. It would be obvious that the house's collapse has resulted from natural forces foreseeable to any levelheaded person.

Jesus tells us that human life is similar. If our lives are not based on the rock who he is, we lack the foundation necessary for enduring life's many floods. Failing to act on his words is equivalent to building our lives on something other than him. No one refusing to build on this foundation can hope to overcome the one natural disaster that awaits us all—death. No such fool can expect to share in the life of God. That anyone who chooses to reject Christ should meet such a catastrophic destiny results not from vindictiveness on God's part, but from his respect for the freedom he has given us.

It is worth noting that our Lord doesn't tell us that if we listen to his words and act on them, we will be like builders of houses that never encounter flood waters. In other words, he makes us no promise of immunity from suffering and death. In fact, throughout Luke's Gospel he assures just the opposite. What he promises those who act on his words is incomparably better: they will be like builders of houses that cannot be shaken by flood waters. Should we be wise enough to build our lives on him, we will have no reason to dread whatever torrents life may have in store for us.

Eternal Father, grant us the grace to allow your saving truth to shine forth in our actions, so that our lives may have as their foundation none other than your Son.

Pagans, Jews, and Jesus

Andrew Matt

When [Jesus] had finished all his words to the people, he entered Capernaum. A centurion there had a slave who was ill and about to die, and he was valuable to him. When he heard about Jesus, he sent elders of the Jews to him, asking him to come and save the life of his slave. They approached Jesus and strongly urged him to come, saying, "He deserves to have you do this for him, for he loves our nation and he built the synagogue for us." And Jesus went with them. (Lk 7:1-6a)

Many of us have friends—pagans, agnostics, atheists—whose acts of self-sacrifice, fidelity, and mercy work on us like magnets. We're naturally drawn to them. They're akin to what the ancient Jews called "God-fearers"—Gentiles who may not formally practice religion, but whose actions spring from a hidden source in God's overflowing goodness.

In Luke's passage, we witness the magnetic effect a pagan has on both the Jews and Jesus. A centurion's slave is about to die and he wants to save him. Having "heard about Jesus" and his power to heal, the Roman enlists the Jewish elders, with whom he's on friendly terms, to serve as mediators. While in Matthew's Gospel the centurion approaches Jesus directly (Mt 8:5-13), the humility he displays here anticipates what he says a few lines later: "I did not consider myself worthy to come to you" (Lk 7:7).

This deep humility, paired with his eagerness to make contact with Jesus, reflects the religious sense Jesus praises in the Queen of Sheba: "the queen of the south... came from the ends of the earth to hear the wisdom of Solomon" (Lk 11:31). This Westerner, part of an invading army, no less, has come to appreciate Jewish wisdom and piety (he's even gone so far as to build a synagogue). Most recently, however, he's caught wind of "something greater than Solomon here" (11:31). Then, suddenly, he needs serious help. Where to turn? He first meets with his Jewish friends, then makes a bee-line for Something Greater.

When Jesus learns about this pagan through the Jewish elders, who are strangely eager to help him, Jesus senses something unusual afoot. Yet he doesn't say a word. Rather, he acts: "And Jesus went with them." Why? "When the Son of Man comes," Christ asks later on, "will he find faith on earth?" (Lk 18:8). Catching wind of some serious faith, Jesus makes a bee-line for it.

Loving Father, your Son is ever on the lookout for sparks of faith that he can fan into flame. Give us this same sensitivity to your Spirit at work in pagans and believers alike.

The Good Roman Shepherd
Andrew Matt

When [Jesus] was only a short distance from the house, the centurion sent friends to tell him, "Lord, do not trouble yourself, for I am not worthy to have you enter under my roof. Therefore, I did not consider myself worthy to come to you; but say the word and let my servant be healed. For I too am a person subject to authority, with soldiers subject to me. And I say to one, 'Go,' and he goes; and to another, 'Come here,' and he comes; and to my slave, 'Do this,' and he does it." (Lk 7:6b-8)

Have you ever received confirmation of being on the right track from an out-of-the blue encounter? Most of us can recall a time a friend, relative, or even a stranger suddenly showed up, inspiring us to keep going full steam ahead. Something similar happens to Jesus with the Roman centurion.

When the centurion asks Jesus to "come and save the life of his slave," he immediately goes. On the way, Jesus receives a message from him, containing a kind of parable: "Lord,… say the word and let my servant be healed… For I too am a person subject to authority, with soldiers subject to me. And I say to one, 'Go,' and he goes…"

Listening to this parable, Jesus suddenly catches a mirror-like reflection of his very own mission. How so? When he hears this pagan address him as *Kyrios* (Lord), and then discovers how he willingly subordinates his worldly power before the spiritual power and authority he senses in Jesus, it's like heavenly music to his ears. Music? Listen to the notes of Saint Paul's kenotic hymn to Christ who, "though he was in the form of God,/ did not regard equality with God something to be grasped./ Rather, he emptied himself,/ taking the form of a slave" (Phil 2:6-7). Jesus does not lord his divinity over us, but rather becomes a slave to show us that true power consists of self-emptying or kenotic love. Thus, he is acutely aware of the love that moves the centurion to leave his authority behind for the sake of his suffering slave.

Suddenly the sparks fly in Jesus' imagination. The pagan who leaves his "century" of a hundred Roman soldiers out of love for his slave becomes the model Jesus uses for his famous parable: "What man among you having a hundred sheep and losing one of them would not leave the ninety-nine in the desert and go after the lost one until he finds it?" (Lk 15:4).

Merciful Father, you sent your Son into the desert to bring your lost sheep back to life. May the good centurion's obedience to love inspire us, just as it inspired the Good Shepherd himself.

What Jesus Finds Amazing

Andrew Matt

When Jesus heard this he was amazed at [the centurion] and, turning, said to the crowd following him, "I tell you, not even in Israel have I found such faith." When the messengers returned to the house, they found the slave in good health. (Lk 7:9-10)

There's something amazing about centurions in the New Testament. Did you know that each one—six in all—is described as an honest and kindly man? Let's have a quick look at them. First there's the centurion from our passage above (cf. Mt 8:5ff.). Then there's the commander of Jesus' death squad who declares, "This man was innocent beyond doubt" (Lk 23:47; cf. Mt 27:54, Mk 15:39). Then the four centurions in the Book of Acts: Cornelius, whom Peter baptizes (Acts 10:1ff.); the two centurions who save Paul, one from a scourging (Acts 22:25ff.), the other from a murder plot (Acts 23:17ff.); and finally Julius, who escorts Paul to Rome (Acts 27:1ff.).

Beyond the fact that none of these Romans conforms to the ruthless pagan warrior stereotype, they share something else in common—Saint Luke! Perhaps it's no surprise that the only Gentile author of a New Testament book should have a word to say about all six centurions. What this reveals is the centrifugal movement of Luke's vision—his marvelous embrace of all peoples, from the lowly and marginalized to Rome's military elite. The net of his Gospel is cast far and wide to gather together an international family of faith.

Luke's missionary impulse coincides with an equally pronounced centripetal movement—reeling in the net to the center of the Church. This is where our centurion is utterly amazing, for his words are reeled right into the liturgy: "Lord, I am not worthy that you should enter under my roof, but only say the word and my soul shall be healed." With the exception of "soul" (instead of "servant" [Mt 8:8]), we repeat his prayer verbatim at every Mass. Why? Because of Jesus' reaction: "he was amazed and said... 'not even in Israel have I found such faith.'" Thus the Church molds every generation of Christians according to the mind of this faith-filled pagan.

Loving Father, help us to be real Catholics by being really catholic—ready to embrace everyone we meet with love, ready to be amazed by the faith we encounter in that embrace.

The Lord's Womb

Andrew Matt

Soon afterward [Jesus] journeyed to a city called Nain, and his disciples and a large crowd accompanied him. As he drew near to the gate of the city, a man who had died was being carried out, the only son of his mother, and she was a widow. A large crowd from the city was with her. When the Lord saw her, he was moved with pity for her and said to her, "Do not weep."
(Lk 7:11-13)

The same man who weeps over his dead friend Lazarus (Jn 11:35), and who weeps over Jerusalem (Lk 19:41) and in Gethsemane (Heb 5:7), here tells a widow not to weep over the dead body of her only son. Such words sound strange coming from an only son whose widowed mother will soon weep over his dead body. But Luke gives us some clues as to why Jesus may be giving this seemingly insensitive command.

In verse 13, Luke as narrator identifies Jesus as "the Lord" for the first time. Like a bystander who has admired the centurion so much that he starts using his language (recall that it's a Roman who first addresses Jesus as "Lord" [7:6]), Luke swiftly adopts this title now, and will use it ten more times (7:19; 10:1, 39, 41; 11:39; 12:42; 13:15; 17:5-6; 18:6). What's clear, then, is that Jesus' command does not come from the mouth of a mere mortal, but from the Lord of Mercy himself.

But wait. We don't see much mercy here, do we? Let's look again.

We hear that Jesus is "moved with pity" at the widow's plight, right? Reading this English phrase, compared to Luke's original Greek expression, is like sipping grape juice instead of savoring a full-bodied Merlot. The verb Luke uses is *esplanchnisthe*, whose beautiful root (*splanchna*) means "womb" or "viscera." So what Jesus is doing, far from being moved with mere pity, is that he is literally—viscerally—identifying himself with the poor widow. The sight of this woman fills him with such compassion that his very entrails ache and tremble—*like a mother himself.*

Thus, what we can barely detect at first, Luke's pregnant verb already hints at: from the depths of his divine "womb," Jesus is preparing to give birth to the widow's son. In other words, the Lord of Mercy is about to give the widow a precious gift. It is a time for rejoicing, not weeping (cf. Jn 16:21).

Merciful Father, you sent forth your Son to give birth to us as children through your Spirit. May we be ever attentive to his mysteriously maternal presence in our daily lives.

Jesus, Elijah, and Newborn Mothers
Andrew Matt

[Jesus] stepped forward and touched the coffin; at this the bearers halted, and he said, "Young man, I tell you, arise!" The dead man sat up and began to speak, and Jesus gave him to his mother. Fear seized them all, and they glorified God, exclaiming, "A great prophet has arisen in our midst," and "God has visited his people." This report about him spread through the whole of Judea and in all the surrounding region. (Lk 7:14-17)

The mercy that moves Jesus so viscerally at the sight of the widow of Nain results in the resuscitation of her son from death. This miracle proves to the people that a "great prophet has arisen." Luke now proceeds to paint a very specific prophetic profile of Jesus. It is based on Elijah and an analogous miracle the Old Testament prophet performs for the widow of Zarephath, whose son had died. Let's look briefly at this unusual scene:

"Taking [the dead boy] from her lap, [Elijah] carried him to the upper room..., and laid him on his own bed... Then he stretched himself out upon the child three times and called out to the LORD: 'O LORD, my God, let the life breath return to the body of this child.' The LORD heard the prayer of Elijah; the life breath returned to the child's body and he revived. Taking the child, Elijah... gave him to his mother" (1 Kgs 17:19-24).

Note the immediate similarities: like Elijah, Jesus revives a boy from death and—the phrases in each account are identical—"gave him to his mother." For Luke, Jesus is clearly an Elijah come back to life.

As we saw earlier, the compassion Jesus feels for the widow issues in the birth of her son from the "womb" (*splanchna*) of his infinite mercy. In the "birth" scene with Elijah, the prophet acts as a kind of mystical midwife who restores life to the boy, thus delivering joy to the widow.

Now here's the key: both the old and new Elijah not only bring dead sons back to life, but they breathe new life into the hearts of mothers. In short, their mission is to give birth to a new motherhood.

We see this most dramatically on Calvary. From the sacred "womb" of his bleeding heart, Jesus gives birth to a new son for Mary: "Woman, behold, your son" (Jn 19:26). This is John, who represents us, the Church. Jesus thus delivers us all into the hands of our new Mother.

Life-giving Father, upon the cross your "great mercy gave us a new birth" (1 Pt 1:3). Thank you for your Son, in whom we are continually reborn through the sacraments of the Church.

Fore-Echoes of the Word

Andrew Matt

The disciples of John told him about all these things. John summoned two of his disciples and sent them to the Lord to ask, "Are you the one who is to come, or should we look for another?" When the men came to him, they said, "John the Baptist has sent us to you to ask, 'Are you the one who is to come, or should we look for another?'" (Lk 7:18-20)

The aristocratic old voluptuary lies on his deathbed, tethered to an oxygen tank. His last words come out in gasps: "The wind will come soon, tomorrow perhaps... Better tomorrow." About to expire, he is anointed by the priest: "Suddenly Lord Marchmain moved his hand to his forehead;... the hand moved slowly down his breast, then to his shoulder, and [he] made the sign of the cross." The ripple effects of this gesture in *Brideshead Revisited* will continue, illuminating the very end of the novel. Last words are important, almost prophetic. But a dying man's last act has the final word.

In our passage above, we hear the voice of the Forerunner for the very last time in Luke's Gospel. John's words echo forth as if in stereo, first to a pair of his disciples, then to Jesus: "Are you the one who is to come, or should we look for another?"

Even after hearing these words twice, we may be left scratching our heads. Is this the same Baptist who at the Jordan heard the Father say: "This is my beloved Son" (Mt 3:17; Mk 1:11; Lk 3:22)? How could the man who has prepared the way for Jesus now seemingly doubt that Jesus is the Way?

If John's last words seem puzzling, let's compare them to his first words. As it turns out, John's opening salvo finds an *exact* echo in the first thing Jesus ever says in public: "Repent, for the kingdom of heaven is at hand!" (Mt 3:2; 4:17). Wait. Could it be that the beginning mirrors the end? That John's question, "Should we look for another?" is a prophetic fore-echo of Jesus' excruciating question on Golgotha: "My God, my God, why have you forsaken me?" (Mt 27:46; Mk 15:34)?

Yes. Before handing over his head, John participates in Christ's agony on the cross, where doubts are indeed raised. Yet the final word flickers with the promise of Pentecost: "And bowing his head, he handed over the spirit" (Jn 19:30).

Heavenly Father, from start to finish John's witness points to Christ's love. Thank you for sending us your Son, who is close to us even in our most heart-wrenching doubts and fears.

Seeing, Hearing, Believing, Touching
Andrew Matt

At that time [Jesus] cured many of their diseases, sufferings, and evil spirits; he also granted sight to many who were blind. And he said to [the messengers of John] in reply, "Go and tell John what you have seen and heard: the blind regain their sight, the lame walk, lepers are cleansed, the deaf hear, the dead are raised, the poor have the good news proclaimed to them. And blessed is the one who takes no offense at me." (Lk 7:21-23)

I had just turned eighteen when my faith came alive. Rather than a sleepy Sunday Catholic I was now full of high hopes that the world would be transformed by Christ—and *very soon*. This immature manic phase very soon gave way to the doldrums, for reality wasn't changing as fast as it was supposed to. What got me out of this trough was a book on Mother Teresa serving lepers and other untouchables. Interspersed among the images were scores of her zinger quotes, two of which burned holes through my adolescent brain: "Jesus said love one another. He didn't say love the whole world… In this life we cannot do great things. We can only do small things with great love." What I saw and read in those pages put my faith on a completely new footing.

We're not given any real clues why John the Baptist asks Jesus, "Are you the one who is to come?" (7:20). Is it because Jesus is too slow in revealing his identity and his Messianic plans? Is John perhaps discouraged like Jeremiah (Jer 15:10ff.)? Whatever the reason, Jesus decides that what his cousin needs is some "live video" of his work among the blind, lame, lepers, deaf, dead, and the poor—images that correspond to choice zingers from the Book of Isaiah: "Then will the eyes of the blind be opened,/ the ears of the deaf be cleared;/ Then will the lame leap" (35:5-6; 29:19); "Your dead shall live, their corpses shall rise" (26:19); "He has sent me to bring glad tidings to the lowly" (61:1; 29:18). Note: lepers are absent in Isaiah.

By sending John's disciples back to the prison-bound Baptist with technicolor evidence of what they have "seen and heard," Jesus aims to jog John's prophetic memory, and to fortify his faith for a shining martyr's witness. For if Jesus is healing even the untouchable lepers (Lv 14:45-46), then God's promises are being fulfilled beyond all expectation.

Father of the poor, thank you for sending us witnesses of your Son's hands-on mercy. Give us the courage not to shy away from the "untouchables" in our neighborhoods, parishes, families.

Seeing More than Meets the Eye

Andrew Matt

When the messengers of John had left, Jesus began to speak to the crowds about John. "What did you go out to the desert to see— a reed swayed by the wind? Then what did you go out to see? Someone dressed in fine garments? Those who dress luxuriously and live sumptuously are found in royal palaces. Then what did you go out to see? A prophet? Yes, I tell you, and more than a prophet. This is the one about whom scripture says: 'Behold, I am sending my messenger ahead of you,/ he will prepare your way before you.'" (Lk 7:24-27)

I remember how excited I was to meet him. I was a college kid and had been told what a towering figure in the Church this priest was. But when the time finally came, it was initially a letdown. First, I expected him to be dressed in black clerics rather than a dark suit and tie. What's with this getup, I muttered, completely ignorant that this was common in Europe when priests weren't exercising an explicit pastoral role. Second, instead of speaking to our American group in English, he spoke in French (and was then translated). Finally, he seemed a bit stiff and reserved, so he struck me as impersonal. I just didn't get it—why was this priest such a big deal? Only later, after learning about his life and works, did I have a complete turnaround.

Yet the turnaround began that evening too. As we lined up to shake his hand after the talk, I had a lingering question. Approaching this sequoia of a man (he stood six and a half feet tall), I looked up and piped out my question. Like a gracious ent straight out of Tolkien, Father Hans Urs von Balthasar bent way down and listened attentively to my hobbit-like query, answering with words that pointed to Christ. It was like watching the Baptist's words unfurl in 3-D: "He must increase; I must decrease" (Jn 3:30). Later I learned that "Hans" means "John."

When Jesus asks the crowd what they went out to see, he first addresses their false expectations regarding the Baptist's external manner and appearance. What was he, a swaying reed, a people pleaser? Nope. What did he look like, a prince decked out in royal threads? Wrong. "What did you go out to see? A prophet? Yes," says Jesus, "and more than a prophet."

Why is John "more"? Because he never stops pointing to Christ, even in death. Bowing his head in a dungeon, he dies like a felled oak, pointing to the One who came to die on a tree.

Almighty Father, John came clad in camel hide and feasted on honey-dipped locusts. Jesus feasted with sinners and died naked on a cross. Prepare our eyes for your unexpected guises!

Leaping for Cosmic Joy

Andrew Matt

"I tell you, among those born of women, no one is greater than John; yet the least in the kingdom of God is greater than he." (All the people who listened, including the tax collectors, and who were baptized with the baptism of John, acknowledged the righteousness of God; but the Pharisees and scholars of the law, who were not baptized by him, rejected the plan of God for themselves.) (Lk 7:28-30)

For millennia comets have been observed to display unpredictable behavior. Unlike what the ancients believed, astronomers now know that the source of a comet's energy comes not from itself but from the sun. These erratic celestial bodies are cold objects; when a comet gets close to the sun its icy particles melt, releasing powerful plumes of vapor and dust. This kinetic reaction acts like a rocket engine, causing comets to carom across the sky in eccentric orbital patterns.

Something similar occurs when John the Baptist first comes into contact with the celestial body of Christ. Like a comet heated by the presence of the sun, "the infant leaped" (Lk 1:41) in Elizabeth's womb. This is why Jesus announces that "no one is greater than John": not only is the preborn Baptist granted the singular privilege of encountering Christ in the womb, but John's very role as precursor begins from the womb—with the prophetic act of leaping.

Then Jesus adds, "the least in the kingdom of God is greater than he." Who is this "least" one? It can only point to the greatest one of all: the Word incarnate. Thus John's amniotic leap of joy, reminiscent of David's ecstatic leaps before the Ark, heralds the "least" one who inaugurated the quickening of time itself, when the "all-powerful word from heaven's royal throne leapt" down (Wis 18:15). John's amniotic leaps thus gather their comet-like force from the kenotic heat of the eternally leaping Logos:

> The Logos leapt down from heaven into the womb of the Virgin, he leapt from the womb of his Mother on to the cross, from the cross into Hades and from Hades once more back on to the earth—O the new Resurrection! And he leapt from the earth into heaven where he sits at the right hand of the Father. And he will again leap on to the earth with glory to bring judgment. (Saint Hippolytus of Rome)

Heavenly Father, you baptized the fetal Baptist with your Spirit of joy. May our hearts leap with John's childlike spirit of gratitude every time we approach the Eucharist.

Becoming Wise Children of the Marketplace
Andrew Matt

"Then to what shall I compare the people of this generation? [...]
They are like children who sit in the marketplace and call to one
another, 'We played the flute for you, but you did not dance./
We sang a dirge, but you did not weep.' For John the Baptist
came neither eating food nor drinking wine, and you said,
'He is possessed by a demon.' The Son of Man came eating and
drinking and you said, 'Look, he is a glutton and a drunkard,
a friend of tax collectors and sinners.' But wisdom is
vindicated by all her children." (Lk 7:31-35)

It's not by accident that Jesus depicts the fickle children in his parable as sitting smack dab in the middle of the marketplace. You can picture them immediately: kids shouting back and forth between the merchants' stalls, right in sync with the coins passing to and fro. It's an enduring image, capturing with uncanny accuracy how modern markets resound with similar shouts and hollers bouncing off the digital walls and stock exchange floors of Wall Street and elsewhere.

It's also not by accident that Luke, who otherwise paints an identical portrait of this scene as Matthew (11:16-19), includes one unique detail. While Matthew's children "call to others," in Luke they "call to one another." What's the difference? Luke's reciprocal pronoun adds a note of heightened reflexivity, creating the effect of a self-enclosed echo chamber. This is why Jesus compares the "people of this generation" to the biblical equivalent of "mall rats," for when John and Jesus don't parrot back popular opinion, they're treated in juvenile fashion: the Baptist is labeled a psycho and Wisdom incarnate becomes a social outcast.

One might be tempted to dismiss this self-absorbed marketplace world altogether. But John and Jesus don't do this. Instead, they roll up their sleeves and engage in serious economic debate (see Lk 3:10-14 and the parables of the crafty steward [Lk 16:1-9] and of the talents [Lk 19:12-26]). The Church's robust body of teachings on social justice continues this vital evangelization of the economic sphere. Today, when market forces seem closed in upon themselves, obsessed with technical progress and relationships of utility, the task of establishing economic policies open to ethics, wisdom, and transcendence is more urgent, and demanding, than ever. Jesus' advice? "Be wise as serpents and innocent as doves" (Mt 10:16, RSV).

Heavenly Father, grant us the grace to play wisely among the children of the marketplace, transforming our culture of consumerism through the shrewd exercise of charity in truth.

Letting Your Love Show in Public

Andrew Matt

A Pharisee invited [Jesus] to dine with him, and he entered the Pharisee's house and reclined at table. Now there was a sinful woman in the city who learned that he was at table in the house of the Pharisee. Bringing an alabaster flask of ointment, she stood behind him at his feet weeping and began to bathe his feet with her tears. Then she wiped them with her hair, kissed them, and anointed them with the ointment. When the Pharisee [...] saw this he said to himself, "If this man were a prophet, he would know [...] that she is a sinner." (Lk 7:36-39)

I remember visiting a church in the city of Prague, not long after the fall of the Berlin Wall. The city was gorgeous but grimy, with the dust of Communism still caked on the buildings. Churches were some of the first structures to begin bearing signs of new life and new paint. All of a sudden I hear running foot-steps. I turn to see a young woman racing toward a statue of the Sacred Heart as if sprinting for home plate. Skidding to a stop on her knees, she reaches up to grasp Jesus' plaster foot and starts sobbing. People look around at each other awkwardly. I do too, but I'm also deeply moved.

"*Eine Magdalenerin,*" says a German woman nearby. I'll never forget that comment. And I'll never forget that young weeping woman, who remained etched in my mind as a modern Magdalene, until recently.

The anonymous woman in Luke's passage above is identified as "a sinful woman in the city." For centuries, this woman has been conflated in the popular Catholic imagination with Mary Magdalene, as if we're seeing Mary here weeping in sorrow at Jesus' feet. Yet there's no evidence anywhere in the Gospels to suggest that Mary was a penitent (let alone a public sinner). And the same goes for Luke's anonymous woman: on the basis of Jesus' own logic (see 7:41-42), her actions demonstrate her "great love" for having been forgiven. Known in the city as a public sinner, she was forgiven by Christ at some point and now comes to show him her heartfelt gratitude. So just as there is no reason to consider Mary Magdalene and this anonymous woman as penitential figures, there was never any real reason for me to associate the young church sprinter in Prague with Magdalene—except for one thing, which binds all three women together. Love propels each of them to bear unforgettable public witness to the power of Christ's mercy.

Loving Father, your Son scandalized the Pharisees by letting sinners touch him. Give us hearts unabashed to tell others how your merciful touch has transformed our lives.

Holding Back the Tears

Andrew Matt

Jesus said to [the Pharisee] in reply, "Simon, I have something to say to you." "Tell me, teacher," he said. "Two people were in debt to a certain creditor; one owed five hundred days' wages and the other owed fifty. Since they were unable to repay the debt, he forgave it for both. Which of them will love him more?" Simon said in reply, "The one, I suppose, whose larger debt was forgiven." He said to him, "You have judged rightly." (Lk 7:40-43)

The Gospels report that Jesus wept twice: once before the tomb of Lazarus (Jn 11:35) and once again upon his final approach to Jerusalem (Lk 19:41). Whenever Jesus meets a Pharisee, the tears he sheds over Jerusalem coalesce with the words he addresses to the holy city on an earlier occasion: "Jerusalem, Jerusalem… how many times I yearned to gather your children together as a hen gathers her brood under her wings, but you were unwilling!" (Lk 13:34). In other words, whenever Jesus faces one of his obstinate kinsmen, he is a mother holding back tears for a child she loves.

In Luke's passage above, Jesus addresses a parable to Simon the Pharisee. Up until this point, Simon has been fuming, silently disparaging Jesus for his scandalous acceptance of the public sinner at his feet. Now, as he turns to Simon, the Lord's words coalesce with the parable about a brother scandalized by his father's joy at the return of his prodigal son. We recall that upon catching sight of his son, the father is "filled with compassion" (Lk 15:20). Here again we find the Greek verb we noticed earlier: *esplanchnisthe* with its root word "womb" (*splanchna*). When Jesus thus describes how the father "ran to his son, embraced him and kissed him" (Lk 15:20), he's describing the "mother hen" instinct of all parents—the yearning to "give birth" again, so their wayward child may be nestled anew under the wings of truth and love.

We can therefore imagine the riptide of emotions tearing at Jesus' heart as he finishes speaking with Simon. On the one hand, he's welling up inside with tears of joy over the return of this prodigal daughter at his feet. On the other hand, tears of maternal anguish fall silently against the tomb-like entrance of Simon's heart. For though he "judged rightly," Simon "refused to enter the house" (Lk 15:28) of Jesus' mercy.

Loving Father, when we self-righteously slam the door on a brother or sister, wash us clean with the gift of tears for our sins. Renew our desire each day to live as children of your mercy.

Heart of a Queen

Andrew Matt

Then [Jesus] turned to the woman and said to Simon, "Do you see this woman? When I entered your house, you did not give me water for my feet, but she has bathed them with her tears and wiped them with her hair. You did not give me a kiss, but she has not ceased kissing my feet since the time I entered. You did not anoint my head with oil, but she anointed my feet with ointment. So I tell you, her many sins have been forgiven; hence, she has shown great love. But the one to whom little is forgiven, loves little." (Lk 7:44-47)

Bath time with butterball Louis, our six-month-old, is always a blast. He loves the water, laughing and kicking like a jack rabbit, especially when big brother Samuel jumps in. My wife Martha plays "life guard" and, true to her namesake, does all the hard work.

I marvel at how she takes tender care of Louis, bathing him so attentively, drying him off between kisses to his chubby cheeks, and then rubbing his limbs down with lotion before popping him into his pajamas. I remember how she did this with Samuel six years ago, and realize how lucky my boys and I are to have her. She treats us like three kings.

As I watch the woman's actions in Luke's scene, observing how she bathes, kisses, and anoints the body of Jesus, I can't help but think of Martha's hands-on devotion. It's as if this anonymous woman is lavishing love upon her own Child, as if it's Bethlehem all over again.

The Magi arrive and, like the woman, they pour out their treasures in silent homage at the feet of the infant King. The Church Fathers were fond of interpreting the gifts of gold, frankincense, and myrrh as signs of Jesus' royalty, divinity, and Passion. Similarly, the woman's tears, kisses, and ointment carry hidden meanings. Yet they are more emotionally raw and intense, more physically intimate meanings. Why? Because they reflect what Jesus himself describes as "great love," born of having been forgiven.

Thus, out of the poverty of her pariah status in society, the grace of forgiveness unleashes golden tears of gratitude. Her kisses, like frankincense, express the transfigured *eros* of the Bride-Church for the divine Bridegroom, an *eros* that now coincides with *agape*. And the ointment? Only a love that has submitted to a life-transforming death can anoint a King destined to die on a cross.

And such sacrificial love transforms the anointer into a queen.

Merciful Father, our ecclesial Mother anoints each member of the Mystical Body with sacramental salve. May we in turn anoint our brothers and sisters with mercy and forgiveness.

Fountains of Forgiveness

Andrew Matt

[Jesus] said to [the woman], "Your sins are forgiven."
The others at table said to themselves, "Who is this who even
forgives sins?" But he said to the woman, "Your faith has
saved you; go in peace." (Lk 7:48-50)

One of the reasons Rome is called the Eternal City is that it's perpetually pregnant with sacramental signs of life. Take a walk down any street and beauty greets you around every corner, beckoning you beyond the mundane. Look, there's a fantastic Roman ruin, there's a gorgeous church! In perhaps no other Western city do so many religious people, places, and things blend together in paradoxical harmony with the profane.

Only in Rome, for example, do you find a church (or two) on every corner, but also something else: fountains. Big curvaceous pagan fountains carved in stone, along with the more numerous stumpier fountains affectionately called *nasoni*, big noses. Somehow the churches and the fountains go hand in hand, gushing forth their respective "sacraments" all day long together: the churches pouring forth Christ's sacramental Body and Blood, and the fountains gurgling out refreshing water for thirsty Romans, pilgrims, and tourists. This fountain image is so apt that the poet-saint Ephrem the Syrian describes the Word of God as a continuous cascade of running water. Anyone can come to quench his thirst, and then go away. But the fountain goes on welling up for ever.

At first sight, the woman at Jesus' feet looks more like a fountain than he does. She's pouring forth tears and ointment. In reality, however, she's drinking deeply from the fountain of Christ's forgiveness, for she has just been baptized: "Your sins are forgiven... Your faith has saved you," says the Fountain. She's Jesus' new-born baby.

If we recall that from apostolic times the baptismal font was also called the *uterus Ecclesiae* (womb of the Church), it's no surprise to find this woman in tears at Jesus' feet. Just as babies naturally cry when they issue from the womb, so too does this woman weep as she springs forth from the womb of Christ's infinite mercy.

Loving Father, through your Son you offer us true happiness—
forgiveness of our sins and rebirth as children of freedom. May
our thirst for this gift turn us into oases of love for others.

Jesus Walking By

Father George William Rutler

Afterward [Jesus] journeyed from one town and village to another, preaching and proclaiming the good news of the kingdom of God. Accompanying him were the Twelve and some women who had been cured of evil spirits and infirmities, Mary, called Magdalene, from whom seven demons had gone out, Joanna, the wife of Herod's steward Chuza, Susanna, and many others who provided for them out of their resources. (Lk 8:1-3)

The English language is a sponge which soaks up words from other languages, and so we speak more Greek, for example, than we realize. To speak of someone who walks a lot as "peripatetic" is to use a word straight from the Greek that Aristotle used, along with his disciples Theophrastus and Strato. Aristotle began his school within the colonnades, or *peripatoi*, of the Lyceum gymnasium in Athens, almost four centuries before the Resurrection. The words for walking and colonnade got mixed up, and later on it was thought that Aristotle taught while walking. Whether he did or not, it would have been a wise practice of a wise man, because sluggish students need to have their blood stirred from time to time.

Jesus often talked walking, but not to keep his disciples awake. He was always on the move in order to preach and proclaim the Good News in many towns and villages. Unlike the classical philosophers, Jesus did not draw his followers to one place: he went to them and bid them follow him as he went to "the whole house of Israel." His message was more than wisdom. He was the Wisdom from which all wise thoughts proceed.

Even a teacher as great as Aristotle could not pass on himself. He could only pass on his teaching. The Apostles and the women and others who walked along with Jesus could not replace him and improve upon his teaching. They would not make the mistake of ranking Jesus as a great teacher among many others. The best of teachers show the way to live, while Jesus is the Way. They teach truths, but Jesus is the Truth. They live and die, but Jesus is the Life. He walks through every century and each generation and he passes through our lives, but just once. To us, he says what he said to those who first accompanied him: "Follow me."

Heavenly Father, give me the grace of your Holy Spirit that, when your Son passes through my life, I may recognize him as my Lord and follow him wherever the path may lead.

Jesus Spoke

Father George William Rutler

When a large crowd gathered, with people from one town after another journeying to him, [Jesus] spoke in a parable. "A sower went out to sow his seed. And as he sowed, some seed fell on the path and was trampled, and the birds of the sky ate it up. Some seed fell on rocky ground, and when it grew, it withered for lack of moisture. Some seed fell among thorns, and the thorns grew with it and choked it. And some seed fell on good soil, and when it grew, it produced fruit a hundredfold." (Lk 8:4-8a)

God brought all things into being by saying, "Let there be." We speak to communicate, but there was nothing to hear him when he uttered his "Let there be." God's speech is simply the power of his intention. His word is his will. When the Word became flesh and dwelt among us (Jn 1:14), he spoke words, but he was the Word that gave words sense. There was an orator once who said that if your argument is weak, it will sound strong if you shout it. Our Lord never shouted that way, for he never had a weak thought. By being the Word, and not just words, Christ could have been speechless and still have saved us, just by the Word becoming a man.

Yet there was a power in his speech: "Never before has anyone spoken like this one" (Jn 7:46). The listeners cannot explain it, but it has nothing to do with the power of his voice. It has everything to do with the power that made the world. He conforms to the physical laws of acoustics which he had made, and there is no recorded instance of him miraculously making himself heard beyond the limitations of natural physics. This is why his parables are different from the stories Aesop and Lincoln told to make a point. Christ is the point himself, and when he speaks of seed being sown, he is the seed.

We should never take for granted the ability to write down what was spoken. In the novel by Betty Smith, *A Tree Grows in Brooklyn*, words almost bounce from the page: "Oh, magic hour, when a child first knows she can read printed words!" But when we read the words of Jesus, their grammar is from heaven, and they can only be understood when we realize that he comes from heaven to be heard.

Blessed Father, may I ever be faithful to the blessing I received in baptism, that my ears may be open to hear your Word, and my mouth may always proclaim your Gospel.

Figures of Speech

Father George William Rutler

After saying this [parable], [Jesus] called out, "Whoever has ears to hear ought to hear." Then his disciples asked him what the meaning of this parable might be. He answered, "Knowledge of the mysteries of the kingdom of God has been granted to you; but to the rest, they are made known through parables so that 'they may look but not see, and hear but not understand.'"

(Lk 8:8b-10)

Jesus spends three years among vast crowds, thousands of people on occasion, but he spends most of his time among the Twelve. They will be told the inner workings of Christ's plan, and then they will lead the people into these mysteries. Holy mysteries are not puzzles designed to confuse; they are parts of God's own existence that we are led into by the sound of his voice.

In Christ, God speaks with a human voice, using parables as hints of the glory he has prepared for us. If he described in direct terms the splendor of what he wants us to become, it would seem frightening. Newman longed for the "kindly light" of God, but he did not look for "the distant scene, one step enough for me." The parables lead gradually into that world where there are no more figures of speech, but only the figure of Jesus himself. On Easter morning, Mary Magdalene sees that figure in the distance, but the Voice, calling to her by name, changes her seeing into perception.

Mother Teresa of Calcutta told a priest that if he wanted to preach well, he should put aside his books after reading, and listen to God, and then tell the people what God said. Sometimes God seems to be saying nothing at all, but he does need words. When he seems silent, faith makes the ears listen and the eyes understand. As the veil on the temple was torn when Christ died, so will there be a moment when no parables will be needed to veil us from the shock of his splendor. To take the first step, turn off the television, computer, and iPod—then listen. At the behest of Pope Gregory X, Saint Thomas Aquinas wrote words meant to be heard: "Seeing, touching, tasting, to discern Thee fail/ Faith which comes through hearing pierces through the veil."

Heavenly Father, let me see those invisible things and hear those silent things that can be known only by the love of your Son and by the working of the Holy Spirit.

The Rootless and the Bored

Father George William Rutler

"This is the meaning of the parable. The seed is the word of God. Those on the path are the ones who have heard, but the devil comes and takes away the word from their hearts that they may not believe and be saved. Those on rocky ground are the ones who, when they hear, receive the word with joy, but they have no root; they believe only for a time and fall away in time of trial." (Lk 8:11-13)

Either in whimsy or melancholy, or perhaps both, Abraham Lincoln remarked that after forty every man is responsible for his face. His detractors said that he was remarkably ugly, and even his friends thought that his achievements were in spite of his looks. Now that "he belongs to the ages," his face is a secular icon of kindness and serenity, which cannot be said of another man who died at the same age: Adolf Hitler.

Pope Benedict XVI has frequently meditated on the face of Jesus, drawing on a psalm: "Such are the people that love the LORD,/ that seek the face of the God of Jacob" (Ps 24:6). While Christ is "the face of God," not one of his disciples bothered to describe what he looked like. As the Word, his appearance is sensed through hearing, and not seeing, him. "Blessed are those who have not seen and have believed" (Jn 20:29).

The beauty of Christ's face can be understood only by "the clean of hand and pure of heart" (Ps 24:4). Cleanliness of hand is simply the sanity of the saints. The devil would contaminate the word of God with his lies in the form of false philosophies and religions. The beauty of Christ's word has been trampled like seed on the path. Then there are those whose knowledge of God is just skin-deep. They "have no root" but look upon life itself like bored people constantly changing the television channels. At first they look at God's face with joy, but they lack the patience to study it carefully, and soon enough are distracted by the outward "glamour of evil" which the Church's baptismal promises reject. The devil can make himself attractive to people who do not realize that he has placed his misery on their faces. This is why George Bernard Shaw spoke of a place "where people have nothing to do but amuse themselves," but he was describing hell.

Almighty Father, open my ears to hear your Word and my mouth to speak nothing but the truth which you have made known through your Son, our Savior Jesus Christ.

Thorns in the Soul

Father George William Rutler

"As for the seed that fell among thorns, they are the ones who have heard, but as they go along, they are choked by the anxieties and riches and pleasures of life, and they fail to produce mature fruit. But as for the seed that fell on rich soil, they are the ones who, when they have heard the word, embrace it with a generous and good heart, and bear fruit through perseverance." (Lk 8:14-15)

The seed that falls on thorny ground is the saddest of all because it means sadness, or sloth, one of the deadly sins which is spiritual apathy. The unchallenged soul grows soft and seeks illusory happiness in wealth and fleeting pleasure, which are the prescription for deep disappointment. The idea that Christianity is a "comfort zone" providing spiritual giddiness is what Ronald Knox called "enthusiasm." It is not righteous zeal. It is the illusion that if I feel happy I am happy.

An early Christian text, the *Philokalia,* called sloth "dejection," meaning a loss of interest in life. The slothful person may think he is lively because times are good for him. But when bad things happen, that crust of illusion shatters. When a couple ill-advisedly and illicitly write their own vows, invariably they are floridly and artlessly poetic promises to love for better, for richer, in health, and as long as thorns do not spring up. As a wise mother, the Church knows that the world is not like that. The Church bids bride and groom to vow love "for better, for worse, for richer, for poorer, in sickness and in health, until death do us part."

For the seed of faith to grow to maturity, the field in which it is sown needs to be shoveled and not raked, turned over and not just manicured. Cardinal Wolsey in Henry VIII's England was distracted by the outward pomp of his office, but was not willing to shed his blood as the red of his cardinalatial hat symbolized. So Shakespeare put on his dying lips the fatal words: "Had I but served my God with half the zeal I served my king, he would not in mine age have left me naked to mine enemies." Had he embraced the word of God with an open heart, nothing would have choked him, and he would have died with a smile.

Father of strength and glory, save me from the vain things of this world so that I may delight as you delight in the good things you have made.

Christ the Lamp

Father George William Rutler

"No one who lights a lamp conceals it with a vessel or sets it under a bed; rather, he places it on a lampstand so that those who enter may see the light. For there is nothing hidden that will not become visible, and nothing secret that will not be known and come to light. Take care, then, how you hear. To anyone who has, more will be given, and from the one who has not, even what he seems to have will be taken away." (Lk 8:16-18)

If our Lord sounds harsh when he says that those who have will get more, and those who have not will lose even what they think they have, it is because he is being heard on a wrong frequency. He is speaking of things moral and not material. Those who have Christ in the soul will have more of him as grace increases grace, and those who have made no room for him will find their lives becoming even emptier.

When you help the hungry, homeless, and naked, "your light shall break forth like the dawn" (Is 58:8). Without these "corporal works of mercy," spiritual sentiment falls into the dangerous category of "isms" which weaken what was strong and good, and the sentiment becomes sentimentalism, just as reason without grace becomes rationalism and race without grace becomes racism.

For the light of Christ to shine fully, as "on a lampstand," the corporal works of mercy join with the spiritual works of mercy: helping the ignorant, doubtful, and sinful, while bearing wrongs patiently, forgiving offences willingly, comforting the afflicted, and praying for the living and the dead. Saint Bonaventure said: "Christ is the lamp that illuminates the whole of Scripture; he is its gateway and its foundation. For this faith is behind all the supernatural enlightenments that we receive while we are still separated from the Lord and on our pilgrimage."

Egoism snuffs out the spark of divinity in the soul. To give glory to God is to bask in that glory. The World War II generation, by its heroic sacrifices, has been called "the Greatest Generation." Its narcissistic heirs risk being remembered as "the Smallest Generation." But there is a cure: "Your light must shine before others, that they may see your good deeds and glorify your heavenly Father" (Mt 5:16).

Eternal Father whose eternal Son is Light from Light, let your radiance shine in my mind and will that I may see your truth and follow it along the way.

Mary Help of Christians
Father George William Rutler

Then [Jesus'] mother and his brothers came to him but were unable to join him because of the crowd. He was told, "Your mother and your brothers are standing outside and they wish to see you." He said to them in reply, "My mother and my brothers are those who hear the word of God and act on it." (Lk 8:19-21)

Blessed Mary cannot get near her Son because of the crowd, nor can members of Christ's extended family, for since Mary had no other children that is what "brothers" means here. In our age when the public media often obscure Christ, there is a wry poignancy in the translation in the King James Bible: they "could not come at him for the press."

Christ's words are the opposite of a rebuke to the Lady who gave him birth, and to his kindred. When Christ declares that his mother and brothers are those who hear and do God's word, he is unveiling the mystery of discipleship. Saint Augustine said, "Indeed the blessed Mary certainly did the Father's will, and so it was for her a greater thing to have been Christ's disciple than to have been his Mother, and she was more blessed in her discipleship than in her Motherhood. Hers was the happiness of first bearing in her womb him whom she would obey as her master."

A right understanding of Mary saves us from a wrong understanding of the Church. Saint Augustine also says, "The Virgin Mary is both holy and blessed, and yet the Church is greater than she. Mary is a part of the Church, a member of the Church, a holy, an eminent, the most eminent, member, but still only a member of the entire body."

Mary conceived Christ by accepting God's will. In the garden of the Agony, her Son will pray that the Father's will be done. The Greek *agonia* could mean a gymnastic struggle. All of us, gifted with free will, from time to time wrestle with our conscience. It was said of one cynical statesman that whenever he wrestled with his conscience, he emerged the winner. Mary always let God win, and so at the cross she joined her heart with his in the terrible agony that gained the victory.

Almighty Father, grant that I may hear your Word with such joy that it moves me to do what you will, through the power of the Holy Spirit.

Real Conversation

Father George William Rutler

One day [Jesus] got into a boat with his disciples and said to them, "Let us cross to the other side of the lake." So they set sail, and while they were sailing he fell asleep. A squall blew over the lake, and they were taking in water and were in danger. They came and woke him saying, "Master, master, we are perishing!"

(Lk 8:22-24a)

Even the Blessed Mother is exasperated with her twelve-year-old Son's apparent lack of consideration, when she and Joseph frantically search three days for him: "Son, why have you done this to us?" (Lk 2:48). On Easter, two men walking to Emmaus sound annoyed when they ask the risen Lord if he is the only one in Jerusalem who does not know what has happened. Their question seems foolish only in hindsight. The Apostles express the same frustration when they cry out, not once, but twice: "Master! Master!" when Jesus is asleep in the storm. Saint Mark's Gospel has the Apostles positively indignant: "Do you not care that we are perishing?" (Mk 4:38).

As prayer is conversation with God, Jesus welcomes these appeals, because they are genuine, and not pious platitudes. Frustration with God, born of limited human intelligence, invites him to respond. "I do believe, help my unbelief" (Mk 9:24). That is a prayer wrenched from the heart, and not from a smooth tongue. The Master only asks that we trust that he has an explanation.

Jesus, serenely sleeping on a cushion, is not cushioned from our suffering, like the abstract wisdom of the Greeks, or the oblivion of an oriental Nirvana. His sleep is power waiting to be unleashed. When he seems to snore through the storms of our world and our individual lives, he is listening for us to call on him in faith.

The Creator knows what is happening in his Creation. But he wants us to know that he knows. Then he can begin to save us. In the synagogue, the Apostles had heard many times: "When you pass through the water, I will be with you" (Is 43:2). Not until the end of their stormy lives could they have understood that Jesus really meant it when he said on the shore of the Galilean lake, "Let us cross to the other side..."

Almighty Father, awaken in us the truth that your Only Begotten Son is at work even when he seems to sleep, for his is the peace that passes all understanding.

Calm in Storms

Father George William Rutler

[Jesus] awakened, rebuked the wind and the waves, and they subsided and there was a calm. Then he asked [his disciples], "Where is your faith?" But they were filled with awe and amazed and said to one another, "Who then is this, who commands even the winds and the sea, and they obey him?"
(Lk 8:24b-25)

The first question God asked was spoken to the first man: "Where are you?" (Gn 3:9). That is really the same question he asks the Apostles in the storm, when he asks them where there faith is, for faith is the knowledge of who we are in relation to God. God knew Adam was hiding behind a tree, but he wanted him to know that he knew. Only by finding God could he find himself. Only by admitting that Jesus is the Lord of the wind and waves can the Apostles become as calm as the sea.

Every generation has social and moral storms. Through them all, the Church saves us from drowning, as the First Vatican Council said, "by her marvelous propagation, her wondrous sanctity, her inexhaustible fruitfulness in good works, her Catholic unity, and her enduring stability." Every age asks about Jesus, "Who then is this?" and the saints give the answer.

There is in every saint an unmistakable serenity, an inner peace that is a mental ballast through the many storms raging around them. This is why they are so fascinating to people of faith, who are calmed by their presence, and by people of no faith who become agitated by them. The English author Malcolm Muggeridge had passed through many interior conflicts before accepting once again the Christianity of his youth, but he had held back from being received into the Catholic Church. He argued about this often with friends. But then Blessed Teresa of Calcutta wrote to him: "The real difficulty you have regarding the Church is finite. Overcome the finite with the infinite." And Muggeridge calmed down and became a Catholic. Christ asks us each day, "Where is your faith?" The Bible ends by replacing the question with an exclamation: "Come, Lord Jesus!" (Rv 22:20).

Infinitely loving Father, whose Only Begotten Son calmed the sea, may the Holy Spirit move upon me as first he moved upon the waters, with his peace.

The Agony of Satan

Father George William Rutler

Then [Jesus and his disciples] sailed to the territory of the Gerasenes, which is opposite Galilee. When he came ashore a man from the town who was possessed by demons met him. For a long time he had not worn clothes; he did not live in a house, but lived among the tombs. When he saw Jesus, he cried out and fell down before him; in a loud voice he shouted, "What have you to do with me, Jesus, son of the Most High God? I beg you, do not torment me!" For he had ordered the unclean spirit to come out of the man. (Lk 8:26-29a)

The Satanist who worships evil would seem to be the polar opposite of the secularist who does not believe in evil at all except as discord with abstract standards of right and wrong. While Satanists worship the Evil One as a god, secularists worship the refusal to worship anything in this world except the world itself.

Christ saves us from both forms of credulity: the belief that the Anti-Christ has power equal to the Christ, and the denial that there is any Christ at all. The Anti-Christ knows better: he dreads the power of Christ over him. Like a thief who returns to the scene of his crime, Satan haunts history, afflicting each generation with his lies that go back to the first man and woman corrupted by him. As Christ sums up in his humanity all of human history, the Anti-Christ cannot help but be drawn to him in an agony of hatred. That is why there are so many instances of Christ confronting people possessed by demons. It will not do to dismiss these encounters as misunderstood readings of people with mental illness. That is a nervous kind of "modernism" that also suggested that Christ walking on water was really walking on a ledge beneath the water level, and that the four and five thousands were not miraculously fed, but were so moved by Christ's preaching that they shared their lunches. Perhaps most people who think they are possessed by demons are simply neurotic, but no neurotic was able to identify Jesus as "son of the Most High God."

The man possessed was naked, for Satan mocks man's original innocence which cannot be regained apart from grace. The man had no house but lived among the tombs, for Satan roams the world seeking the death of souls. Christ torments Satan each time we enter the confessional and say, "Bless me, Father, for I have sinned."

Father of all mercies, raise me up in newness of life by the power of your Son whose death rebuked Satan and whose Resurrection destroyed the death that Satan brought into the world.

Into the Abyss

Father George William Rutler

Then Jesus asked [the man possessed by demons], "What is your name?" He replied, "Legion," because many demons had entered him. And they pleaded with him not to order them to depart to the abyss. A herd of many swine was feeding there on the hillside, and they pleaded with him to allow them to enter those swine; and he let them. The demons came out of the man and entered the swine, and the herd rushed down the steep bank into the lake and was drowned. (Lk 8:30-33)

The one place on the eastern shore of the Sea of Galilee that fits the description of this strange scene with its high cliffs is what is now called Kursi in the Golan Heights. The plain fact is, every place is Kursi, and the ugly voices screaming to Christ can be heard everywhere. The powers of evil are "Legion" because Satan's spirits that "roam the world" are many. A Roman legion had five to six thousand soldiers, but there is no mathematics to add up the ways in which evil attacks and corrupts civilizations and its civilian souls. Satan can act through helpless individuals, like the man possessed, and through people who willingly offer themselves to him, and through social structures and movements. In the twentieth century, more than one hundred and sixty million lives were destroyed by wars and genocides, and at least ninety-four million deaths were the direct result of deliberate starvation, forced labor, execution, and violence caused by Communist hatred of God.

Christ gives each of us a name in baptism as a sign of his gift of life to us. The Anti-Christ and his evil spirits try to erase our individual personalities. Evil tries to intimidate us by all forms of Legion: mass movements, opinion polls, fads, and celebrity. Evil dreads being cast "into the abyss" where he has no influence. Jesus gives us our name to remind us that no evil can destroy our identity if we appeal to him. Jesus casts the evil spirits into the prison of the abyss, as he will eventually do for ever at the end of the world (Rv 11:7), and he deliberately mocks the evil spirits by first casting them into pigs. Evil is destroyed by humiliation. To confess our sins in humility is to humiliate the many demons that try to destroy us. Christ casts them out when a priest says, "I absolve you."

Heavenly Father, give me the humility to know that evil is real and the grace to choose the good, so that I may not be cast out but rejoice with you for ever.

The Two Fears

Father George William Rutler

When the swineherds saw what had happened, they ran away and reported the incident in the town and throughout the countryside. People came out to see what had happened and, when they approached Jesus, they discovered the man from whom the demons had come out sitting at his feet. He was clothed and in his right mind, and they were seized with fear. Those who witnessed it told them how the possessed man had been saved. The entire population of the region of the Gerasenes asked Jesus to leave them because they were seized with great fear. So he got into a boat and returned. (Lk 8:34-37)

Holy fear is the awe that moved Jacob to bow down at Bethel on the place where he had dreamt of angels on a ladder to heaven, and made the face of Moses radiant with light on the holy mountain of Sinai, and cast the Apostles to the ground at the sight of Christ transfigured in radiance on the mount of Tabor. This fear of God which "is the beginning of knowledge" (Prv 1:7) is one of the seven gifts of the Holy Spirit. Its opposite is the "servile fear" of one who does not know what his master is doing, and its tone is not blissful awe but miserable fright. Holy fear makes the fearful shimmer in astonishment, while mere fear of the unknown makes the ignorant shiver.

The Gerasenes should be awestruck when they see the perfect calm of the man who had been violently deranged. Instead, the change frightens them. They had become accustomed to madness, and are shaken by sanity. They cannot deny what happened, so they try to alter the conversation. Their slavish fear is an inversion of holy fear: they ask Jesus to leave them.

Sanctity is perfect sanity, and in an imperfect world it is tempting to think that it is eccentric. It is the only balance in an unbalanced world. The fact that there are saints is the most practical and present proof for the truth of Catholicism. The one reasonable choice is to rejoice with the saints rather than ignore them. But in an irrational culture, the saints are deliberately ignored.

The cure of the demoniac shows the power of Christ to perfect human nature, and to put us in our "right mind." Holy fear bows before Christ who is the Way. Servile fear nervously asks the Way to please go away.

Almighty Father, may your Son and Holy Spirit give me the grace to worship your holiness which passes all understanding.

Tell What God Has Done

Father George William Rutler

*The man from whom the demons had come out begged
to remain with [Jesus], but he sent him away, saying,
"Return home and recount what God has done for you."
The man went off and proclaimed throughout the whole town
what Jesus had done for him.* (Lk 8:38-39)

There are some personalities who are admired most by those who know them least. The case is the opposite with Jesus. The attraction of his human nature increased people's desire to stay with him. There is no record of any flaws in him that admirers excused because "he's only human, after all."

When he would not remain in one place, people followed him. On Easter morning, Mary Magdalene tried to cling to him, and in the same day's sunset on the Emmaus road, the two men begged, "*Mane nobiscum*"—"Stay with us"—as he gave the impression of moving toward the horizon, just as he had on that day when he walked on the water past the Apostles in their boat. The Gerasene man, now healed, begs too. He wants to remain with Jesus, which is a human appeal to tag along with Jesus on his mystic journey. Instead, Jesus tells him to go back to his own town and spread the news of what had happened.

Jesus often tells people whose bodies he has healed to keep secret what he has done, lest others focus on their physical health. With the Gerasene it is different. His people had grown so accustomed to neighborly evil that they could not imagine what their neighborhood might be like without it. So Jesus tells him to publish the secret.

Jesus saves the cured man from the solitary piety of "me and my God," oblivious to others. The fruit of true encounter with Jesus is evangelization. Contemplative prayer spends time privately with Jesus and then goes public. The best way to "keep the faith" is to spread it. Salvation in not preservation: "Whoever seeks to preserve his life will lose it, but whoever loses it will save it" (Lk 17:33). We can stay with Jesus for ever, but only if we have brought others to him.

Almighty Father, as you never leave me, save me from ever leaving you, and help me to bring others into your joy.

Down in Adoration

Father George William Rutler

When Jesus returned, the crowd welcomed him, for they were all waiting for him. And a man named Jairus, an official of the synagogue, came forward. He fell at the feet of Jesus and begged him to come to his house, because he had an only daughter, about twelve years old, and she was dying. (Lk 8:40-42a)

An early desert father in Upper Egypt, Abba Apollo, claimed to have seen an apparition of Satan who had no knees. It is a graphic description of haughty pride. Humility is all about kneeling, and angels are described far more often kneeling than flying.

What we know as pews became widespread only with Protestantism's emphasis on instruction over adoration. Kneeling is easier without pews, and prostration on the ground is not possible with them. Jairus uses his knees. He flings himself at the feet of Jesus the way true worshipers should bow before the Blessed Sacrament.

Jairus is a man of prominence, an "official" of the synagogue, but he is not stiffened by his own importance. Moved by his desperate love for his daughter, his only daughter, he flings himself at the feet of Jesus and begs a favor. Here is the self-abandonment which the spiritual writer Lorenzo Scupoli marked as an essential ingredient in winning the spiritual combat against vain pride. Were he self-conscious, Jairus would not be conscious enough of the power of Jesus. If he thinks first about the impression he makes on others, he will not impress Jesus. Jesus accepts the homage as his due, for perfect humility casts out false modesty. He is the Lord and expects to be worshiped, for by that worship the worshiper learns his own true worth.

Contrast this with the scene later in Caesarea. An important man, a centurion named Cornelius, flings himself at the feet of Peter who raises him up: "Get up. I myself am also a human being" (Acts 10:26). Protocol forms of respect in daily life, social courtesies and salutes and bows, are valid when they are understood as tributes to the authority behind the figure being respected. The Church teaches the world what knees are for.

Merciful Father, I kneel before you in adoration, for your Son took flesh and touched the ground he created so that his creatures might be raised in glory.

137

God Is in the Details

Father George William Rutler

As [Jesus] went, the crowds almost crushed him. And a woman afflicted with hemorrhages for twelve years, who [had spent her whole livelihood on doctors and] was unable to be cured by anyone, came up behind him and touched the tassel on his cloak. Immediately her bleeding stopped. Jesus then asked, "Who touched me?" While all were denying it, Peter said, "Master, the crowds are pushing and pressing in upon you." (Lk 8:42b-45)

There are no throwaway lines in the Gospel. There is not even a single dispensable word. Everything recorded is there for a reason. There are some words and phrases we may be inclined to skim over, but they are the very ones we should pay special attention to. A venerable saying insists: "God is in the details." It has variously been attributed to an artist, Michelangelo; and a writer, Flaubert; and an architect, Mies van der Rohe. All of them may have said it in one form or another, because it is true of all that we see and do and touch. God is not an abstraction, nor does he affect us in vague ways. As he knows every hair on every head, so also does he reveal his nature most precisely in matters that mere mortals might pass off as trivial.

This passage is replete with very important details. "Crushed": that is how big the crowd was. "Hemorrhages": the woman has an illness that is clinically identifiable, and not just a poetic metaphor for sickness in general. "Twelve years": this has burdened her for a long time, racking up big medical bills. "Tassel": Christ follows the dress code (Nm 15:37-41) by wearing ornaments as reminders to keep the great commandments. "Immediately": when the Master wills something, he can make it happen at once.

The biggest little detail is Peter's common sense. Jesus, who knows all things, asks who touched him in order to provoke the hesitant woman to approach him. While others think they are being scolded, Peter simply responds with logic: How can we possibly know, since so many people are crushing him? If we innocently put our earthly logic at the disposal of the logic of heaven, Christ the Logos will show us why details are important.

Almighty Father, creator of all things, who despise nothing that you have made, I rejoice that your love holds together all things great and small in one great hymn of praise.

What Our Hands Have Handled

Father George William Rutler

But Jesus said, "Someone has touched me; for I know that power has gone out from me." When the woman realized that she had not escaped notice, she came forward trembling. Falling down before him, she explained in the presence of all the people why she had touched him and how she had been healed immediately. He said to her, "Daughter, your faith has saved you; go in peace."
(Lk 8:46-48)

If there were a million in that crowd, the Master would know each one. Mere mortals may speak of "someone," but he knows who that one is. The woman hides from the crowd by blending into it, but she cannot hide from the Master, nor can we. In confession, we cannot tell him anything he does not already know. By telling him in trust, the Lord we touch touches us.

If we do not understand that God knows us, we might get nervous when he tells us what he knows. That is "servile fear." If we trust that God knows us and wants us to know that he knows us, then we bow down in awe—holy fear. The woman bows down and confesses before the whole crowd that she is the "one" who touched him, and then she broadcasts that she was healed. Here at work is the love that casts out fear. She does not care what the onlookers think: she only has eyes for Jesus.

The power that goes out from Jesus at her touch is the love that made the universe and each of us. Love has no limits, and so the Lover is not weakened when love "goes out" from him, but the beloved is strengthened. The others in the crowd do not receive this power because they are pushed against Jesus by others. The sick woman has deliberately sought to touch him, and that act of faith heals her. When we receive communion, we should tremble joyfully like that woman.

As Christ heals real people and not abstract figures of speech, we can receive his power when we cease treating him as an abstraction and try to touch him so that he might touch us. We become real when we approach him as the ultimate reality, as did Saint John who "touched with our hands" (1 Jn 1:1) the Word of Life.

Almighty Father, I bow down before you in thanks for having let your Word of Life come to your holy Church and to me.

Never to Die Again

Father George William Rutler

While [Jesus] was still speaking, someone from the synagogue official's house arrived and said, "Your daughter is dead; do not trouble the teacher any longer." On hearing this, Jesus answered him, "Do not be afraid; just have faith and she will be saved." When he arrived at the house he allowed no one to enter with him except Peter and John and James, and the child's father and mother. All were weeping and mourning for her, when he said, "Do not weep any longer, for she is not dead, but sleeping."
(Lk 8:49-52)

The dead daughter of Jairus is no longer capable of an act of faith, but the faith of her parents brings the power of Jesus to her, quite as we in the Church pray in faith for the faithful departed. Saint Athanasius said that our Lord requires faith from those who ask him for favors, not because he needs their faith (since he is the Lord and Giver of faith), but so that the recipient of a benefit from him will not lose it because of unbelief. Faith prevents us from forgetting his gracious acts.

The parents are admitted into the house, for they will have the care of rearing the girl. Peter, James, and John also are allowed to watch, for they will be witnesses to the world of the two most revealing moments in the life of Christ before his death and Resurrection. They will see the ineffable brightness of the Transfiguration, and the horrible darkness of the Agony.

Jesus does not indulge in the awkward bromides often heard at funerals. When he says that the girl is not dead but sleeping, he does not pretend that she has turned into a rainbow or will live on in others. Christ is deeply moved by the weeping of the mourners gathered around the girl's house, as he will groan at the weeping of those at the tomb of Lazarus. But his raucous weeping opens graves. He resuscitates the child and she will die again sometime, but after he has conquered death. He will resurrect those who believe in him never to die again. Then, as John Donne prayed, "there shall be no darkness nor dazzling, but one equal light; no noise nor silence, but one equal music; no fears nor hopes, but one equal possession; no ends nor beginnings, but one equal eternity."

Eternal Father, grant that I may serve you in this world as you will, so that I may become what you conceived me to be, and rejoice in your glory for ever.

From Ridicule to Worship

Father George William Rutler

*And they ridiculed [Jesus], because they knew that [Jairus'
daughter] was dead. But he took her by the hand and called to
her, "Child, arise!" Her breath returned and she immediately
arose. He then directed that she should be given something to
eat. Her parents were astounded, and he instructed them
to tell no one what had happened. (Lk 8:53-56)*

"Ridicule" may have come from Latin into the English
language as late as the 1680s, but people have made fun of
others since our first parents in Eden learned how to do it
from the Liar who ridiculed them, saying they could live as gods.
He smirked as he said it. There is a tone of despair in the strained
laughter behind ridicule, as a French saying has it: "I force myself
to laugh so as not to cry."

The soldiers who dressed Christ as a clown before his crucifixion
were sad men, for in their joyless world they had to force themselves to laugh. Those who are insecure create a false confidence
by cruelly mocking what threatens them. The Nazis made elderly
Jewish women chirp like birds from tree branches.

When Jesus says that Jairus' daughter is not dead, the people's
laughter is sour, born of a dreary sense that life cannot conquer
death. They force themselves to laugh so as not to cry.

The joy of Jesus is impervious to ridicule, because he holds the
secrets of eternal life. When he speaks to the girl as "Child," there
is a joy inside him which he communicates by taking the girl by
the hand. No one saw God breathe life into Adam, and so the
Lord wants no one outside the house to know what has happened
here. The parents and the three Apostles will remain silent until
the Resurrection when the hand that touched Jairus' daughter will
touch the whole world. The parents are frozen with surprise, and
only the divine Wisdom has the common sense to know that the
child is hungry. He knows our hunger too, and now he gives us the
Bread of Life, changing ridicule to worship. "I have told you this
so that my joy might be in you and your joy might be complete"
(Jn 15:11).

*Almighty and eternal Father, as your Son raised the dead, so may
he raise me from sin to virtue, and by so doing, open to me the
gates of everlasting life.*

Called to Poverty of Spirit

Father Michael L. Gaudoin-Parker

[Jesus] summoned the Twelve and gave them power and authority over all demons and to cure diseases, and he sent them to proclaim the kingdom of God and to heal [the sick]. He said to them, "Take nothing for the journey, neither walking stick, nor sack, nor food, nor money, and let no one take a second tunic." (Lk 9:1-3)

Why does Jesus instruct his disciples to take nothing for the journey on which he was sending them? The answer is found in the words "power and authority." In the New Testament this phrase signifies anything but worldly domination, prestige, and privilege. Jesus is adamant that his missionaries be poor in spirit.

He reproves the disciples for being place-getting, power-seeking, and slow to learn the principle that he eminently exemplifies without fuss or fanfare: that of service-leadership. Jesus' own majestic authority will be shown when Pilate presents him stripped of his garments to the mob: "Behold, the Man." In sending his disciples to proclaim God's kingdom, he tells them to take nothing, neither a prop nor even a change of clothes.

By following in the simplicity of Jesus' lifestyle, the disciples gradually learn the truth he points out in the Sermon on the Mount: reliance solely on God our Father's providential love. This provides everything needful for all creatures, especially for the renewal and wholeness of being human. Everything is created out of nothing by him, the divine Word. Later, empowered by the risen Jesus' communication of the new creation, the disciples call all to believe in the real presence of his kingdom always with them. They baptize people into this new creation and lead them to celebrate and live its fullness through the Eucharist.

People listen more readily to witnesses of this civilization of love, as Pope Paul VI says, rather than to teachers. Francis of Assisi powerfully witnesses to complete reliance on God. Stripping himself of his heritage and claiming only God as Father, he shows the beautiful truth of brotherhood. This means sharing God's gifts in poverty of spirit, the first of the beatitudes of the kingdom. This attitude flows from the transforming power of the Eucharist.

God our Father, fill us with the Lord Jesus' brotherly love, so that we may give without counting the cost, care for others lovingly, and thus bear witness to the transforming power and authority poured out by your Holy Spirit.

Welcoming Good News

Father Michael L. Gaudoin-Parker

"Whatever house you enter, stay there and leave from there. And as for those who do not welcome you, when you leave that town, shake the dust from your feet in testimony against them." Then [the Twelve] set out and went from village to village proclaiming the good news and curing diseases everywhere.
(Lk 9:4-6)

Saint Luke's Gospel is characterized by the universal scope of hope offered to those who are weak, ill, or marginalized, such as women and the poor. This feature is evident in the attention Luke, whom Saint Paul calls the "beloved physician" (Col 4:14), pays to Jesus' acts of healing, which draw people to him as the compassionate Savior.

Jesus entrusts his disciples with the task of carrying out a mission that is identical with his own: to awaken and stir up hope by proclaiming humankind's well-being, signposted by the corporal and spiritual works of mercy. Among these, the work of healing holds a privileged place. It has many forms, corresponding to various situations and needs. The healing that is closely linked here with offering people "the good news" is first and foremost that of curing the division between people and God, among and in themselves. For, as Saint Paul says, Christ in reconciling us to God gave his followers the ministry of reconciliation (cf. 2 Cor 5:18).

In the footprints of the Apostles, the Church's particular grace and vocation is to evangelize. It exists above all to spread abroad the "good news" that Jesus is himself the unique Savior of all humankind's ills. In the Church's history, which is a story offering salvation or genuine health, there are numerous instances of miraculous cures—such as at Lourdes.

Apart from these, various persons show the revitalizing touch of Christ the Wounded Healer. There are, for instance: Damien the Belgian priest living among the lepers of Molokai; Mother Teresa of Calcutta lifting the untouchables out of the gutters or giving unwanted children a home; Jean Vanier reaching out to disabled persons. These reveal clearly the "good news" of the risen Lord Jesus bringing about *in deed* a welcome healing to the world's wounds and woes.

May we always welcome, Father, the Bread of Life that we receive through the Spirit of your Son in the holy Word and sacrament, to strengthen us to live the healing reconciliation we proclaim and celebrate.

Believing Is More than Seeing

Father Michael L. Gaudoin-Parker

Herod the tetrarch heard about all that was happening, and he was greatly perplexed because some were saying, "John has been raised from the dead"; others were saying, "Elijah has appeared"; still others, "One of the ancient prophets has arisen." But Herod said, "John I beheaded. Who then is this about whom I hear such things?" And he kept trying to see [Jesus]. (Lk 9:7-9)

The tyrant Herod, confused by reports, is curious to see Jesus. He is trapped by his guilt about executing John who prepared the way to recognize Jesus, which requires a conversion of heart. Later, through Pilate, Herod does get to see Jesus, and dismisses him as a fool.

Quite different is the attitude of the tax collector Zacchaeus, who likewise wants to see Jesus. Luke describes how this man's effort to do so is perceived by Jesus, who then calls him to salvation.

But, Jesus Christ is not out to gain mere popularity. Everything about him is fascinating. His teaching is impressive. Prophets and kings, he says, were longing to see what is shown to persons who have childlike hearts. Like the shepherds and angels at his birth who praise God for the good news of great joy, Simeon rejoices to see him, the light of the nations. The disciples rejoice at seeing him, the risen Lord. His attractiveness never fades.

The true grandeur of his mystery has inexhaustible divine depths. Saint Augustine states that believing *that* God exists is not enough. It is needful to keep exploring *into* him. For God etches an unquiet desire into our hearts, which finds rest only through total commitment to his design that Jesus reveals. This entails more than seeing or just hearing the Word. It demands listening and keeping it, like Mary, with joy. This joy costs "not less than everything"—the condition of complete simplicity. The cost, however, is not too high or impossible to pay, because it is inspired and sustained by God's grace, his gift gratuitously and generously given to everyone. It is not a question only of speaking *about* Jesus, but of encountering and conversing *with* him. In a Eucharistic hymn Saint Thomas Aquinas says that all our senses, except hearing, are deceived. No one but Jesus, as Bach puts it in a famous musical piece, is the joy of human desiring.

Eternal Father, we thank and praise you for your beloved Son who opens our eyes to your immense love and to walk always in the light and joy of the Holy Spirit.

No Prize, but Surprise
Father Michael L. Gaudoin-Parker

When the apostles returned, they explained to [Jesus] what they had done. He took them and withdrew in private to a town called Bethsaida. The crowds, meanwhile, learned of this and followed him. He received them and spoke to them about the kingdom of God, and he healed those who needed to be cured. As the day was drawing to a close, the Twelve approached him and said, "Dismiss the crowd so that they can go to the surrounding villages and farms and find lodging and provisions; for we are in a deserted place here." (Lk 9:10-12)

The disciples return to Jesus their teacher full of excitement about being involved in his work. They are no doubt weary from their labors. Jesus, on the other hand, continues to attend to the people, who seek him because of their hunger for what he is showing them of the healing power of God's kingdom.

Jesus hardly needs to be reminded by his disciples of the time or the crowd's need for food and rest. He isn't so wrapped up in what he wants to say or do that he is lacking common sense, oblivious or insensitive to basic human necessities. Thus, the disciples' suggestion or request that he send the people away seems superfluous, even somewhat impertinent. While their words sound as if motivated by concern for the crowds, they no doubt are also tinged with self-interest. While they imply a desire to have a break from others' pressing demands, they also voice a yearning to enjoy the company of their teacher for themselves away from the surging multitude.

The issue, however, is not about the quality of the disciples' compassion, but the surprising way Jesus is going to deal with their request. He understands that their practical-mindedness is the best they can muster, given their perception of the critical moment.

Jesus' way of surprising is illustrated in the lives of persons who closely follow him, like Mother Teresa. Once a successful businessman went to work in one of her shelters for the poor in India. His frustration at not finding the little woman there was overturned on the day before his departure when she returned. He was moved to tears of joyous surprise when, on admitting that his whole life was self-concerned, instead of being like hers, she held his shoulders and looked deep into his eyes saying: "Know that God appreciates you are doing the best you can."

Loving Father, knowing all things about us, you surprise us by filling us with the joy of praising you, especially when what we can't achieve becomes realized through the Spirit of Jesus' love.

Nourishing the Hungers of Humanity
Father Michael L. Gaudoin-Parker

[Jesus] said to [the Twelve], "Give them some food yourselves."
They replied, "Five loaves and two fish are all we have, unless
we ourselves go and buy food for all these people." Now the
men there numbered about five thousand. Then he said to his
disciples, "Have them sit down in groups of [about] fifty."
They did so and made them all sit down. (Lk 9:13-15)

Jesus defies the disciples' quantitative calculation by a higher logic—that of love's quality to give freely and generously without stint. This entails giving of oneself, becoming bread broken for a new world. Jesus' compassion for the people could not have them sent away hungry or disappointed or being denied hospitality. He provides for them because he himself feels for them. He becomes one of the poorest of the poor. He knows what it is to be turned away, as when there was no room for him at Bethlehem. John, the disciple of divine love's truth, says that the Word is not received even by his own people, but whoever welcomes him has power to become God's children.

Jesus' words to the Twelve are poignant. They are prophetic of what all members of his community of hospitality are to offer. The very poverty of every disciple becomes enriched by the Lord outpouring himself as the Host of Love's banquet. The feeding of the multitude takes place in the city of Bethsaida, which is called a "deserted place." This significantly recalls how God feeds his people with manna from heaven. John links this occasion to Jesus' promise of the Eucharist. The desert can symbolize our conurbations, where people are hungry and lonely because of the greed of consumerism.

In 1976 at the International Eucharistic Congress of Philadelphia—the city of "brotherly love"—the future Pope John Paul II spoke powerfully about the importance of raising awareness about basic human yearnings today. Jesus alone uncovers the depths of these. He shows that it is not sentimental pity, but solidarity with others in striving freely and generously for justice that can satisfy the heart's hope for communion. He expresses the depth of this in his heartfelt yearning on the cross: "I thirst"—words inscribed in the chapels of Mother Teresa's Missionaries of Charity.

Father, since you created our hearts with an insatiable thirst for communion, fill us with the generosity and joy of freedom flowing from becoming sensitive to the yearnings of our brothers and sisters.

Not Ritual, but Sacramental Reality

Father Michael L. Gaudoin-Parker

Then taking the five loaves and the two fish, and looking up to heaven, [Jesus] said the blessing over them, broke them, and gave them to the disciples to set before the crowd. They all ate and were satisfied. And when the leftover fragments were picked up, they filled twelve wicker baskets. (Lk 9:16-17)

Jesus' manner of dealing with the critical situation is more than a ritual gesture foreshadowing his actions at the Last Supper. He shows that the sacramental significance or sacred meaning of sharing requires thanksgiving. He involves his followers in the divine network of generous gift-giving, handling and sharing the fruits of the earth and the work of human hands. He draws them into his own incarnational reality of emptying himself utterly for humankind.

The Evangelist Luke states that the crowd is "satisfied." This suggests that they are already given a foretaste of the characteristic reality of the fellowship of the Christian community, namely, that of being one in heart and soul, rejoicing to share all things in common (cf. Acts 4:32).

True joy is the fruit of the quality of *being related*. This being-in-communion is incomparably deeper and qualitatively richer than a rejoicing over possessing a superabundance or even a contentment about merely *having* sufficient for oneself.

The paschal joy of thanksgiving or "Eucharist" springs from *being* united to God, from whom all blessings come. The greatest of these is communion in the Blessed Trinity's eternal life of love.

Mother Teresa has many stories illustrating this celebration of life. Thus, she recalls that one day she saw a woman, to whom she had given some rice, divide it and go out. Later when she asked the woman where she went, Mother Teresa was amazed to hear that she shared the rice with neighbors who were also hungry. The saint of Calcutta remarks that although want and suffering often make for self-centeredness, poor people can be exemplary in thoughtful generosity. Saint Paul reminds the leaders of the Ephesus community of Jesus' counsel: it is more blessed to give than to receive (Acts 20:35). Christian tradition means handing on to others the spiritual riches received.

Gracious Father, we thank you for your Son Jesus' self-emptying and for impelling us by his Spirit, your first Gift to believers, toward the true meaning of paschal joy—being related to one another in your mystery of communion.

Jesus' True Divine Identity

Father Michael L. Gaudoin-Parker

*Once when Jesus was praying in solitude, and the disciples were
with him, he asked them, "Who do the crowds say that I am?"
They said in reply, "John the Baptist; others, Elijah; still others,
'One of the ancient prophets has arisen.'" Then he said to them,
"But who do you say that I am?" Peter said in reply,
"The Messiah of God." He rebuked them and directed
them not to tell this to anyone. (Lk 9:18-21)*

Jesus prays for the disciples to believe in him as the one sent to
reveal God's love. After this he asks them directly about how
they regard him. He isn't interested in others' opinions. The
disciples see and are involved in his compassionate action of feeding the crowds. But, when they see him praying, absorbed in god-
liness, they can't doubt his true identity. Peter, their spokesman,
replies to Jesus' question: he is God's "anointed one" or "Christ."

Despite this profession of faith in him, however, the disciples
are slow to grasp the vital connection between three realities: his
action of breaking bread, his Passion and Resurrection, and also
his presence in all his followers.

These realities are clearly brought out in John's Gospel. Here the
miraculous feeding of the multitude is linked with Jesus' teaching
that he himself is the true Bread come down from above for the
life of the world. Because he carries out the work of God, the disciples are drawn to recognize his divine being. He shows the Father's
desire of love for all to be saved. He comes to do the Father's will,
which is his real food.

Jesus often has recourse to God's sustaining will in solitary
prayer. Especially in the garden of Gethsemane while wrestling
with God's will, he submits to it. If God were to remove the chalice
of suffering from him, there would be no Mass, through which
we have the joy of tasting the soul-nourishing fruits of his paschal
mystery and his abiding presence.

The second-century martyr-bishop of Antioch, Ignatius, understood well it is better to witness by one's life to Jesus' sacrificial
gift, than merely to profess belief in him in words, no matter how
eloquently. He thus pleaded not to be prevented from witnessing
by martyrdom what he celebrated and handed on to others in the
Eucharist.

*Father of love, in praising and thanking you for showing us your
will for our peace, may we live our profession of faith by imitating
your Son Jesus' docile submission to your loving design for the
world.*

Call to Become Christian in Deed

Father Michael L. Gaudoin-Parker

[Jesus] said, "The Son of Man must suffer greatly and be rejected by the elders, the chief priests, and the scribes, and be killed and on the third day be raised." Then he said to all, "If anyone wishes to come after me, he must deny himself and take up his cross daily and follow me. For whoever wishes to save his life will lose it, but whoever loses his life for my sake will save it." (Lk 9:22-24)

At first sight, the condition Jesus sets for following him sounds absurd. It seems that he is fostering crass, disguised selfishness and self-deception. What's the point of giving up one's life, if at the same time one sets an eye on reward or on getting it back? In any case, what's so extraordinary about this? Aren't mothers daily self-forgetting? Don't soldiers risk their lives for their nations?

In issuing this challenge, however, Jesus calls all who listen to it to confront the meaning of their lives in relation to him. His words present many levels of meaning. Apart from their obvious moral implications, they have profound depths pertaining to our very Christian identity and mission.

The stakes are high: it is all or nothing. His challenge certainly has nothing to do with hero-worship. It isn't about being for or against him or of admiring him as a wise, inspiring teacher. These attitudes can be passing as fads tend to be.

Discipleship of Christ signifies something far deeper than feelings. He asks for our very selves. This entails being integrally at one with him, intimately bonded with him and one another. For this reason, before inviting the disciples to share his life, he foretells for the first of three times how his earthly existence is to end as Yahweh's Suffering Servant. He hides nothing. He doesn't promise a path strewn with roses or one leading to success.

Yet, he does guarantee something truly lasting, eternal. John's Gospel gives this teaching a particularly Eucharistic flavor in recalling Jesus' words about the abundant harvest coming from the single grain falling into the ground and dying. We become Christian in *deed* by living his mystery of death and Resurrection, into which we are plunged at baptism. In responding "Amen" at communion we affirm, as Saint Augustine says, that we are the "Body of Christ."

Father, may we not balk at the cost of being witnesses of your Son's paschal mystery, living truly faithful to the life-transforming power of communion that we celebrate in the Eucharist.

Discerning Purity of Heart
Father Michael L. Gaudoin-Parker

"What profit is there for one to gain the whole world yet lose or forfeit himself? Whoever is ashamed of me and of my words, the Son of Man will be ashamed of when he comes in his glory and in the glory of the Father and of the holy angels. Truly I say to you, there are some standing here who will not taste death until they see the kingdom of God." (Lk 9:25-27)

Hope springs eternal in the human heart. Hope for what? Human hopes take many forms. They shape the ways people seek to work out their lives. There are long and short term goals. The shape of hope, however, is determined by what is loved, and loved according to what is believed. Apart from ambition for personal gain, achievement, and success, the objectives of hope stretch people in altruistic efforts to realize plans and projects for a welfare state, a more humane and better world of justice and peace. But, the human heart's mixed motives are notoriously deceptive. Not to admit this is self-delusory.

Jesus clarifies that the meaning and purpose of human life is to seek the perspective of God's design for the coming of the kingdom. With utter conviction he points out that even the best hopes crumble if this perspective and scope is denied. At the Last Supper, knowing that through weakness Peter would deny him out of human respect, Jesus prays for his faith to be strengthened to be a rock for all the brethren (cf. Lk 22:31f.).

Not only perspective, but perseverance is necessary to integrate all personal desires, aspirations, ambitions into God's great desire to share his glory with human beings. This glory is being fully alive in the vision of God.

Various persons lived this. Thus, the brilliant law student Francis Xavier was converted by his countryman Ignatius of Loyola, who kept putting to him Jesus' question about the profit he hoped for in pursuing a worldly career.

Earlier, Saint Thomas à Becket the martyr knew a dilemma deeper than that requiring him to oppose the unjust rule of his king, Henry II. He anguished about the inner drama of discerning whether or not he was doing the right thing for the wrong reason. To enter into God's kingdom within and among us, he needed purity of heart coming from Jesus' paschal mystery.

Glorious Father, draw us to you, font of holiness, by purifying our hearts so that we may discern your gracious design and desire to do your will, always led by the Spirit of truth promised by your Son Jesus.

Transfiguring Hope

Father Michael L. Gaudoin-Parker

About eight days after [Jesus] said this, he took Peter, John, and James and went up the mountain to pray. While he was praying his face changed in appearance and his clothing became dazzling white. And behold, two men were conversing with him, Moses and Elijah, who appeared in glory and spoke of his exodus that he was going to accomplish in Jerusalem. (Lk 9:28-31)

The memory of this event always remains part of the disciples' proclamation of Jesus' mystery. All the Synoptic Gospels present it, as Peter does also (cf. 2 Pt 1:16f.). While John doesn't describe this amazing moment, his entire Gospel reveals Jesus' glorious truth of gracious beauty. This shines through the "signs" that Jesus gives, from the miracle at Cana to the raising of Lazarus. This disciple's narrative gives way to breathless witness to the Word of Life that he heard, beheld, and touched (cf. 1 Jn 1:1-4).

Luke recounts that the representatives of the law and the prophets are conversing about Jesus' "exodus." This word indicates not merely his departure from sight, but offers a clue to the inner significance of the Transfiguration as pointing to his way of the cross. The same three disciples learn to appreciate this when Jesus pleads with them to watch with him in his agonized prayer in Gethsemane. Because of Jesus' exodus they, like a child at birth, come to see the light and colors of day amid life's uncertainties.

Alluding to God's creation of light and perhaps his encounter with the risen Lord on the Damascus road, Saint Paul compares himself to a fragile terracotta lamp that brings people to acknowledge God's glory on Christ's face (cf. 2 Cor 4:6). This is no mere abstract knowledge, but an experiential and personal going out of oneself to reveal Christ to others.

Dostoevsky's insight about the world being saved through beauty best applies to Christ. Oscar Romero of El Salvador uplifted his people's faltering hope by focusing on the meaning of the Transfiguration of Christ, the true Light of the world and the Splendor of Truth. He issued three Pastoral Letters on this feast. His last homily on the Sunday before being gunned down denounced the "gods of power and money" as unable to destroy Christ's resplendent truth.

Father of true beauty in the world, enlighten our sin-darkened minds and open our closed hearts to behold the work of your Spirit transforming and transfiguring our doubts and fears through Christ's paschal mystery.

Awakening to Jesus' Transforming Presence

Father Michael L. Gaudoin-Parker

Peter and his companions had been overcome by sleep, but becoming fully awake, they saw [Jesus'] glory and the two men standing with him. As they were about to part from him, Peter said to Jesus, "Master, it is good that we are here; let us make three tents, one for you, one for Moses, and one for Elijah." But he did not know what he was saying. (Lk 9:32-33)

The three disciples awake from no dream. They really see Jesus' splendid reality. Like the two disciples on the road to Emmaus, their eyes are opened. They realize how good it is to recognize Jesus in a new way. They don't want their experience to fade. Impetuous Peter exclaims in bewilderment his intention to set up three tents as tokens of the beauteous sight he and his companions are delighted to behold.

Peter doesn't fully understand the implications of what he says. His proposal, nevertheless, has a deep meaning. It signifies that the law and the prophets point to Jesus, whose presence on the other hand illumines the whole of the Old Testament.

By being drawn into the inner significance of the amazing event of Jesus' Transfiguration, the disciples can no longer be bystanders. Their lives are no more the same. From being spectators they become witnesses. Their entire relationship to Jesus is changed. They can't regard Jesus merely from a human viewpoint: their outlook is new. Moreover, they are able to perceive everything in a different light as a new creation. So too, God's Spirit enables us to recognize Jesus' coming as fulfilling and relating everything in harmony.

Eucharistic adoration isn't, as Saint Peter-Julian Eymard teaches, only staying at Tabor, but it awakens us to Jesus' presence illumining the ordinary circumstances of living. Being struck by the splendor of the truth of God's closeness to humankind, this apostle of the Eucharist worked to prepare the waifs of Paris for their First Communion. He taught them to regard this as the life-transforming experience of Tabor, paradise on earth.

The celebration and adoration of the Eucharist leads even to something deeper and more wonderful than the togetherness experienced in the closeness of camping. This is a sense of communion with Christ and one another.

Father of all goodness, we praise and thank you for refreshing our way of seeing by showing us Jesus' presence in your holy Word and sacraments, so that we may serve him with renewed enthusiasm in people longing for hope.

Awesome Revealing Word
Father Michael L. Gaudoin-Parker

While [Peter] was still speaking, a cloud came and cast a shadow over them, and they became frightened when they entered the cloud. Then from the cloud came a voice that said, "This is my chosen Son; listen to him." After the voice had spoken, Jesus was found alone. They fell silent and did not at that time tell anyone what they had seen. (Lk 9:34-36)

The most important words in the whole of the Tabor-event are not what Peter declares about building three tents. Rather, they are the mysterious revelation and the command from on high: "This is my chosen Son; listen to him."

These words echo what is described earlier in the Gospel, on the occasion of Jesus' baptism at the beginning of his public ministry. Then the disciples didn't understand the implications. But from now on they are told that their lives are intimately involved in making known Jesus' mystery.

Their encounter with Jesus is awesome. It fills them with fear. It isn't without darkness and obscurity. It plunges them into a cloud of unknowing, like that which mystics write about. But it is also paradoxically full of light. It is symbolically similar to Moses' meeting with God on Sinai. They begin to see Jesus in a new light as the life-giving Word. They are told to listen to him more attentively. For, in the presence of the divinely revealed mystery, as a chant of the Eastern liturgy puts it, all mortal flesh falls silent, as the disciples do.

God's Word impels us, as Saint Paul says, to work toward our salvation "with fear and trembling" (Phil 2:12). This is not a groveling servility, which love casts out (1 Jn 4:18). Rather it is holy fear, that gift of God's Spirit (cf. Is 11:2-3) leading to wisdom (cf. Ps 111:10). Recognizing the transcendent light of Christ's Eucharistic presence, the Word made visible, as Saint Augustine says, entails adoring what is revealed and received. Pope John Paul II, therefore, emphasizes the crucial importance of experiencing the wonderment of adoration before the gift of the Eucharist, in which God's love while mysterious becomes tangible. Through this we are enabled to discover a sense of amazement about God's revelation of humankind's true meaning and ultimate purpose.

Eternal Father, as in the past you spoke in various ways, teach us now to listen reverently to what your Spirit is saying so that our lives may proclaim coherently the Good News of your Son to the world.

A Tale of Descents

Father Albert Trudel, O.P.

On the next day, when [Jesus, Peter, John, and James] came down from the mountain, a large crowd met [Jesus]. There was a man in the crowd who cried out, "Teacher, I beg you, look at my son; he is my only child. For a spirit seizes him and he suddenly screams and it convulses him until he foams at the mouth; it releases him only with difficulty, wearing him out. I begged your disciples to cast it out but they could not." (Lk 9:37-40)

Perhaps it is just the thinness of the air at altitude, but the descent from a long hike past the treeline down to the beginning of a trail seems anticlimactic in more than just the obvious way: at altitude, an unrestricted vision allows one to look at life below with a seemingly God-like eye. The distance, the sunlight, and the fresh air erase the problems and difficulties of life below. The descent means a return where life's problems take on, once again, their former proportions as the eye loses its aerial perspective.

How much more must this have been the case with Jesus, Peter, John, and James, after the Apostles had seen the Lord's glory firsthand at the top of the mountain. The contrasts between the Transfiguration and what follows are even more profound: from relative isolation, Jesus and his three Apostles descend into a large crowd. From a vision of Christ's divinity, they descend to a case of apparent demonic possession. From the Father's voice declaring his pleasure with his only Son, they descend to a father pleading for his son's life. The descent from heaven to earth could not be more complete.

Descending from moments when we encounter Christ in a dramatic or meaningful way can resemble the Apostles' journey down Mount Tabor. Life's ordinary (or in the case of the Gospel, extraordinary) challenges and tragedies meet us, sometimes in great and overwhelming numbers. At the center of the crowd, at the focus of the pleading, the cries, and the noise, however, stands Jesus, our life-line. The Lord, present in moments of intense encounter, prepares us to meet the challenges, ordinary or extraordinary, with confidence in his power, not our own. Just as Jesus descended to become one like us in all things but sin, we can descend to share the Lord, and allow him to set others free.

Heavenly Father, who sent your beloved Son to save us, illumine our lives that we might reflect the light of your Son's Transfiguration in the darkness around us.

The Nobility of God

Father Albert Trudel, O.P.

Jesus said in reply, "O faithless and perverse generation, how long will I be with you and endure you? Bring your son here." As he was coming forward, the demon threw him to the ground in a convulsion; but Jesus rebuked the unclean spirit, healed the boy, and returned him to his father. And all were astonished by the majesty of God. (Lk 9:41-43a)

Nobility in a person is hard to define. We might think of some member of the aristocracy, given to public service, or someone who does some extraordinarily selfless deed. Nobility expresses something of the highest part of human nature, something that really sets the human person apart and above all the rest of creation. We Christians might identify total selflessness in the service of Christ as part of human nobility. Watching Blessed John Paul II go out of his way, even in his later years, to greet the sick and the infirm wherever he went to say Mass marked him out as a noble human person. In the parish where I serve, a man is dying of cancer who has spent his illness reaching out to others who share his disease, organizing people to provide for their needs. That is not only noble, but majestic.

The Greek word used in the Gospel for what astonishes the crowd, the "majesty" of God, really means something regal. It can be used as a title—"your Highness"—or as an adjective describing excellence in action. Jesus' miracle, restoring the son to the father, impresses the crowd as a manifestation of God's highness, his nobility, toward humanity. The crowd clearly associated the boy's illness with darker, supernatural forces that could only be repelled by divine power; both the nature of the illness, then, and the simplicity of Jesus' rebuke indicate, for the crowd, God acting directly in Jesus. That degree of power, exercised for the good, could itself be majestic. But the comment about the crowd's astonishment comes after a significant observation: Jesus not only healed the boy, but he also "returned the boy to his father." This restoration involves not only physical healing, but social restoration, a symbol, perhaps, of Jesus restoring us in redemption to union with our heavenly Father.

Heavenly King and Father of all, grant that we might accept your noble offer of redemption, and express the dignity of our Christian vocation in selfless charity.

Master Full

Father William M. Joensen

While [the people] were all amazed at [Jesus'] every deed, he said to his disciples, "Pay attention to what I am telling you. The Son of Man is to be handed over to men." But they did not understand this saying; its meaning was hidden from them so that they should not understand it, and they were afraid to ask him about this saying. (Lk 9:43b-45)

God's grace remains amazing only when people are not content to remain amazed. The cocktail of wonder and awe can intoxicate and leave folks frozen in their tracks, where they remain distant from the source that has stirred them. I have led parties abroad who agree when I propose the "four churches and two museums per day" rule—perhaps projecting my own limited capacity to remain struck by the sublime significance embedded in the material forms composed by master artists. Amazement is the admission ticket to an experience that is meant to leave us for ever changed, ready to peel back the drape of fear and ignorance, and become ourselves the canvas through whom Christ draws others to Gospel life. The Master beckons for a response beyond amazement. Our consent to heed the tug on our heart, accept Christ, and offer ourselves with glad abandonment is the proper succession of grace that amazes, unites, and, finally, saves.

Jesus' words fall on the deaf ears of those who would prefer to settle for being perpetually amazed, for whom the pursuit of happiness is sold out for the pursuit of novelty or pleasure. Jesus stands ready to hand over himself, but is able to do so only as we consent to his presence and allow him to apply his healing power to our lives, to chisel away at our inert preconceptions, and impress the brushstrokes of his features upon our self-image. Blessed John Paul II contends the principal reason that people fear faith in Christ is not because of the exceptional evils inflicted by so-called Christians in human history, but because they fear what faith and a commitment to the Son of Man would ask of them: to come out of the hidden recesses of the crowd, to hand over their lives to him, and receive his self-gift with open minds and hearts, where at last we understand what we mean to God.

You are wonderful in all your works, Father of my Master, Jesus. Inscribe the meaning of his death deeper in my heart, so that I might commit myself more completely to you.

Great with Children

Father William M. Joensen

An argument arose among the disciples about which of them was the greatest. Jesus realized the intention of their hearts and took a child and placed it by his side and said to them, "Whoever receives this child in my name receives me, and whoever receives me receives the one who sent me. For the one who is least among all of you is the one who is the greatest." (Lk 9:46-48)

I have a nephew in elementary school named Maximilian. His name literally means the "great one." And being partial as any uncle, I think he's pretty great for lots of reasons, including his love for all the animals God created—except wasps.

Max's older sister Natalie and younger brother Timothy don't always think that Max is so great. It often seems their life mission as siblings is to make sure he knows his place, or to remind him that he's not as strong or clever or cute as they are. It's not easy being a middle child. In fact, it's not easy being a child, period, especially when we have supposedly reached adulthood. The mind games people play can easily make us forget that God's preferential option is for the child—in each of us. Yet Jesus keeps reaching out for children and reminding us that when we receive the child in another—whose "leastness" consists primarily in the simple fact that they are not us—then we begin to approach the greatness that only God can bestow. Jesus' own receptivity redeems the child who has yet to be made whole, even if that child is carrying an AARP card.

Max's parents had another Maximilian in mind when they named him: Saint Maximilian Kolbe. At the Auschwitz death camp where he volunteered to take the place of a father selected to die by his Nazi warlords, Maximilian was consigned to a protracted death that was hastened only because his executioners became impatient. Maximilian permitted this man's children eventually again to be embraced by their father. And Maximilian, faith attests, has been embraced by the Father of the Son who really knew how to hug. Maybe when young Max is on the verge of another squabble with his siblings, it will be occasion again to share the story of Saint Maximilian, and remind him what his name really means—something more than merely great.

Your Son embraces me, most kindly Father, and helps me overcome my fear of being a child before you. Help me to accept the least ones in my life, so that they, too, might know that they are your own sons and daughters.

Casting for Communion

Father William M. Joensen

Then John said in reply, "Master, we saw someone casting out demons in your name and we tried to prevent him because he does not follow in our company." Jesus said to him, "Do not prevent him, for whoever is not against you is for you."
(Lk 9:49-50)

The Church maintains that there is a perennial need for exorcists and the rites they perform. She thereby alerts us to the reality of evil and of those spiritual powers that remain "on the prowl" (see 1 Pt 5:8) for unguarded hearts who presume God will protect them even if they do not take heed to live for Christ. Luke's Jesus cautions us about the more subtle workings of the evil one, where disciples empowered to carry out his mission become self-appointed deputies issuing cease-and-desist orders to every person who does not exhibit full adherence to their own particular company of faith.

Though the desire for the fully visible unity of persons who confess and worship Christ as Lord in word and sacrament is God's own intention, human beings can have a tendency to misappropriate this desire, and will that other people follow themselves. The perfection of communion among persons still in need of conversion and conversation remains a work-in-progress. We can too hastily dismiss fellow workers who have not paid their dues to our particular fishermen's union, prematurely drawing in the net so tight that it both constricts the circulation of Spirit among those already caught up in Christ's Church, and ruling out the prospect that those who are swimming in other schools might be gathered into the fold of God's redeeming grace.

Christ's counsel to John and his company in effect reminds us that our habitual attitude is to look for the signs of God's Spirit present in those who bear fruit that confirms that they are already with and for God. Our sacred mission is to do all within our power to draw ever closer to them, since God has already anticipated our hope that all who bear Christ's name might be one. Persons who display signs of God's power are not against us, but for us—to love and labor in harmony.

Father for ever for us, you do not compete with your Son or Spirit in relieving the afflicted, but are perfectly united in yourself. Cast out any rivalry or conceit that would fragment the company I keep, so together we might follow only you.

Spreading the Message of Love
Heather King

When the days for his being taken up were fulfilled, [Jesus] resolutely determined to journey to Jerusalem, and he sent messengers ahead of him. On the way they entered a Samaritan village to prepare for his reception there, but they would not welcome him because the destination of his journey was Jerusalem. When the disciples James and John saw this they asked, "Lord, do you want us to call down fire from heaven to consume them?" Jesus turned and rebuked them, and they journeyed to another village. (Lk 9:51-56)

Thus Christ begins his journey to Jerusalem where, nailed to the cross, he will subvert the age-old cycle of eye-for-an-eye, tooth-for-a-tooth, retributory violence. The Jews and Samaritans have been at odds for centuries, just as, our whole lives, we have been at odds with our neighbors, God, ourselves.

Like the disciples, our solution is often to call down fire on our "enemies." Our impulse is to annihilate all who stand in our way. The way of Christ is infinitely gentler and infinitely more difficult. Christ calls us to overlook mercifully the faults of others and to examine fiercely our own. Christ calls us to discover the power of humble charity. Christ calls us to look at the violence within ourselves.

In 1953, a woman named Mildred Lisette Norman gave up all her worldly belongings, took on the name "Peace Pilgrim," and, starting in Pasadena, California, walked for the next twenty-eight years: fasting until she was given food, walking until she was given shelter, speaking to all who would listen about peace. "This has been our trouble down through the ages—we have given only lip service to Christian values, and lived by the jungle law of tooth and claw," she observed. "We have quoted '*Be not overcome of evil, overcome evil with good*' and then attempted to overcome evil with more evil, thereby multiplying the evil."

Christ knows that we are never converted by violence. We are converted by being accepted: all the good and all the bad. We are converted by being welcomed, by being invited to contribute our gifts, by being willing to be called to our highest selves. We don't convert others by telling them they are wrong; we convert others by showing them Christ.

"Who are you?" his disciples ask him (Jn 8:25). And in reply, Christ asks, over and over again: Who are *you*?

Heavenly Father, help me to refrain from calling down fire on my enemies. Teach me to turn to you for help with the many things that I can't do by myself.

Nowhere to Lay Our Heads
Heather King

As [Jesus and his disciples] were proceeding on their journey someone said to him, "I will follow you wherever you go." Jesus answered him, "Foxes have dens and birds of the sky have nests, but the Son of Man has nowhere to rest his head." And to another he said, "Follow me." But he replied, "[Lord,] let me go first and bury my father." But he answered him, "Let the dead bury their dead. But you, go and proclaim the kingdom of God." (Lk 9:57-60)

One of the great temptations for a follower of Christ is to come up with a formula. Publishers like authors to have a "platform." We want to have a foothold from which we can dispense spiritual wisdom. We strive for bullet points and a brand.

I once watched a documentary on Dietrich Bonhoeffer, the Lutheran minister and prisoner of conscience during the Nazi regime. One scene was a clip of Hitler before a maniacally enthusiastic crowd, shaking his fist at God and saying, "We're ready! We're in control! We have a plan! *Now bless it!*" Later the camera panned to a photo of Bonhoeffer, taken at a family gathering during the time when he and several of his male relatives were plotting to assassinate Hitler. The contrast was striking. While Hitler's face bore the bloodless, single-minded stare of the fanatic, Bonhoeffer's was marked by uncertainty and conflict. That's just it: as followers of Christ, we don't get to have a foothold. We have nowhere to lay our heads.

To be a follower of Christ means being certain that we are to love each other as he loved us, and being very uncertain what that means in any given situation. It means being certain that the light will prevail, and then consenting to walk in almost complete darkness. It means being certain about Christ, and very, very uncertain about ourselves.

Bonhoeffer, like Christ, put his family in potential danger. Bonhoeffer was eventually caught by the Nazis and, like Christ, executed. But first, he wrote a book called *The Cost of Discipleship* in which he spoke of the danger of "cheap grace." "Cheap grace is the preaching of forgiveness without requiring repentance, baptism without church discipline. Communion without confession. Cheap grace is grace without discipleship, grace without the cross, grace without Jesus Christ."

That's not a formula, that's a call. And as Dietrich observed, "When Christ calls a man, he calls him to die."

Blessed Father, teach us to refrain from counting the cost. Let the lives of those who died in your name bear fruit in me.

Saying Farewell

Heather King

And [someone else] said, "I will follow you, Lord, but first let me say farewell to my family at home." [To him] Jesus said, "No one who sets a hand to the plow and looks to what was left behind is fit for the kingdom of God."
(Lk 9:61-62)

T he genius of the Gospels is that they address us wherever we are. They tell us how to act prospectively and they give us a picture of an authentic conversion in progress. "For [Christ's] vitality consists in this," writes Father Hans Urs von Balthasar: "that he always stands at the level of the person he is educating and yet always is to be found as well at [as!] the final goal of his education."

The final goal of our education is always love. When you lock eyes with the person with whom you're about to fall madly, deeply, in love, you don't stop to wonder how the folks at home are going to feel. You don't pause to calculate the labor that went into those many-times-mended nets that heretofore meant your livelihood. You're not concerned with who's going to feed the ox from now on. As if in a trance, you drop the handle of the plow and start walking.

To set our hand to the plow means to begin to walk among the people of the world but with our lives based on an entirely different order from that of the world. We learn to accept scorn, betrayal, and meager results. We begin to acknowledge our deep imperfection. We become willing to accept any number of unpromising people and situations.

Not to look behind means foregoing all earthly security. But this is where things get interesting. We're given all kinds of signs to let us know when we're onto Christ, and almost the first sign is that the Way, the Truth, and the Life are *interesting*. We start to change: that's interesting. We forgive someone when we thought forgiving was impossible: that's interesting. We start to see that lack of security is not an obstacle to the path: it is the path. And after awhile we're no longer tempted to look to what we left behind. We're too vitally interested in what's up ahead.

Almighty Father, teach us to keep our hand to the plow. Teach us that to leave our family behind for your sake means to come awake to the human family in a new way.

The Big Bad Wolf

Anthony Esolen

After this the Lord appointed seventy[-two] others whom he sent ahead of him in pairs to every town and place he intended to visit. He said to them, "The harvest is abundant but the laborers are few; so ask the master of the harvest to send out laborers for his harvest. Go on your way; behold, I am sending you like lambs among wolves." (Lk 10:1-3)

In her youth, my wife took part in a tent revival, called Christ is the Answer. The name was apt, because Christ is the answer to all the questions the human heart can pose. So the young Christians tried to bring that answer home to people in cities like Nashville. The leaders sent them out, two by two, for the spreading of the Word is always an invitation to belong to a people, bound in friendship with one another and with God. One might think that Nashville was already filled with such friends, but we should never forget how easily we take God for granted, and slowly, half-consciously, fall out of friendship with him.

So the harvest was great! There were many souls to win. There always will be. Then what keeps us from taking our faith to the streets?

Jesus suggests the answer when he says, "Behold, I am sending you like lambs among wolves." The command to *behold* is not idle. "Open your eyes!" he says to us. "Pay heed!" There are wolves everywhere. Who or what are they? The people of Nashville, minding their business, caught up in the daily round of love, or duty, or boredom, or greed? Or those spiritual wolves that prowl about, seeking to tear the lambs to pieces? Or our own fears and sins, skulking behind our back, laying a rough paw on our shoulder, slavering at our feet? Or all of these?

Yet the miracle is that the Lamb has overcome the wolf! Many were the souls in Nashville that the young laborers brought to Christ, including their own. If we try to bring Christ to the world, we can rest assured that we will see some fangs. But that chief of wolves, Satan, who Jesus says was a liar and a murderer from the beginning, has fallen like lightning from the sky. There is, finally, nothing to fear.

Eternal Father, master of the harvest, hearten our love for our neighbors, so that we will go forth without fear or shame to give them the best of gifts, the Lamb, your Son, through the same Christ, our Lord.

The Son of Peace

Anthony Esolen

"Carry no money bag, no sack, no sandals; and greet no one along the way. Into whatever house you enter, first say, 'Peace to this household.' If a peaceful person lives there, your peace will rest on him; but if not, it will return to you."
(Lk 10:4-6)

This is another of Jesus' hard sayings. First he tells the disciples that they will be lambs among wolves, and now he tells them that they will be destitute to boot. They may not even greet someone along the way, presumably to gain an invitation for a place to sleep and food to eat.

He is pressing them not to rely upon things, even if they are offered to them by a friendly fellow-traveler, but upon God alone. And since God is love, all is oriented toward that moment when they suddenly enter a man's dwelling and say, "Peace to this household." That unexpected blessing is an act of love, and the very fact that the disciples own nothing but this love is their invitation. For God not only loves us. He grants us the great joy, denied to the beasts and rejected by the devils, of loving him, by his grace.

Now do heaven and earth await the reply! When we bring Jesus before a man who does not know him, will we be laughed at? Will he treat us as quaint survivors of a bygone age? Will he lash out against us? We are not to worry about these things. They are in the hands of God.

All depends upon whether the person we invite is "peaceful." The actual words Jesus uses, however, are "the son of peace." That is not a description of someone's natural inclinations, as some people are placid and others are impetuous (Peter comes to mind). It names a personal relationship. The "son of peace" is already responding to the call of the Father, the giver of the peace that passes all understanding. Then to accept the preachers of Jesus is to affirm that call to peace, and to join with them—perhaps not yet knowing exactly what it means—in a greater household, a more intimate circle of love.

Loving Father, calm the troubles of our hearts and silence the grumbling of sin, that with free hearts we may greet people who do not know you and invite them to share your peace, through Christ our peace.

Commanded to Work Wonders

Anthony Esolen

"Stay in the same house and eat and drink what is offered to you, for the laborer deserves his payment. Do not move about from one house to another. Whatever town you enter and they welcome you, eat what is set before you, cure the sick in it and say to them, 'The kingdom of God is at hand for you.'"

(Lk 10:7-9)

The people of my sister's parish, Our Lady of Mount Carmel, celebrate the patronal feast for two weeks, concluding in a procession that winds its way up and down the hills of the old quarry town. Hundreds walk behind the figure of our Lady, with hundreds more lining the streets to join in praying the rosary. The tradition is more than a century old. Miracles have been associated with the procession. One man, deaf from birth, recovered his hearing. I've been told so by my sister, a physician of extraordinary talent and responsibilities.

"Do you believe that miracles happen?" I asked a friend of mine, a Dominican priest and world-class scientist. It was a period of weakness and trial for me. "Oh yes, all the time," he replied. "Some are incredibly obvious"—he mentioned the inexplicable vanishing of cancer and replacement with bone in a recent patient at Lourdes—"while others require love to see them."

Jesus here sends his disciples not only to preach, but to heal; and his command is as matter-of-fact as can be: "Cure the sick." How can they do that? Only by the power of God. They are called to be wonder workers, so that the people may gaze in admiration of God, and know that his kingdom is near.

That commission has not lapsed. We too are called to manifest the mighty works of God. Prayer can achieve astonishing things. If many such things are too subtle for those who do not love, that's only to be expected, since the wonders themselves point to love. When the disciples cured the sick, it was not so that they could then go about their worldly business. It was a sign that a new reality was among them, as subtle perhaps as a mustard seed, or the yeast that quietly and wondrously works in a measure of flour: the kingdom of God.

Father all-powerful, for whom a grain of sand is as a universe, and a universe as a grain of sand, give us the love to see your wonders and to share the vision with others, through Christ, our Lord.

Shaking the Dust

Anthony Esolen

"Whatever town you enter and they do not receive you, go out into the streets and say, 'The dust of your town that clings to our feet, even that we shake off against you.' Yet know this: the kingdom of God is at hand. I tell you, it will be more tolerable for Sodom on that day than for that town." (Lk 10:10-12)

Can a whole city be damned?

When I'm in an airport, I sometimes feel I've entered a hostile world. People look harried. They don't talk to one another. They shout into telephones, on business. They type at computers. The television blares above. The chic newsstands are laced with pornography.

God will judge us as individuals. But he made us social beings, and we will be judged as such, also. The retort of Cain should ring in our ears: "Am I my brother's keeper?" The answer is yes, we are. Cain's contempt for fellowship with Abel results in murder, in his becoming an outcast, and then, of all things, in his becoming the first founder of a city in Scripture.

If we were not responsible for one another, why would Jesus entrust us to preach his Word? It's a fearful responsibility. All we do among our fellows can help lead them to God, or away from him. If the Lord does not build the city, they labor in vain who build it. But if he does build the city, then its laws and customs will assist the people, singly and together, in leading a godly life. Our lives in the city and our prayer before God cannot be separate.

What happens when a city plainly rejects the Lord? Jesus, who descended among the dead, does wish to send us into such places, as Jonah was sent to Nineveh. If Cain is responsible for Abel, how much more is the just Abel responsible for Cain! Yet Jesus did not remain among the dead. Nor does he require his disciples to remain there.

What brings joy to those who seek the face of God brings loathing to those who reject him. The kingdom is the same; the cities are different. The same fire cheers Jerusalem and destroys Sodom. Jesus warns us that not one evil custom, not one unjust law, can partake of his kingdom.

Father of mercy and justice, give us the courage to proclaim your word from the housetops, that we may come safely to your kingdom in company with our neighbors, through Christ our Lord.

What Happens to Capernaum?

Anthony Esolen

"Woe to you, Chorazin! Woe to you, Bethsaida! For if the mighty deeds done in your midst had been done in Tyre and Sidon, they would long ago have repented, sitting in sackcloth and ashes. But it will be more tolerable for Tyre and Sidon at the judgment than for you. And as for you, Capernaum, 'Will you be exalted to heaven? You will go down to the netherworld.'"

(Lk 10:13-15)

In *The Great Divorce*, C. S. Lewis dramatizes the moment when souls from the netherworld, arriving by bus on the borderland of paradise, are invited to remain and not return below. We might suppose their hearts would leap at the invitation. Not so. Heaven will not allow itself to be infected with the merest germ of lust, greed, envy, pride, or hatred. God will not be wedded to sin. All who seek heaven will find it. All who knock at the door will enter. But all must be made pure.

So there are those who do not seek, do not knock. Why not? Lewis suggests two reasons. The first is that the soul loves something else more than God. That idol may be noble in the world's eyes: business sense, mother-love, intellectual renown. And because the idols are respected, the soul runs the risk of the second danger. He may be satisfied with himself as he is.

Such self-satisfaction is deadly. Jesus warns us against it here. He had performed many miracles near Capernaum, and what was the response? Large crowds followed him, but many people stayed home. Perhaps they thought they had better things to do than listen to a country preacher. Perhaps they were preoccupied with worldly matters. But perhaps they said, "What he's doing is fine, but I'm all right as I am."

Are we all right as we are? The people of Tyre and Sidon worshiped Moloch, a fertility god to whom they sacrificed their infants, making them "pass through fire" to the idol. Such was their bargain for rich harvests. Yet Jesus says that their fate will be more tolerable on judgment day than the fate of Capernaum. It is wicked to seek God in evil places. It is worse to fail to seek him at all, acknowledging neither his wonders nor one's sins. Moloch was a grim idol indeed. But Capernaum rouses the sterner condemnation.

Father in whom there is only light, grant us such fervor of love that, when we are attracted by sin, we may turn away from it because we love you far more, through Jesus your beloved Son.

Welcoming the Messenger
Anthony Esolen

"Whoever listens to you listens to me. Whoever rejects you rejects me. And whoever rejects me rejects the one who sent me."
(Lk 10:16)

Who can see God? Because he loves us, he doesn't abandon us to our imaginations. We needn't have a powerful intellect, waiting for special inspiration, seeking to solve the mysteries of the world. Instead God meets us in our weakness. He reveals his will through the law and the prophets. Christ takes flesh of the Virgin and dwells among us, knowing hunger and thirst, joy and sorrow, and even temptation, like us in all things but sin. After he ascends to the right hand of the Father, he is still with us, in the sacraments, and in his mystical Body the Church. He sends us messengers.

I recall one such, a holy priest, who came to dinner at my house and in a kindly way recalled me to the Catholic faith. The word he used was "apostate." I admired him for it. Because we are human and sinners to boot, the Word of God can never be exactly what we'd expect or want it. We wouldn't have made the cross a symbol of divine love. We wouldn't have cried, "Blessed are the poor, for theirs is the kingdom of God." Once we accept these things, we see their truth and beauty, but before we do so they remain a scandal. We stumble over them. The wisdom of God is foolishness in our eyes.

We need to take care. If God's Word often surprises us, then so will his messengers. Saint John Vianney was a poor scholar, and cut a ridiculous figure among the sophisticated. But he revived the faith in France after the Revolution. Saint John Bosco attracted the homeless boys of Turin by juggling and athletic tricks. He was scorned by his superiors. The next person you meet, maybe a devout old lady with rosary beads, may be the very messenger God has sent to you. Let's not turn away in pride. If we welcome his messengers, we welcome him.

Almighty Father, send down your Spirit upon us, so that we will be wise to recognize the messengers you send, and humble enough to heed their message, through Christ our Lord.

I Saw Satan Fall

Anthony Esolen

The seventy[-two] returned rejoicing, and said, "Lord, even the demons are subject to us because of your name." Jesus said, "I have observed Satan fall like lightning from the sky. Behold, I have given you the power 'to tread upon serpents' and scorpions and upon the full force of the enemy and nothing will harm you. Nevertheless, do not rejoice because the spirits are subject to you, but rejoice because your names are written in heaven."
(Lk 10:17-20)

No devout Jew would cast out demons in the name of Moses or Elijah, as venerable as they were. There is only one name in heaven and earth by which man may be saved. It is, under the old law, the name of God, too sacred to be uttered except by the chief priest, on the Day of Atonement, in the holy of holies. We will learn that it is also the name of Jesus, which means, simply, Savior. That name the disciples are granted the right to utter, for the conquest of all the demon-riddled world. When they return to Jesus and report that the demons are subject to his name, Jesus cries out, "I saw Satan fall like lightning!"

Recall when Satan led Jesus to the top of the temple. "Hurl yourself down from here," he said. "God will not allow you to dash your foot against a stone." The temptation was demonic in its worship of sheer power, divorced from love and obedience. It's as if Satan were to say, "Force the Father's hand! Make yourself the chief priest, and reform the worship of these lowly people! Play the benevolent tyrant! Seize the opportunity!" But Jesus did not fall. It is Satan who falls, or is hurled headlong.

Why here, why now? God saves us not only by dwelling among us, but by descending into the depths of our sinful and divided hearts. He humbles himself so far as to grant us the authority, in his name, to preach the Word and heal the sick. It is the military move that Satan cannot answer, because the devil cannot renounce his pride. So Jesus instructs the disciples not to rejoice in their power—that's what Satan would like—but in the fact that their names too have been made holy. They are warriors in Christ's Church, and the gates of hell do not prevail against them.

Father, Lord of hosts, enroll us in the army of your saints, that we may go forth preaching and healing, and ridding the world of demons, not to boast, but to give you glory, through Christ our Lord.

Out of the Mouths of Babes

Anthony Esolen

At that very moment [Jesus] rejoiced [in] the holy Spirit and said, "I give you praise, Father, Lord of heaven and earth, for although you have hidden these things from the wise and the learned you have revealed them to the childlike. Yes, Father, such has been your gracious will. All things have been handed over to me by my Father. No one knows who the Son is except the Father, and who the Father is except the Son and anyone to whom the Son wishes to reveal him." (Lk 10:21-22)

This may be my favorite verse in all of Scripture. It concentrates in a few luminous words all of the revelation of God. He is the maker of heaven and earth, who appeared to Elijah not in the earthquake or the whirlwind, but in a mysterious still small voice. He awoke not the high priest Eli but the boy Samuel, who responded, "Speak, Lord, for your servant is listening." He chose the youngest of Jesse's sons, David, who defeated the giant of the Philistines armed only with the name of God and a few pebbles from the brook. His beloved Son is the Suffering Servant, rejected by his own people, and put to an ignominious death upon a cross. The great Apostle to the Gentiles is a homely little man with a weak voice, but the heart of a lion, who echoes these words of Jesus when he says that God has chosen the foolish things of the world to confound the wise. The world worships power, in whatever form it can obtain it, but we preach Christ crucified.

Jesus is at once too profound for the sophisticated, and simple enough for a child. That's why, when the disciples were quarreling over who would be greatest in the kingdom, he took a little child and set him in their midst. Everywhere in the world we teach children to be adults, but Jesus goes us one better, and teaches adults to be like children new-made. A man may pride himself on his knowledge, but the child doesn't even know what it is to know, and looks upon all the world with wonder. A man may pride himself on being important, but the child's most blessed haven is that he isn't important, that he is only a child. Jesus appears among the great, and they ask for his credentials, but all the child sees is Jesus, the youngest among us.

Father, you who bring joy to our youth, make us to grow ever younger in wonder and love, and clear away the age of pride from our eyes, that we may see Jesus, in whose name we pray.

What the Eyes Have Seen

Anthony Esolen

Turning to the disciples in private [Jesus] said, "Blessed are the eyes that see what you see. For I say to you, many prophets and kings desired to see what you see, but did not see it, and to hear what you hear, but did not hear it." (Lk 10:23-24)

The poet Dante imagines the joy of an old man from far across the sea, who travels to Rome to see the image of Jesus on the cloth that wiped his face as he carried the cross. "And did you look like this, was this your face," the pilgrim cries out, "O Jesus Christ my Lord and very God?" We are fascinated by the Shroud of Turin, not simply because it is an inexplicable artifact from a miraculous event, but because in it we see dimly the one face we long to behold, the face of Jesus.

We don't know what the disciples were thinking when they heard Jesus speak these words. Did the words refer to the miracles? To the sense of a new beginning, a covenant in the name of the Messiah? What did prophets and kings long to see?

When the old prophet Simeon beheld the infant Jesus in the temple, he rejoiced, saying that he had seen the salvation of Israel, and a light to shine upon all nations. Perhaps he was imagining events to come that would shake the world to its foundations. But perhaps he was gazing upon the beauty of the child. Jesus performs wonders as signs of who he is; but he and not they must be the object of our wonder. More glorious than news of a healing are the words of Jesus, revealing eternal life to those who have ears to hear. What a great blessing it was for those disciples, to walk with Jesus, to eat with him, to hear his words, and to look upon his face! But Jesus has given us a great blessing too. "Blessed are those," he says to Thomas after the Resurrection, "who have not seen, but who have believed." The disciples learned to call "Lord" the man they had seen; and we long one day to see him whom we call Lord.

Father of lights, giver of every good thing, help us to see your Son in all whom we meet, that one day we may see all of the saints in the light of his countenance, through the same Christ our Lord.

You Shall Have Life

Anthony Esolen

There was a scholar of the law who stood up to test [Jesus] and said, "Teacher, what must I do to inherit eternal life?" Jesus said to him, "What is written in the law? How do you read it?" He said in reply, "You shall love the Lord, your God, with all your heart, with all your being, with all your strength, and with all your mind, and your neighbor as yourself." He replied to him, "You have answered correctly; do this and you will live."
(Lk 10:25-28)

The Jews considered that the greatest gift God gave them was not the land of Canaan, but the law. God had favored no other people so! The Psalmist says he delights to meditate upon it, to proclaim it, and to follow it. It's interesting that the Jews don't evaluate the law according to practical measures. They don't say, "If we follow these commandments, there will be less crime among us." Instead the law is an object of wonder, because it is a way for man to approach the heart of God. His words are sweeter than honey. They are a lamp unto our feet. They rouse us to songs of praise.

The law, then, springs from love, and is fulfilled in love. So when the scribe answers Jesus, saying that the greatest commandment is to love the Lord with all our being, he is right, and Jesus commends him. A slave obeys because he fears punishment. But a loving son obeys, and thinks it a privilege, because he wishes to share in the wisdom of his father. A philosopher may do right because his reason persuades him of it. But the lover of God cannot stop there. He seeks no less than friendship with God, so he prays to be filled with his overflowing goodness, which he then wishes to share with his neighbor, whom God also loves abundantly.

When Mother Teresa went to Calcutta, what did she seek to bring the destitute and the dying? Medicine, food, shelter, no doubt; but something else that no merely human law can prescribe. She brought them love, the love of God. The human law can keep me from shooting my neighbor. It cannot keep me from hating him. The human law can tax me to support a soup kitchen. It cannot make me love the hungry. Only God's love for us penetrates so deeply, and so we should love him in return, with all our heart.

Father of love, grant us the love to seek your will in all things and to obey it cheerfully, drawing our fellows to you by the beauty of that love, through your beloved Son, Jesus our Lord.

Averting the Eyes

Anthony Esolen

But because [the scholar of the law] wished to justify himself, he said to Jesus, "And who is my neighbor?" Jesus replied, "A man fell victim to robbers as he went down from Jerusalem to Jericho. They stripped and beat him and went off leaving him half-dead. A priest happened to be going down that road, but when he saw him, he passed by on the opposite side. Likewise a Levite came to the place, and when he saw him, he passed by on the opposite side." (Lk 10:29-32)

Who is my neighbor?

I cannot read the parable of the Good Samaritan without feeling ashamed. It's because I understand why the priest and Levite passed the beaten man, walking "on the opposite side." Perhaps the priest was in a hurry to officiate at a celebration of the law. Perhaps the Levite was in a hurry to meet a rabbi, and discuss the finer points of worship. Maybe they thought, or half hoped, that the man was dead. Maybe they feared to become enmeshed in violence.

What's long troubled me is that Jesus does not say that they pass the man as if he weren't there. They are not cold and vicious by nature. They are moved by the sight. That's why they take the opposite side of the road. If they stop to look at him, they will see the blood seeping from his wounds. They will hear the labored breathing. They will *feel* the shame of a man made in God's image, stripped naked, crumpled in pain, falling into the chasm of death. They will have a decision to make.

We cannot save the world. But Jesus doesn't ask us to save the world. He commands us to love our *neighbor*. It's easy to love mankind; we can do that at a comfortable distance, sending money. But the neighbor is all too *near*. He's the person whom God has sent us to. He's right there, at the side of the road, bleeding. Is he a good man, deserving our help? Better not ask; we don't deserve the grace God showers upon us. Will he thank us for saving him? Better not ask that either; what return do we make to our Savior? Can we assist him conveniently, and go on our business? Was Calvary convenient?

Alas, I take the opposite side because I want to choose my neighbors, rather than have God choose them for me.

Merciful Father, open my eyes and ears and touch my heart; teach me not to fear love, that I may welcome the neighbor, seeing in his poverty my own, and the poverty your Son assumed for us on the cross.

Who Is the Samaritan?

Anthony Esolen

"But a Samaritan traveler who came upon [the victim] was moved with compassion at the sight. He approached the victim, poured oil and wine over his wounds and bandaged them. Then he lifted him up on his own animal, took him to an inn and cared for him. The next day he took out two silver coins and gave them to the innkeeper with the instruction, 'Take care of him. If you spend more than what I have given you, I shall repay you on my way back.'" (Lk 10:33-35)

Who is that beaten man at the side of the road, and who is the Samaritan?

There's no question that Jesus is encouraging us to be like that good traveler, who helped the man who had fallen among thieves. But Jesus' parables are rich and profound. We never come to an end of meditating upon them. So too here.

I am a man on my way *from* the city of God, Jerusalem, "City of Peace," to Jericho. It's a highway infested with evil. Why I'm taking that route and that direction, Jesus does not say. Then I am waylaid. The robbers steal everything I have, and strip me, and beat me within an inch of my life. I am left in a ditch. I can't go one step farther on my own. I have nothing on my person to purchase balm for my wounds. I have not even the wherewithal to hide my shame. I can cry, with the Psalmist, "I am a worm and no man."

I am the one who has fallen among thieves. I've been robbed by my greed, bruised by my violence, stripped naked by my pride, and left for dead by my hardheartedness. Devils surround me; I know, because my sins have given them shelter. I am the man in the ditch.

The priest and the Levite cannot help me now. Only the Lord, rejected and despised just as the Samaritans were, can help me. He does so by entering into my shame. He touches my body. He pours oil and wine into my wounds: and the wine is his own blood shed for me. He lifts me in his arms. He walks beside the lowly animal that carries me to the inn. What I need most of all is love, and this he gives me, not because I deserve it, but because he loves me first and has compassion upon me.

Father, you who heard the cries of your people and sent to them your Son to heal their wounds: bring us also to the haven we seek, no earthly inn but your eternal dwelling, through Christ our Lord.

Drawing Near

Anthony Esolen

"Which of these three, in your opinion, was neighbor to the robbers' victim?" [The scholar of the law] answered, "The one who treated him with mercy." Jesus said to him, "Go and do likewise." (Lk 10:36-37)

As we proceed through this parable, we suppose that the man beaten at the roadside is our neighbor, and we should help him. But Jesus doesn't ask the scribe, "Which man understood that the victim was his neighbor?" He asks instead, "Which man was a true neighbor to the victim?"

That's not exactly the same thing. It's one thing to say, "This man is near to you," and another to say, "You should draw near to this man."

I have a friend who has the knack of seeking people whom everyone else shuns. One day while we were sitting at a luncheonette he introduced me to a woman who was fifty years old and looked seventy. She cadged a few dollars from him to buy a pack of cigarettes. Meanwhile she complained about the people in the store, who had told her to get lost. The townsfolk had tagged her with an ugly name, referring to what she did to make a buck now and then. She didn't smile once. She looked as if harassed by demons. But she knew she could come to my friend. She wanted the money, sure. She also wanted someone to share her unpleasant company.

Saint Augustine says that God is closer to us than we are to ourselves. That being so, when God calls us to *be a neighbor* to others, he doesn't mean something breezy and efficient and impersonal. That would be to keep them at a safe distance. But love is far from safe; the cross proves that. Even the scribe admits that the neighbor is he who treated the man *with mercy*. The man in the ditch was beaten, but the Samaritan who drew near him was pierced with compassion. The word "mercy" describes both the Samaritan's action and that willingness to suffer, to draw near. It is to share the heart of Jesus, pierced with a lance.

Loving Father, pierce our hearts with compassion, not to draw life from us, but that your life-giving Spirit may enter there to dwell for ever, through Christ, our Lord.

In Rest You Shall Be Saved

Anthony Esolen

As [Jesus and his disciples] continued their journey he entered a village where a woman whose name was Martha welcomed him. She had a sister named Mary [who] sat beside the Lord at his feet listening to him speak. Martha, burdened with much serving, came to him and said, "Lord, do you not care that my sister has left me by myself to do the serving? Tell her to help me." (Lk 10:38-40)

I imagine a brash young man saying to Jesus, "Lord! I will climb mountains for you! I will brave the tempests of the sea! I will face down enemies from earth and hell!" To which Jesus replies, "Yes, but suppose I ask you for something more difficult? Will you sit still for me? Will you listen to my words? Will you wait in peace?"

Poor Martha believes she has good reason for complaining. She's bustling about the house, trying to prepare and serve food for Jesus and his disciples. That would be no small undertaking. What's in her mind? Is she immersed in the delight of serving? Or has she made her service an object of pride, as forgivable as that may be? Is the service something she wishes to possess, like a precious ring, to be cherished and shown to one's neighbors?

What's gone wrong? There's a note of hurt feelings in her plea to Jesus. "Don't you care about me?" she asks. It isn't enough just to serve Jesus. Martha needs to be noticed as serving Jesus. At the least, she has for a moment lost the person in the event.

My wife always takes the part of Martha. I understand that, because Martha is a good woman, and women assume the care of others with a readiness that astonishes the ordinary man. But the care is not the same as the person. It isn't, I think, that Mary has forgotten Martha, but that Martha has in some small part forgotten Jesus. So she asks the Lord to make Mary take her attention away from him. "Tell her to help me," she says. It would be better if Martha should let the dishes go for awhile, and sit beside her sister, or rejoice, that her humble task had given Mary the incomparable opportunity to drink in the words of the Lord.

Heavenly Father, help us to delight in serving you at all times, and in the favor you show to others whose service is not as ours, for even to serve you is your own gift to us, through Jesus Christ, our Lord.

The One Thing Needful

Anthony Esolen

The Lord said to [Martha] in reply, "Martha, Martha, you are anxious and worried about many things. There is need of only one thing. Mary has chosen the better part and it will not be taken from her." (Lk 10:41-42)

This is a moment whose beauty breaks the heart. Imagine what it must have been like to be Mary, sitting at the feet of Jesus. She isn't mulling over how great she will be in the kingdom, as James and John did, whom Jesus with teasing irony called the Sons of Thunder. She isn't counting out the money in the purse, as Judas did. She is so wholly rapt in contemplation of the Lord that she has forgotten everything, even the obvious tasks of serving the food and clearing the dishes.

What does anything matter, when Jesus is here? How much we would give to be in Mary's place, looking intently into the eyes of the Lord, understanding at once but little of what he says, yet treasuring it, taking it into the heart where it will bear much fruit! Surely it would be wrong to break that rapture. It is "the better part," the burning love for Jesus, made manifest in obedience so complete that acting is superseded by *being*.

But there's something else here. It's easy to miss, if we focus on the lesson, and not on the tenderness of Jesus the teacher. Jesus speaks the name of the woman twice, "Martha, Martha." In just that moment he brings her back to him, assuring her that he knows her and loves her. If it is good to be in Mary's place, it is also good to be in Martha's, even if we take Jesus' words as a gentle rebuke. What would it be like, to hear such a rebuke from those lips? Or even to hear Jesus speak our name, twice? I had rather be rebuked by Jesus than praised by kings. I had rather dispense with every empty title I've ever earned, and hear Jesus simply say my name in the way he said the name of Martha long ago.

Father, shower your grace upon us that we may seek the one thing needful, which is to be indwelt by the Spirit of love that proceeds from you and your Son, our Lord, in whose name we pray.

The Need to Pray

Father Emmerich Vogt, O.P.

[Jesus] was praying in a certain place, and when he had finished, one of his disciples said to him, "Lord, teach us to pray just as John taught his disciples." He said to them, "When you pray, say: Father, hallowed be your name,/ your kingdom come./ Give us each day our daily bread/ and forgive us our sins/ for we ourselves forgive everyone in debt to us,/ and do not subject us to the final test." (Lk 11:1-4)

The followers of Jesus see him praying and are touched by the experience. Seeing Jesus in private converse with his Father, the disciples are moved to want to do the same.

As a young boy, I had the good fortune of being close to my mother's sister, a devout Catholic, whom I would visit often during vacation. Every evening at a certain hour, while my cousins and I would be enjoying a good movie or playing cards, my aunt would excuse herself and go into her bedroom for a private holy hour. It touched my child's heart and gave me the desire to know God.

Jesus teaches first by example and then, when asked, he gives his followers a simple prayer to learn by heart. The first petitions have to do with God and the glory of God. The second three petitions have to do with our needs and necessities. I must put God first and only then turn to my needs. When God is given his proper place in my life, all things fall into their proper places.

The second part of the Our Father—which deals with our needs and necessities—is a beautifully constructed unity dealing with the three essential needs of man and the three spheres of time within which man moves. It asks for bread—what is necessary for the maintenance of life, thereby bringing the present to the throne of God. Next it asks for forgiveness, thereby bringing the past into the presence of God and his forgiving grace. Lastly, it asks for help in temptation, thereby committing the future to God's providential care.

Someone once told me that anger isn't getting my way in the present; resentment isn't getting my way in the past; and fear isn't getting my way in the future. With this simple prayer, Jesus teaches me to place the present, the past, and the future in God's loving hands.

Loving Father, help me to be a prayerful and virtuous person who gives good example in all I say and do.

The Need for Persistence

Father Emmerich Vogt, O.P.

And [Jesus] said to [his disciples], "Suppose one of you has a friend to whom he goes at midnight and says, 'Friend, lend me three loaves of bread, for a friend of mine has arrived at my house from a journey and I have nothing to offer him,' and he says in reply from within, 'Do not bother me; […] my children and I are already in bed. I cannot get up to give you anything.' I tell you, if he does not get up to give him the loaves because of their friendship, he will get up to give him whatever he needs because of his persistence." (Lk 11:5-8)

Man was not made for defeat. The prince of this world, who seeks to thwart the designs of God, puts it into people's minds to give up. Our Lord, true lover of souls, teaches the value of persistence. The saints are people who trust in the will of God and persist in seeking it.

When Mother Teresa had her first heart attack, people thought her end was near. Her response was that she needed to bring her sisters to Albania and China, then she would "go home." People wagged their heads, "She'll never get into Albania." Albania was the strictest of the Communist countries, but before long, Mother Teresa established a convent of her sisters in Albania. And at the time of her death, she had convents both in Macao and Hong Kong, which at that time belonged to Communist China. Mother Teresa never took no for an answer.

To persist means resolutely to pursue the goals we have set in spite of opposition. We see this quite often in news stories of athletes who, despite setbacks and hardships, keep on struggling no matter the cost. We see it in soldiers who return home from a war severely wounded and yet, persisting through strenuous routines of recovery, overcome all odds to walk again. We see it in the Paralympics where those who are handicapped compete in sports.

Jesus' message is a call for me to be a disciple of persistence. A Christian is persistent. A Christian does not give up on life. If a friend can be imposed upon and coerced into giving bread in the middle of the night, how much more generous and gracious is God to give me what I need if approached with ardent and persistent desires! Jesus makes a startling claim: How much more will our heavenly Father give! Saints, as with Mother Teresa, take Jesus at his word. And so must I.

Father, you bless those who with ardent and persistent desires seek your blessings in this life. Help me to remain your faithful disciple who never gives up despite daily challenges to Gospel living.

The Need to Seek

Father Emmerich Vogt, O.P.

"And I tell you, ask and you will receive; seek and you will find; knock and the door will be opened to you. For everyone who asks, receives; and the one who seeks, finds; and to the one who knocks, the door will be opened."
(Lk 11:9-10)

Our blessed Lord teaches me that if I want to develop a vital prayer life, I must bring my will into conformity with the will of God. Jesus stressed this in the prayer he taught his disciples and in his own life, "Father... not my will but yours be done" (Lk 22:42). It is an essential aspect of my life of prayer. God is shown to be a fulfiller of *holy* desires, i.e., desires for his will.

In 2 Corinthians 12:7, Saint Paul prays three times that the Lord remove his "thorn in the flesh." Paul does receive, he does find, and the door is opened to him—but in a way he never expected. What was the response to his prayer? The Lord enlightened Paul that it was God's will that he bear with his thorn in the flesh, that it was intended by God to keep Paul humble and always close to Christ. Paul learned then to boast gladly of his weaknesses, because with grace weaknesses become strengths.

God knows what I need before I ask. My yearning and seeking for answers sensitizes me to the Spirit's influence. I learn both from Paul's experience and from this Lucan passage that God always answers my heartfelt prayers, but in ways that I never expect. An old saying goes, "I asked God for strength that I might achieve great things, yet I was given weakness that I might learn humbly to obey."

My life of prayer is part and parcel with my life of virtue. In asking God for something, I cannot ask only with my lips. I must always do the works Jesus expects of me: spurning worldly pleasures, giving to the poor, loving my enemies. These are the works my life should never be without. This must be the attitude of my heart when I seek answers to my prayers.

Father, all wise counselor, help me to seek and find your will in all things, never counting the cost of doing what is right and good.

179

The Need to Trust

Father Emmerich Vogt, O.P.

"What father among you would hand his son a snake when he asks for a fish? Or hand him a scorpion when he asks for an egg? If you then, who are wicked, know how to give good gifts to your children, how much more will the Father in heaven give the holy Spirit to those who ask him?" (Lk 11:11-13)

A snake instead of a fish, a scorpion instead of an egg—how cruel! Yet sometimes in my life it appears God is doing just that.

In remarking about the evil things people do, the Lord says to Saint Catherine, "Imagine what these people wouldn't do, if they found perfect pleasure in the world." Because of sin, there is suffering. Jesus comes, not to take away the suffering (the less suffering, the greater is man's evil) but to make the suffering redemptive.

Trust in God's providence teaches me that he would never allow anything to happen in the past that's not part of his loving plan for the future. He is a loving Father. And my love for others is but a participation in God's love, for I am not greater than God. He must love them more.

All of my life I have had the privilege of knowing a certain married couple with six children. I also knew the husband's only sibling, a sister. This sister never married and so always remained close both to her six nieces and nephews and their children. Years later we discovered she was not the man's sister. She was his mother. She was cruelly raped as a young teenager, and her parents thought it best to raise the child as their son instead of their grandson.

"Woe to that man by whom the Son of Man is betrayed," Jesus warns (Mt 26:24). Nonetheless, that betrayal leads to salvation. Nothing can thwart God's loving plan. Not only is the raped woman's son glad to be alive, so are his six children and his many grandchildren.

At times it may seem God is handing me a snake instead of fish, a scorpion and not an egg. Faith trusts in his plan. He sends his Spirit to bring a greater good out of the troubles of my life, a good that would never have happened had the troubles not happened.

Loving Father, help me to see your hand at work in my life. Give me the grace to trust in your loving and providential care for me.

The Need for Deliverance

Father Emmerich Vogt, O.P.

[Jesus] was driving out a demon [that was] mute, and when the demon had gone out, the mute person spoke and the crowds were amazed. Some of them said, "By the power of Beelzebul, the prince of demons, he drives out demons." Others, to test him, asked him for a sign from heaven. But he knew their thoughts.
(Lk 11:14-17a)

Note the irony in this passage which takes place as Jesus journeys to Jerusalem. Jesus' goal in going to Jerusalem is to give his life out of love for sinful man, wherein Satan will be defeated—and yet here Jesus is accused of healing in and through the prince of demons!

How does the "prince of demons" exercise his power over me? I am deeply wounded, both by original sin and by my personal sins. These wounds have made me vulnerable to the fear of being unlovable and the fear of dying. The message from the world, over which Satan is prince, is that love must be merited. The Gospel shows the lie. "God proves his love for us in that while we were still sinners Christ died for us" (Rom 5:8). God does not love me because I am lovely or lovable, because of something I have done, or because of who I am. His love exists, not on account of my character but on account of his. It is his grace that makes me lovable. Acting on that knowledge I can be delivered from the power of Satan.

Once I met a drug pusher in a big city. He led a very corrupt life. Then one day he met Mother Teresa's Missionaries of Charity and the encounter changed his life. He told me, "Father, the sisters knew what I was doing and they loved me anyway." This man found healing in and through love. He was loved "while still a sinner."

Being touched by Christ, either through his disciples or in and through the sacraments, can deliver me from the power of the "prince of this world." Freed from my preoccupation with what others think of me, I am free to love troubled and difficult people. In my sinfulness I am loved by Christ. I can now offer the same love to others and set them free from the prince of this world.

Heavenly Father and Lord of mercy, let your love shine through me that others may feel your loving touch and be delivered from the power of sin and death.

The Need for Unity

Father Emmerich Vogt, O.P.

[Jesus] said to them, "Every kingdom divided against itself will be laid waste and house will fall against house. And if Satan is divided against himself, how will his kingdom stand? For you say that it is by Beelzebul that I drive out demons. If I, then, drive out demons by Beelzebul, by whom do your own people drive them out? Therefore they will be your judges. But if it is by the finger of God that [I] drive out demons, then the kingdom of God has come upon you." (Lk 11:17b-20)

No kingdom at war with itself can survive an outside attack. If the devil is giving his power to someone in order to defeat himself, he cannot win. Jesus was not the only exorcist in his day, and so he asks of them if they were driving out Satan with Satan's own power? He thus confronts their slanderous attacks.

A common means of opposing an enemy is demonic slander. We see it all the time in today's news reports. It is a grave evil. Saint Paul points out that people nourish hostility because of their own evil deeds (cf. Col 1:21). And so it is with me in my own sinfulness. Any derogatory remarks toward others derives from my own sinfulness, causing me to think the worst of others. Knowing this to be the case, I can take an honest assessment of myself, and in all honesty admit that I am the source of my false interpretation of others.

Is there a civil war going on in me? Am I a kingdom divided? It is only too obvious when I see myself judging others and attributing entirely false motives to their behavior, or seeing myself concentrating on the speck in their eyes while avoiding the plank in my own (cf. Lk 6:41). With such division in the kingdom of my soul, there is no chance of my defeating the real enemy—the prince of this world. I need first to clean house.

Getting closer to Christ through the sacraments, especially the sacrament of reconciliation, which requires that I make amends, heals me from the inside, and I can let go of my compulsion to slander. Indeed, I can love my enemies and not hate them for what they've done. Such is the power of Christ's healing touch in my life.

Loving Father, make me sensitive to the promptings of your Spirit that I may guard against false judgment and detraction. May the healing touch of your Son free me to love as you love.

The Need to Gather with Christ

Father Emmerich Vogt, O.P.

"When a strong man fully armed guards his palace, his possessions are safe. But when one stronger than he attacks and overcomes him, he takes away the armor on which he relied and distributes the spoils. Whoever is not with me is against me, and whoever does not gather with me scatters." (Lk 11:21-23)

There is no place for neutrality in the Christian life. I am either for what is right, and therefore Christ and his kingdom, or I am against it. The devil is fully armed with all sorts of weapons for the destruction of a soul. The soul in the grasp of evil is his kingdom. Christ comes with his Power to despoil Satan. Satan has power over me because of slavish fear and arrogance. Pride causes me to place myself above others and fear keeps me from doing what is right.

This passage teaches that when the Word of God, the Giver of all good gifts and the Lord of all power, became man, he overcame the strong arm of Satan. Christ's Gospel is stronger than Satan's evil. I must embrace Gospel truth in the daily living out of my life and so disarm Satan.

In his incarnate life we see that God's distinctive greatness is manifest in powerlessness: the powerlessness of dying as a criminal on Golgotha. In essence we are shown that the least amount of love is already stronger than the greatest power of destruction. By loving my enemies and learning how to return blessings to those who are against me, I avail myself of the spoils Christ has rescued from Satan.

Can Christ save me from the strong arm of Satan? He could and he would, provided I incarnate his Gospel principles in my life: to turn the other cheek, to love my enemies, to do good to those who persecute me, to give alms to the poor, to instruct the ignorant, to guard against lust. I must live by Gospel principles, for the devil has no power over the strength of Christ.

If I have been dishonest and unloving, Christ can save me, but he cannot save me in my dishonesty. He forces no one to come to him. Absolute candor is required of me—and Satan is overcome once again.

All-powerful Father, you sent your Son to rescue me from Satan's grasp. I beg for the strength that comes from Gospel living. May I put you and your kingdom first in my life and be freed from Satan's grasp.

The Need for Asceticism

Father Emmerich Vogt, O.P.

"When an unclean spirit goes out of someone, it roams through arid regions searching for rest but, finding none, it says, 'I shall return to my home from which I came.' But upon returning, it finds it swept clean and put in order. Then it goes and brings back seven other spirits more wicked than itself who move in and dwell there, and the last condition of that person is worse than the first." (Lk 11:24-26)

What a great lesson for me that if I sweep the house of my soul clean—in my self-righteous need to feel good about myself, or to look good to others—I am doomed to be possessed by more and worse spirits than before. Any self-denial I practice in my spiritual life must not be for the sake of vanity. The cleansing of my soul through mortification is a dying that I might live, a refraining from evil that I may do good.

It is not uncommon for Christian people, influenced by cultural trends, to get involved in the latest fads to lose weight. Flip through a magazine, scan a newspaper, or watch the television ads and you see them everywhere—ads that promise quick and easy weight loss without diet or exercise. This industry makes millions promoting these diets. And yet everywhere we look, food indulgence is promoted. Gas stations even offer food! But often the purpose in dieting is simply health or vanity or a combination of both. This is not Christian mortification.

To die to evil—such as gluttony—is good but does not go far enough. I must turn my energy into doing good, not simply avoiding evil. If there is no direction to doing good into which my energy is turned, it is to be feared that evil will regain control. The unclean spirit that is cast out when I set my house in order—in my determination to deny myself—waits until he finds the house of the soul empty. Then he returns with seven worse spirits, and they enter in and my situation becomes worse. This is often the case with dieting, for example.

My hardest struggle is with self, because self is striving against self. The goal of my asceticism is to overcome self and to love more.

Loving Father, increase my desire to die to self that I may live more for you and share your love with those you put in my life.

The Need for True Blessedness

Father Emmerich Vogt, o.p.

While [Jesus] was speaking, a woman from the crowd called out and said to him, "Blessed is the womb that carried you and the breasts at which you nursed." He replied, "Rather, blessed are those who hear the word of God and observe it."
(Lk 11:27-28)

It is very common for people to seek their justification in those they are related to or descended from. "My son's a doctor!"; "My ancestors came over on the Mayflower"; "My cousin is the Mayor"—as if these relationships are enough to satisfy them. "We have Abraham as our father," Jesus' people boast. Jesus is not impressed. "And do not presume to say to yourselves, 'We have Abraham as our father.' For I tell you, God can raise up children to Abraham from these stones" (Mt 3:9). The privilege of my relationships avails me nothing where there is no virtuous life.

From my window late one night in a rectory in the downtown area of a big city, I heard a woman screaming. I ran downstairs and out the back door to discover a man, sorely inebriated, assaulting a woman, equally inebriated. His response to my attempts to intercede on the woman's behalf: "I'm Catholic!" Although an extreme example (yet a true one), nevertheless it demonstrates that people regard their position or relationships as of importance. Rather, true blessedness is found in hearing the good news of salvation, keeping it in a holy heart, and practicing it in a blameless life. This is the true dignity of the Blessed Virgin Mary, a dignity to which the Word of God is calling me. And this, too, is our Lady's call to me, "Do whatever he tells you" (Jn 2:5).

It is only when I surrender my need to impress others with my achievements or my relationships or my acts of devotion that I gain the humility to accept what is truly important: listening to the Word of God, meditating on it, and then seeking to live it. This is true blessedness and the path to lasting happiness and peace. The dignity to which God calls me is found in keeping his commandments and in being prepared for heaven.

Heavenly Father, I pray for the grace to find my dignity, not in human respect, but in carrying out your will on a daily basis. I now surrender my need to impress others.

The Need for the Sign of Faith

Father Emmerich Vogt, O.P.

While still more people gathered in the crowd, [Jesus] said to them, "This generation is an evil generation; it seeks a sign, but no sign will be given it, except the sign of Jonah. Just as Jonah became a sign to the Ninevites, so will the Son of Man be to this generation." (Lk 11:29-30)

Through two thousand years of lived Christianity there have been many signs given by heaven to confirm the Gospel. Christ's followers have been the privileged recipients of special signs from our Blessed Mother—as at Lourdes and Fatima. Do I need any more signs of God's loving providential care?

The people of Jesus' own day also had been blessed with many signs throughout their history. Even though privy to Jesus' cure of the mute, they seek more signs!

Jesus gives an everlasting sign—the sign of Jonah. Jonah was caught in a storm and was sacrificed to save the men on board from devastation and certain death. Jonah struggled three days and three nights. He beseeches God from whom salvation comes, and the Lord of salvation commands the whale, and Jonah rises to life on dry ground! This is the sign Jesus offers in his own life.

My enemies are threefold: the world, the flesh, and the devil. I look to the world for my happiness and self-worth. Christ offers me a far deeper happiness and genuine self-esteem. The sins of the flesh are the hardest for me to overcome. In their hold over me I lack the grace to love as God would have me. So I need to submit the flesh to a life-giving fast: fast of the eyes, fast of touch, etc. It is a death that redeems. The devil has power over me because of fear—my fear of dying and my fear of being unlovable. I need to die in order to rise, redeemed.

Christ has given the sign that takes away fear: he triumphed over the power of sin and death. He has shown me that my lovableness is on account of his character, not mine, and so I can accept myself as I am and be freed from my enemies: the world, the flesh, and the devil, freed by an asceticism of love.

Loving God and Father, through the sign of his death and Resurrection, your Son and my Lord has taught me the way to salvation. May I embrace this truth by all I say and do.

The Need for Repentance

Father Emmerich Vogt, O.P.

"At the judgment the queen of the south will rise with the men of this generation and she will condemn them, because she came from the ends of the earth to hear the wisdom of Solomon, and there is something greater than Solomon here. At the judgment the men of Nineveh will arise with this generation and condemn it, because at the preaching of Jonah they repented, and there is something greater than Jonah here." (Lk 11:31-32)

The references above are to Gentiles who were more attentive to the Word of God than were God's own people. These Gentiles were moved to repentance when they encountered the Word of God.

Years ago a young African-American woman was enrolled in our RCIA process. When she heard that our Lady had appeared to various people throughout the history of the Church, she was stunned. I showed her the old Hollywood movie about our Lady's appearances at Fatima. She was thrilled. It deepened her conversion. Also in the program was a young Japanese woman, a Buddhist. Her attraction to Catholicism was a photo of our Lady of Fatima that her Buddhist mother allowed her to buy. This attracted her to Catholicism.

When I see so many converts deeply in love with the truths of the Catholic faith, it puts me to shame. Through their conversion stories, I recognize that with the privilege of the faith comes the responsibility to live it.

Today's Lucan passage is a call for repentance. It fills me with the desire to recommit to my baptismal promises. These promises are renewed every Easter—in word but not necessarily in deed. Now I need to come up with a practical plan to live out these promises in my daily life. Today in true repentance I renew my promise to reject sin so as to live as a child of God. If there is something in my life that draws me away from God, it is sinful. I reject the glamour of evil and refuse to be mastered by sin. To do this I must commit to ascetical practices such as fasting on Fridays since the Lord died for my sins on that day. I reject Satan, the father of sin and the prince of darkness. The devil has power over me because of my fear of dying. I commit myself to dying to self that I may do God's will.

Father of heaven and earth, for so long you have sent the Mother of your Son to call us to repentance. Make me attentive to her voice that I may be the instrument of your grace and her devoted child.

The Need for the Light

Father Emmerich Vogt, O.P.

"No one who lights a lamp hides it away or places it [under a bushel basket], but on a lampstand so that those who enter might see the light. The lamp of the body is your eye. When your eye is sound, then your whole body is filled with light, but when it is bad, then your body is in darkness. Take care, then, that the light in you not become darkness. If your whole body is full of light, and no part of it is in darkness, then it will be as full of light as a lamp illuminating you with its brightness." (Lk 11:33-36)

It is a frightening experience to be in total darkness. One time when visiting Mammoth Cave, I was paralyzed with fear as the guide turned off all the lights leaving us in total darkness. I could not even see a hint of my hand waved in front of my eyes. Yet as frightening as physical darkness is, moral darkness is even more frightening.

The body depends on the eye to see the world. My heart depends on the light of faith to see as God sees. If my heart is darkened, nothing can turn out good. If it seems to me that the sun isn't shining, most probably the windows need cleaning.

The spiritual life is said to consist of three parts: the purgative, the illuminative, and the unitive. Eternal life, eternal happiness is my goal. But I'm wrapped in darkness because of sin. When I cooperate with grace and begin to purify my desires and control my senses, using them for whatever leads me to God and denying to them whatever keeps me from God, I begin to see. Purgation leads to illumination, and illumination to a deepened union with God, who is love. The more I experience God's love, the greater my desire to embrace purgation. If seeing something does not help me to love God, I pray for the grace not to see it. Likewise with hearing something. In this way I purge my senses of what is not God—and I am able to see what is hidden from me.

A man once commented to Mother Teresa, "How can you see God in someone who does evil?" Mother Teresa responded, "If you are clean of heart, you can see." The light of faith revealed to her that every person is created in the image of God. Faith gave her the grace to attend lovingly to that image, and love is what causes the evil person to emerge from the darkness.

Father, that I may see! I pray for the strength to cooperate with your grace for the cleansing of my soul that I may see as you see, that I may love as you love and so help others emerge from the darkness.

The Need for a Deep Interior Cleansing

Father Emmerich Vogt, O.P.

After [Jesus] had spoken, a Pharisee invited him to dine at his home. He entered and reclined at table to eat. The Pharisee was amazed to see that he did not observe the prescribed washing before the meal. The Lord said to him, "Oh you Pharisees! Although you cleanse the outside of the cup and the dish, inside you are filled with plunder and evil. You fools! Did not the maker of the outside also make the inside? But as to what is within, give alms, and behold, everything will be clean for you." (Lk 11:37-41)

For the Pharisee to omit the slightest detail of ritual cleansing was a serious offense. Jesus often reprimands the people for placing perfect ritual observance above moral goodness that springs from the inside—from the heart, and not from exterior observance. This behavior was not simply characteristic of the religious people of Jesus' day, but it is a common practice in every age.

In our parish I once met a married man who was proud to tell me that he grew up in a perfect family, where things were neat and orderly. For example, when you borrowed a pair of scissors, you opened the drawer, took the scissors out, *and closed the drawer.* Well, his wife was not like that. He came home from work one night and was horrified—and angry—to find his wife cooking *with every drawer and cabinet wide open!* There were other things she did that, to his mind, were not right. He couldn't cope. The poor man became an alcoholic.

The founders of Alcoholics Anonymous, in being honest about themselves, admitted that in addition to having the compulsion to drink, they had the compulsion to be right. I can see this compulsion in my own life. A need for things to go right; a need to be treated right; a need to look right; a need to worship right. What a fool! If only I were as particular about cleansing my soul as I am about having things right in my life. If I could have the same desire to be morally right, i.e., to cleanse my heart of all sin and all affection for sin, then I would be following the Lord's commands.

I can go to Holy Hour, daily Mass, pray novenas—all worthy practices—but if there is no interior conversion toward virtue, I am a noisy gong (1 Cor 13:1). It is mere religiosity as it was for the Pharisees in their religious practices.

Loving Father, guide me to put into practice the saving Mystery I celebrate each time I go to Mass so that my life may be a witness of the power of your grace.

189

The Need for Moral Character

Father Emmerich Vogt, O.P.

"Woe to you Pharisees! You pay tithes of mint and of rue and of every garden herb, but you pay no attention to judgment and to love for God. These you should have done, without overlooking the others. Woe to you Pharisees! You love the seat of honor in synagogues and greetings in marketplaces. Woe to you! You are like unseen graves over which people unknowingly walk."
(Lk 11:42-44)

No matter what their moral lives were like—neglecting justice and forgetting love—the Pharisees never omitted the tithe, while seeking worldly honors. This, too, is something with which I am tempted: the need to be thought well of, to have a place of honor so that I may feel good about myself. Such vanity. May the Lord deliver me from it and give me the soundness of moral character.

Very early in her new life as a Missionary of Charity, Mother Teresa was confronted by someone who said to her, "Do you know how many people are starving in the world, yet you help but a few?" She replied, "If I can take one person from the gutter and he dies being loved, then I am fulfilling God's will. God called me not to be successful but faithful." Do I accept that same call to be faithful? What I am in the eyes of God is what is of importance. How I am viewed in the "marketplace" is of little value.

When Jesus compares the Pharisees to people touching unnoticed graves, he is saying that they are unclean. The Levitical law (Nm 19:16) stipulates that to touch a grave made one unclean, even if the person did not know he had touched a grave. The Pharisees are unclean in their hypocrisy.

Jesus confronts me to assess honestly my dependence on externals as a way of living my faith, while ignoring the interior state of my heart. Am I lacking in charity and justice? There is an old expression, "Mr. Business went to church; he never missed a Sunday. Mr. Business went to hell for what he did on Monday." Do I seek to live the mystery I celebrate at holy Mass, the mystery of Christ's Passion, Death, and Resurrection? Am I willing to die to all that is not God and so rise to the newness of life that comes from the cross?

Gracious Father, in your providential care lead me to a renewal of heart that all my actions may be in conformity with your will.

The Need to Bear One Another's Burdens

Father Emmerich Vogt, O.P.

Then one of the scholars of the law said to [Jesus] in reply, "Teacher, by saying this you are insulting us too." And he said, "Woe also to you scholars of the law! You impose on people burdens hard to carry, but you yourselves do not lift one finger to touch them. Woe to you! You build the memorials of the prophets whom your ancestors killed. Consequently, you bear witness and give consent to the deeds of your ancestors, for they killed them and you do the building." (Lk 11:45-48)

How little things have changed in two thousand years as "experts" in the law continue to impose heavy burdens. Jesus reproves them for making the services of religion more burdensome, while neglecting to help them. Do my religious practices grace me with the ability to help bear others' burdens, or do I inflict heavy burdens upon them because of my needs and desires?

I saw a woman in a certain parish holding her small children to a fast she had decreed for her family while they mingled in the church hall with other families who were celebrating together with food and drink. She brought her children, but they couldn't participate in the fun of the event. Needless to say, as adults they turned away from the faith of their mother.

The essence of the prophetic message was to love mercy, to deal honestly with one's fellows, and secure rights for the widow and the orphan. In preaching against abuses, the prophets were often persecuted and even killed. The lawgivers of Jesus' day honored those prophets by building memorials in their honor, and yet they will persecute Jesus just as the prophets had been!

When I contemplate the moral beauty of the saints, I have the privilege of honoring them. But do I honor only with lip-service, practicing devotions like praying a novena to them with the self-serving motive of having my will done? And then do I go about my lukewarm Christian existence instead of seeking to imitate the virtues that stand out in the lives of the saints whom I honor? True devotion is never cold and withdrawn.

Whatever devotions I utilize, I must do so with the goal of imitating the message of the saints and leading a Christ-like existence. Otherwise in honoring the saints I am like the scholars of the law who honored the prophets while at the same time opposing their message.

Father of Life, you have called me to be of service to you and my neighbor. Help me to be a source of your love that I may help others with their daily burdens.

The Need for Reparation

Father Emmerich Vogt, O.P.

"Therefore, the wisdom of God said, 'I will send to them prophets and apostles; some of them they will kill and persecute' in order that this generation might be charged with the blood of all the prophets shed since the foundation of the world, from the blood of Abel to the blood of Zechariah who died between the altar and the temple building. Yes, I tell you, this generation will be charged with their blood!" (Lk 11:49-51)

All the prophets were precursors of the Messiah. Their preaching and teaching pointed to his coming as Savior of his people. And when he came, these same self-righteous followers of the law ridiculed him and put him to death. Now he holds them responsible even for the past.

Am I cognizant of the need to repair the misdeeds and sins of my past? Part of my recovery from the effects of sin in my life is to strive with ever greater zeal to cleanse my soul from the blemishes of my past life. Confession of sin is a sacrament that brings me God's forgiveness. To avail myself of that grace I must have a firm purpose to change, otherwise there is no forgiveness. And I must make amends. I am responsible for the harm that has come to others from my sins and I need to repair the damage I've done. The sacrament of reconciliation does not repair the past. I must make reparation. How?

A young father with his kids on a Saturday afternoon is playing ball in the back yard, when all of a sudden one boy sends the ball clear through the neighbors' picture window! The father leads the boys over to the neighbor to own up and to ask forgiveness. But the next week the same thing happens. Will the neighbor continue to forgive if there is no evidence shown of a sincere desire to change? Now if the man and his sons ask for forgiveness and move to the park down the street, they have demonstrated a firm purpose of amendment, of changing. But is that all? Aren't they responsible for repairing the damage they've done?

This is true of me in my moral life. My sins have caused damage. I go to confession and am sincere about amending my life, but the sacrament of confession does not repair the damage I've caused. I must make acts of reparation.

Provident Father, you have given me the great grace of atoning for my sins and for the sins of my family and friends. I beg you not to let me forget this great gift by which your mercy is extended through me, a repentent sinner.

The Need for the Key

Father Emmerich Vogt, O.P.

"Woe to you, scholars of the law! You have taken away the key of knowledge. You yourselves did not enter and you stopped those trying to enter." When [Jesus] left, the scribes and Pharisees began to act with hostility toward him and to interrogate him about many things, for they were plotting to catch him at something he might say. (Lk 11:52-54)

The key of knowledge was given by God to Moses in and through the law. The scholars of the law not only failed to live by that law, but they inhibited others from doing so. And now they reject the Lawgiver himself in the person of Jesus and plot against him.

God in and through his Son, Jesus, has left the key to his kingdom in the hands of Peter and his successors, whom I am bound to obey. Is my life in keeping with the wisdom of God as expressed in the teaching of his representatives on earth? Jesus and his bride are perfectly one. To hear the Church is to hear Jesus. Jesus opens to those who knock, gives to those who ask, but the asking and knocking must not be with words only but with deeds, as we see in the parable of the Last Judgment (Mt 25:31-46). Living the Gospel is often painful. It can be painful for me in my pride to ask forgiveness, to own up to something wrong I've done, to be loving to an enemy. These are the works my life should never be without. But the suffering that living the Gospel entails ultimately gives life.

A movie was made recently about the early life of Saint Josemaría Escrivá (*There Be Dragons*). It shows some of the horrors of the civil war that Escrivá witnessed in his native land. At one point Monsignor Escrivá encounters a young woman bearing terrible wounds inflicted on her in the course of the war. It was very moving to hear her whisper to Escrivá about God, "But I still love him!" When one can suffer and still love, one is imitating the sacrifice of Christ. This is the sacrifice that saves. It is the wisdom of God and the key to heaven.

Govern me by your wisdom, O Father, so that my soul may always be serving your law. Do not grant me what I ask or seek, if it offends your love, which should always live in me.

The Ceiling of the Confessional

Father James M. Sullivan, O.P.

Meanwhile, so many people were crowding together that they were trampling one another underfoot. [Jesus] began to speak, first to his disciples, "Beware of the leaven—that is, the hypocrisy—of the Pharisees. There is nothing concealed that will not be revealed, nor secret that will not be known. Therefore whatever you have said in the darkness will be heard in the light, and what you have whispered behind closed doors will be proclaimed on the housetops." (Lk 12:1-3)

The crowd is massive as it surrounds Jesus and his disciples. It is an awesome sight and yet Jesus remains perfectly unimpressed. He warns against being puffed up by false leaven, namely, that of the hypocritical Pharisees. Jesus is not opposed to true leaven, that which lifts up all that it touches. He simply wants that "raising up" to be genuine and long-lasting as opposed to short-lived and superficial.

The clue to finding this true leaven for our own lives can be found in Jesus' words about secrets, darkness, and closed doors. To the Catholic soul these words point to only one place: the confessional. It is in the confessional where we regularly receive the sacramental grace of God, which forgives our sins, heals us of sin's damage, and strengthens us for the future against those same temptations. That is the leaven for which our hearts hunger.

As we progress in the spiritual life we often come to realize that our sins are really anything but secret. We might think that others do not see them, but in fact they are revealed in almost everything that we do. Regular confession helps us to take account of our life and recognize where and when we have failed, how we have offended God, the ways in which we have hurt others. Regular confession helps us to be lifted up by God's grace to see the reality of our sins, not to be deflated by them but rather to be freed from them. Christ brings that freedom in the secrecy of the confessional, in the darkness behind its closed doors. Only Christ can be the leaven that lifts up our whole life. This truth is what we proclaim from the housetops in the revelation of our life in the light of a new day.

Loving Father, give me the desire to frequent the sacrament of reconciliation on a regular basis. Help me to avoid always false leaven in my life.

Freedom from Fear

Father James M. Sullivan, O.P.

"I tell you, my friends, do not be afraid of those who kill the body but after that can do no more. I shall show you whom to fear. Be afraid of the one who after killing has the power to cast into Gehenna; yes, I tell you, be afraid of that one. Are not five sparrows sold for two small coins? Yet not one of them has escaped the notice of God. Even the hairs of your head have all been counted. Do not be afraid. You are worth more than many sparrows." (Lk 12:4-7)

There is a terrifying scene in Walt Disney's *Fantasia*. Surprisingly, the scene itself seems to embody these words from Sacred Scripture and at the same time teaches us a lesson for a lifetime as if it were drawn from the very pages of a Catholic catechism.

In the animation that accompanies Modest Mussorgsky's "Night on Bald Mountain," a new Disney villain is introduced in the form of Chernabog, a demon who appears in all of his blackness calling forth the dead and other creatures of the night to terrorize the people of a local village. There is soon fire and calamity as the little town is engulfed in evil and all sorts of things that would cause fear to any normal person.

Believe it or not, but the answer to these fears is found in the very next scene that follows "Night on Bald Mountain," and that relief is in the words of Franz Schubert's "Ave Maria." The one thing that stops Chernabog from wreaking havoc is the first bell of the Angelus. After a night of terror, the peal of the Angelus bell causes all of the demons to stop, and as the volume of the bell increases, the demons begin to flee in their own terror because of what that bell means.

Simply put, it rings in the new age of the Incarnation, of God taking our human nature as his own, and becoming man for our salvation. This is where we find our freedom from fear, in Christ. This is how we live without fear, in Christ. The "Ave Maria" signals that the night is over and the darkness has been vanquished. The Blessed Virgin Mary is the Morning Star announcing the dawn of a new day, her Son, who casts out all fear.

Heavenly Father, free me from all fear by giving me the grace to meditate more profoundly on the lives of Jesus and Mary. Remind me always of your love.

Denying the Undeniable

Father James M. Sullivan, O.P.

"I tell you, everyone who acknowledges me before others the Son of Man will acknowledge before the angels of God. But whoever denies me before others will be denied before the angels of God. Everyone who speaks a word against the Son of Man will be forgiven, but the one who blasphemes against the holy Spirit will not be forgiven." (Lk 12:8-10)

The traditional way of understanding this passage interprets blasphemy against the Holy Spirit as being the denial that God can forgive my sins. It is a blasphemy in the sense that we are speaking falsely of God in limiting his power, while in truth he is all-powerful. If we do not believe that God can forgive our sins, then we will never be able to receive his forgiveness.

One way to think of the forgiveness of sin is looking out a window on a perfectly sunny day. Then after closing the blinds, pulling the curtains, shutting off all the lights in the room, we begin to curse God for the darkness in which we now find ourselves. So begins the long list of woes and complaints that we have about our lives. This never happened the way I wanted. That other thing was denied me. I still want this to take place.

The truth of forgiveness is that God has already forgiven us for all of the sins that we have or ever will commit. This is the great truth of Christ's salvific death on the cross. What is awaiting us, though, is the reception of that forgiveness—the opening of the blinds and curtains, and the turning on again of the lights. We receive God's forgiveness at definite moments in definite places. Regularly, and for all mortal sins, we receive his forgiveness in the sacrament of reconciliation. But we also receive his forgiveness when we receive Holy Communion. We receive his forgiveness when we perform an act of charity for someone in need. These are the times when we are opened by God's grace to receive his grace, when the curtains part and the sunlight comes in.

It is simply undeniable that God loves us and forgives us. Sadly, however, what we can deny is our ability to receive that forgiveness.

Most merciful Father, make me receptive always to the grace of your forgiveness so that I might never sin against the Holy Spirit in any way.

The Best Defense

Father James M. Sullivan, O.P.

"When they take you before synagogues and before rulers and authorities, do not worry about how or what your defense will be or about what you are to say. For the holy Spirit will teach you at that moment what you should say."
(Lk 12:11-12)

Throughout the twelfth chapter of Saint Luke's Gospel, Jesus is inviting us to a greater trust in himself while necessarily having a lesser confidence about our own ability. This is not to dismiss the individual talents that God has given to each of us, but rather to keep them in perspective, and also to be reminded of the One who gave us these gifts in the first place.

One recent phenomenon in the Church is the rise of apologetics, the art of explaining and defending the teachings of the Church. While study of the faith is a necessary part of growing in the faith, it is especially necessary in growing in love for the Lord, and this love is the surest defense of the faith that we have.

There are times when we have to say something to defend the faith, and for that Christ assures us of the guidance of the Holy Spirit. "For the Holy Spirit will teach you at that moment what you should say." But for most times in our lives, it is not our words that the Lord needs, but our witness.

A missionary priest was being prepared for a new assignment. He was to study the language and customs of a people that had never been evangelized. In the midst of his preparations, though, his superiors decided to send him earlier than planned—he was not ready, he did not know enough, he had not even learned their language. In obedience he went to his new assignment and realized almost immediately that all he had to offer them was his example of life. He had nothing else. And that is exactly how he preached the faith. Over time he had learned their language and their ways, but that was only after he had taught them his, without using any words.

Almighty Father, defend me by the power of the Holy Spirit. Make me an instrument for your truth and love in the world around me.

Telling Jesus What to Do

Father James M. Sullivan, O.P.

Someone in the crowd said to [Jesus], "Teacher, tell my brother to share the inheritance with me." He replied to him, "Friend, who appointed me as your judge and arbitrator?" Then he said to the crowd, "Take care to guard against all greed, for though one may be rich, one's life does not consist of possessions."
(Lk 12:13-15)

Jesus continually offers us divine intimacy. He desires to make us one with himself so that we can share in all that is properly his. We become co-heirs with him and so through him and in the Holy Spirit we begin to call God our Father.

This divine intimacy, however, does not make us a divine Person of the Trinity. It does not afford us god-like qualities such as omnipotence or omniscience. It does not allow us to begin to tell Jesus what to do. Yet too often we may find ourselves in prayer doing just that. Before we dismiss those "self-fashioned" commands, though, maybe we can learn something from them.

Think of the examples in the Gospel where those closest to Jesus tell him what to do. What happens in turn is that he tells them what to do, and even something true about themselves—perhaps something they never would have otherwise known. Martha tells Jesus to have Mary help her with the housework. Jesus tells Martha she is anxious and worried about many things. Peter tells Jesus to leave him, after the miraculous catch of fish, because he is a sinful man. Jesus tells Peter to stop being afraid. Then there is today's passage of the brother telling Jesus to settle a dispute over money. Jesus tells him to watch out for greed. Jesus responds not to the request that is made, but more so to the needs of the person's heart—Martha's need for prayer, Peter's need for courage, the brother's need for generosity.

Telling Jesus what to do may have one benefit: it opens our mouth and our heart to the Lord. He then can tell us what to do and what we really need. Of course, all of this only happens if our ears are open too.

Eternal Father, open my ears to the voice of Christ so that my soul might be filled with whatever grace I need to be faithful to you.

The Order of Ordering

Father James M. Sullivan, O.P.

Then [Jesus] told [the crowd] a parable. "There was a rich man
whose land produced a bountiful harvest. He asked himself,
'What shall I do, for I do not have space to store my harvest?'
And he said, 'This is what I shall do: I shall tear down my barns
and build larger ones. There I shall store all my grain and other
goods and I shall say to myself, "Now as for you, you have
so many good things stored up for many years,
rest, eat, drink, be merry!"'' (Lk 12:16-19)

Ordering the desires of our lives is not an easily accomplished task. We want many things and seemingly we want them all at once. We also want competing and conflicting things at times too, and this is where the presence of sin is so often found. If the rich man had known that his night ahead would have been other than what he had planned, he might have planned it differently. He might have made the virtuous choice of generosity, or he might have made sinful choices and chosen debauchery.

In our own lives we might not often think that each of our actions, no matter how small, is making a choice of what we desire more than something else. We choose to stay after Mass for a mere minute to offer a prayer of thanksgiving, and thus we grow in our desire for God. We choose to keep the wrong change that was given to us at the coffee store, and thus we grow in our desire for money. The actions we choose all affect us in some way.

While on summer vacations my sisters and I would often play (and they would cheat) at a card game called Rack-O. Ten cards, numbered anywhere from one to sixty, are dealt and you insert them upright into your rack in the order they are dealt. It is a mess of numbers. The goal is to order them by choosing a new card and replacing one of the "out of order" cards.

This game is a great deal like our lives in that we are given a certain "starting deck" in life. Some people find themselves in more disorder than others, but the challenge is the same: to choose the right card to go in the right place. Making the sixty card the first in the order of cards will guarantee a loss just as choosing anything but God as first.

Loving Father, order the desires of my heart. Free me from the disorder of my sins so that I may always choose you above all the goods of this world.

God Always Provides

Father James M. Sullivan, O.P.

"But God said to [the rich man], 'You fool, this night your life will be demanded of you; and the things you have prepared, to whom will they belong?' Thus will it be for the one who stores up treasure for himself but is not rich in what matters to God."
(Lk 12:20-21)

Throughout these verses of the Gospel of Saint Luke, Jesus is calling us to rely on him for everything, and he is giving us his answer to all the possible objections we might raise. "I need this or that to get a better job." "I really need to have more money in order to compete." "We need to be financially secure for twenty years after retirement."

To all of these objections, Jesus simply responds: "Do not worry about your life and what you will eat, or about your body and what you will wear. If even the smallest things are beyond your control, why are you anxious about the rest? Do not worry anymore. Can any of you by worrying add a moment to your lifespan?"

One of the most fruitful Lents I ever had was one in which I rotated throughout the forty days a penance of prayer, fasting, or almsgiving. I did not decide beforehand what the specific penance would be, such as an extra rosary or one of the psalms for a day of prayer, just that it would be a day for extra prayer. The same was true for fasting or almsgiving.

What was truly remarkable was that I did not even need to plan it out. On a day of almsgiving, for example, some request would come to me either in person or in the mail asking for some material help. On a day for fasting, some sacrifice was obvious, as was the addition of some prayer for a day of prayer.

Living in the knowledge that God always provides whatever it is that we need, frees us in a way like nothing else. The lesson that Lent was more in the letting go of planning things than it was in the actual penances of each day.

Heavenly Father, free me from all worries of this world, and give me a greater confidence in you and your will for my life. Provide always what I truly need.

Self-Storage Units

Father James M. Sullivan, O.P.

[Jesus] said to [his] disciples, "Therefore I tell you, do not worry about your life and what you will eat, or about your body and what you will wear. For life is more than food and the body more than clothing. Notice the ravens: they do not sow or reap; they have neither storehouse nor barn, yet God feeds them. How much more important are you than birds!"
(Lk 12:22-24)

Driving on any highway no doubt brings with it the sighting of self-storage units. Fields of them at times, neatly packed together in rows, and awaiting their owners' planting or harvesting. "What is in them all?" I often think. "How can people have so much stuff that it will not fit in their closets, attics, and basements?"

Storage Wars is a popular cable television show that reveals exactly what is in these storage units! And on this show these storage units are being auctioned off to the highest bidder, because for one reason or another they have been abandoned by their owners. It remains a mystery to the bidder what is exactly inside of these units, but they nonetheless try their luck, bid away, and get the reward or the revenge of the previous owner.

Obviously all of us need some storage, a place for winter clothes, another place for Christmas decorations, and another place for the lawn furniture. But if we were to be honest, do we still have too much stuff? Do we keep things for too long just in case we might need it again at some time? Do we need these things for a false sense of security or an overbearing growth of greed?

It seems from this passage that Jesus wants us to store up nothing in this world which does not help us live life in the next world. Instead of sweaters and scarves, we can store up chastity and compassion. Instead of wreaths and ornaments, we can store patience and generosity. Instead of umbrellas and deck chairs, we can store up faith, hope, and charity.

I would not wish *Storage Wars* to go off the air, but if we all began to store up only treasure for heaven, the surprises inside our self-storage units might be even greater!

Most merciful Father, fill me with the treasures of heaven so that each of my possessions here on earth will only help me find my way to you.

True Thanksgiving

Father James M. Sullivan, O.P.

"Can any of you by worrying add a moment to your lifespan? If even the smallest things are beyond your control, why are you anxious about the rest? Notice how the flowers grow. They do not toil or spin. But I tell you, not even Solomon in all his splendor was dressed like one of them. If God so clothes the grass in the field that grows today and is thrown into the oven tomorrow, will he not much more provide for you, O you of little faith?" (Lk 12:25-28)

One of the best remedies for worry or anxiety in the spiritual life is gratitude. Giving thanks to God possesses a quality that wards off undue concern for the future. We are so grateful for what we have in the present that we are not even aware of what we do not yet have, or what we are missing.

The pilgrims of that first Thanksgiving Day are a good example of this grateful mentality. Half of their "fleet" never left England. Their other ship, the *Speedwell*, had to remain behind, and they had to sell off a great deal of their cargo so that they could all fit onto the *Mayflower*.

Half of the one hundred and two passengers were not even "pilgrims"; they were referred to as the "strangers" by William Bradford (later, the governor of the Plymouth Colony for thirty-three years) while he saved the name "saints" for those who were the true pilgrims. More than half of the pilgrims' congregation in Holland, their land of English exile, could not travel or chose to remain behind. Half of the one hundred and two passengers died that first winter, in the dead of winter as many as three a day at its worst.

Even with half of what they intended, half of what they planned, half of what they had hoped for taken away, lost, or never given at all, they were still thankful. They thanked God for what they had and, it seems, even for what they had not. They were not thanking him because they liked what was happening to them, but rather because they loved him.

Thanksgiving Day can still conjure up images of pilgrims and Indians, of turkeys, squash, and cranberry sauce. But what it most especially means is thanking God today and not worrying about tomorrow. If he provided today for all we need, he will surely do the same tomorrow.

Almighty Father, today I thank you for all that you have given me. I offer it back to you for the building up of your kingdom here on earth.

Tell That to the Bank

Father James M. Sullivan, O.P.

"As for you, do not seek what you are to eat and what you are to drink, and do not worry anymore. All the nations of the world seek for these things, and your Father knows that you need them. Instead, seek his kingdom, and these other things will be given you besides." (Lk 12:29-31)

There are some verses of Scripture that I would love to attach to the non-payment of bills and see how long it takes the collection agency or the police to show up at the door. This is one of those verses. Christ is not calling us away from responsibility in the world, but he is helping us to recognize that it is just the world. It is not heaven, and therefore we live our life here on earth *for* our life in heaven.

There are two extreme pitfalls in the spiritual life that become very common as one progresses in sanctification. One is believing that nothing that I do matters; God's will has power over everything and therefore he should feed me, clothe, and shelter me. Never mind the fact that I refuse to look for a job, continue to use my credit card without regard for debt, and blame everyone else for my problems.

The other extreme is just as damaging. I believe that everything that I do matters, to the point that it is determinative for God's will. He does things because I make it possible for him to act. I have to work hard, pray hard, and make sacrifices that are truly heroic if I want things in my life to change.

The problem with both of these extremes is that they exclude God's grace from my life. They rob me of a true sense of responsibility and of personal worth. They leave me with no other option but "giving up." The first pitfall's "giving up" comes earlier, and the second's is through exhaustion, but it is the same ending for both.

To paraphrase a familiar quote of Saint Teresa of Ávila: Pray as if everything depends on God; work as if everything depends on yourself. Keeping the right mind when we need to make the right decisions in life is only possible by God's grace: "Seek his kingdom, and these other things will be given you besides."

Eternal Father, give me all the things that you know that I need. Help me to seek your kingdom every day, and fill me with your grace.

The Treasures of the Kingdom

Father James M. Sullivan, O.P.

"Do not be afraid any longer, little flock, for your Father is pleased to give you the kingdom. Sell your belongings and give alms. Provide money bags for yourselves that do not wear out, an inexhaustible treasure in heaven that no thief can reach nor moth destroy. For where your treasure is, there also will your heart be." (Lk 12:32-34)

In the life of Saint Dominic there was one moment in particular that must have broken his heart. It was August 15, 1217. Saint Dominic was dispersing his brethren to the major cities of Europe to spread the Order of Preachers beyond the roots of its foundation in south-eastern France.

It must have been heartbreaking, not for the fact of being separated from the men with whom he made this foundation, but particularly because one of them would not "go" in the manner that Saint Dominic had asked him. Saint Dominic sent out his band of preachers the same way Christ did: without money. They were to rely fully on God.

That was acceptable to all the friars except for one, John of Navarre. He refused to leave without a moneybag. Saint Dominic pleaded with him, but John refused and so Saint Dominic begged him with tears. John still refused. Saint Dominic, being the loving father that he was, gave in to John's request and let him take money with him on his journey.

Jesus gives us the quickest way to know the reality of our heart—that is, the treasures in our lives. What are they, really? Who are they, really?

The wisdom of Saint Dominic in letting John take money was born of the saint's knowledge of the human heart. It is not instantaneous in changing. It takes time and it takes grace to bring about conversion. Saint Dominic knew that it would not happen that day. A conversion did happen, though, in John's life. Where and when is not known, but for the rest of his years in the Order he confessed openly that he was sinful in his greed on August 15, 1217. Christ had become his treasure once again.

Loving Father, open my heart to your treasures. Help me to be generous with all that you have given me so that you may be the one lasting treasure in my life.

The Sound of Arrival

Father James M. Sullivan, O.P.

"Gird your loins and light your lamps and be like servants who await their master's return from a wedding, ready to open immediately when he comes and knocks. Blessed are those servants whom the master finds vigilant on his arrival. Amen, I say to you, he will gird himself, have them recline at table, and proceed to wait on them. And should he come in the second or third watch and find them prepared in this way, blessed are those servants." (Lk 12:35-38)

Whatever nights the babysitter would come over to watch me and my brother, our parents' arrival home was always accompanied by typical sounds that we could hear from our beds. There were the sounds of the car driving up to the house, the shutting off of the engine, the closing of the car doors, and the opening of our front door. There were also the sounds of the babysitter shutting off the television and the cleaning up of the living room. Then there would be some talking (and the exchange of money, I assume) and then the front door again as the babysitter would leave to walk home. The last sound of the night would be my mother walking down to our room to look in on us, while we each pretended to be asleep.

With each of the sounds of our parents' arrival, our anticipation grew, but that anticipation was disappointed at times. For example, many cars might have parked on the street that night. If it were only one car door that closed, then we knew it was not our parents. If it were two car doors but no front door, then we knew it must have been a neighbor. The difficulty of waiting is simply not knowing the exact moment. But somehow all of the previous disappointments made the joy of their arrival all the greater. We had seemingly waited for ever for them to get home, and when they finally did, the time we waited seemed as nothing.

"Blessed are those servants whom the master finds vigilant on his arrival." Jesus tells us to wait for him with all of our attention. We are to remain vigilant and watchful. There might be times, though, when we expect him and he does not seem to come to us, but the assurance of Christ is that he is always coming to us. We perhaps just need to listen for the sound of that arrival.

Heavenly Father, help me to hear your arrival in each instance in my life so that I might be assured of your presence and serve you as a faithful servant.

The Wonder of Vigilance

Father James M. Sullivan, o.p.

"Be sure of this: if the master of the house had known the hour when the thief was coming, he would not have let his house be broken into. You also must be prepared, for at an hour you do not expect, the Son of Man will come."
(Lk 12:39-40)

The best commercial I've seen recently is one in which the expressions of children are captured on film as they find out that they are going to Disney World. My favorite is one of a little girl with her littler sister being told by their father of their upcoming trip. The littler sister just stands there frozen with joy with dazed eyes and a huge smile. The older sister stares at her father with an even bigger smile on her face. She is full of excitement, as she begins to jump up and down. She then asks her father in complete seriousness: "Daddy, is this true?"

Somehow this little girl could ask no more important question. She did not ask, "When are we leaving?" "Who is coming with us?" "Can I take my friend?" She just wanted to know: "Is this true?" "Could this be true?" "How is this true?"

Christ's command of vigilance is not born of obedience. It does not come from will power or forcing ourselves into something. This vigilance comes forth from wonder. It comes from amazement of what the Lord has done in our lives and in anticipation of what he will do next. We are always prepared for him if we know that we can never be fully prepared for what he has in store for us next.

"You also must be prepared, for at an hour you do not expect, the Son of Man will come." We await his coming just as that little girl began to await her trip to Disney World. We imagine all of the blessings that the Lord will bestow upon us, all of the graces that we will receive, all of the sins from which we will be healed. We await the Lord's coming with longing, not simply for what he will do for us, but longing just for him.

"Is this true?" Nothing else is more true.

Most merciful Father, keep me always convinced of the truths of my faith. Make me prepared for the coming of your Son simply by sheer wonder.

The Property of the Lord

Father James M. Sullivan, O.P.

Then Peter said, "Lord, is this parable meant for us or for everyone?" And the Lord replied, "Who, then, is the faithful and prudent steward whom the master will put in charge of his servants to distribute [the] food allowance at the proper time? Blessed is that servant whom his master on arrival finds doing so. Truly, I say to you, he will put him in charge of all his property." (Lk 12:41-44)

There is an account from the life of Saint Lawrence that captures the essence of this passage from Saint Luke's Gospel. A certain Roman official had threatened Saint Lawrence with death unless he turned over to him all the treasures of the Church. Saint Lawrence, a deacon who had been entrusted with the care of the Vatican's treasury, asked for a few days to get it all together. Saint Lawrence arrived as scheduled for his meeting with a mass of people surrounding him. The official asked for the treasures, and the saint pointed to the poor and the sick that he had brought with him. The official was not amused, yet Saint Lawrence could not have been more serious. The saint was martyred but the treasures were protected.

If there is any sense of a treasure in the Church, it is the treasure of the human person believing in Jesus Christ. Nothing is of more value to the Lord than one soul who comes to him seeking mercy and a new life in his grace.

Yes, the Church does have "prime real estate" throughout the world, it has golden chalices, and precious jewels. It possesses art from every age of the Church's existence and classics of literature, architecture, and knowledge from every people it has evangelized. Yet none of these treasures—not one of them—measures up to the real wealth the Church possesses in one person.

We likewise in our own lives have many possessions and treasures, but none of them adds up to the value of one person: our spouse, our children, our parents, our friends. Even people we do not know well are more valuable than the possessions we have had for a lifetime.

Saint Lawrence was not willing to give away the riches of the Church to the Roman official. He just wanted to be sure that the Roman official knew how rich the Church really was.

Almighty Father, help me always to treasure the people in my life, those whom you have entrusted to me to remind me of your love, both given and received.

Home or Away

Father James M. Sullivan, O.P.

"But if that servant says to himself, 'My master is delayed in coming,' and begins to beat the menservants and the maidservants, to eat and drink and get drunk, then that servant's master will come on an unexpected day and at an unknown hour and will punish him severely [...]. The servant who was ignorant of his master's will but acted in a way deserving of a severe beating shall be beaten only lightly. Much will be required of the person entrusted with much, and still more will be demanded of the person entrusted with more." (Lk 12:45-46, 48)

One of the sad situations that sin often leads us to is the false notion that we can divide our life into different subsections, each with its own code of behavior: "My master is delayed in coming." We can falsely believe that this is my private life and that is my public life. I can choose to do different things depending on who is around me at the time. In truth, all we are confirming is our distance from God: This is my "supposed life" with Christ and that is my life without him.

Christ wants the union we have with him to be the union we have with everyone, in the sense that the love which binds us to Christ draws other people to him through us. There are no times when I am on the clock for Christ and others when I am not. So, whether or not the Master is home or away, my behavior is the same. In truth, my whole life is seen as one, not little bits tied together somehow.

In some icons of the archangels, Saints Michael, Gabriel, and Raphael are depicted in a certain manner and order. Saint Michael is dressed as a soldier indicating military authority, Saint Gabriel is dressed as a prince indicating civil authority, and Saint Raphael is dressed as a priest indicating religious authority. Each of those depictions can easily be deduced from the archangels' appearances in the pages of Sacred Scripture. What is unique, however, about these icons is the placement of Raphael. He is in the center because religious authority is the highest authority and that which is to be followed more than any other. "Much will be required of the person entrusted with much, and still more will be demanded of the person entrusted with more."

Eternal Father, you have given me much in my belonging to Christ. Give me even more so that I might always act in accord with your authority in my life.

The Fire of Baptism
Father James M. Sullivan, O.P.

"I have come to set the earth on fire, and how I wish it were already blazing! There is a baptism with which I must be baptized, and how great is my anguish until it is accomplished!" (Lk 12:49-50)

Fire is often a source of danger, yet in the spiritual life it is more often seen as a source for strength and purity. It is in this sense that Christ describes the force of fire in this passage.

I do not often save forwarded e-mails, jokes, cartoons, articles on every topic imaginable, but one e-mail caught my eye. It was an explanation about Malachi 3:3 describing how the Lord sits before us as a refiner of silver. In this scriptural example we are the silver; the flame and the fire refine us; and the Lord, of course, is the refiner. Each of these three "characters" is necessary.

Most likely, all of us have experienced the purifying fire of the Lord. It could be times of suffering, loss, dryness in prayer, or even a weakening of our faith. Why does the Lord not save us from these "flames"? What are we supposed to gain from all of this "fire"? It seems that the answer itself is found in the midst of the flames and the fire.

When a refiner has to purify silver he has to hold it to the hottest part of the flame. He does this so that he can guarantee all of its impurities have been burned off. He personally has to hold it there as well, because if it is unattended it might be left in too long and the silver itself would be lost. And how does the refiner know that all of the impurities are burned off? He can begin to see his own reflection in the silver.

The fire that purifies us, however, also causes pain. We have to sacrifice many good things so that we can love all the more. The baptism which Jesus offers, though, comes not only with the promise of restoring the image of God to us, but also the cooling and refreshing presence of water.

Loving Father, set me on fire with love for Christ and his Church. Make me a vessel of love for the world purified by the flames of your Holy Spirit.

The Divisive Peace

Father James M. Sullivan, O.P.

*"Do you think that I have come to establish peace on the earth?
No, I tell you, but rather division. From now on a household of
five will be divided, three against two and two against three;
a father will be divided against his son and a son against his
father, a mother against her daughter and a daughter against
her mother, a mother-in-law against her daughter-in-law
and a daughter-in-law against her mother-in-law."*
(Lk 12:51-53)

It is perhaps not a stretch to imagine a mother-in-law not getting along with her daughter-in-law, but a mother and her daughter are a different story. In fact, Jesus' reference to the division in a family sadly might not be all that surprising these days anyway. But what remains at the heart of this Gospel passage is that Christ alone can bring peace—Christ alone is the peace and unity for which we long. There is nothing else but him who can hold our lives, our families together.

A famous quote from Saint Augustine reminds us: "Peace is not the absence of war, but the tranquility of order." In other words, you do not just have a wonderful family reunion because no one throws food at each other in a fit of rage (which, by the way, had happened for the past seventeen years), but rather because as a family you celebrate a day together and share your lives in a more meaningful way.

The "tranquility of order" to which Saint Augustine refers is first the order within myself—the ordering of my emotions and passions, the ordering of my thoughts and opinions. This ordering within myself due to his grace and my fidelity to him brings his order to everything that is around me. The offer of "family peace" then starts with peace with God—with peace within myself. The division that Christ calls me to face is the clear division between sin and sanctity in my life. Too often we live blind to our own disorder, and yet bemoan the fact that those around us lack the virtues we think they need to have.

Christ always shows us that false peace is no peace at all. Only when he is in our midst can we have lasting peace.

Heavenly Father, bring peace to my life, to my family, and to my world. Free me from all division and unite me all the more to Jesus Christ.

The "Whether" of Our Lives

Father James M. Sullivan, O.P.

[Jesus] also said to the crowds, "When you see [a] cloud rising in the west you say immediately that it is going to rain—and so it does; and when you notice that the wind is blowing from the south you say that it is going to be hot—and so it is. You hypocrites! You know how to interpret the appearance of the earth and the sky; why do you not know how to interpret the present time?" (Lk 12:54-56)

I had stopped one blustery night to fill up the gas tank. I was tired and the trip had just begun. I was in no mood to stop. As I waited for the next available pump I noticed that one pump was free. Why had no one else chosen it? I thanked God for my good fortune and drove over to it. As I went to put the pump into the gas tank it wouldn't fit. I thought, what's wrong now?! Did something get stuck in the gas tank? What's the problem here? The nozzle just would not fit in, no matter how hard I tried, and I did try pretty hard. Then for some unknown reason I just happened to look up at the sign above the pump itself: Diesel Fuel. I did not know it at the time, but luckily diesel gas pumps are made not to fit into regular gas tanks—good thing, too!

Jesus became man so that it would be obvious to all of us how to get to heaven—namely, through him. Just like the gas station and this Gospel passage, however, we have to read the signs, and usually the signs are pretty obvious.

God is a mystery, but he is also obvious in some ways to those with faith. We certainly will not know him perfectly as he knows himself, but we will know him perfectly according to our own abilities for ever in heaven. God has chosen to reveal himself to us so that we might know him. The "whether" of our lives is not whether or not we will ever figure out the mystery of God, but rather it is whether we will live by that mystery, looking for all of his signs and following them. Sometimes those signs are right there in front of us, just waiting to be noticed.

Most merciful Father, thank you for revealing yourself to me and for the gift of faith. Fill me with a great faith so that I might always see your signs in my life.

Great Power

Father James M. Sullivan, O.P.

"Why do you not judge for yourselves what is right? If you are to go with your opponent before a magistrate, make an effort to settle the matter on the way; otherwise your opponent will turn you over to the judge, and the judge hand you over to the constable, and the constable throw you into prison. I say to you, you will not be released until you have paid the last penny."
(Lk 12:57-59)

I know that he is not the most often quoted "father" of the Church, mainly because he is only an "uncle," but still one quote of his to his young nephew, Peter Parker, stands out among all the others: "With great power comes great responsibility." Thus Uncle Ben reminds Spiderman of the life that is before him.

Words from a comic book or movie are not all that important when weighed against the treasure of our faith, yet these words do highlight something true about our faith. We have been given a gift that is literally beyond this world; we have a power and a responsibility because of what has been given to us, of what has been revealed to us.

Our faith unites us here on earth with the loving God whom we profess to be Father, Son, and Holy Spirit. He has given us his words in Sacred Scripture and his Word incarnate as our Savior. He has promised the forgiveness of our sins through the cross of his Son, and has filled us with the power of his Holy Spirit. He has given us the Church and the graces of the sacraments that flow through this Church. He has offered us eternal union with him in the joys of heaven.

There is no aspect of our life that our faith is not meant to transform, even legal proceedings such as the one Jesus mentions above. Because of the power of our faith, we have a responsibility to use it in a way that conforms the world more perfectly to Christ, and that helps others to come to an encounter with Christ because of the way that I live my life. Living according to the world's standard just robs us of the power of our faith.

Uncle Ben might have taught catechism class after all.

Almighty Father, help me to use the power of my faith for the good of your name and the building up of your kingdom here on earth.

Jesus Has a Vision for Us

Douglas Bushman

At that time some people who were present there told [Jesus] about the Galileans whose blood Pilate had mingled with the blood of their sacrifices. He said to them in reply, "Do you think that because these Galileans suffered in this way they were greater sinners than all other Galileans? By no means! But I tell you, if you do not repent, you will all perish as they did!" (Lk 13:1-3)

From beginning to the end, Jesus calls his disciples to conversion. It is because he has a vision for us, an ideal "me" that he desires to see realized. His Passion confirms how intense that desire is. It is said that the greatest of Renaissance artists, Michelangelo, did not consider himself a creator of his sculptures. When viewing a block of marble he would envision a form as if it were trapped inside. The *Pietà*, the *David*, begin as imprisoned shapes, and his task is to liberate them by removing all that does not belong, all that obscures the essential form and keeps it hidden. Conversion is like that. Jesus is the divine sculptor, his love is the chisel, and his cross the mallet that powers each strike of love to take away what covers over the ideal "me" that he envisions. Only, unlike marble, which must be forced to relinquish the form it holds captive, we are called to cooperate in the process. And so conversion begins with accepting the Artist's sketch, his vision for our fulfillment. There is no more profound way to die to ourselves than to redefine what we consider to be our ultimate happiness.

The obstacle to this ultimate happiness is called sin. Sin is everything that veils the ideal "me" envisioned by God. This is why sin can only be known for what it is in contrast to the ideal, the perfect "me" that our divine Sculptor desires to manifest to the world. Conversion, then, begins with the identification of all that extra weight of marble that we carry and that conceals the ideal. In today's reading, Jesus confronts perhaps the greatest obstacle to identifying sin, namely, speculation about the sin of others. God has given us our own chisel to cooperate with his. It is called the conscience, and our consciences are made only for chipping away at our own marble, not that of others.

Eternal Father, I thank you for your purifying love, for the gift of conscience, and for your great vision for my fullest happiness. Mold me, shape me according to your wisdom.

Catastrophes Are a Call to Conversion

Douglas Bushman

"Or those eighteen people who were killed when the tower at Siloam fell on them—do you think they were more guilty than everyone else who lived in Jerusalem? By no means! But I tell you, if you do not repent, you will all perish as they did!"
(Lk 13:4-5)

Jesus does not dodge the difficult question of death. Rather, the finality of death is a call to conversion, as in the parables of Dives and Lazarus (Lk 16:19-31) and the man who built huge barns to store a great harvest (Lk 12:16-21). Jesus confronts us with the finality of death to elicit our longing for eternal life. His own death is the unsurpassed call, a divine plea to come to our senses and to get a proper perspective on life.

Reports of increased church attendance following the terrorist attacks of 9/11 confirm that catastrophes, especially fatal ones, move people to turn to God. This is a very good thing. But it is a better thing to remain close to God always and to be prepared for catastrophes before they happen. This is the point Jesus makes when he calls his listeners to repent lest their death take them by surprise. He challenges us to be ready for death by engaging in conversion. Non-repentance will not result in being crushed by a tower, but it will guarantee that one is caught off guard when death comes.

To be prepared for death is the fruit of conversion. Conversion brings peace of conscience because it is always a matter of putting the truth first. Those who live in the truth need not fear a final judgment by the truth, because they have already submitted themselves to truth's judgment. For there is one thing only that defies the axiom, "You can't take it with you." We cannot take across the frontier of death what we have accumulated in terms of wealth, power, or prestige. But we cannot not take our consciences with us. With his solemn warning, call to conversion, and his own death, Jesus calls us to be people of conscience. In this way, even an unanticipated death is only a catastrophe of the physical order. With consciences purified by conversion, death cannot take us by surprise.

Father of faithful love, help me to be a good steward of the gift of conscience by recognizing your voice in its every dictate.

Fig Trees, Patience, Love, and Wisdom
Douglas Bushman

And [Jesus] told [the people] this parable: "There once was a person who had a fig tree planted in his orchard, and when he came in search of fruit on it but found none, he said to the gardener, 'For three years now I have come in search of fruit on this fig tree but have found none. [So] cut it down. Why should it exhaust the soil?' He said to him in reply, 'Sir, leave it for this year also, and I shall cultivate the ground around it and fertilize it; it may bear fruit in the future. If not you can cut it down.'"

(Lk 13:6-9)

The story is told about Satan summoning his top demons to devise a new strategy, since too many people were entering heaven. One recommends telling people that there is no heaven, a second that there is no hell. That way, people will have no motive to reform their lives. But Satan dismisses these, saying that no one is gullible enough to doubt that heaven and hell exist. The third demon says, "Let's tell them there is no hurry." Voilà, the adopted strategy, a direct attack on the wisdom: "Oh, that today you would hear his voice:/ Do not harden your hearts" (Ps 95: 7-8). Today's reading reveals God's counter-strategy that there is a "today" of salvation, a "now" for producing fruit. Because his love is limitless, God's patience cannot be limitless.

Farming has a bottom line, an objective limit that cannot be neglected. A farmer knows that a fig tree producing no fruit in four seasons never will. His patience is subject to the four-year limit, lest he cling to a foundationless hope. If the fig tree overhears the exchange between proprietor and gardener, it would realize it has one final season to produce fruit—or else. God's patience is perfect, but it does not cancel out his wisdom.

The same wisdom and love govern intervention for alcoholics and other addicts. It becomes clear that the bond of slavery is so strong that nothing will change without an intense moment of truth, a realization that it is a matter of life or death. A life of addiction is a fruitless, unhappy life. Those who love cannot stand by and watch; they cannot live in denial, hoping for a change that never comes. When God intervenes on behalf of sinners, whose humanity has not yielded the fruit of the happiness he desires for us, it is a call of the paschal mystery. It is God's great reminder: "If today you hear his voice…"

Father of perfect patience, my desire to produce fruit for your glory is your gift. Forgive me, yet again, for failing to be fruitful. Do not abandon me, but in your mercy transform me.

215

The Language of the Body

Douglas Bushman

[Jesus] was teaching in a synagogue on the sabbath. And a woman was there who for eighteen years had been crippled by a spirit; she was bent over, completely incapable of standing erect. When Jesus saw her, he called to her and said, "Woman, you are set free of your infirmity." He laid his hands on her, and she at once stood up straight and glorified God. (Lk 13:10-13)

A little girl, old enough to be aware of her parents' dire financial situation, yet young enough to desire a doll for Christmas, kept her wish to herself. She thought that by remaining silent her desire would remain a secret. But her father could easily interpret the longing look of her eyes when she passed by the display. To her surprise and joy, that Christmas she received just what she wanted, thanks to her father's attentive discernment of her desire.

Prayer of petition verbalizes the desires of the heart. Throughout his life Jesus was bombarded by pleas for healing, but he does not need to hear words in order to know the hidden movements of hearts. In today's reading he takes the initiative to heal without any prior petition. He did the same in raising a widow's son (Lk 7:11-15). In these instances does he violate people's free will? Of course not! Jesus knows the human heart. What mother would not be ecstatic to have her dead son return to life? What cripple does not dream of full health? Jesus knows what they would ask if they believed that someone had the power. And after the exercise of that power, they do believe.

Those who witnessed Jesus' raising of the widow's son glorified God, and the first use the healed woman makes of her newfound wholeness is to glorify God. Though he does not state it, Jesus clearly desires us to give glory to God. The demonstration of Jesus' saving power in these miracles unleashes our capacity to praise and to thank God. He heals in order to make us aware of God's love, and this is why all the miracles point to and find in his death and Resurrection their full meaning. The paschal mystery is the definitive demonstration of God's love for man: in the Son's love "to the end" for us, and in the Father's love for the Son in the Resurrection.

Praise and thanks to you, eternal Father, for sending your Son to teach us how to pray. Through him, with him, and in him, for your glory, I offer to you all my prayers and desires.

216

Jesus Is Lord of the Sabbath

Douglas Bushman

But the leader of the synagogue [...] said to the crowd in reply, "There are six days when work should be done. Come on those days to be cured, not on the sabbath day." The Lord said to him in reply, "Hypocrites! Does not each one of you on the sabbath untie his ox or his ass from the manger and lead it out for watering? This daughter of Abraham, whom Satan has bound for eighteen years now, ought she not to have been set free on the sabbath day from this bondage?" When he said this [...] the whole crowd rejoiced. (Lk 13:14-17)

Timing, they say, is everything: in delivering comedic lines, in the stock market, in coordinating intricate maneuvers in war, and complicated plays in sport. If comedians, investors, generals, and coaches attend so closely to timing, there is nothing accidental about Jesus timing this healing to occur on the sabbath. The synagogue official's negative reaction does not surprise him. It fits into a strategy, but what is it? The theme of conversion is center stage in this sabbath healing. Jesus confronts his listeners with an inconsistency in their practices. They accommodate attending to their animals' needs, yet they would neglect a crippled woman's need for healing love. One can almost hear the echo of Jesus' teaching about men being more valuable than sparrows (Lk 12:7).

The sabbath means imitation of God's rest after creation, but it cannot be perfect rest and enjoyment, since even God continues to provide for his creatures. "My Father is at work until now, so I am at work" (Jn 5:17). Watering animals is a form of cooperation with God in this ongoing work of providing for his creatures. Jesus calls us to rethink what it means to imitate God. It means to love as God loves. There is no rest from love! One may rest from the ordinary work of providing for a family's needs, but not from the corporal and spiritual works of mercy.

Now we see why the woman does not ask to be healed. She knows that a healing would bring the condemnation of not imitating God's rest. She puts Jesus ahead of her desire to be healed. Out of love she is willing to delay being healed, or perhaps to miss altogether her once-in-a-lifetime chance. How could he not be moved by such selflessness? Jesus knows her heart's desire, her hidden prayer to receive God's healing love. What better day than the sabbath for that prayer to be fulfilled?

Merciful Father, grant me the wisdom to seek my rest only in your love. Through the intercession of Saint Luke, transform me into a bearer of your love for those who need it most.

217

How Does God's Kingdom Grow?

Douglas Bushman

Then [Jesus] said, "What is the kingdom of God like? To what can I compare it? It is like a mustard seed that a person took and planted in the garden. When it was fully grown, it became a large bush and 'the birds of the sky dwelt in its branches.'" Again he said, "To what shall I compare the kingdom of God? It is like yeast that a woman took and mixed [in] with three measures of wheat flour until the whole batch of dough was leavened."
(Lk 13:18-21)

Preaching to an audience familiar with banking, Jesus might compare God's kingdom to compounding interest. The kingdom is like a young person who works hard and invests his money to earn compounding interest. Years later he will have a fortune. Seeds and yeast work on their own. Once a farmer plants and a baker puts dough in the oven, nature takes over. God's kingdom is like that. It requires some action on our part, yet it is something God does. It won't happen without our effort, but our effort is tiny—like a seed, some yeast, a modest initial investment—compared to the outcome.

We see this in the divine maternity of the Virgin Mary. Gabriel reveals God's plan and invites her to take her place in it. Mary immediately realizes that this vocation is beyond her. She knows it is impossible for her, on her own, to become the Mother of God—just as a farmer cannot make seeds grow or a baker make dough rise. But, Mary is not on her own. The Holy Spirit overshadows her and she conceives. The divine maternity is the joint work of God and Mary. From Mary's small, unassuming, humble virginity comes the fruitful seed of God's kingdom, Jesus Christ.

We enter into this mystery at Mass. In the Liturgy of the Word, God discloses his plan of love, calls us to holiness, and invites us to embrace the role he assigns to us, our vocation. We become aware of our weakness and make Mary's words our own: "Lord, how shall this be?" In response, the Holy Spirit overshadows the bread and wine offered in sacrifice. He transforms bread ("fruit of the earth and *work of human hands*") and the wine ("fruit of the vine and *work of human hands*") into the supernatural nourishment we need. God grows his kingdom in the Eucharist. The Eucharistic Jesus is the mustard seed and leaven of God's kingdom.

Gracious Father, conscious of the beatitudes and your call to be holy, I can only say: "How shall this be?" Through Mary's intercession, overshadow me with the power of your Spirit.

Passing Through

Douglas Bushman

[Jesus] passed through towns and villages, teaching as he went and making his way to Jerusalem. Someone asked him, "Lord, will only a few people be saved?" He answered them, "Strive to enter through the narrow gate, for many, I tell you, will attempt to enter but will not be strong enough." (Lk 13:22-24)

Who could count the encounters that make up our lives? The majority of people we meet simply pass through our lives: four years of high school and college, so many polite exchanges, so many short-lived acquaintances and temporary projects that bring us together. How do we evaluate these encounters? Probably not in terms of the questions people inspire us, or challenge us, to ask. Perhaps we should.

In today's reading what stands out is the impact that Jesus has on the person who asked a question about salvation. By his presence, words, and demeanor Jesus elicits from us the all-important question about salvation. This means that he is not just passing through our lives, because the question of salvation is not just a point of passing curiosity. It goes to the depth of what it means to be human. It is equivalent to the question of the meaning of life. If there is no salvation, there is no ultimate meaning to life.

Everything about Jesus provokes the question about salvation. He wants us to ask because he has the answer. But the question has to be formulated properly. The question about how many will be saved seems rather secondary in comparison to the question whether *I* will be saved. This is where Jesus' response leads us, right straight to the ultimate question: Will *I* be saved? Too few people ask this question. Blessed are those who ask it, and ask it often! To discern the answer we have to read Saint Luke carefully. Jesus is "making his way to Jerusalem." The way to Jerusalem holds all the answers because that is where Jesus' mission of salvation is fulfilled. There, in all of the drama of Jesus' last days, the ultimate realities are revealed. Will *I* be saved? It depends on the answer to another question: Will Jesus be for me only a passer-by, or will I follow him all the way to Jerusalem?

Heavenly Father, I praise you and thank you for sending Jesus to bring me to salvation. Never let me be parted from him; sustain me in following him through the paschal mystery.

On the Outside Looking In

Douglas Bushman

"After the master of the house has arisen and locked the door, then will you stand outside knocking and saying, 'Lord, open the door for us.' He will say to you in reply, 'I do not know where you are from.' And you will say, 'We ate and drank in your company and you taught in our streets.' Then he will say to you, 'I do not know where [you] are from. Depart from me, all you evildoers!'" (Lk 13:25-27)

The magician Houdini wowed audiences by escaping from straitjackets, handcuffs, jails, and safes. No man-made device, it seems, could restrain him. Reading today's text he might think: "I would find a way through that door." In reality, only Jesus can unlock the door to the Father's house. He does this by his death on the cross. To know him only as teacher but not to follow him to the cross is not to know him fully. That is why he says that he does not know them. Jesus' cross, that is, God's merciful love that forgives sins, is the key to God's kingdom. Jesus is a great teacher, indeed the greatest. He is a miracle worker, again, the greatest. He is a holy man who attracts disciples, unrivaled. But, one can know Jesus as teacher, miracle worker, and master to imitate, yet not know him as redeemer. To know him as redeemer one must know oneself as sinner. Repentance from sin is the key that unlocks the door to his mercy.

"Oh, that today you would hear his voice:/ Do not harden your hearts" (Ps 95:7-8). True disciples are not surprised by the closing of the door because they are not surprised by the call to repentance. Attentive to every knock of God's truth, they rush to open the door of conscience and extend the most lavish hospitality to this truth. Because conversion is a way of life they are at home in the Lord's house. By dying for all Jesus invites all to use the two keys of divine mercy and repentance to enter the Father's house. Without these, eating with him and hearing his teaching do not matter. Indeed, this is the indictment against them. If they really understand his teaching, they will be people of conscience and follow him to the cross. If not, they have locked themselves out and find themselves on the outside looking in.

Almighty Father, forgive me for all the times I have neglected to seek the truth. Create in me a clean heart, that I may not harden it when I hear your voice.

A Tale of a Bishop and a King

Douglas Bushman

"And there will be wailing and grinding of teeth when you see Abraham, Isaac, and Jacob and all the prophets in the kingdom of God and you yourselves cast out. And people will come from the east and the west and from the north and the south and will recline at table in the kingdom of God. For behold, some are last who will be first, and some are first who will be last."

(Lk 13:28-30)

The papal nuncio called to inform a priest that the pope had selected him to be a bishop. This model priest and dedicated pastor was taken totally by surprise. He was so busy serving the flock of his parish, so preoccupied with fulfilling the duties of his priesthood, and so humble in realizing his unworthiness before the splendor of the priesthood, that in his own eyes he was not even last among priests who might be called to be a bishop. He was not even on the list!

King David comes to mind. When Samuel comes to the house of Jesse, everyone presumes the eldest son is the Lord's choice. But God does not judge by appearances. Though the last and least of Jesse's sons, David is God's choice to be king of Israel. David is not even present when Samuel arrives. He is busy tending sheep. He is busy, like the parish pastor, dutifully fulfilling the demands of his vocation. This is the lesson for us. What looks insignificant, mundane, too small to be of importance, counts for a great deal in God's eyes. What is last in human reckoning is first in God's!

Throughout this chapter of Luke's Gospel, Jesus' words are intended to shake up consciences. They challenge us to re-examine our way of thinking, our criteria of judging things. The thought of being on the outside looking in upon the joy of the patriarchs and prophets in the kingdom should provoke an examination of conscience: Do I really know what the values of the kingdom are? Is my standard of judging the importance of things the same as God's standard? Do I value daily fidelity to the seemingly insignificant, routine, humdrum events of my life as God does? Do I really understand what Jesus means when he says: "The person who is trustworthy in very small matters is also trustworthy in great ones" (Lk 16:10)?

Praise and thanks to you, eternal Father, for valuing little acts of fidelity so greatly, because that is all I have to offer to you. I long to be faithful in all things; sustain me by your grace.

Who Wants to Kill Jesus?

Douglas Bushman

At that time some Pharisees came to [Jesus] and said, "Go away, leave this area because Herod wants to kill you." He replied, "Go and tell that fox, 'Behold, I cast out demons and I perform healings today and tomorrow, and on the third day I accomplish my purpose. Yet I must continue on my way today, tomorrow, and the following day, for it is impossible that a prophet should die outside of Jerusalem.'" (Lk 13:31-33)

Reading today's text we might be tempted to see it only as an account of that villain, King Herod, and think: "How could he kill John the Baptist and threaten Jesus too? If I were a king, I would act differently." This reminds me of my children, years ago, learning about the consequences of Adam and Eve's sin. "How could they be so dumb? We could still be in the garden if only…" If only what? At their young age my children's grasp of the mystery of sin was not deep. If they had been Adam and Eve would it have been different? Experience has taught them humility. They are just as likely to sin were they in Adam and Eve's place. But our sins weigh more heavily because we believe in God's love revealed in Jesus' suffering and death. Yet we still manage to misuse our freedom.

Jesus knows he has come to die for sinners. He is conscious of the link between sin and his death: "Now you are trying to kill me, a man who has told you the truth" (Jn 8:40); "You are trying to kill me, because my word has no room among you" (Jn 8:37). Those with a mature sense of sin also realize the connection. "He was pierced for our offenses,/ crushed for our sins" (Is 53:5). Saint Paul makes it brutally personal: Jesus loved *me* and gave himself up for *me* (Gal 2:20). There is something of Herod in everyone. So, the Lord's crucifixion is not an event that remains exterior to us. In our sins we are there as those who want to kill Jesus. His words from the cross apply: the Roman soldiers, those who conspired to have him crucified, and *me*. Especially for those with an acute sense of sin, which is the gift of the Holy Spirit, Jesus' words are the hope for salvation: "Father, forgive them, they know not what they do" (Lk 23:34).

Father of our Lord, Jesus Christ, grant me the grace of an ever deeper contrition for my complicity in your Son's suffering and death. By his infinite merits, make me his faithful friend.

The Great "I Told You So!"
Douglas Bushman

"Jerusalem, Jerusalem, you who kill the prophets and stone those sent to you, how many times I yearned to gather your children together as a hen gathers her brood under her wings, but you were unwilling! Behold, your house will be abandoned. [But] I tell you, you will not see me until [the time comes when] you say, 'Blessed is he who comes in the name of the Lord.'"
(Lk 13:34-35)

When we disregard a friend's warning and things turn out badly, the words "I told you so" are not really necessary. A look in the eyes suffices to recall the words and to trigger a sense of humiliation. Jesus' warning in today's reading is an anticipatory "I told you so," designed not to humiliate but to lead to repentance. His mission will end in rejection, torture, and death, and Jesus knows that this means disaster for the people. Hanging on the cross, he takes this disaster upon himself. Looking upon the crucified one should make us remember his words, which express the interior warning of conscience that accompanies every sin. Jesus teaches us to heed the voice of conscience before it becomes the dreaded "I told you so."

But "I told you so" is not the last word regarding sin. The cross makes this clear, and this is why Jesus' warning cannot be separated from the cross. The cross means that the "I told you so" of an accusing conscience is accompanied by an even more powerful "I told you so" of love. Jesus says: "I told you that I love you, and I mean it." This witness to love is greater than the "I told you so" of our own hearts (1 Jn 3:20). This is the source of our hope. From the cross Jesus meets us in that intense moment of consciousness of sin. He invites us to contemplate him on the cross and hear him say: "I told you that I love you!" This harmonizes with the prodigal son's father, image of the heavenly Father, who never says a word to his son about his foolishness. In Jesus, God meets us in the twin truths that echo as a twofold "I told you so." First, the "I told you so" of conscience, and second, the "I told you so" of forgiving love.

Merciful Father, my hope is in your love. Keep me close to your love in the Eucharist, and grant me the grace of frequent sacramental confession and the grace of final perseverance.

Jesus at Table: Healing and the Law

Father Francis Martin

On a sabbath [Jesus] went to dine at the home of one of the leading Pharisees, and the people there were observing him carefully. In front of him there was a man suffering from dropsy. Jesus spoke to the scholars of the law and Pharisees in reply, asking, "Is it lawful to cure on the sabbath or not?" But they kept silent. (Lk 14:1-4a)

Jesus, still on his way to Jerusalem, accepts an invitation to a sabbath repast at the home of one of the leading Pharisees of that district. He goes, still on his mission to the lost sheep of the house of Israel. Perhaps we get a glimpse of their spiritual state from Saint Luke's observation that the guests "were observing him carefully," and that the sick man was right there "in front of him."

Jesus went to this meal with the same motive of compassion that inspired his meals with tax collectors and sinners: he went to offer them the Father's love. He comes to us, in prayer, in the Scriptures, and in the Eucharist with the same motive.

Now we see humility and compassion. Instead of using the presence of the sick man as an occasion to condemn his host for allowing, or causing, this challenge, Jesus, the Son of God, takes the trouble to reason with "the scholars of the law and Pharisees." He initiates a discussion on a still nebulous question among the Pharisees, yet they refuse to engage him.

This glimpse into our Lord's heart can teach us many things: zeal for the salvation of others, a tactful way of approaching them, and mostly, confidence in the Jesus who answers our invitation to come to us. I am still learning from Jesus how to enter any situation with an open and expectant heart.

Father of compassion, you send your Son as Physician of our souls and bodies alike. May we always remain receptive to his healing touch in our lives.

Jesus Keeps the Discussion Open

Father Francis Martin

So [Jesus] took the man [suffering from dropsy] and, after he had healed him, dismissed him. Then he said to [the scholars of the law and Pharisees], "Who among you, if your son or ox falls into a cistern, would not immediately pull him out on the sabbath day?" But they were unable to answer his question.
(Lk 14:4b-6)

One would think that, after side-stepping Jesus' first question, the gathered group of legal experts would rise to the invitation to continue the discussion. After all, they had just witnessed with their own eyes a man healed from a serious disease (an abnormal accumulation of fluid beneath the skin or in one or more cavities of the body). Surely this Galilean peasant deserves some answer.

But there is more. The sabbath observance itself is not a division of time that owes its existence to the movement of the sun, the earth, or the moon, as do our days and months and years. The sabbath was created by divine decree: "Take care to keep my sabbaths, for that is to be the token between you and me throughout the generations, to show that it is I, the LORD, who make you holy" (Ex 31:13). Thus, when Jesus makes his claim that "the Son of Man is lord of the sabbath" (Lk 6:5), he is asserting a divine authority. Yet here, in his mercy, he is willing to debate with his interlocutors in order to win them over. His question to them places him among the legal experts who were still pondering what could be legitimately done on the sabbath.

I have learned that our Lord Jesus Christ is the best person to go to in order to understand him. I have spent fifty-five years of my life studying and teaching Sacred Scripture. Almost every day, when all the historical and literary work is done, I need to ask Jesus to help me understand *the reality* brought to me by his words. Sometimes I receive an answer right away and, at other times, I have to keep asking because the answer is not a new concept but a deeper knowledge of Jesus himself. Try it and you will see.

Gracious Father, it is such a privilege to learn from Jesus your divine Son. I ask you to look on all those who believe in him and give us your Spirit who can make Jesus' words and actions come alive.

The Emptiness of Vainglory

Father Francis Martin

[Jesus] told a parable to those who had been invited, noticing how they were choosing the places of honor at the table. "When you are invited by someone to a wedding banquet, do not recline at table in the place of honor. A more distinguished guest than you may have been invited by him, and the host who invited both of you may approach you and say, 'Give your place to this man,' and then you would proceed with embarrassment to take the lowest place." (Lk 14:7-9)

This passage is the first part of a two-part parable (in the sense of "proverb") concerning conduct at banquets. Given the fact that our social norms governing gatherings such as banquets are not nearly as rigid as those of the Middle East, it is hard to place ourselves in the situation envisaged by our Lord. However, to get some idea, just imagine seating yourself at table number 3 at a wedding reception and then being told by the host that you belong at table 17.

In an ancient Middle Eastern context, the values of honor and shame govern most social interaction. This, along with the social laws governing reciprocity (an invitation *requires* a comparable invitation) make a highly codified, if unspoken, manner of acting. Jesus sees the social stratification, the snobbery, the self-centeredness of such a societal arrangement and, almost humorously, points God's people away from them. Such attitudes indicate that, over time, his people have forgotten their own poverty and need for rescue. Thus says the LORD: "You shall not molest or oppress an alien, for you were once aliens yourselves in the land of Egypt. You shall not wrong any widow or orphan. If ever you wrong them and they cry out to me, I will surely hear their cry" (Ex 22:20-22). It has come to such a point that his opponents actually make an accusation out of his continued act of caring for the poor as he had done for their forefathers in Egypt: "This man welcomes sinners and eats with them" (Lk 15:2).

Jesus' advice, then, is not merely counsel on proper social conduct. It is founded on and flows from that same act of divine humility that reigns between the three Persons of the Trinity and flows over into our world as we consider Jesus who now invites us to his heavenly banquet.

Thank you, heavenly Father. You loved the world so much that you gave your only Son as our Redeemer and eternal Host.

How to Get Ahead

Father Francis Martin

"Rather, when you are invited, go and take the lowest place so that when the host comes to you he may say, 'My friend, move up to a higher position.' Then you will enjoy the esteem of your companions at the table. For everyone who exalts himself will be humbled, but the one who humbles himself will be exalted."

(Lk 14:10-11)

Jesus, the Wisdom of God, expressed himself in the same vein as the Old Testament wisdom tradition: "Claim no honor in the king's presence,/ nor occupy the place of great men;/ For it is better that you be told, 'Come up closer!'/ than that you be humbled before the prince"(Prv 25:6-7; see also Sir 3:17-20). The Lord is telling us that the way to be exalted is to follow him in humility. He first illustrates the principle with a humorous simile: "your reward for not being pushy at a big dinner party will be that the host will invite you, in the sight of all the guests, to come occupy a better position." Jesus himself, for the joy set before him, endured the cross, despising its shame (see Heb 12:2).

Saint Teresa of Ávila is often quoted as saying that humility is not thinking little of yourself; it is not thinking of yourself at all. Such an interior peace is the fruit of a steady life of prayer. As we come to know Jesus personally, our attention becomes more fixed on him and we find our peace in his company. It is principally in this company that we are not restless. Then we understand that we do not take the lowest place hoping to get a promotion: the last place *is* the promotion because we share it with Jesus who said of himself: "For the Son of Man did not come to be served but to serve and to give his life as a ransom for many" (Mk 10:45).

Finally, our Lord states his principle: self-exaltation leads to humiliation; self-humbling leads to exaltation and respect. I still remember my meeting Pope John XXIII. I was just a graduate student at the time, but the love and respect with which he treated me gave a glimpse into the power and beauty of a humility raised to a universal love.

Most blessed Father, Creator and Sustainer of the whole of creation, you are the first place. Please raise us up to you.

The Imitation of Christ

Father Francis Martin

*Then [Jesus] said to the host who invited him, "When you hold
a lunch or a dinner, do not invite your friends or your brothers
or your relatives or your wealthy neighbors, in case they may
invite you back and you have repayment. Rather, when you
hold a banquet, invite the poor, the crippled, the lame, the blind;
blessed indeed will you be because of their inability to repay you.
For you will be repaid at the resurrection of the righteous."*

(Lk 14:12-14)

It is Easter Sunday afternoon in Rome, 1972. A young couple
has just been married. The groom is Italian and the bride is
American, part of a group of young evangelists. There is a
reception just starting in a hall that is part of the convent at the
top of the Spanish Steps. The "tables" are planks mounted on saw-
horses and covered with paper tablecloths. The banquet is simple
food and some wine. All of a sudden, one of the young evangelists
jumps onto a table and reads this Gospel passage from Luke. At
that, everyone picks up the "tables" and the food, sets everything
up in the small piazza at the top of the Spanish Steps, and invites
everyone to come and join the celebration.

The joy, and the interest in hearing about Jesus on the part of the
intrigued, the bemused, and the open-hearted are singular confirmation of the words of Jesus: it is Good News. The only people
unhappy are the merchants with their wares spread out on rugs all
up and down the Spanish Steps. I could only think of the riot in
Ephesus as a result of Paul's successful efforts to preach the Good
News: "'This Paul has persuaded and misled a great number of
people by saying that gods made by hands are not gods at all. The
danger grows, not only that our business will be discredited, but
also that the temple of the great goddess Artemis will be of no
account...' When they heard this, they were filled with fury and
began to shout" (Acts 19:26-28).

What would happen if more of us took these and other words
of Jesus and gave them existence in our words and actions?
Remember that Jesus told us that those who really listen to his
words and act on them are building their house (their life) on a
solid foundation (see Mt 7:24).

*Loving Father, give flesh to my faith today by helping me reach
out to a person in need of food or money, of encouragement or
sympathy, of a loving touch or a simple smile.*

Left Out

Father Francis Martin

One of his fellow guests on hearing this said to [Jesus], "Blessed is the one who will dine in the kingdom of God." He replied to him, "A man gave a great dinner to which he invited many. When the time for the dinner came, he dispatched his servant to say to those invited, 'Come, everything is now ready.' But one by one, they all began to excuse themselves. The first said to him, 'I have purchased a field and must go to examine it; I ask you, consider me excused.'" (Lk 14:15-18)

Our Lord's parable reflects his Middle Eastern milieu. Notice that the man first "invited many"—this is the first step in organizing a banquet. Then, when the time came, he sent his servants a second time to announce the "great dinner." Holding banquets was a means of demonstrating, as well as furthering, one's social standing. Turning down such an invitation was a serious insult. The allusion to the announcing of the banquet by the prophets and the invitation by the Apostles is clear.

The first of the reasons for turning down the invitation was the trivial fact that the man wanted to look at his newly bought field. What is our Lord telling us in setting forth such disproportion? His immediate audience in the narrative are the guests invited to the table; his ultimate audience includes ourselves.

Sometimes our Lord's invitation is a quiet but insistent call to some action. It could be seeking reconciliation with someone estranged. I once suggested in a homily a few weeks before Christmas that people think about some relationship that had become strained or perhaps non-existent and that they call that person and invite him or her to Christmas dinner. For weeks afterward I heard beautiful stories of reconciliation and joy.

There is one standing invitation to a banquet that requires a serious response, and that is the invitation (and requirement) to participate in Sunday Mass. We should reflect on the fact that, for eternity, we will remember that Mass and see it for what it really was: a time to join the angels, listen to Jesus, the Word of God, in the Scriptures, and take his glorious Body and Blood into ourselves as the seed of an eternal resurrection.

Heavenly Father, let us hear your voice calling us to the eternal banquet even now.

Missing Out on the Banquet and More

Father Francis Martin

"And another [of those invited] said, 'I have purchased five yoke of oxen and am on my way to evaluate them; I ask you, consider me excused.' And another said, 'I have just married a woman, and therefore I cannot come.' The servant went and reported this to his master. Then the master of the house in a rage commanded his servant, 'Go out quickly into the streets and alleys of the town and bring in here the poor and the crippled, the blind and the lame.'" (Lk 14:19-21)

The first superficial excuse, inspecting a field, marks the man who made the refusal as quite wealthy, probably an absentee landlord who is traveling to see his new acquisition. The second is the same: five yoke of oxen would be needed to work a property of over one hundred acres, a sizeable piece of real estate. The third man places family ahead of the invitation to the kingdom, something our Lord warns us about: recall his words about following the homeless Jesus, letting the dead bury their dead, and not turning back in the midst of plowing (Lk 9:57-62).

It seems that the only way to implement this teaching of Jesus, leaving everything to partake of the banquet, is to be so bound in love to him as to realize that he is enough and that he will take care of anyone close to us. He will care for our needs in keeping with our state in life. To be invited, even in this life, to share in the Messianic banquet is such a privilege and a joy that it places everything else in perspective. There was an article in a big city newspaper recently, one that is definitely not pro-life. It warmly described the good order and the joy of a Christian family of rather modest means that counted eleven children from the ages of one to twelve. Clearly this family understood that commitment to marriage did not impede joining the Lord's heavenly banquet even now.

Now the action of the parable changes. The master of the house, "in a rage," tells the servants to go out into the town, into the "slum area," and bring in exactly those people whom Jesus recommended earlier in his discussion of whom to invite to banquets. Luke, in recording this invitation, is inviting us to see ourselves as among the poor and disqualified, the uninformed and inept. Such a recognition is the work of the Holy Spirit.

Merciful Father, we are so grateful to be brought to your banquet. Every Sunday we recognize ourselves as the poor and the crippled, the blind and the lame invited to your table.

Fill My House

Father Francis Martin

"The servant reported, 'Sir, your orders have been carried out and still there is room.' The master then ordered the servant, 'Go out to the highways and hedgerows and make people come in that my home may be filled. For, I tell you, none of those men who were invited will taste my dinner.'"
(Lk 14:22-24)

The city slums have contributed what they could; now the servants must look elsewhere. They go to the outer-city slums, to the ramshackle dwellings like those one can see outside some cities in India or Latin America. These are the poor whom even the poor try to avoid. The rich householder tells his servants to "make" them come to his house: they are too embarrassed to be in such company. We can almost feel the faster heartbeat of Jesus as he thinks of his brothers and sisters, too poor ever to be included, now being "compelled" to come to the banquet, his banquet. He hears the words he had uttered long ago: "This is the one whom I approve:/ the lowly and afflicted man who trembles at my word" (Is 66:2).

Who is a poor man? Someone who delights in the experience of dependence upon God. A harsh life coupled with the action of the Holy Spirit can bring this about. When we are sick, experiencing loneliness or failure, we are "deprived." We are only "poor" when this experience of dependence upon God brings us joy: this too is a gift made to those who seek it and the road to it may be harsh. At the end of this road, Saint Francis assures us, lies "pure joy."

Our Lord's words, then, are describing how the banquet hall of the kingdom is filled. They are a parable, but they are more than that. They are a revelation of the Father's plan: "I do not want you to be unaware of this mystery, brothers, so that you will not become wise [in] your own estimation: a hardening has come upon Israel in part, until the full number of the Gentiles comes in, and thus all Israel will be saved"(Rom 11:25-26).

Let us not be among the self-satisfied rich who "will never taste my dinner."

Loving Father, your preferences, revealed in the life and words of your Son, are a challenge to our small pride but they are also a bubbling spring of hope.

The Cost of Discipleship
Father Francis Martin

Great crowds were traveling with [Jesus], and he turned and addressed them, "If anyone comes to me without hating his father and mother, wife and children, brothers and sisters, and even his own life, he cannot be my disciple. Whoever does not carry his own cross and come after me cannot be my disciple." (Lk 14:25-27)

The scene changes. Jesus is on the road to Jerusalem and all that awaits him there. Great crowds accompany him and he turns to point out to them that "traveling with him" is one thing, being a disciple is another. In that context Jesus begins by challenging people to "hate" their immediate family. This has nothing to do with emotions: it is a question of reordering allegiances. The Jewish scholar Jacob Neusner (whom Pope Benedict XVI quotes) understands what is implied. Jesus is reordering the priorities ordered by God. Who, then, can he be, this man who claims that he must be ahead of any other ties of family and affection? Who is he who calls himself the "lord of the sabbath" (Lk 6:5), thus putting himself ahead of what was considered another divine ordinance? The answer is that he is, literally, the Son of God.

But there is more: discipleship means taking up one's own cross and following Jesus. People carrying crosses are on their way to death. The glitter, the fame, the comfort available in this life are not for such a person. Such a one is on the way to an identification with Jesus whose love for his Father and for us moves him forward to offer his whole life for us. "Or are you unaware that we who were baptized into Christ Jesus were baptized into his death? We were indeed buried with him through baptism into death, so that, just as Christ was raised from the dead by the glory of the Father, we too might live in newness of life" (Rom 6:3-4).

The secret of the saints, lay or clerical, active or contemplative, is the same: they obeyed the Holy Spirit who led them into a love relationship with Jesus. From then on, even when we feel crucified, there is joy.

Heavenly Father, teach me the truth of your Son's words as he made his way to Jerusalem and to death on the cross for us. Let us glimpse your heart in his, and learn to put you first as you put your Son first for us.

Looking for Resources

Father Francis Martin

"Which of you wishing to construct a tower does not first sit down and calculate the cost to see if there is enough for its completion? Otherwise, after laying the foundation and finding himself unable to finish the work the onlookers should laugh at him and say, 'This one began to build but did not have the resources to finish.'" (Lk 14:28-30)

After having described the nature of the calling, our Lord gives two examples of people undertaking a large project and therefore needing to count the cost. He is hoping that we will see that what he is calling us to far exceeds our resources, and then turn to him for all we need. In these verses we meet the tower builder. Saint Cyril of Alexandria puts it this way: "Those who choose to live a glorious and blameless life should store up beforehand in their mind a sufficient zeal."

Another saint who clearly counted the cost was Saint Thérèse of Lisieux. Recall her image of a child trying and trying to mount the stairs in order to be with her father. Finally the father descends, picks her up, and carries her to the top. I once had a similar experience of what it means to measure our resources and then go ahead, relying on God. I had injured my wrist and opening jars was very difficult for me. I prayed to my guardian angel for help. I had the distinct impression that he would indeed help me, but that I had to try hard myself. I would lay hold of the jar and turn as hard as I could, against the real pain, and then the jar would open. From this small experience I learned that trying amidst pain is often the way that we arrive at a success brought about by God.

Our efforts give joy and glory to God. Even in difficult circumstances we are promised divine aid: "When they hand you over, do not worry about how you are to speak or what you are to say. You will be given at that moment what you are to say. For it will not be you who speak but the Spirit of your Father speaking through you" (Mt 10:19-20).

Thank you, Father, for your Son's clear words and the promise of help they bring to us.

Learning to Listen

Father Francis Martin

"Or what king marching into battle would not first sit down and decide whether with ten thousand troops he can successfully oppose another king advancing upon him with twenty thousand troops? But if not, while he is still far away, he will send a delegation to ask for peace terms. In the same way, everyone of you who does not renounce all his possessions cannot be my disciple." (Lk 14:31-33)

After giving us the example of the tower builder, our Lord repeats the illustration, this time with a king marching out to battle. Then, he applies it to us: "Everyone of you who does not renounce all his possessions cannot be my disciple."

One Sunday morning I was driving to the parish where I was doing weekend help. The last line of the Gospel that Sunday was precisely the last line of our text. I had studied it and prayed about it, but I was still at a loss as to what to say. I was praying to our Lord: "Lord, most of the time both we and the congregation just duck this text. These people have families. They have to feed, clothe, and educate their children. What can you possibly mean, that they have to renounce all their possessions? I don't want to duck this text again and have the most serious and fervent among them leave after Mass with an uneasy feeling that they are not obeying you and yet be at a loss as to what to do."

The Lord in his mercy answered me. He said in a calm and loving voice: "Look, I know that these people have responsibilities to their families, especially their children whom they are obliged to feed, clothe, educate, and generally care for their needs. What I am telling them is that they must come to me and learn from me how and upon what I want them to spend their money. Their life is compartmentalized. They pray and come to church and they try to train their children in the Gospel, but when it comes to their finances they act as though I were not their Lord and as though I did not love them. Selfishness and short-sightedness can creep in and subtly disturb the family's peace. Tell them to come to me with their plans for their money. Is this not to renounce responsibly?"

Thank you, Father for your love and your patience. There is no one like you!

Tasteless Christians?

Father Francis Martin

"Salt is good, but if salt itself loses its taste, with what can its flavor be restored? It is fit neither for the soil nor for the manure pile; it is thrown out. Whoever has ears to hear ought to hear."
(Lk 14:34-35)

Salt preserves and enhances. Christians are meant to preserve all that is good in human nature and raise it higher. If we are not doing that, we are unfit for anything. I think our Lord wants us to appreciate the enormous privilege that is ours as well as the stakes involved in our call to be Christians. If we are faithful to the Lord, we bring an inestimable blessing to the world; if we are non-committal, we are, literally, useless.

How do we bless the world? First, by being a "place" where Christ dwells and acts. This is true of us individually, but also as families and parishes. Let us think first of a parish Sunday Mass where the people come properly dressed, attentive, and prayerful. The music here enhances prayer, the priest mediates the Word of God and leads the congregation in prayer and adoration. The assembled community is brought into union with Jesus Christ, glorious, still fixed in the act of love in which he died, and leading us now to join in his act of love. Anyone entering such an environment, even if he be a non-believer, is "salted" with a touch from Christ.

Now think of the opposite scenario: "The Amen, the faithful and true witness, the source of God's creation, says this: 'I know your works; I know that you are neither cold nor hot. I wish you were either cold or hot. So, because you are lukewarm, neither hot nor cold, I will spit you out of my mouth'" (Rv 3:15-16).

In addition to being a "place" where Christ dwells and radiates his peace and friendliness through us, we are also meant to be a "voice" for him. Think of the occasions when we are with others, a check-out line in the grocery store, or sitting next to someone on a bus or plane, etc. Perhaps Jesus wants a friendly greeting from you; at times he wants to change a life.

Heavenly Father, salt us with your Son's Word, so that through our lives of faith we may help others to "taste and see the goodness of the Lord."

Lost and Found

Father Lawrence Donohoo

*The tax collectors and sinners were all drawing near to listen
to [Jesus], but the Pharisees and scribes began to complain,
saying, "This man welcomes sinners and eats with them."
So to them he addressed this parable. "What man among you
having a hundred sheep and losing one of them would not
leave the ninety-nine in the desert and go after the lost one
until he finds it?" (Lk 15:1-4)*

Once when lost at night in a dangerous city, I took a chance and asked the only man within eyeshot for directions. His slurred speech and staggering stumble told me that I was not alone in needing help. "Where's the highway?" he asked, repeating my question. "I first have to find out where I am!"

How right he was. I can only find my way if I first know where I am, and I can only learn where I am if I recognize that I have lost my bearings. Who will lead me out of this circle of darkness? The One who in the very act of finding me teaches me that I've been lost.

The Pharisees want to talk about sin, but Jesus translates their speech into the new category of lost and found. Their dispute arises in the first place from the fact that Jesus has been searching for sinners at the dinner table. He helps them to see that salvation is not primarily a moral attitude that aspires to a blessed and unattainable state of sinlessness. It's rather a matter of learning that one is loved enough to be pursued and found.

Little wonder that all sorts of findings permeate the Gospels: the shepherds and the Magi find an infant in a manger, Mary and Joseph retrieve their missing child, Philip tells Nathanael he has found the Messiah, the woman at the well secures her past and future, Peter finds God's saving arm as he sinks into the waves, some disciples locate the merchant who finds them an upper room, and Mary Magdalene finds the Gardener she wasn't looking for. "The Son of Man has come to seek and to save what was lost" (Lk 19:10). This is what Jesus wants us to see: look at salvation primarily as a *finding*, because it is a personal Lord who tracks you down and a loving God who carries you home.

Loving Father, help me to see that I'm constantly being lost, especially when I think I'm safe with the herd. Thank you for putting your Good Shepherd on my trail.

This Is All about You

Father Lawrence Donohoo

"And when he does find it, he sets it on his shoulders with great joy and, upon his arrival home, he calls together his friends and neighbors and says to them, 'Rejoice with me because I have found my lost sheep.' I tell you, in just the same way there will be more joy in heaven over one sinner who repents than over ninety-nine righteous people who have no need of repentance."
(Lk 15:5-7)

My memory still tracks the long-haired evangelist in the trench coat on the college campus anywhere, anytime in search of God's stray sheep. "Have you accepted Jesus as your Lord and Savior?" he would shamelessly ask student and professor alike while whipping out from the coat's deep pocket his "sword"—a well-worn copy of the King James Version—to follow up with a convicting word. It took me time to learn that my Catholic faith allowed, indeed mandated, that I accept God's righteousness through faith in Jesus Christ. And it took time to learn that accepting Jesus personally as my Lord and Savior was a different act from accepting Jesus as my *personal* Lord and Savior.

This is what the parable of the lost sheep clarifies. While all of us need the common salvation that God offers us in Christ, we also need this salvation in the unique way that fits our individual situation. No other person is lost, disobedient, forlorn, troubled, wounded, smashed, and disfigured in exactly the same way as I. Accepting God's universal salvation offered to all as my personal act can then be joined to accepting his personal act of saving me just as I am. Happily, my problem invites his solution, and his solution clarifies my problem. This is the reason that the old spiritual masters linked God-knowledge with self-knowledge.

And so it's true that the more desperate my situation, the more willingly I may be led to seek the divine rescue. But it's equally true that the divine rescue can show me as for the first time that Jesus found me in the nick of time bending backwards over the ravine. At least for now, then, my strong-armed Savior coming over the hill is here for me alone as if no one else mattered. Pretend that everyone back in the flock is doing just fine. Salvation for me, for here, for now, for keeps is this divine personal lift.

Heavenly Father, keep me from turning my personal faith in you, your Son, and your Spirit into an abstraction or method or ethic. It is you Three I wish personally to grasp.

Finding Joy in Finding Us

Father Lawrence Donohoo

"Or what woman having ten coins and losing one would not light a lamp and sweep the house, searching carefully until she finds it? And when she does find it, she calls together her friends and neighbors and says to them, 'Rejoice with me because I have found the coin that I lost.' In just the same way, I tell you, there will be rejoicing among the angels of God over one sinner who repents." (Lk 15:8-10)

Call in your friends and neighbors to celebrate the occasion of the finding and you'll likely spend more on the wine and cheese than what it's worth—unless the coin is really rare. So throwing a party to celebrate the finding of the coin is quite absurd unless it's really valuable or it has some intrinsic worth to the woman that sparks her boundless joy. We haven't a clue about the coin's objective value, so we must settle for her joy as the evidence of its worth.

Stopping right there, I must be quite exceptional for God to make such an astounding effort in tracking me down and sponsoring a rollicking party to celebrate the occasion. And it is God's joy that the angels share which is our sign that these coins he has fashioned, lost, and found—these human images stamped with the divine nature—are worth all the ecstatic fuss. For this reason it pays to search the Scriptures to learn our true worth by finding out what really makes God happy in the act of finding us. When we grasp our importance to him, we can be confident that we're closer to understanding the heart of God, "for where your treasure is, there also will your heart be" (Lk 12:34).

This gives me a positive reason to receive his salvation for me with the same vigor as the woman scouring her house for the missing coin. In a word, God wants me to understand that my letting him pursue me should be seen as giving him delight. Jesus expresses this in his closing prayer at the Last Supper when he prays that his disciples may share his joy completely (Jn 17:13). And when I catch a glimpse of this divine joy, I am invited to examine my own joys in life and see how they may be founded, purified, strengthened, and found in the ecstatic joy of God.

Loving Father, my joy will be complete when I rejoice in the same things that you do in the same way that you do. Purify my joy and make me worthy of its divine expression.

First Things Last

Father Lawrence Donohoo

*Then [Jesus] said, "A man had two sons, and the younger
son said to his father, 'Father, give me the share of your estate
that should come to me.' So the father divided the property
between them. After a few days, the younger son collected all his
belongings and set off to a distant country where he squandered
his inheritance on a life of dissipation." (Lk 15:11-13)*

Like any good parable, the image suffers from the fact that our ways are not God's ways. For even the faithful son there is life beyond the estate's boundaries and a future after his father's death, but "[t]he Lord's is the earth and its fullness" (Ps 23:1, Grail), and our God is deathless. There is nowhere to go and no time to go to that utopia, rooted only in our free-falling imagination, that appears perfect because we form it ourselves. All the more reason to admit that whenever I scorn the first commandment, that is, every time I sin, my act is effectively one of desperate solitude, of lone-ranger salvation seeking, of incredible self-deception in a futile attempt to make off alone with the family goods.

To be sure, God created the problem in the first place by giving us legs and by making himself our highest but not our only good. So blame the divine humility in setting up a world in which created goods share the limelight with him and tempt us to keep them in the spotlight. We know we may and must respond to legitimate needs and desires of our God-given nature, but we also know how prone are our wayward hearts to prefer the Lord's gifts to the Lord who bestows them.

The truth of the matter is that even my rusty conscience knows I've compounded the problem by loving things and using persons, whether divine or human. To help me, then, Jesus presents Lesson One whereby he identifies himself with his created brothers and sisters who need the things I love. In this way I learn to love the ones who need and the One who became needy.

If I'm going to stay on the farm, I can begin with these earthly priorities. By learning to put God's images before the goods of the earth, I make progress in the never-ending struggle of putting the Exemplar before even them.

Eternal Father, I recognize the difficulty of loving all things in you and loving you above all things. Help me to give priority to your images on earth in my expressions of love for you.

He'll Handle This Himself

Father Lawrence Donohoo

"When [the younger son] had freely spent everything, a severe famine struck that country, and he found himself in dire need. So he hired himself out to one of the local citizens who sent him to his farm to tend the swine. And he longed to eat his fill of the pods on which the swine fed, but nobody gave him any."

(Lk 15:14-16)

In Elisabeth Kübler-Ross's celebrated five stages of grief—denial, anger, bargaining, depression, and acceptance—only the third explicitly involves interaction with a "higher power." The other steps one can do alone. And that's precisely the temptation when we're confronted with death and dying in our daily life, even in non-emergency cases.

Even before I get started on first-stage denial, I mutter to myself: "There's a problem here—no, I mean there's no problem here." So I'll take care of the non-problem myself. Well, that doesn't last long, so now I'm tempted to bring God into the picture, but under the rubric of half-conscious anger toward him. Now it enjoys the status of problem, and he could have solved it because he's almighty, but I have to all by myself! I'm not talking *to* God at this stage; I'm talking *about* him to myself. Both myself and I agree that there is a fundamental wrong here that God's not righting. So we all need to talk. More precisely, I want to talk. Lord, here's how you're benefited if you remove this cross… But the cross remains, and I'm not happy about this. At this point I could in fact accept my lot, or… I could start over.

The best course of action is to head back to the ranch at the first hint of hunger, which tells us we never should have left in the first place. The younger son that we are needs to start thinking far ahead in a full rejection of earlier blind moves. The Father can be sought out even when it's still an issue and not yet a crisis. We don't have to show him that we tried and failed. We can succeed much earlier—if we're willing to admit our predicament and our responsibility, and honestly say to him: "I got myself into this mess, and now—not later—please get me out of it."

Almighty Father, I need to engage your help from the start when things go awry, which happens all the time. Remind me that without your grace I can do nothing.

Upward Mobility

Father Lawrence Donohoo

"Coming to his senses [the younger son] thought, 'How many of my father's hired workers have more than enough food to eat, but here am I, dying from hunger. I shall get up and go to my father and I shall say to him, "Father, I have sinned against heaven and against you. I no longer deserve to be called your son; treat me as you would treat one of your hired workers.""
(Lk 15:17-19)

The wayward son's reasoning is helpful for grasping the Church's teaching on imperfect contrition, a fancy term for admitting that sometimes I'm sorry because it's to my benefit. Granted, it's not ideal, and it's not genuine love of God. But it's something, and by its fruit you shall know it. Imperfect contrition is good because it's a form of self-love, and we're commanded to love ourselves.

Think of all the parables where Jesus lauds prudence: the contractor who builds on rock, the tower builder who counts his supplies, the general realistic about impending defeat, the wise virgins who bring enough oil, the servants keeping the house in order, the man who finds a treasure and hides it, the go-getters making cash with cash. Jesus knows his Scriptures: Proverbs is almost exclusively devoted to praising the wise against the foolish. And recall his consistently positive response to all those assertive enough—and sometimes aggressive enough—to seek his healing touch. Consider Jesus' invitation to us to ask, seek, knock.

Pristine self-love is very far from spiritual perfection, but it is something we can build on. Jesus will take what he can get: "A bruised reed he shall not break" (Is 42:3). For that reason, we shouldn't despise self-love, whether in ourselves or others. Instead of casting it out, cast it in—in that more perfect self-love that has learned the lessons of sacrifice, altruism, and charity. For if I love myself enough to sacrifice today's pleasures for tomorrow's good, I can take the next step and begin working toward perfect contrition for the love of God. There is no better way to love myself truly than to receive the gift of being loved and loving the Father with no thought of gain. He'll take care of you: "Whoever loses his life for my sake will save it" (Lk 9:24). If you love him, you just can't lose.

Loving Father, I thank you for giving me a commandment that I can naturally obey. Purify my self-love so that I may love you, my neighbor, and myself more perfectly.

Suffering Fools Gladly

Father Lawrence Donohoo

"So [the younger son] got up and went back to his father. While he was still a long way off, his father caught sight of him, and was filled with compassion. He ran to his son, embraced him and kissed him. His son said to him, 'Father, I have sinned against heaven and against you; I no longer deserve to be called your son.'" (Lk 15:20-21)

The prodigal father is sometimes pictured as a doddering old man who just doesn't get it. Such a portrait is paradoxically meant to highlight our Father's unreasonably extreme love for his children. But let's not be fooled. The wayward son might be as young as eighteen and his father a robust man in his early forties. And note he knew his son would be back: he was constantly scanning the horizon for the returnee. So we go back to the beginning and conclude that the father expected a total failure at the outset, but freely let his son depart with the inheritance money in his back pocket. Yet the father apparently kept the land: he and the elder son are still farming and the servants are still at work. Income is being produced, and a future inheritance is being generated.

So it appears that our heavenly Father knows what he's doing, even when he lets us toy with trouble and play with fire. The naïve Lord who is expected to deliver the goods and then get out of the way is just a façade of human fabrication. God only apparently allows his children to take advantage of him: "Make no mistake: God is not mocked" (Gal 6:7).

I need to remind myself of the constant temptation to think that I can outsmart God, even in the simple sense of believing I have a better handle on what's good for me. Almost unconsciously I can imagine myself as ardently seeking the Father's will and yet be surreptitiously at work behind his back. To free myself from this illusion and temptation, I can learn the art of constantly gliding from thinking, planning, and reflecting to surrendering my interior life to the divine gaze. When the Holy Spirit is given permission to scrutinize everything in me, even the shallow depths, I'll be quicker to agree with Paul that divine foolishness is always smarter than it looks.

Eternal Father, the secret to a loving relationship with you is to remind myself continually that you are closer to me than I to myself. Tear down any barriers I set up.

The Death of the Party

Father Lawrence Donohoo

"But [the younger son's] father ordered his servants, 'Quickly bring the finest robe and put it on him; put a ring on his finger and sandals on his feet. Take the fattened calf and slaughter it. Then let us celebrate with a feast, because this son of mine was dead, and has come to life again; he was lost, and has been found.' Then the celebration began." (Lk 15:22-24)

After committing a wicked act as a young boy, I expected the mother of all punishments from my father. Instead, I was not punished at all. After the dreadful interim period of waiting for the ax to fall and realizing it never would, I faced the awful experience of trying to exorcise the demon myself, but to no avail. It is a horrible thing to long for the cleansing balm of punishment and simply to be ignored.

Now compound the pain by placing oneself in the sandals of our lavishly dressed young man. Imagine how it feels to be feted in grand style after showing up at home as a rag-tag loser, a wasteful scoundrel, a derelict good-for-nothing. The younger son's scripted line about desired servanthood was memorized not because he wasn't sincere but because he was: he couldn't afford to get it wrong. However, only we now know his dirty little secret about working with the swine, but this filthy tidbit that must not come out only adds to the weight of an already over-burdened conscience. The son can only redeem this dark feast by enduring the celebration as a form of lavish punishment and a call to ongoing conversion.

In view of all the pain he would experience with such a distasteful welcoming, we are happy to report that the parable and the reality must go separate ways. Our heavenly Father goes further than his earthly double: he loves us enough to punish us when we sin. Satisfaction for our sin is the way we receive his forgiveness; restitution for our waywardness is our cooperation in being restored.

We can experience the joy of satisfaction even when not coming fresh from sinning ourselves. We can fill up "what is lacking in the afflictions of Christ" (Col 1:24), and make reparation for the sins of others through prayer and acts of penance. Then let the celebration begin.

Almighty Father, you discipline every child you receive because you want the very best for me and the very best from me. Help me to learn and grow from your just punishments.

243

A Just Return
Father Lawrence Donohoo

"Now the older son had been out in the field and, on his way back, as he neared the house, he heard the sound of music and dancing. He called one of the servants and asked what this might mean. The servant said to him, 'Your brother has returned and your father has slaughtered the fattened calf because he has him back safe and sound.' He became angry."
(Lk 15:25-28a)

At first sight, the faithful son and the wayward son appear to have little in common. One is faithless, the other faithful; the one lives a loose life, the other works hard. One asks for his share of the estate, the other asks for nothing. One feeds forbidden swine; the other cares for lawful cattle.

But a closer glance reveals a startling similarity: both are men of justice. The prodigal son wants *his* share of the estate that is due him. He wants to be treated as an adult, to dispose of *his* property as he sees fit—and dispose of it he will. Upon his return, he wishes to be treated with justice, not mercy, as a servant, not son.

For his part, the faithful son is scandalized at his father's injustice in slaughtering the fattened calf for this gaunt miscreant. He is livid that his younger brother whose inheritance is spent is now dipping into his own share. He bitterly contrasts his own fidelity with his brother's infidelity. Far from asking for what is due him, the elder brother asks for nothing—and receives nothing in return. Justice is the virtue appropriate to the fair distribution of material, measurable goods. Both brothers have the same desires; both are concerned with goods before all else. One labors in the hope of receiving it at a later time, the other has the audacity to waste his share right here and now.

Their limited take on justice points to the failure of both brothers in preferring the estate of the father to the father himself, his gifts to his affection, measurable goods to immeasurable love. They don't see that love must enclose justice rather than the other way around. Justice must take its moorings from love because material goods are ultimately in the service of persons, and persons cannot be relegated to a formula. Only when justice does justice to love can it order goods aright.

Loving Father, your prodigal love is seen in accepting my imperfect contrition and taking me back home time and time again. Let me never tire of the well-worn pathway.

Go for It

Father Lawrence Donohoo

"When [the older son] refused to enter the house, his father came out and pleaded with him. He said to his father in reply, 'Look, all these years I served you and not once did I disobey your orders; yet you never gave me even a young goat to feast on with my friends. But when your son returns who swallowed up your property with prostitutes, for him you slaughter the fattened calf.'" (Lk 15:28b-30)

So what's the real difference between the two brothers if they're both motivated by a strict definition of justice? Quite simply, the younger son gives in to his desire and goes out into the world. The older son stays home, works, and never asks for anything. With the news of the slaughtered calf wafting through his angry consciousness, memories bring him back to the day when that feast with his friends never took place. Both brothers have deep yearnings, but only one was able to act on them.

What's wrong with this man? The elder brother is the most intriguing person in the parable because it's not clear what makes him tick. Why does he work year after year without asking for anything? What went through his mind while his brother was away? Was he working for the future? Was he trying to win his father's approval? Why all this pent-up hostility? Why *didn't* he ever ask for a fattened calf or young goat? Is he envious that his carefree brother went out and lived it up? All we know is that he keeps all these injustices in mind and that it's mindless justice that keeps him going.

So there's our man: brimming with desires, totally unfulfilled. He really needs to walk into his heart and survey all these urges. They require identification, labeling, evaluation, processing. And then it's a matter of deciding which of these should see the light of day.

In some ways it's easier to put Danger: No Trespassing signs on all the warehouses of our desires since a few of them may in fact contain explosives. But shutting down the whole enterprise is to forget that God is creator of the human heart and maker of energy. If the Holy Spirit is Lord of our desires, then we need his counsel and his strength in knowing when and how we should let in the light and let out the fire.

Loving Father, I need to reflect continually on the constantly changing desires of my heart and submit them to your lordship. Help me to do so.

The Man Who Never Was

Father Lawrence Donohoo

"[The father] said to [the older son], 'My son, you are here with me always; everything I have is yours. But now we must celebrate and rejoice, because your brother was dead and has come to life again; he was lost and has been found.'"
(Lk 15:31-32)

Recall the parable of the son who said he would but didn't, and the son who said he wouldn't but did (Mt 21:28-32). Now we're faced with two brothers in similar straits. One was disobedient and reckless, but now returns in humility and contrition. The other is the model of obedience and industry, but refuses to come home. "There is none that does good, no, not one" (Ps 14:3, RSV).

So who is this elder son anyway who looks so virtuous from afar, but paints such a picture of disobedience, envy, and anger up close? He is nothing other than an illusion, the wayward son when he imagines he isn't a sinner. Lacking the courage to face his own sinfulness, he hides behind the façades of virtue and retreats to the safe haven of the fields—that in-between no-God's-land on the fence between foreign country and home. Distant from both father and brother, he creates his own standard of salvation that he alone measures up to. He works his entire life trying to possess what he cannot rightfully claim, while missing the father's offer to accept what is there waiting for him.

Because of sin, we can easily overlook the fact that in strict justice nothing is given us, but through divine love we have been given all things. Because of sin, grace now expresses itself, not simply as love, but as forgiving love. This happens through the truly prodigal Son, not the one with such narrow interests as the fast life, nor the one who lived a life of fasting. This is the prodigal Son who came to serve, and not to be served, who ran from village to village proclaiming the Father's love, who stretched forth his hands to heal others only to have them nailed, who threw his life into the arms of God and through his death saved us. This is the kind of wild prodigality to which we might aspire.

Heavenly Father, when I'm doing well and others aren't, it's so easy to canonize myself. Free me from self-delusion and the dangers that are most acute when unrecognized.

The Real Steward of the Story

Regis Martin

Then [Jesus] also said to his disciples, "A rich man had a steward who was reported to him for squandering his property. He summoned him and said, 'What is this I hear about you? Prepare a full account of your stewardship, because you can no longer be my steward.' The steward said to himself, 'What shall I do, now that my master is taking the position of steward away from me? I am not strong enough to dig and I am ashamed to beg. I know what I shall do so that [...] they may welcome me into their homes.'" (Lk 16:1-4)

One does not have to be a Carthusian monk subsisting on a diet of soda water and saltines to notice that the age in which we live is awash in avarice, positively lousy with loot. The shrieking sound of so many Wall Street Gordon Gekkos—"Greed is good!"—reminds us that in a world where money never sleeps, the gospel of ill-gotten gains remains firmly in the saddle. A stern sense of justice, in other words, puts us immediately at sword's point with the Unjust Steward of Saint Luke's Gospel. How eagerly we await the promised comeuppance! Will the outraged Owner send him to the slammer? There will be no passing Go and collecting two hundred dollars for this guy. And yet the Owner does nothing. Oh, sure, he'll fire him for having frittered away company funds, making him pony up an account of his failed stewardship. But, really, for someone both too wimpy for honest hard work, and too bloody proud to beg, one ought to be able to come up with a punishment more condign than that.

Ah, but that would be to miss the point of the story, which is deeply, unmistakably parabolic. Because it is we, fallen humanity, who are the real villains of the piece. The Unjust Steward is the perfect symbol of ourselves, for whom all that we have represents so much largesse given us by God. An overflow of sheer divine generosity to which we have absolutely no prior claim, no entitlement whatsoever. "All is grace," as that improbable Doctor of the Church, the Little Flower, tells us. The poet Pavese is surely right, then, to remind us, "What a great thought it is that truly *nothing is due* to us," that we have never been promised a thing. He is wrong, too: we have been promised something, namely, the grace to become, not money managers, but stewards of the kingdom, deploying our skills to otherworldly ends.

Eternal Father, enable us by your ever abundant grace always to be good stewards of your mercy, which alone may surpass all the riches of the world.

Feathering God's Nest

Regis Martin

"[The steward] called in his master's debtors one by one. To the first he said, 'How much do you owe my master?' He replied, 'One hundred measures of olive oil.' He said to him, 'Here is your promissory note. Sit down and quickly write one for fifty.' Then to another he said, [...] 'Here is your promissory note; write one for eighty.' And the master commended that dishonest steward for acting prudently. For the children of this world are more prudent in dealing with their own generation than are the children of light." (Lk 16:5-8)

In *The Republic*, Plato's seminal study of the meaning of justice, power is given only to those wise enough to disdain its exercise. Only the truly disinterested are qualified, he argues, because they alone have resisted the temptation to lust after it. Not so in the case of "the dishonest steward," whom the master strangely commends for "acting prudently" in giving away large chunks of his money. Surely, we protest, one should never grant responsibility for the management of another's wealth to someone whose earlier indiscretions placed him beyond the pale. For all that the wily steward succeeds in ingratiating himself with those whose load of debt he considerably lightens, we mustn't forget that it is all done at the expense of what is owed to the master. And yet the master appears not the least bit put off by the objections we raise. Indeed, having determined that the behavior of this scamp be praised, he grants him favorable status compared to "the children of light," who haven't the wit to augment their savings.

What is going on here, we want to know? This is hardly the stuff of Horatio Alger, where plucky young lads rise triumphant from rags to riches. This guy is a complete crook, bent on shamelessly feathering his own nest. There is nothing in him to commend. Yes, but we had better trust the teller if we're to explain this tale. And because it is a tale told by Christ himself, we need to pay close attention to the point he's making. And the point is this: we, the so-called children of light, need to apply the same foresight in relation to heavenly affairs as this clever chap showed in relation to earthly and material concerns. In heaping praise on his cooking the books, Jesus is not excusing the conduct of a crook; instead, he is urging us to show a comparable zeal when laying hold of the kingdom.

Heavenly Father, grant us the grace always to look after the needs of others, especially the poor, and not the insular and petty concerns of the self.

Inheriting What Is Yours
Regis Martin

"I tell you, make friends for yourselves with dishonest wealth, so that when it fails, you will be welcomed into eternal dwellings. The person who is trustworthy in very small matters is also trustworthy in great ones; and the person who is dishonest in very small matters is also dishonest in great ones. If, therefore, you are not trustworthy with dishonest wealth, who will trust you with true wealth? If you are not trustworthy with what belongs to another, who will give you what is yours?"
(Lk 16:9-12)

In lines written by that most gentle of Elizabethan poets, George Herbert, attention is paid to the great cleverness of God in arranging our salvation. Entitled "The Pulley," the poem shows God in the very act of bestowing his gifts. It is an impressive inventory, too, including great dollops of strength, beauty, wisdom, and honor. But not the gift of rest, which God chooses to withhold lest man be tempted to find rest in nature, rather than the God of nature. "Yet," says God, who enjoys a good pun, "let him keep the rest,/ But with repining restlessness:/ Let him be rich and weary, that at least,/ If goodness lead him not, yet weariness/ May toss him to my breast." It is a lovely little conceit, allowing God just enough leverage to lift the sinner safely into his arms.

The account in Luke's Gospel is along very much the same lines, revealing another striking instance of divine adroitness. What exactly is Christ getting at in offering us encouragement to become friendly with "dishonest wealth"? Only that when it all comes to grief, as all things human and material must, we may then turn from the world of mammon and find welcome amid the dwelling places of God. For some of us, I suspect, it will be the only way the crooked lines we've written will finally be made straight.

In addition, Christ tells us that unless we've proven ourselves "trustworthy in very small matters," why should the Father be moved to give us the kingdom? What he really means, of course, has to do with faithfulness in all the details, yes, even when they appear soiled and mud-splashed from contact with this all too grubby world in which we live. Nothing is ever too small or unimportant for Christ-bearers anxious to acquire the kingdom.

Most loving and generous Father, continue to pour out your blessings upon us, including especially the gift of your Son, who often awaits us in the details.

The Two Standards
Regis Martin

"No servant can serve two masters. He will either hate one and love the other, or be devoted to one and despise the other. You cannot serve God and mammon." The Pharisees, who loved money, heard all these things and sneered at [Jesus].
(Lk 16:13-14)

In the Vestibule of Hell, a most useful invention by Dante to designate the fate of those who will not hitch their wagon to any particular star, preferring endlessly to dither rather than to decide, we find those who, in trying to serve both God and mammon, merely succeed in splitting the difference between the two. Like the proverbial politician whose personal abhorrence for abortion never gets in the way of an equal and public defense of it, such humbuggery amounts to the homage vice invariably pays virtue. These are damned souls, declares Dante, who, quoting both Aristotle and Aquinas, have lost the good of the intellect and must therefore go and make their beds in Hell. "The dismal company/ Of wretched spirits/ Whose lives knew neither praise nor blame." Heaven will not have them, says Dante, their presence there would only diminish the light. "Deep Hell rejects so base a herd,/ Lest sin should boast itself because of them." It is an old story. In the end we shall all be forced to choose between God and mammon— *caritas* vs. *cupiditas*—and there can be no outcome more certain to fix our place in eternity.

How entirely disproportionate the two choices are. What possible attraction can nothingness offer? It is no more than love's shadow. Isn't this why the pharisaical never offer reasons to justify their greed (there aren't any), but instead "sneer" at those who refuse to be mastered by it? In Luke's account, the standard to be upheld is precisely God himself. Indeed, the Standard has come among us in the flesh. He is the real target of their ridicule, the Lord who enjoins us to decide. The sword that sunders is Christ himself. Constrained thus to choose between two competing attractions, of which only one can lay claim to an absolute love and loyalty, there is simply no contest.

Father of truth and justice, instruct us in the ways of wisdom and light; grant us the courage always to choose you over against the darkness.

Costing Not Less than Everything

Regis Martin

And [Jesus] said to [the Pharisees], "You justify yourselves in the sight of others, but God knows your hearts; for what is of human esteem is an abomination in the sight of God. The law and the prophets lasted until John; but from then on the kingdom of God is proclaimed, and everyone who enters does so with violence."

(Lk 16:15-16)

Which is easier? To convert an honest pagan, or a dishonest prig? The problem the prig has is that the hours are long and there's never a day off. A life for ever spent in scrubbing down one's moral façade is hard work. Who wants to appear obnoxiously virtuous all the time? How long can you keep that soufflé from collapsing? And then of course everyone knows what an awful fraud you've been. Like that hilarious humbug Tartuffe, preening himself on virtues he'll never practice. Or the real Pharisees, who affect a level of righteousness to which they would never dream of aspiring. Jesus, who has their number, does not hesitate to pronounce sentence, calling them "an abomination… in the sight of God." A real knuckleduster. It means they worship idols, which is certainly loathsome enough since the idolater aims to dethrone God. But positively ludicrous when they dare to substitute themselves in his place. As an exercise in infidelity it was sufficiently wicked to warrant divine condemnation before the coming of Christ.

But now that the preparatory phase of revelation has given way to the fulfillment brought by the Way himself having come among us, anyone wishing to enter the realm of grace and glory will first have to reckon with the One who pitched his tent in our midst. Here, as the poet Eliot reminds us, "The hint half guessed, the gift half understood, is/ Incarnation." With the shattering addition of Christ we come to "the still point of the turning world," without which, "There would be no dance, and there is only the dance." Only by violence may we bear away this kingdom. What that means is that we to whom the promised salvation has been given, must with utmost zeal and intensity seize the opportunity to enter therein. Heaven is only for those who most ardently desire to go there.

Heavenly Father, you have granted me a great longing for you. Enable me by your grace to reach the glory you have promised.

Not a Jot Shall Be Jettisoned

Regis Martin

"It is easier for heaven and earth to pass away than for the smallest part of a letter of the law to become invalid. Everyone who divorces his wife and marries another commits adultery, and the one who marries a woman divorced from her husband commits adultery." (Lk 16:17-18)

There once was a rabbi who lived during the reign of Herod, which puts him within a half-century of the birth of Christ, whose position on marriage was so bizarre that he would regularly permit divorce in cases where the wife's cooking was not up to speed. A slightly burnt blintz, one supposes, would be sufficient to nullify the union. And then there was another rabbi who lived a half-century after Christ, who allowed for divorce in the event a husband were to find a woman prettier than his wife. It was dangerous nonsense like this that Jesus decisively put an end to, enjoining men never to abandon their wives. The penalty for doing so, he declared, was adultery. What a sweeping change wrought by God's Word! And yet, notwithstanding this seeming departure from the practices of Judaism, Jesus insists that nothing in the law, not the least scintilla, is destined to fall away.

The truth of the indissolubility of marriage, its binding sacramental character, does not invite wholesale revisions of the law. Grace perfects nature, it does not abolish it. But now and again, as Chesterton reminds us, it becomes necessary to exaggerate in order to tell the truth. Hence the ease with which heaven and earth will pass away before even "the smallest part of the letter of the law" will undergo repeal. Here Jesus has recourse to that wonderful rhetorical device known as hyperbole, whose exercise enables him to emphasize the enduring importance of the moral law. It is not rendered obsolete by the coming of the kingdom, he tells the Pharisees, who were for ever devising evasive measures to circumvent it. So binding is the law, in fact, that its protections extend even to the maintenance of the marital bond. To think otherwise, says Jesus, is not an honest reading of the text, but instead a falsification prompted by self-serving motives. In short, a stolen base.

All-powerful God and Father, help us to reverence your law in every circumstance of our lives, observing it with exacting fidelity and love.

The Truth of Lazarus and Ourselves

Regis Martin

"There was a rich man who dressed in purple garments and fine linen and dined sumptuously each day. And lying at his door was a poor man named Lazarus, covered with sores, who would gladly have eaten his fill of the scraps that fell from the rich man's table. Dogs even used to come and lick his sores."

(Lk 16:19-21)

"We may see the small value God has for riches," wrote Alexander Pope, "by the people he gives them to." And, to be sure, the tendency among many to whom much is given is that they are for ever on the lookout for opportunities to flaunt it. Like the rich man in Luke's Gospel, arrayed in purple and fine linen, whose sumptuous suppers stand in stark contrast to poor Lazarus lying in misery outside his door. Not only has Lazarus nothing to eat, the rich man disdaining to share even the scraps that fall from his table, but he must suffer the dogs to come and lick the sores that cover his body as well.

Yet while we are moved to pity poor Lazarus, whose arms appear always outstretched, we recognize at the same time that here, as Monsignor Giussani so often reminds us, is the real protagonist of human history. For are we not all beggars before the Lord, asking for what we could never ourselves give? And what does the name bespeak but that he, Lazarus (from the Hebrew Eleazar, "God has helped"), will be the very one whom God helps? It is no mere accident, in other words, that he bears a distinct name, whose meaning provides an immediate connection to God, to the One on whom he depends for everything. He will never be wholly destitute so long as he cries out to God. The ladder that leads to complete human fulfillment is there before us all; Lazarus at least realizes that he is too poor to climb it alone. Not so the rich man, who thinks he has already reached the top. It is right that we remain indignant with him, because by his refusal to help his stricken brother he will never climb the ladder. Indeed, he has broken the deepest bond of all, that in the sight of God we beggars are all one.

Merciful Father, full of compassion for Lazarus, help us to see that we are as poor as he, and teach us to call on you for all that we need of life, of love.

The Peril of Ignoring the Poor

Regis Martin

"When the poor man died, he was carried away by angels to the bosom of Abraham. The rich man also died and was buried, and from the netherworld, where he was in torment, he raised his eyes and saw Abraham far off and Lazarus at his side. And he cried out, 'Father Abraham, have pity on me. Send Lazarus to dip the tip of his finger in water and cool my tongue, for I am suffering torment in these flames.'" (Lk 16:22-24)

It was Chesterton who once said that he could never quite understand the necessity people felt to heap honors upon a man simply because at some point in his life he had managed to corner the soybean market. And we all know Lenin's wry prediction that when the last bourgeois is hanged, it will have been another capitalist rogue who sold the hangman the rope. We are not told what market the rich man in Luke's Gospel contrived to corner, only that he appeared to be obscenely rich as a result. Egregiously indifferent to the sufferings of poor Lazarus, too, whose abject state he had done nothing to relieve. And while he may have skipped the rope in this life, he will almost certainly get it in the next. For it is from that place, the seeming depths of the netherworld where he lay in torment, that he now cries out to father Abraham, to whose bosom Lazarus has at last come, carried thereto by the very angels of God, imploring him to send Lazarus down into Sheol to assuage the flames he is forced to suffer.

What dreadful punishments await those who will not feed the hungry, nor comfort the afflicted. Indeed, the text here is very clear on two things: one, that the soul of man is imperishable, it will survive the dissolution of death; two, that there will be a reckoning on the other side, the wicked shall not escape justice. Those who think God bestows rectitude upon the rich because of the fortunes they amassed, while the poor are made to suffer because they hadn't the wit to corner a single market, will find, in the fiery encounter with Judgment, second of the Four Last Things ever to be remembered, that not to look upon one's neighbor as another self, to ignore the cries of God's children, is to court an eternity of loss for oneself.

Heavenly Father, teach us to hear the cry of the poor, heeding in their voice the sound of your Son, who calls us to serve all who suffer.

Severe Mercy
Regis Martin

"Abraham replied, 'My child, remember that you received what was good during your lifetime while Lazarus likewise received what was bad; but now he is comforted here, whereas you are tormented. Moreover, between us and you a great chasm is established to prevent anyone from crossing who might wish to go from our side to yours or from your side to ours.'"
(Lk 16:25-26)

A colleague of mine likes to tell his students on the first day of class that if they only show up, they can expect mercy. And the others? They get justice. The students of course find this hilarious. But they come to class. The Gospels reveal a God rather more demanding. It is not enough merely to show up to receive the promised mercy; we need to dispense it as well. "For the judgment is merciless to one who has not shown mercy," we are told in the Letter of Saint James, even as, "mercy triumphs over judgment." Far better for the rich man, writhing in eternal torment on the far side of death, had he but tried to lift the sufferings of poor Lazarus in this life. The fate of the poor must not be left to the ministrations of unclean dogs who come to lick their sores.

The poor are everywhere, their presence mute testimony to the dolorous disguise Christ wears in their midst. It will be too late on reaching the shores of the netherworld for the rich man to ask Abraham to send Lazarus "to dip the tip of his finger in water," and thus allay his thirst. So vast will be the differences between them be—a chasm indeed of sheerest incommensurability—that nothing and no one will be able to cross from one to the other side. What else is hell but that which stands justly condemned by the good God who casts it out of his creation for ever. All that cannot be reconciled with the exigencies of love is hell. "In the evening of our lives," Saint John of the Cross reminds us, "we shall be examined on love." Hell is the condition of those unwilling to love, the self-inflicted pain of those who take themselves to hell. Because God, as C. S. Lewis reminds us, paid us "the intolerable compliment" of taking seriously the choices we make.

Merciful Father, move us to show mercy to others, and so become beneficiaries of your Son's mercy, whom we truly see and serve in the poor.

Warnings from the Underworld

Regis Martin

"[The rich man] said, 'Then I beg you, father, send him to my father's house, for I have five brothers, so that he may warn them, lest they too come to this place of torment.' But Abraham replied, 'They have Moses and the prophets. Let them listen to them.'" (Lk 16:27-29)

The cleverest ruse of the devil, who was a liar from the beginning, is to tell us that he does not exist. Or that anyone actually goes to hell in order to keep company with him. The Scriptures tell a different story. They awaken us to the terrifying news that a place of torment does exist, inhabited by those who will not serve God, who refuse the summons to joy and love. As a wise and humane retreat master used to say, hell is the place where the damned announce over and over: "I do not want to love. I do not want to be loved. I want only to be left alone." The doors, therefore, leading into hell are locked on the inside.

Is this where the rich man in Luke's Gospel languishes in blackest misery? And if so, why does he entreat Abraham to send Lazarus to warn his brothers of the punishments to come? If hell, as the saintly Father Zossima reveals in Dostoevsky's *The Brothers Karamozov*, "is the suffering of being unable to love," why this concern for others? Besides, isn't it too late on reaching the shores of the netherworld to send warnings to anyone, much less those who scorn the practice of charity? If the Mosaic law and the warnings of the prophets were not sufficient to disabuse the wicked, how would the testimony of one damned soul succeed in moving their hearts? Virtue is not knowledge, despite the protestations of philosophers like Plato. Still, how strangely out of character he is to evince so sudden and unexpected a seizure of concern to avert another's damnation! How right Saint Gregory the Great was in telling us that, in each encounter with the scriptural Word, one does not so much solve a problem as deepen a sense of mystery. Here is a mystery so deep that only grace may enable us to endure it.

Father of heaven and earth, send us the grace of clarity to see Christ in all that awaits us, and the courage to choose him in all that we do.

The Urgency of the Choice

Regis Martin

"[The rich man] said, 'Oh no, father Abraham, but if someone from the dead goes to them, they will repent.' Then Abraham said, 'If they will not listen to Moses and the prophets, neither will they be persuaded if someone should rise from the dead.'"
(Lk 16:30-31)

In every life, however fleeting, there is one essential drama, played out against an absolute horizon constantly beckoning us to one or another eternal possibility. Either the company of God and his angels and saints in heaven, or the infernal isolation of the self-centered self in hell. We hope for the one even as we fear the other. As for the denizens of either place, there can be no communication between them. This of course is what lends so surreal a quality to the exchange between Abraham and the rich man. How is it that the two are able to speak across so fixed and immutable a divide, representing two entirely disparate, discontinuous realms? Or that it would be possible for the rich man, reaching back into the world he left behind, there to send Lazarus in order to set his brothers straight? Surely he must see the unreality of what he is proposing. And, more to the point, even if a dead man were suddenly to decamp in their midst, armed with copy book reminders regarding the wages of sin, why should they listen to him any more than they heeded the warnings of Moses and the prophets? It will do them no good, Abraham seems to suggest, even if Christ himself were to rise from the dead. Mercy deferred in this world means mercy denied in the next.

Yet the dialogue between the two is intended to dramatize, to heighten, the importance of deciding right now, of making choices whose outcome will determine the place where we spend all of eternity. The teaching of Christ and his Church is very clear: the need for repentance is right now when, during this brief respite, there is still time enough to change course. "Let us be converted," exhorts Saint John Chrysostom, "so that we will not have to lament uselessly like that rich man when we die and tears can do us no good."

Merciful Father, help us to allay the sufferings of the poor, and in looking after them may we recognize the sorrows of your Son, and so bring comfort to him.

Insinuated Woe

Father William M. Joensen

[Jesus] said to his disciples, "Things that cause sin will inevitably occur, but woe to the person through whom they occur. It would be better for him if a millstone were put around his neck and he be thrown into the sea than for him to cause one of these little ones to sin. Be on your guard!" (Lk 17:1-3a)

Sin happens. But Jesus alerts us to the fact that we cannot erase the distinction between the "things that cause sin" and sinners themselves. We cannot claim to be flotsam in the sea of life when we consent to precursors that cannot explain our conscious choices to depart from the sensible human good, freely to misuse people and things for our own selfish purposes.

In our own time, incarcerated criminals employed in prison food services find their kitchen utensils (such as knives, tongs, and tenderizers) chained to the grills and ovens to which they are posted as a protective measure so they might not wreak further havoc rather than simply put food on the table. The tools meant to nourish life can be transformed into weapons of death.

Even if we have never succumbed to using lethal force against another innocent life, we know some of the tools that are the stock-in-trade of our self-imposed estrangement from God and one another: words, gestures, affected indifference, outright disobedience, blame, blasphemy, possessiveness, ingratitude are the more subtle instruments that assault the spirit and progressively constrict the range of our relationships. Sin is no stranger to us. Actual sin does not arise in a vacuum; we can trace the bloodlines of sin back to the beginning of humanity. We are the recipients of potentially lethal alleles of a spiritual nature (antagonism toward God, conceit, cold-heartedness, lust, laziness, as well as other so-called "deadly sins").

Christ died and rose so that human freedom might be restored, and the toolbox entrusted to us might serve its appointed end. We guard ourselves against the presumption that God's mercy will moss over our stony hearts; our default attitudes do not automatically guarantee that we will lead others to God, instead of drawing them down with us into the depths.

The weight of my guilt would crush me, heavenly Father, but the stone rolled before your Son's tomb has ground all sin as fine as sand. Let me stand upright today, so that others might not be led astray.

Losing Count

Father William M. Joensen

"If your brother sins, rebuke him; and if he repents, forgive him.
And if he wrongs you seven times in one day and returns to you
seven times saying, 'I am sorry,' you should forgive him."
(Lk 17:3b-4)

Priests can readily testify to the dynamics of a sort of "sacramental amnesia" whereby they do not keep track of individual sins of persons who regularly go to confession—even for habitual sins toward which most of us tend. Each encounter, each declaration that "I am sorry" occurs in an original moment, a novel event whereby all that has taken place since the last confession is reconfigured, joined to the lively influx of the Holy Spirit in the perpetual now of God grafted onto our personal history. The Spirit does not call us to become preoccupied or tentative based on how many times we have fallen and needed forgiveness, but catalyzes a sacramental "an-amnesia" that calls us to remember the immeasurable mercy-love of Christ.

This same Spirit empowers every baptized person to exercise his or her baptismal priesthood in the ordinary calendar days that present us with innumerable chances perhaps first to rebuke, but then remember mercy, and be reconciled with one another. This Spirit converts us from a small-minded, petty, and spiteful way of being, where we initially find ourselves replaying words said or unsaid, constructing witty and caustic replies, and thus capitalize on the misgivings and ugliness of others. Instead, we drink from the draught of genuine prayer and sense the opportunity to allow divine Charity to flow and reform us, willing to "for-bear" grace even when none has been tendered to us—and thus slipping beyond the world's way of assessing credit and blame. For we know all too well how the sinner suffers while also recalling the precedent of the One whose loving forgiveness is the credit rating upon which we rely. We are not afraid to depend on a God who freely depends on us to keep drawing a world gone broke into the account of the kingdom.

Infinitely merciful Father, you do not dwell on my sins, but seek me out in the person of your Son. Rebuke me if you will, but only to convert me from my reluctance to forgive others as you forgive me.

Trees, Not Hedges

Father William M. Joensen

And the apostles said to the Lord, "Increase our faith." The Lord replied, "If you have faith the size of a mustard seed, you would say to [this] mulberry tree, 'Be uprooted and planted in the sea,' and it would obey you." (Lk 17:5-6)

A couple whose wedding was eventually called off involved a very successful hedge fund trader who was asking his fiancée to sign a prenuptial agreement—"just in case." Her misgivings centered on the fact that though they were about to enter into a communion of love where they would honor and obey one another, he was reserving what was "mine," and denying that all would be "ours." Any sharing would be hedged by an escape clause signifying a lack of faith that their love would endure.

One cannot gauge a personal faith portfolio based on amount or duration; faith that dots the exclamation point at the end of this sentence is potent enough to transplant a tree into the sea! But we must constantly allow the tree doctor to graft his cross onto our own hearts, transforming our ability to trust by centering all we do in the awareness of his ever-increasing, enduring presence within us.

Faithful persons risk letting God draw them beyond the shoreline of their own security without the ready consolation of feeling their roots touch or tread along a false bottom they have constructed—the basis of a shallow life. We agree through daily decision become perpetual dedication to the "our-ness" that is a compact between Christ and us, making the same sort of exchange as Jesus did with his Father, even if our mutual fund is hardly of the same degree. We cling tenaciously to the tree that is often partially submerged by worry and worldly demands, but which also keeps us from drowning in the deceit born of an over-calculating self-sufficiency. Persons of faith are like birds who are able to taste the mulberries from a tree they did not plant, except that the fruit they are privileged to sample is something far sweeter: to know themselves judged faithful to the Faithful One.

Faithful Father, you heed the seeds of prayers that could fill the sea. Unsnarl roots that would cling to a shallow life, and graft me more firmly by faith to the Tree of Life which is your Son's cross.

Truly Over Time

Father William M. Joensen

"Who among you would say to your servant who has just come in from plowing or tending sheep in the field, 'Come here immediately and take your place at table'? Would he not rather say to him, 'Prepare something for me to eat. [...] You may eat and drink when I am finished'? Is he grateful to that servant because he did what was commanded? So should it be with you. When you have done all you have been commanded, say, 'We are unprofitable servants; we have done what we were obliged to do.'" (Lk 17:7-10)

We tend to dismiss good deeds performed primarily from a sense of duty in contrast to those done out of a felt sense of love and compassion. But Jesus corrects our tendency to underestimate the value of doing our duty by supplying lines that will come in handy for those who might flag in their kingdom commitment: "When you have done all you have been commanded, say, 'We are unprofitable servants; we have done what were we obliged to do'" (Lk 17:10). Whether we are self-employed or not, we are challenged to consider whether we have yet truly to order all our time to Christ, so that all we are is employed for the sake of our relationship with him.

Are lifestyle demands driving the number of hours we work? Do we expect others to work odd or long hours so as to be available to us 24/7— obliging them to curtail family time in the face of scant consumer loyalty? And closer to home: how good are we at transitions during the course of the day? Do we pray as we move from home to field or office, from desk to lunchtime conversation, from sports practice to supper table? In the process, do we find ourselves "passing over" or passing on our pent-up frustrations that we unload on others whom we expect to serve us by their forbearance, sitting there and taking our misdirected anger because we have failed to consult our confidant Christ, who stands always ready to attend to us?

Patience may not win us plaudits or quiet the grumblings of our stomachs, but the ability to wait and keep working is itself a profound form of suffering. We take part in the Passion of the Servant who continues to toil until the end of time, when he will turn over his timesheet and those who have dutifully collaborated with him to his heavenly Father, and all will receive their proper recognition.

Father of every age, you are not finished with me, even when I anticipate only my own satisfaction. Bind me more perfectly to you in patient toil and trust that you will fill me at the appointed time.

Showing Sin Off

Father William M. Joensen

*As [Jesus] continued his journey to Jerusalem, he traveled
through Samaria and Galilee. As he was entering a village, ten
lepers met [him]. They stood at a distance from him and raised
their voice, saying, "Jesus, Master! Have pity on us!" And when
he saw them, he said, "Go show yourselves to the priests."
As they were going they were cleansed. (Lk 17:11-14)*

Jesus knows the afflictions and guilt that would drive us into
the remote reaches of community, where misery does not
really love company, but tolerates it as less than the evil of
complete isolation. We readily limit ourselves to persons whose
story more closely matches our own and live in a contracted zone
of life. Jesus asks the lepers to change course as part of a process of
making their way back into the midst of community.

It is a sad fact that though modern medicine can cure Hansen's
Disease (leprosy), there are global sites where the disease endures
because of inadequate treatment. It is a more tragic fact that
though ample remedies for venial sin are available (e.g., personal
acts of reparation, prayer, participation in Eucharist), there is still
widespread reluctance in some quarters for persons to avail themselves of the most direct means to cure us from the wounds of sin:
the sacrament of reconciliation. Jesus wants poor souls to become
pure souls. He hears our cries for mercy. And his healing grace is
already in motion when we aim these cries toward him, without
shouting down his own immediate response: "Go show yourselves
to the priests."

Jesus charges priests to administer his saving forgiveness, for
they uniquely represent both himself and the larger Church from
which one has become estranged by sin. The examination of conscience according to the number and species of sins, the intention to approach Christ in confession, and the steps we take to
get there are parts of the healing process where God's power is
at work. Mercy lines the entire way to mercy. Repentance tends
toward reconciliation with the visible Church. God is justified in
asking us to incarnate this therapeutic encounter in sacramental
form. And we are justified in the course of heeding his command
to show ourselves to the priests.

*Father of my life, how often I raise my voice to you, and yet drown
out your Son's response. Speak to me today in the key of his compassion, and I will heed whatever you ask me to do.*

Return to Sender

Father William M. Joensen

And one of [the lepers], realizing he had been healed, returned, glorifying God in a loud voice; and he fell at the feet of Jesus and thanked him. He was a Samaritan. Jesus said in reply, "Ten were cleansed, were they not? Where are the other nine? Has none but this foreigner returned to give thanks to God?" Then he said to him, "Stand up and go; your faith has saved you." (Lk 17:15-19)

It may seem to squelch our childlike spontaneity when we have to be taught to say "thank you." But for at least one man for whom the scourge of leprosy was removed, thanksgiving is a mark of a fully restored childlike spirit. His act of return and glorification of his Lord and Savior is a pleasing sacrifice to God.

Healing is part of, but not synonymous with, being saved. Gratitude is a necessary ingredient that perfects the process of salvation, realized by abiding with Christ and every other soul who has been afforded reason to give thanks, to make sacrifice. Jesus is the source of salvation for which we give thanks most perfectly in the celebration of Eucharist, the thanksgiving sacrifice in which Christ's death on the cross delivers us from the affliction of sin and confirms us in the communion he shares with the Father in the Spirit. Gratitude is not reserved until all has been made perfectly whole. The Mass is the heart of a process that completes, where God's children reflect God's goodness as they say "thank you." Saint Francis de Sales holds out to us the image of a little child who desires nothing except to be with his mother, with whom he thinks himself to be one being. The child does not even think he has his own will, and so leaves care to his mother, to will what she finds good.

We want to be united to One worthy of all respect, attention, and gratitude, who conducts us to worship and back home and everywhere in between. Christ's will is that we become a perfect sacrifice in ourselves. Jesus himself is the means by which we offer thanks. He is the God in whom thanksgiving and faithfulness are met. Jesus gives us himself as one to whom we return, and in doing so, nudges us further along the way to salvation.

Most glorious Father, how often I forget to thank you. Grant me a Eucharistic heart, always grateful that I can come and praise you in the midst of your assembly, the Church.

Closer than It Appears

Father William M. Joensen

*Asked by the Pharisees when the kingdom of God would come,
[Jesus] said in reply, "The coming of the kingdom of God cannot
be observed, and no one will announce, 'Look, here it is,' or,
'There it is.' For behold, the kingdom of God is among you."*
(Lk 17:20-21)

Visitors flock to the city of Krakow, Poland, from which Pope John Paul II was called as archbishop to become Saint Peter's successor. The exquisitely beautiful medieval "old city" is not marked off from the surrounding "new city" by massive fortified walls but by a verdant park that forms a green ring around the *centrum*, through which people freely stroll and linger on benches under the leaves.

The Pharisees who engage Jesus on a kingdom reconnaissance mission sense that their grip on the city is slipping away. They seek to specify the boundaries of God's activity so that they can fortify and reassert their control over all that lies within their purview. They look for a physical locus where they can declare who lies within and outside God's righteous protection, who are "citizens" of the covenant and who are aliens. They would draw arbitrary lines that evaporate in thin air as the wind of the Spirit rustles through the leaves of human lives.

Jesus is not interested in building walls that restrict access to the reception of God's promise, or demarcating the dignity of human lives based on developmental trimesters, country of origin, or how many carbon credits their existence consumes. He advances a society where both the old and the new contribute to the flourishing of persons whose function may be compromised in the world's eyes, but who serve God's providential purpose by calling us to look within more deeply. Merle, a person with Down syndrome who served Mass for many years and eventually died of natural causes in his late fifties, was such a man. Merle's transparency and truthfulness revealed his heart, captured in comments like: "You're late"; "I'm hurting"; "That was good"; "I'll miss you." One did not have to be either a scientist or a scholar to sense the kingdom in Merle's midst.

You reign, O God! Like the air in which birds fly, your kingdom surrounds me. Help me attend to your subtle presence in persons whom I meet today, Lord, and I will announce what I have seen and heard.

Ground Lightning

Father William M. Joensen

Then [Jesus] said to his disciples, "The days will come when you will long to see one of the days of the Son of Man, but you will not see it. There will be those who will say to you, 'Look, there he is,' [or] 'Look, here he is.' Do not go off, do not run in pursuit. For just as lightning flashes and lights up the sky from one side to the other, so will the Son of Man be [in his day]. But first he must suffer greatly and be rejected by this generation." (Lk 17:22-25)

Fierce thunderstorms roiling on the horizon draw many of us outdoors to behold nature's fireworks display. Yet weather experts remind us of the fact that many of the farmers, golfers, and other persons hit by lightning in the midst of a storm are not struck from above, but by current coursing from the ground below. Storm chasers who look to the heavens for spectacular displays or more mild types who seek reassurance that they are out of harm's way would do well to realize that "acts of God" frequently surface beneath one's own feet.

Spiritual storm chasers who zealously seek cauldrons of controversy, who look to make some volatile prophetic statement that charges the atmosphere and flashes for a few fleeting moments, will never be satisfied in their pursuits. They ultimately are trying to shine the spotlight on themselves, rather than on the Son of Man.

Jesus realizes that the path he has adopted spells certain death, but he does not hasten the process by provoking a premature end. Along the way, he has to deal with disciples such as James and John, the "sons of thunder," who are spoiling for a fight, who want to turn the wrath of God loose like so much fire from the sky. But Jesus knows which storms to engage and which ones to let pass. Saint Ignatius of Antioch would later observe, "Christianity is not the work of persuasion, but, whenever it is hated by the world, it is a work of power." God's wisdom flashes from disciples who eventually became martyrs, who endured periods where grace prompted them to walk—even run—away from conflict, until the day the Spirit spoke to them and said: "Thus far, and no further. Stand your ground. I am with you. Stake your claim. Suffer now, and no longer. And the light of your witness will roil around the world."

Ignite my heart, Father of Light, not so that I can run to perform projects of my own design, but so that I will gladly remain where you would set me, and serve you to the end of my days.

Wedded to the Familiar

Father William M. Joensen

"As it was in the days of Noah, so it will be in the days of the Son of Man; they were eating and drinking, marrying and giving in marriage up to the day that Noah entered the ark, and the flood came and destroyed them all. Similarly, as it was in the days of Lot: they were eating, drinking, buying, selling, planting, building; on the day when Lot left Sodom, fire and brimstone rained from the sky to destroy them all. So it will be on the day the Son of Man is revealed." (Lk 17:26-30)

When we attend a wedding reception, we basically know the drill: mingle and sip until being invited to take our seats to dine; welcome and toasts by father of the groom, best man, and maid of honor; bouquets and garters tossed, cutting of the cake, and dancing and conversation for as long as we care to linger. There is a ritual that relieves some discomfort and suspense about how we are to act. But this wedding reception ritual, like other activities in life, can be drained of significance and reduced to mere routine by persons who drift complacently through the motions as spectators or set pieces.

Jesus rouses us from our senseless conceit with words that are more acrid than burning leaves, that should cause our eyes to tear, our souls to shudder. He does not threaten or scold, but simply reminds us of past perils that should seize our attention and awaken us to the vivid possibilities that each day presents to meet and wed ourselves more deeply to the living God. The Son of Man establishes a new protocol of involvement with the humanly familiar by uniting himself habitually to our situation. Jesus releases the potential of each and every choice we make to deepen our intimacy with God, to sustain the ingrained disposition to engage the Bridegroom beyond pre-scripted compliance. He infuses existence with elements of good ritual: a sense of mystery, reverence, and gratitude. All our life rituals are like the parquet floor for God to dance with us, to free us for worship in Spirit and truth, as we expect the in-breaking presence of a God who is not content to reign remotely from above. Even our sense of past and pending peril can be transformed into hope that today God stands ready to reveal his embedded, burning presence, and will not leave us like so much burnt toast.

O Father of my ancestors, do not let me become flooded by preoccupations with my daily affairs. Grace me to recognize your hand at work amidst my familiar routine; I celebrate your steadfast love today and always.

Standing Offer

Father William M. Joensen

"On that day, a person who is on the housetop and whose belongings are in the house must not go down to get them, and likewise a person in the field must not return to what was left behind. Remember the wife of Lot. Whoever seeks to preserve his life will lose it, but whoever loses it will save it."
(Lk 17:31-33)

My mom has started divesting herself of items and images that she wants her children to have. Despite our protests that her largesse is morbidly premature, she claims, "Better when alive than dead!" Among the items I have received is a porcelain bowl and pitcher that belonged to her own mother—that was given to my grandma by her priest son, my uncle, when he was stationed close to where I presently serve. What goes around, comes around!

Jesus warns us against the tendency to construct our own personal museums in which we stand like some wax figure preserved for perpetuity. While we do not disdain the items we possess with an affection that is part sentimental, part sacramental, we press on through the seasons of life ready to release what has been handed on to us, rather than salting it away for some rare occasion that never arrives. We intentionally check the tendency to become possessed by the tangible things and memories that will despoil us of our share of our heavenly inheritance.

Christ's mother Mary, the Pillar of Wisdom, stands as the antitype to Lot's wife, a notorious member of the "left behind" crowd. As much as Mary cherishes her Son and takes every word and gesture to heart, she resists the temptation to possess and overprotect him. In tandem they daily hand over their respective wills—the sole possession we might think we are entitled to retain at all cost. Jesus and Mary are like pitchers pouring themselves out into the bowls of our being, enabling us to bless others as we do the same. While I might presently possess the pitcher and bowl my mom has given, I know that I, too, will pass them on to others. For as any good mother teaches us, there is a world of difference between offering everything as gift versus the living death that eventually just leaves it all behind.

Blessed, beautiful Father, you place so much into my possession that I can barely keep track. Free me for what lies ahead; do not let me cling to the past, or forget that all is gift, especially my life.

Observation Deck

Father William M. Joensen

"I tell you, on that night there will be two people in one bed;
one will be taken, the other left. And there will be two women
grinding meal together; one will be taken, the other left."
[… Jesus' disciples] said to him in reply, "Where, Lord?"
He said to them, "Where the body is, there also
the vultures will gather." (Lk 17:34-37)

A solitary bike accident on a rural highway left one side of my body looking like so much hamburger. I called a friend on my mobile phone to come pick me up and take me to the emergency room. While I waited, I watched several hawks circle above me, chuckling to myself that from their vantage point they must have regarded me as a particularly hefty piece of road kill.

From his heavenly throne, God does not view us as a species of cosmic road kill. To us, God seems to let death swoop in arbitrarily upon paired persons doing the same thing, with earthly reward and punishment doled out absent rhyme or reason. Some of the greatest saints had to confront the siren song of despair which claims that life leads only to death, and that we daily grind meaning into mush until we fall exhausted into the bed of oblivion. Persons whose celestial navigation affirms that there is more beyond the horizon of mortal death, in contrast to those who reject God and the afterlife, seem to operate in parallel universes whose interface consists of our daily tasks and obligations.

Luke takes us to the heavenly observation deck as he challenges us to work zealously within the world as a form of kingdom service. Persons who make their living on the land, who work around heavy machinery, who defend public and global peace, and who serve on emergency rescue teams are daily reminded that life is fragile and too often short. But we do not simply roll on until we hit the deck of fate: our acts of friendship and love display the truth that we are in this for the long haul, no matter when death occurs. God does not spare us from accidents, but tenders a life assurance policy that we will only appreciate when we expire—not from exhaustion or neglect, but from hope finally fulfilled.

You watch over me, loving God and Father, as your Son tends to my wounds and restores me to his Body. Take what you will from me, and leave only what is not from you in the first place.

A Just Decision
Heather King

Then [Jesus] told [his disciples] a parable about the necessity for them to pray always without becoming weary. He said, "There was a judge in a certain town who neither feared God nor respected any human being. And a widow in that town used to come to him and say, 'Render a just decision for me against my adversary.' For a long time the judge was unwilling, but eventually he thought, [...] "Because this widow keeps bothering me I shall deliver a just decision for her lest she finally come and strike me."' (Lk 18:1-5)

A child will tug and tug at his father's pants leg to get attention. A child will set up an unholy wailing in order to be heard.

As adults, we want to appear seemly. We want to keep our desperate longing under wraps. We're embarrassed by the intensity with which we hunger for righteousness.

One of the reasons I find Saint Thérèse of Lisieux so compelling is that she was just like the importunate widow. Even as a child, Thérèse yearned to enter the cloistered convent at Carmel. So determined was she to enter at fifteen in fact—three years earlier than the minimum age—that as a teenager she traveled to Rome with her father, and on November 20, 1887, knelt at the feet of Pope Leo XIII.

In spite of having been given strict orders on no account to speak, she pleaded: "Most Holy Father, I have a great grace to ask of you!... Most Holy Father, in honor of your jubilee, allow me to enter Carmel at the age of fifteen." The Pope, startled, responded, "Well, my child, do what your superiors tell you." At which point, not satisfied with that remark, Thérèse placed her hands on his knees and in a pleading voice begged, "'Oh! Most Holy Father, if you were to say yes, everyone would be willing!'... He looked at me fixedly and pronounced these words, emphasizing each syllable: 'All right... All right... *You will enter if it is God's will.*'" Still loath to leave without having received a definite yes, Thérèse was then taken beneath the arms by the Papal Guards, lifted up, and forcibly torn away, sobbing.

Christ knew the love required to overcome the fear of being considered a pest.

"Woman's will, God's will," the French say: Thérèse entered Carmel, at the age of fifteen, on April 9, 1888.

Loving Father, give us the courage to ask again and again and again. Protect us from a lukewarm, timid faith.

Faith on Earth

Heather King

*The Lord said, "Pay attention to what the dishonest judge says.
Will not God then secure the rights of his chosen ones who call
out to him day and night? Will he be slow to answer them? I tell
you, he will see to it that justice is done for them speedily. But
when the Son of Man comes, will he find faith on earth?"*

(Lk 18:6-8)

So much of life is waiting, and how impatient we are! How quick we are to think God is slow, but how slow we are to turn to trust and love him! Like the importunate widow, we beg and beg, and he showers us with gifts. The real question is: When we get what we want, what do we do with it?

I once heard a woman say, "I used to stay up all night doing crack, then lie down at 4 AM and say, 'God, please help me sleep!'" I so related. When I was in the throes of my own addiction, if I managed to get any kind of sleep, I'd get up, light a cigarette, and start drinking again.

We want God to do for us, and then to forget him. We want a magician, a miracle worker. If we really knew how little was due us, maybe we wouldn't quite so insistently ask for it. As Oscar Wilde observed in *De Profundis*, "The people who work for an hour in the vineyard in the cool of the evening receive just as much reward as those who have toiled there all day long in the hot sun. Why shouldn't they? Probably no one deserved anything."

That we don't deserve anything and yet are freely given everything is the whole radical basis of Christianity. Through absolutely no virtue of my own, my obsession to drink was finally lifted. I could hardly believe that my bad track record was not going to be used against me. I could start falling asleep instead of passing out. I could start seeking God and helping another alcoholic.

Christ wants not justice, but mercy. He wants us to give what we've been given away. He wants us to come awake in love.

*Heavenly Father, help us to have faith. Help us call to you day
and night, not with demands, but with thanks and praise.*

The Rest of Humanity

Heather King

[Jesus] then addressed this parable to those who were convinced of their own righteousness and despised everyone else.
"Two people went up to the temple area to pray; one was a Pharisee and the other was a tax collector. The Pharisee took up his position and spoke this prayer to himself, 'O God, I thank you that I am not like the rest of humanity— greedy, dishonest, adulterous—or even like this tax collector. I fast twice a week, and I pay tithes on my whole income.'" (Lk 18:9-12)

Rules make us feel safe. Rules make us feel like if we follow them, we get a gold star. "What would happen if everyone started bending the rules?" a certain kind of person indignantly asks. But if anyone bent the rules, it was Christ. The rule that says if you catch a woman in adultery, you gather in a circle and heave stones at her until she's dead was one of the rules Christ bent. The rule that says to shine up your eating vessels on the outside was the rule Christ bent when he told the Pharisees: Your dishes are clean, but inside, "you are filled with plunder and evil" (Lk: 11:39).

The minute we start trying to build a case for ourselves based on our perfect adherence to the law, we're in trouble. We don't get to despise anyone. We don't get to think our spiritual practice makes us one iota holier than the next person. Attending Mass in order to get a gold star avails us nothing. Fasting and tithing are meant to unite us to the rest of the world, not separate us from it. In fact, the real fruit of the spiritual path is that we start to become more compassionate, more humble, more aware of the fact that we are not only not better than everyone else, but if anything, worse.

The cramped, rigid letter of the law crowds us up so that the only part of the church available is the front row. It fools us into thinking that we can become one with Christ without becoming one with his people.

By contrast, the expansive, resilient spirit of love opens up the whole church. Now we can sit in the front, the middle, either side, the balcony, even the back. We can mingle. We can look our brothers and sisters in the eye, and breathe freely.

Blessed Father, help us to remember that Christ came not to abolish the law but to fulfill it. Help us to remember that we are just like the rest of humanity.

The One Who Humbles Himself
Heather King

"But the tax collector stood off at a distance and would not even raise his eyes to heaven but beat his breast and prayed, 'O God, be merciful to me a sinner.' I tell you, the latter went home justified, not the former; for everyone who exalts himself will be humbled, and the one who humbles himself will be exalted."

(Lk 18:13-14)

Not long ago a friend, disabled since birth, left a movie theater one night and was verbally and almost physically attacked by a gang of thugs. He was shaken, angry, and hurt. "The worst thing," he said, "was that I felt completely powerless."

At the time, I happened to have been receiving a series of anonymous hate mails on my blog. I was pretty sure I knew who the person was and my impulse was to attack back verbally. I had some information with which I could have embarrassed him. I could put him in his place. But listening to my disabled friend, I realized that I would then become the attacker of a person with a disability. Because clearly, people don't leave anonymous hate comments unless they feel deeply disenfranchised. People don't blindly, unreasoningly lash out at others unless they feel desperately lonely, unloved, and powerless themselves.

The truth is we are all disabled, all broken, all wounded. That doesn't mean we allow people to hurt us. That doesn't mean we invite people to hurt us. That doesn't mean we excuse them or condone their behavior or instantly forgive them if they do hurt us.

But there is one power greater than the power of hate, and that is the power of love. The rule that says the way to get ahead in the world is by power and force was the rule Christ blew to smithereens. The rule that says hate your enemies and do everything in your power to do violence to them was the rule that Christ blew to smithereens on the cross.

Maybe the operative phrase in the passage above is "went home." Luke doesn't just say the tax collector was justified, he says he went *home* justified. Humility brings us home. Love brings us to Christ.

Dearest Father, help us be willing to stand with the tax collector in the back of the church. Help us to remember that your mercy alone allows us to live.

Let the Children Come

Heather King

People were bringing even infants to [Jesus] that he might touch them, and when the disciples saw this, they rebuked them. Jesus, however, called the children to himself and said, "Let the children come to me and do not prevent them; for the kingdom of God belongs to such as these. Amen, I say to you, whoever does not accept the kingdom of God like a child will not enter it."
(Lk 18:15-17)

One morning, at the conclusion of morning Mass at Saint Francis here in L.A., the priest invited the people who take the Eucharist to the sick and shut-in to come forward for a blessing. One stooped, elderly lady began to make her way toward the altar, and walking tall right behind her came a strapping gal with an infant carrier who proceeded to have a lively conversation, right up on the steps of the altar, with the priest. This was very out of order; the alarm registered among us parishioners with much shifting of feet and clearing of throats.

"Oh, both you AND the baby!" we presently heard the priest say. "Okay, then, come any time," and he made the sign of the cross over their foreheads, and blessed the meek old lady, too.

I felt deeply moved by this mother with her baby who had "stepped outside the lines." So afterwards I went up to her, and she launched into a whole story about how she had always loved Christ, and now she wanted to come into the Church, and her husband, who partied too much, was not interested (she herself used to steal but she was over that now), and she had two other boys besides the baby, one special-needs at the school across the street, and she was enrolled in RCIA, and she came to Mass every chance she got because she "just wanted to be with Jesus." Placing the chintzy blanket just so over little Adam, she chattered away, *beaming* with joy.

All the way home I thought, "Let the children come to me." I thought of how children don't care about making fools of themselves. Children aren't thinking of what people will say. Children don't count the cost, and plan and weigh, and draw back in fear. They just want to be loved. They just want to run toward the light. They just want to get close to Christ.

Eternal Father, give us the courage of children. Let our hearts burn with such love that we run toward you headlong and unheeding.

Inheriting Eternal Life

Heather King

An official asked [Jesus] this question, "Good teacher, what must I do to inherit eternal life?" Jesus answered him, "Why do you call me good? No one is good but God alone. You know the commandments, 'You shall not commit adultery; you shall not kill; you shall not steal; you shall not bear false witness; honor your father and your mother.'" (Lk 18:18-20)

C hrist didn't go against the structure; he went beyond the structure. But to go beyond the structure, we need first of all, for ever and always, a structure. One of the paradoxes of Christianity is that it is both utterly revolutionary and utterly practical. We never go off on a frolic of our own. We are always grounded in community, in family, in the moral law.

Just in case we're trying to veer off onto some "new" spiritual path, here's how we know whether it's valid: we don't steal, murder, lie, covet. Just in case we think we can bypass the basics and launch into some ersatz spiritual ether, let's not forget that we refrain from adultery. We remember the Sabbath and keep it holy.

To say, "It's settled: I consent to live by the teachings of the Church," affords a tremendous freedom. We voluntarily harness ourselves to the discipline and self-renunciation to which Christ, the disciples, and the saints have harnessed themselves. We begin to walk the road by which we come to the next phase: more freedom, more love. "Moving easy in harness" is how Robert Frost described the rules of poetry. And once the harness is in place we find it is guiding us where we wanted to go, perhaps unbeknownst to ourselves, all along.

We wonder, too, what Christ means when he asks, "Why do you call me good? No one is good but God alone." Perhaps the supplicant, an "official," approached Christ with an air of toadying. Officials, like most of us, tend to order their lives to power, status, and prestige. Perhaps Christ was reminding us that obeying the commandments in and of itself avails us nothing. Perhaps Christ was saying: This isn't about hiding even from ourselves the gods we *really* worship. Perhaps Christ was saying that if we want to inherit eternal life, we have to be willing to allow our souls to lie stripped before the Father.

Almighty Father, help us to remember that the commandments are the solid rock on which our house is built. Help us to let our souls lie open before you.

Come, Follow Me
Heather King

And [the official] replied, "All of these I have observed from my youth." When Jesus heard this he said to him, "There is still one thing left for you: sell all that you have and distribute it to the poor, and you will have a treasure in heaven. Then come, follow me." But when he heard this he became quite sad, for he was very rich. (Lk 18:21-23)

"Very rich." In other words, very attached. Very afraid. Very divided.

We look for loopholes. Well, the poor, yes. A buck or two, maybe a hundred, a thousand bucks here and there, but "*all* that you have"? We like to think he meant give to the poor metaphorically—our prayers, our good thoughts. He meant that but he also meant in certain circumstances, for some people, at a certain stage, literally.

Christ didn't so much mean things literally or metaphorically as he meant them supernaturally. Christianity is not about learning a new way to count the cost; Christianity is to stop counting the cost. Christ didn't say to give a little more than everyone else; he said to give everything. Christianity is not "balanced" or "healthy" or "sane"; Christianity is of an entirely different order. Was Saint Francis of Assisi "balanced"? Was Saint Rose of Lima, who disfigured herself to save men from being tempted by her beauty, "sane"?

Simone Weil (1909-1943), the French intellectual and mystic, took on a variety of tasks in order to be in solidarity with the poor, often with such ineptitude that she seemed to make things harder, not easier, for the folks she was trying to help. She worked on an assembly line in a factory, suffering the existential despair of a slave. She went to the front during the Spanish Civil War and stuck her foot in a pot of boiling oil. She died, possibly of self-imposed starvation.

A convert to Christ, she never officially joined the Church. That was her loss, and ours. But she also offered up her wounds, her neuroses, her weaknesses, her motives, and her body. She "sold" all that she had and distributed it to the poor. That is more than many of us do. That is about as Catholic as you can get.

Loving Father, give us the courage to sell all that we have. Kindle our desire to have treasure in heaven.

Possible for God

Heather King

Jesus looked at [the official] [now sad] and said, "How hard it is for those who have wealth to enter the kingdom of God! For it is easier for a camel to pass through the eye of a needle than for a rich person to enter the kingdom of God." Those who heard this said, "Then who can be saved?" And he said, "What is impossible for human beings is possible for God."
(Lk 18:24-27)

When "those who heard" asked, "Then who can be saved?", what did they mean? Not everybody is rich. In fact, most people aren't rich. So why did they ask, "Then who can be saved?" Maybe they meant that the people who are "saved," who are "favored," often seem to be the ones who have already been saved in a worldly sense. Perhaps they were asking if being together and successful and admired in the eyes of the world doesn't give us an advantage, what does?

Christ turned all that upside down. That blessed are the poor, not the rich; that the last shall be first; that we are saved not by anything we do or earn or achieve but by the merciful love of God are radical notions.

In one way, of course, we are all "rich." To be poor is to realize our limitations. To be poor is to realize that God doesn't protect us from our limitations: he suffers them with us. To be poor is to realize that God's ways are not our ways. Neither are they senseless or absurd. But to accept God's ways means consenting to have our old ideas, our identities, and our egos continually shattered.

To help the process along Christ often "answered" a question, as he did here, with a riddle. To the question "Then who can be saved?" Christ didn't answer, "Rich people who love God more than they love their wealth." He didn't answer, "Poor people." He answered: "What is impossible for human beings is possible for God."

To picture a camel passing through the eye of a needle requires a complete subversion of time and space. Either the camel would have to be disassembled and reassembled, or the needle would have to become gigantic! The kingdom of God is not like this world, Christ tells us, but better, fairer, with more money: the kingdom of God is of a different order altogether.

Dearest Father, help us to be willing to be poor. Help us to allow you to shatter and reassemble us, again and again.

Giving up Our House

Heather King

Then Peter said, "We have given up our possessions and followed you." [Jesus] said to them, "Amen, I say to you, there is no one who has given up house or wife or brothers or parents or children for the sake of the kingdom of God who will not receive [back] an overabundant return in this present age and eternal life in the age to come." (Lk 18:28-30)

For years I lived in a below-market-value but beautiful apartment in a section of L.A. called Koreatown. I had Oriental and kilim rugs, paintings, icons, and crucifixes. I had French windows, hand-painted tile, a plant-filled balcony. I had a living room with crown moldings, a fireplace mantel carved with cherubs, and walls painted a contemplative gray-green. People walked in and said, "It's so you!" They said, "It's so warm!" They said, "*You'll never find another place like this.*"

Something about that last remark began to irk me. Perhaps I never would, but perhaps seventeen years in any apartment—especially one that was pretty much in the ghetto—is also long enough. I'd come in some sense to believe that my identity lay in that apartment. The apartment, with its emotional weight of decades of mementoes, photos, keepsakes, and journals had become a kind of psychic albatross.

I didn't understand why, but I needed to pare down. So I sold or gave away three quarters of my belongings and set off on a six-month cross-country sabbatical. I prayed, I went to Mass, I stayed at retreat houses and hermitages. I worked through a very old wound, and when I returned to L.A., a house-share opportunity materialized before I even had to begin looking for an apartment.

I now live in a better part of town, with more peace and quiet, in a house with a huge back yard, a washer-dryer, and free Wifi. I have access to a vacation home in the desert. I'm paying less than I did in my old place. I've had to stretch myself to adjust to a roommate, and best of all, my writing has flowered.

I don't know where I'll be a year from now, but I'm pretty sure I'll be able to bear fruit there as well. Giving up our house doesn't give us more security; it gives us more faith.

Blessed Father, give us the eyes to see and ears to hear that an overabundant return comes in many forms. Help us to grow in courage so that we, too, are willing to give up houses, lands, and even family for you.

Going up to Jerusalem
Heather King

Then [Jesus] took the Twelve aside and said to them, "Behold, we are going up to Jerusalem and everything written by the prophets about the Son of Man will be fulfilled. He will be handed over to the Gentiles and he will be mocked and insulted and spat upon; and after they have scourged him they will kill him, but on the third day he will rise." But they understood nothing of this; the word remained hidden from them and they failed to comprehend what he said. (Lk 18:31-34)

"They understood nothing." Not they understood only in part. Not they understood as through a glass darkly. They understood nothing. Not that Christ was the fulfillment of the Old Testament law. Not that he was the Savior of the world. Not that he would rise and thereby vanquish death, imbue our suffering with meaning, and show us how to love each other as he loved us: by laying down his life for his friends.

He took them aside, all Twelve of them. He must have been in desperate dread of the fearsome physical agony that lay in store. He must have been bursting to impart something of the magnificent glory in which he was about to enter. He must have longed for them to say, "Oh, dearest, most sublime friend! We will stay by your side." He must have longed for them to respond, "The mystery! The wonder! Do you actually mean to say that you will rise *from the dead*?"

But nothing. After all the parables about selling all you have, and giving up house and parents and children, and humbling ourselves for the kingdom of God, they understood nothing. He would go to his crucifixion without a single disciple understanding or believing in his mission.

Perhaps the word had to remain hidden from them. Perhaps we are only given to comprehend when we are emotionally and spiritually ready to comprehend. But one thing this passage reveals to us is the almost unbearable moral loneliness in which Christ lived—and in which we are called to live, too.

They understood nothing, yet they were his closest friends. And so on the night before he died, it was the disciples with whom he shared his last meal, the disciples whose feet he washed, the disciples, in the garden of Gethsemane, whom he asked to sit with him for an hour.

They understood nothing—and he loved them anyway. That is very good news for us.

Heavenly Father, inflame our hearts with the desire to understand Jesus, even though we never fully will. Give us the love to go up to our own Jerusalem.

Approaching Jericho
Heather King

Now as [Jesus] approached Jericho a blind man was sitting by the roadside begging, and hearing a crowd going by, he inquired what was happening. They told him, "Jesus of Nazareth is passing by." He shouted, "Jesus, Son of David, have pity on me!" The people walking in front rebuked him, telling him to be silent, but he kept calling out all the more, "Son of David, have pity on me!" (Lk 18:35-39)

Back in the late eighties, in the depths of my alcoholic drinking, I happened to be visiting some friends in Tennessee. One afternoon, I wandered outside, headed toward the woods, and sank to my knees beneath a towering pine. Ants swarmed the trunk like black stars; a clump of gray-green lichen bloomed: wondrous things I had lost the capacity to wonder about. *I'm dead inside*, I thought. *If I don't stop drinking I'm going to die.*

The very next instant I felt a force—there is no other word for it—physically pulling me down. I didn't stop to think. I opened my mouth and said: "Our Father, who art in heaven, hallowed be thy name…" I hadn't said the words since Sunday school, but there they still were, within easy reach: "Thy will be done…" "Give us this day…" "Forgive us our trespasses…"

I'd always thought of people who believed in evil as religious crackpots, but what was it but evil that I was obsessed with something that was killing me? What was it but evil when I longed with all my heart to be good, useful, loved, and was compelled to do this thing that made me feel bad, exiled, hated? "Deliver us from evil!" I implored loudly, as if speaking through a door to someone I wasn't sure was there. "Deliver us from evil," I whispered, burying my head in my sweaty, shaking hands.

After awhile my usual self-consciousness returned. "Did I just… pray?" I thought. Then I got up, walked back across the field to the house, and mixed another pitcher of gin and tonics.

But for once, the Inner Crowd had been stilled. For once, I had turned my back on The Accuser. Three months later, my family held an intervention and shipped me off to rehab. That was twenty-four years ago.

I haven't had a drink since.

Almighty Father, help us to hear the cry of our own hearts. Give us the courage to resist both outside peer pressure and the "peer pressure" of our inner selves.

Please Let Me See

Heather King

Then Jesus stopped and ordered that [the blind man] be brought to him; and when he came near, Jesus asked him, "What do you want me to do for you?" He replied, "Lord, please let me see." Jesus told him, "Have sight; your faith has saved you." He immediately received his sight and followed him, giving glory to God. When they saw this, all the people gave praise to God.
(Lk 18:40-43)

"What do you want me to do for you?" Jesus asks, and interestingly, often we don't know what we want. We know we want money, or to be admired, or for a certain person to love us, but what do we really want? What do we want Christ to do for us?

Several years ago, I embarked on a cross-country pilgrimage. I found myself in a kind of dark night of the soul, a situation I couldn't see my way out of, and so I decided to drive from Los Angeles to my childhood home of New Hampshire and back, going to Mass every day. I wanted to get closer to Christ. I knew Christ was my only answer. All I knew was to drive and stay close to Christ.

In Spencer, West Virginia, I stayed with third order Franciscan contemplative hermit Sister Jeanne McNulty. One night she made dinner and I poured out my heart, and at the end she looked at me very gently, and said, "You need to know what you want. When you know what you want, God will lead you to it. God will open the way. But you have to ask yourself, *What do I want?*"

I'd thought I knew exactly what I wanted. But I sat there for a minute, stunned, and then I said wonderingly, "I don't know what I want."

Notice, too, that the blind man didn't say, "*Make me see.*" He said, "*Let me see.*" Even in his blindness, he "saw" that Christ doesn't work from the outside; he works from the inside. Saint Thérèse of Lisieux wrote, "My God, you know the only thing I've ever wanted is to love you; I have no ambition for any other glory except that."

That's a pretty good ambition for all of us. Let me see. Open the eyes of my heart.

Most merciful Father, allow us to have the faith of the blind man. Lead us to ponder what we want Jesus to do for us.

A Preeminent Attraction

Father Richard Veras

*[Jesus] came to Jericho and intended to pass through the town.
Now a man there named Zacchaeus, who was a chief tax
collector and also a wealthy man, was seeking to see who Jesus
was; but he could not see him because of the crowd, for he was
short in stature. So he ran ahead and climbed a sycamore tree
in order to see Jesus, who was about to pass that way.* (Lk 19:1-4)

At a concert at my parish school, I noticed that there was only
one eighth-grader playing in the band. The other musicians were underclassmen, mostly fifth and sixth-graders.
This lone eighth-grader was a girl who had taken up clarinet the
year before. She was a popular girl in school, a cheerleader in fact.
I asked her mother who told me that she was needled by a lot of
her classmates for doing something so "geeky." Performing in the
spring concert in seventh grade was somewhat permissible, but
to do such a thing in the eighth grade was to break all the rules
of cool.

Her mother also told me that her daughter was looking for a
high school with a good music program. She may or may not
pursue cheerleading, but she absolutely wanted to pursue music.

I was moved by this girl who was so taken by something that it
had become for her more important than even her image among
her peers.

This seems to be what happened to Zacchaeus. Climbing trees
is something that little boys do, not something for grown men—
certainly not grown men who want to be taken seriously. Zacchaeus was the chief tax collector, and even if he was not hated he must
at least have been feared. In fact, to be in such a hated position it
would seem necessary that the people have a certain fear of you.
Zacchaeus' desire to see Jesus is so great that he sacrifices his image. Once he climbs that tree there is, somehow, no turning back.

What was the promise that Zacchaeus expected in the person
of Jesus? What was it that so drew him beyond himself? Jesus is
moved by the fact that Zacchaeus is so taken by him; just as he is
moved by our desire to see him in our lives and know him better.
Jesus continually approaches us as he approached Zacchaeus.

*Loving Father, awaken my heart that I may be moved by the
presence of Christ with the same hope that moved Zacchaeus
beyond all other concerns.*

Called by Name

Father Richard Veras

When he reached the place, Jesus looked up and said to [Zacchaeus], "Zacchaeus, come down quickly, for today I must stay at your house." And he came down quickly and received him with joy. When they all saw this, they began to grumble, saying, "He has gone to stay at the house of a sinner."

(Lk 19:5-7)

In the film *Decalogue V*, one of Krszysztof Kieslowski's film series on the ten commandments, a lawyer calls out to his client, who had just been condemned to death, as he is being taken away from the courthouse. The young man is clearly startled, and the next day, before his sentence is carried out, he tells the lawyer with great affection and gratitude, "You called me by name!" That had not happened to him in many years.

How much it must have meant to Zaccheaus when Jesus called out his name! The announcement that he would come to his house was equally important, but Zacchaeus must have remembered over and over that moment when Jesus called his name.

The entire announcement that the angel Gabriel gave to Mary was extremely important, but our Lady must have never forgotten that first greeting, "Hail, full of grace." A greeting the Church calls us to repeat over and over.

Jesus' love for each of us is personal. He loves all of us, but not in the way we love all the sand on the beach or all the coins in the jackpot. His love for us is particular and unique. What unites us is that each of us experiences this particular love and it draws us together in an experience that only disciples of Christ can understand and share.

Did Zacchaeus notice the grumbles of the crowd? Even if he heard them, those grumbles probably faded into nothingness. What would never fade is the affectionate voice of Jesus who had called him by name. This is an experience beyond all of his expectations. It is the beginning of the new life that Zacchaeus is now born into, the same life to which the grumblers are also invited, if they will only stop their grumbling and be as attentive to the desire of their hearts as Zacchaeus has been to his.

Gracious Father, let me know of your personal and tender love for me, especially through those you have given to accompany me as I follow your Son to my destiny.

Love Offered, Salvation Accepted

Father Richard Veras

But Zacchaeus stood there and said to the Lord, "Behold, half of my possessions, Lord, I shall give to the poor, and if I have extorted anything from anyone I shall repay it four times over." And Jesus said to him, "Today salvation has come to this house because this man too is a descendant of Abraham. For the Son of Man has come to seek and to save what was lost." (Lk 19:8-10)

Monsignor Paul Andrews was the saintly pastor for many years of my current parish, Saint Rita's on Staten Island. Many of our long-time parishioners who have become pillars of the parish have told me that they never expected to become so active in the church. Over the years, they gave so much of their time and of themselves because "Monsignor asked me!" From the president of the Ladies' Guild to the man who established the Holy Name Society, from the bingo workers to lectors, cantors, and choir members, they all did what they did because they were invited by their much beloved pastor, who loved them like a father, like "another Christ." They found these time-and energy-consuming tasks to be easy and light, because they were done as a response to a love that moved them deeply.

We know that Zacchaeus was not a generous man. In fact, it was likely that his lack of generosity and his self-centeredness brought upon him the intense resentment of his fellow Jews. So from where does his magnanimous promise of charity arise? It arises from the charity he first receives from Jesus. Saint John tells us, "In this is love: not that we have loved God, but that he loved us and sent his Son as expiation for our sins" (1 Jn 4:10).

How has salvation come to Zacchaeus' house? This salvation was made possible by the loving initiative of Jesus, Love itself who has become flesh and graced Zacchaeus' house with his presence. Salvation actually happened because Zacchaeus accepted this love. The chief tax collector didn't do anything to deserve Jesus' love. True love is not deserved, it is freely given; and it reaches its goal when it is freely, humbly, joyfully, and gratefully accepted.

Zacchaeus was a true "charity case." Salvation comes to each of us when we humbly, joyfully, and gratefully accept to be Jesus' "charity cases."

Heavenly Father, your love is the source of my existence. Consciously accepting your love allows me not merely to exist, but truly to live. May I always accept gratefully the love you are always giving.

283

The Unexpected King of Love
Father Richard Veras

[Jesus] proceeded to tell a parable because he was near Jerusalem and [the people] thought that the kingdom of God would appear there immediately. So he said, "A nobleman went off to a distant country to obtain the kingship for himself and then to return. He called ten of his servants and gave them ten gold coins and told them, 'Engage in trade with these until I return.' His fellow citizens, however, despised him and sent a delegation after him to announce, 'We do not want this man to be our king.'" (Lk 19:11-14)

The priest who served as dean of discipline at the boys high school absolutely did not want the priest who was the school's president to accept the new priest that the diocese offered to send to them to teach religion. Father Discipline made the case with Father President that Father Religion, while perhaps adequate for parish ministry, did not have what it took to control classes of teenage boys, some of whom were from tough neighborhoods. Father Religion had neither the experience nor, it seemed, the personality for this kind of high school work.

Father President ultimately, and reluctantly, accepted Father Religion (there were no other candidates proposed). Three years later, Father Discipline would tell Father Religion that he was a treasured part of the faculty. Speaking as Father Religion, I can say that I was as surprised as anyone else that things worked out. Any classroom control I had at that school, as well as any success I may have had in communicating the faith, are due to the merciful workings of God's grace in my life.

As they near Jerusalem, the people are expecting the kingdom of God to appear, and for Jesus himself to appear as a king according to their images of how a king should be. In Jerusalem, however, Jesus is not going to fit their kingly ideas. He will not lord it over his subjects and make his authority felt as we would expect of a king. Like the king in his parable, Jesus will give his subjects freedom… even to despise and reject him.

He is not a king who wields power, but rather a king who depends upon his Father's Love, and offers this love freely, allowing his subjects to accept or reject him. In the end it will be up to each of us to decide if Jesus is the treasure for which we are willing to sell everything, even our preconceptions.

Merciful Father, your thoughts are beyond our thoughts and your ways are beyond our ways. Grant me the simplicity of heart to love you more than I love my ideas of how things should be.

Given in Trust

Father Richard Veras

"But when [the nobleman] returned after obtaining the kingship, he had the servants called, to whom he had given the money, to learn what they had gained by trading. The first came forward and said, 'Sir, your gold coin has earned ten additional ones.' He replied, 'Well done, good servant! You have been faithful in this very small matter; take charge of ten cities.' Then the second came and reported, 'Your gold coin, sir, has earned five more.' And to this servant too he said, 'You, take charge of five cities.'"
(Lk 19:15-19)

Jesus told his disciples that they would do even greater things than he (see Jn 14:12). Saint Paul, in many missionary journeys, must have encountered more people than Jesus did. Later Saint Francis of Assisi would reach greater numbers than Saint Paul. Due to modern communications technology, Mother Teresa and Pope John Paul II reached people all over the world during their lifetimes.

But what is it that made all of these disciples of Christ attractive, each in his own unique way? They proclaimed unabashedly that they were followers of Christ. Whatever goodness and truth they conveyed came not from themselves, but from Jesus. They were witnesses, not creators. They were continuing, extending, making present the love that came from their beloved Lord and King.

These two servants are images of every true disciple. The money they invested was not theirs; it had been entrusted to them by the nobleman who had become king.

Christ has become our King through his suffering, death, and Resurrection. He pours out his love to us and invites us to cooperate with him in pouring out his love to all ages and all places. He chooses to entrust himself to us because he wants to build his kingdom in union with us.

Through the sacraments and through the Christian community, Christ invests us with his love. His love generates us and makes us a new creature, and our newness can become a witness and an invitation to others if we treat Christ's love with the same freedom and certainty with which these servants treated the gold coins.

Everyone recognizes the value of gold. Likewise, although Christians live out their faith in different times and circumstances, and with very different personalities, the newness to which we witness is the same, for it emanates from our One Lord, Jesus Christ.

Father, you continuously entrust your love to us through your Son. May we receive your love with joy, trusting that you will bring to completion all the works that your love begins in us.

Engage!

Father Richard Veras

"Then the other servant came and said, 'Sir, here is your gold coin; I kept it stored away in a handkerchief, for I was afraid of you, because you are a demanding person; you take up what you did not lay down and you harvest what you did not plant.' [The nobleman] said to him, 'With your own words I shall condemn you, you wicked servant. You knew I was a demanding person; [...] why did you not put my money in a bank? Then on my return I would have collected it with interest.'" (Lk 19:20-23)

A n old friend who had been living a non-committal and worldly life once ventured to bet that my life as a priest was easier than his. For years he had admired me for what he saw as my "altruistic sacrifice," but finally came to the conclusion that I, along with other "serious" Catholics that he knew, had much happier lives. I agreed with him completely, my life was much richer... I didn't envy him at all.

Similarly, I was once watching a Woody Allen movie with my mother; it was a later film in which the director/actor must have been in his sixties. His character was chasing women with the maturity of a teenager, and my mother commented on how sad it was. As faithful wife, mother, and grandmother, she enjoyed more happiness in her modest home on her modest income than this successful moviemaker might ever know.

When you verify your Christian faith in the reality of day-to-day life, you can become more certain of its truth. You grow in the realization that following Christ and the teachings that flow from his presence in the Church makes life a hundred times more bountiful than a life that is unaware of the greatness of Christ and thus of the greatness of the human heart. The lesser things that the world offers are seen for their lack of substance.

The king told the servants to "engage in trade"; two did engage and discovered the fruits. One decided at the outset that it was too daunting, or perhaps not to be taken too seriously, and so he stored away what he had received in a handkerchief. Had he taken the risk of engaging himself with what he had been given, he would have discovered the fruits. Christianity is not a quaint heirloom that has been left to us. It is given to us *for life*, and it flourishes in the engagement with life!

Dear Father, help me to be open to the ways that you provoke me through the circumstances of life, so that I may recognize Christ in reality and grow in the certainty of his living, abiding presence.

Poured out and Flowing Over

Father Richard Veras

"And to those standing by [the nobleman] said, 'Take the gold coin from him and give it to the servant who has ten.' But they said to him, 'Sir, he has ten gold coins.' 'I tell you, to everyone who has, more will be given, but from the one who has not, even what he has will be taken away. Now as for those enemies of mine who did not want me as their king, bring them here and slay them before me.'" (Lk 19:24-27)

When Pope Benedict XVI visited Saint Patrick's Cathedral in 2008, he noted that from inside the church the stained-glass windows shine with luminous splendor, while from outside they look dark and dreary. He used these images to contrast those for whom the Church is a life full of joy and grace as opposed to those who see it only as a legalistic institution.

If I am graced with witnesses who provoke me to enter more deeply into the communion of the Church and the new life that animates that communion, then the life I have becomes more profound, more vibrant, ever more alive. My faith in Christ increases and my desire for his continued presence grows. In short, if I have faith and live it, more faith will be given to me.

If I reduce the Church to a set of rules or to a merely human institution, then I have very little. Even if I know Church teachings and the traditions well, if an experience of the living Christ is not at the center of my life in the Church, then the superficial or partial religiosity I practice is not Christianity at all. There is outward show, but no faith, no hope, no charity. What little I have is founded on nothing, and will fade away.

Many lapsed or "former" Catholics will tell you that they know all about the Church they have rejected because they were altar boys, or they went to Catholic school; but the way they speak about the Church makes clear that they never really entered inside, never experienced the beauty of the encounter with Christ. They didn't have faith, and so faith never flourished. The dark and dreary institution they saw could never give them hope. May the splendor of God's love one day illuminate their lives so they may enter fully into the Church they have never known, and experience God's superabundant, overflowing blessings.

Almighty God, may you pour out your blessings upon your Church so that your faithful love may enter more deeply into your Life, and your lost sons and daughters may know the joy of calling you our Father.

The Seeds of Certainty

Father Richard Veras

After [Jesus] had said this, he proceeded on his journey up to Jerusalem. As he drew near to Bethphage and Bethany at the place called the Mount of Olives, he sent two of his disciples. He said, "Go into the village opposite you, and as you enter it you will find a colt tethered on which no one has ever sat. Untie it and bring it here. And if anyone should ask you, 'Why are you untying it?' you will answer, 'The Master has need of it.'" (Lk 19:28-31)

Not long before their engagement, two friends of mine were traveling to his hometown so that she could meet his parents. At a certain point during the flight, she began to cry. When he asked her what was the matter, she explained that things seemed to be happening quickly, evidenced by the fact that she was on a plane going to meet his family. She didn't know if she was certain enough to be taking such serious steps, to which he responded, "I'm certain enough for the both of us!" Twenty years and five children later, they are continuing to live and to share a very joyful marriage.

Jesus is approaching Jerusalem. He has predicted his suffering, death, and Resurrection three times, and three times the disciples didn't seem to understand. Peter even rebuked Jesus when he prophesied that he would suffer in Jerusalem.

It is likely that the disciples are anxious about entering Jerusalem and of what might lie ahead. Yet in the midst of their anxiety and confusion they remain with Jesus. They have spent time with him and their certainty about him has increased, just as happens as any friendship or loving relationship grows. At this point they have thousands of reasons to trust and to follow.

Jesus sends two disciples ahead of him and describes to them what they will find. The two go forward, confident that they would find things just as Jesus said, and ready to respond in his name to any who question them. Jesus is certain enough for both of them, and they are participating in his certainty.

The moment will come when fear will eclipse the certainty of most of the disciples, and they will falter. But for most, fear will pass and their certainty will bring them together again, and they will witness the basis of all their future certainty, the one reason to trust and follow: the Resurrection.

Loving Father, when I falter and forget the wonders you work in salvation history and in my own life, awaken me to the reasons I have to be certain of your love, continually given and deepened through your risen Son.

Inviting Us to Help

Father Richard Veras

So [the two disciples] who had been sent went off and found everything just as [Jesus] had told them. And as they were untying the colt, its owners said to them, "Why are you untying this colt?" They answered, "The Master has need of it." So they brought it to Jesus, threw their cloaks over the colt, and helped Jesus to mount. (Lk 19:32-35)

The mother puts the sugar into the measuring cup and lets her young daughter pour the pre-measured sugar into the mixing bowl. The daughter has helped bake the cake.

The father allows his young son to pull the cover off the gas grill. The son has helped to barbecue.

Jesus has arranged his entry into Jerusalem. He has understood that now is the time. His Father's design has led him to this entrance which will lead to the saving culmination of his ministry. In his love for his disciples, he allows them to help him mount the colt that will bring him into Holy Week.

Matthew, Mark, and Luke tell us about Simon of Cyrene who helped Jesus to carry his cross. John, on the other hand, tells us that Jesus carried the cross himself. Both accounts reveal the truth. Simon of Cyrene was pressed into service and did indeed help Jesus carry the wood up to Calvary. At the same time, neither Simon, nor any other man or woman, could have helped Jesus to bear the weight of sin that only he could take upon himself for our salvation.

And after we have been saved, Saint Paul teaches us that, as members of Christ's Mystical Body, we can unite our sufferings to his and participate in his saving act, even more profoundly than the disciples were able to participate in Christ's entry into Jerusalem.

Jesus alone is able to bring us the salvation for which our hearts yearn. But with the tenderness of a parent toward a beloved child, Jesus does not want to place a limit on our desire to be with him. He invites our "help," he lovingly accepts our "help," and he transforms our love into his love, our desire into his desire, that we may be one with him. For this unimaginable cooperation and intimate union with God through Jesus Christ is our salvation.

Heavenly Father, may all my joys and sufferings be lived through Christ your Son in the unity of the Holy Spirit, so that I may live in Christ and Christ may live in me.

What Eyes Have Seen

Father Richard Veras

As [Jesus] rode along, the people were spreading their cloaks on the road; and now as he was approaching the slope of the Mount of Olives, the whole multitude of his disciples began to praise God aloud with joy for all the mighty deeds they had seen. They proclaimed: "Blessed is the king who comes/ in the name of the Lord./ Peace in heaven/ and glory in the highest."

(Lk 19:36-38)

I once had a high school student complain to me that his mother didn't love him. I answered the complaint with a question: "You mean the mother who is working two jobs to keep you in this school? Is that the mother who doesn't love you?" He looked down at the floor and smirked, because he knew that the simple fact I had recounted was clear evidence of his mother's love, a love that needn't be argued about or doubted, because it could be seen.

At Jesus' entry into Jerusalem the disciples cry out with joy and praise God because of all the mighty deeds they have seen. He might not look like the king they expected, but through his authoritative words and merciful deeds, through his very presence, it is clear that Jesus is a king. He is a king different from and beyond all their expectations. And their certainty is not a matter of theological understanding, but rather a matter of having eyes to see.

Recall that when John the Baptist's disciples ask Jesus if he is the one who is to come, Jesus tells them to tell John what they hear and see. In his letters, the Apostle John will emphasize that when he speaks of Christ, he speaks of what he has heard and seen.

Jesus doesn't merely know about God, he knows God as Father. Jesus is the very face of the Father, a face that can be seen!

At my grandfather's funeral my great-aunt was staring at me because she said I looked just like her brother when he was my age. She looked upon me with love. So the disciples look upon Jesus, who has made God's love present in the flesh.

God's love is not something reserved for the scholarly or religious, for it can be seen by anyone. And anyone who sees this love with simplicity of heart cannot help but praise God joyfully.

Almighty God and Father, may neither sin or cynicism ever blind me to seeing and recognizing with purity of heart the tangible faces and circumstances through which you reveal to me your loving presence.

The Peace He Gives

Father Richard Veras

Some of the Pharisees in the crowd said to [Jesus], "Teacher, rebuke your disciples." He said in reply, "I tell you, if they keep silent, the stones will cry out!" As he drew near, he saw the city and wept over it, saying, "If this day you only knew what makes for peace—but now it is hidden from your eyes." (Lk 19:39-42)

I often participate in vacations and retreats for high school students, and I have seen many miracles of conversion and transformation. Yet my temperament is not one that normally enjoys a lot of loud and raucous activity, the precise type which tends to emerge from happy teenagers.

There has been many a bus ride in which I wanted to rebuke students for singing on and on and on, or for joking and talking loudly and incessantly. In the midst of my mild misery I sense the Pharisee in my heart. I see it in my reaction which is partly selfish, because I want my own "peace" rather than to rejoice in the signs of Christ's miraculous presence which is redeeming and healing these young people who live in an impossibly inhuman culture. And I think my reaction is also partly jealous, because I am a religious "professional" who can allow my heart to get old— to forget the enthusiasm that flows from encountering Christ and flourishing in his love.

The Pharisees thought that what makes for peace is the status quo. Everyone is in his place, which means that the Pharisees are secure in their position just like the "religious" ones, who know more than most everyone else about God. A "peace" in which we have God figured out, and he will never do anything to surprise us or revive us. In their selfish arrogance and, perhaps, their jealousy, they do not see that true peace comes from the stirring entry of Christ into our lives. Christ, whose love is so unpredictable and so beyond our categories that it cannot be conquered or compromised by any cynicism, anger, or resistance: "Even the very stones will cry out!"

We cannot "beat" or even slightly limit the superabundant love of Christ, so why not join him? Let us live in the peace of Christ that breaks so raucously and inconveniently into our lives.

Almighty and eternal Father, in your mercy continue to break into my life with the unbridled power of your love, that I may break out of my preconceptions and experience the peace which comes through Christ alone.

The World Closing In

Father Richard Veras

"For the days are coming upon you when your enemies will raise a palisade against you; they will encircle you and hem you in on all sides. They will smash you to the ground and your children within you, and they will not leave one stone upon another within you because you did not recognize the time of your visitation." (Lk 19:43-44)

I don't know about other parts of the country, but on Ash Wednesday a priest in New York City is a marked man. As soon as you clean your thumb after Mass more people come into the church looking for ashes, and an invitation to come back to the next Mass or service is never warmly received. If you bring ashes to the nursing home, workers come out of the woodwork before and after the general service and during the room visiting rounds. The rectory doorbell will likely ring even after you have closed up the church at 8:30 PM.

My first Ash Wednesday as a pastor, I was overwhelmed. I began the day with the idea to fend people off, rather than minister to them. That day I perceived myself as alone with my plans and strategies. My patience was already spent by late morning.

What was really happening that day? The Catholic faith was moving people, literally moving them to come for ashes. I don't know what was in each person's heart, but it was certainly interesting that even non-practicing Catholics felt an intense need to receive this sign of penitence, this sign of belonging.

Christ was attracting all kinds of people to himself that day; people who were somehow recognizing their need for Christ, to whatever degree. Not to mention it was the beginning of the holiest season of the year.

Christ was exerting the attractiveness of his presence right in front of me, and I never even noticed him.

When I forget Christ and conceive of myself as alone, it doesn't take long for the world to encircle me and hem me in. When I remember Christ, I am able to stand in wonder and gratitude before his presence. Subsequent Ash Wednesdays were more truly lived, not because I tried to be patient or kind, but because I remembered Christ who was visiting me in a particular way on that day.

God our Father, may our eyes and hearts be open to recognize your many and varied visitations. When we forget you, let the disturbance in our hearts stir us to turn back to you yet again.

Depending on the Word
Father Richard Veras

Then Jesus entered the temple area and proceeded to drive out those who were selling things, saying to them, "It is written, 'My house shall be a house of prayer, but you have made it a den of thieves.'" And every day he was teaching in the temple area. The chief priests, the scribes, and the leaders of the people, meanwhile, were seeking to put him to death, but they could find no way to accomplish their purpose because all the people were hanging on his words. (Lk 19:45-48)

I remember Pope John Paul II's 1993 visit to Denver for World Youth Day. There were reporters working the crowd who had gathered there. Two of my friends were asked, "How do you feel about being women in the Catholic Church?" To which they answered, "We like it!" The reporter had asked a leading question and did not get the controversial answer he was looking for. He didn't realize that he had stumbled upon two pilgrims who, like most of the others, had a love for Jesus that he did not understand. This love for Jesus made it difficult for the reporter to accomplish his purpose of reducing the event to ideological concerns.

When Pope John Paul II visited New York in 1995, I was one of the seminarians chosen to be interviewed by a major newspaper. The journalist asked, "Why have you decided to study for the priesthood?" My answer was, "Jesus Christ—he is the only reason this vocation makes any sense; I'm not good at helping people and the job description seems pretty demanding." My answer was not printed in the article. In fact, I don't think the name of Jesus appeared anywhere in the article.

Today's culture does not so much seek to kill Jesus as to ignore him and relegate him to irrelevance. We readily analyze and argue over every detail of the Church except that which is most essential: that Christ is Present among us.

Let us not forget that we, too, are influenced by this culture. We would never think of wanting to kill Christ, but how often and easily do we conceive of the Church, the world and, indeed, our very selves without an awareness of him or a desire for him.

Let us be converted to the point that we hang on his every word and his every way of revealing himself to us in the Church, in the world, and in our lives.

Merciful Father, your Word made flesh promises to remain in the Church until the end of the world. Let us remain constantly aware of Christ's presence without whom we are nothing.

The Kingdom Come

J. David Franks

*One day as [Jesus] was teaching the people in the temple area
and proclaiming the good news, the chief priests and scribes,
together with the elders, approached him and said to him, "Tell
us, by what authority are you doing these things? Or who is the
one who gave you this authority?" He said to them in reply,
"I shall ask you a question. Tell me, was John's baptism
of heavenly or of human origin?" (Lk 20:1-4)*

Here it is: the endgame of God's ancient plan for the salvation of all flesh is being enacted. Passion Week. Jesus has entered Jerusalem, acclaimed by the crowds as the King who comes in God's name. He cleanses the temple of dishonest commerce so that the Father's Word of boundless mercy toward all may be heard. Jesus has always been that Word, as he was the twelve-year-old boy who just had to be in his Father's house. His heart is full; he burns to speak to the world what is in the heart of his Father.

The religious elite in control of Jerusalem and the temple have authorized none of this. Who does this blue-collar nobody from Galilee think he is?

If they had been paying attention to John the Baptist, when all Jerusalem and environs flocked to the Jordan under the spell of John's preaching and seeking his baptism of repentance, they would have heard the answer to their question about Jesus' authority. The Word of God had never waxed stronger in a man than in John the Baptist, but John's ministry merely prepared the way for the Word to come in Person, enfleshed in the womb of the Virgin Mary.

As Matthias Grünewald so powerfully portrays him in the Isenheim Altarpiece, John the Baptist's whole life is a finger pointing to Christ: "Behold, the Lamb of God, who takes away the sin of the world" (Jn 1:29). The authority of Jesus is the authority of total, sacrificial, self-giving love: love minus zero/no limit (to borrow a Bob Dylan title).

The wise and loving will of the Father is for every human being's salvation and ultimate fulfillment. When the Father reigns, this is the will that reigns. This is the kingdom of God. The Good News Jesus preaches is that the kingdom of God's love is coming; indeed, it has arrived in his very Person. That is why Jesus speaks with authority.

Beneficent Father, who desire our true happiness more than we desire it ourselves, move us to cooperate in the expansion of the kingdom of your Son in our own hearts and in the hearts of others.

No King but God

J. David Franks

[The chief priests, scribes, and elders] discussed this among themselves, and said, "If we say, 'Of heavenly origin,' [Jesus] will say, 'Why did you not believe him?' But if we say, 'Of human origin,' then all the people will stone us, for they are convinced that John was a prophet." So they answered that they did not know from where it came. Then Jesus said to them, "Neither shall I tell you by what authority I do these things." (Lk 20:5-8)

By what authority do we act? Those opposing Jesus stumble upon a question fundamental to "the discernment of spirits." Am I seeking my true good when I choose to do something, moved by the merciful and wise Spirit of God? Or is the Adversary of my true happiness deluding me? Is Satan enticing me to reach out and pick the pretty bauble of the moment—even if I thereby forfeit the real good that would bring lasting happiness?

Do our desires flow from the Father, the Source of all true good? Or do our desires bubble up like foam on the ideological currents of the world, a consumerist desire that takes and does not give?

The Christian knows by faith that Jesus provides the authoritative measure for discernment. By the Holy Spirit incarnate of the Virgin Mary, Jesus is the living Criterion because he is true God and true man: his authority is *both* heavenly and human. He loves us with his Sacred Heart, a human heart. And when Jesus is baptized by John, God the Father attests his heavenly origin: "You are my beloved Son; with you I am well pleased" (Lk 3:22).

Because of the baptism of Jesus in the Jordan, consummated on the cross, we who are baptized in the name of the Father, Son, and Holy Spirit now also have a birth from on high. Baptized into the death and Resurrection of Jesus, we are made real members of his Body, intimately joined to Christ's life—a life of self-squandering love. The Father now says to us: you are my beloved son (or daughter), with *you* I am well pleased!

Formed in the womb of Mary-Church, we are called to love every human as completely as the Father does (Lk 6:35-36). Am I acting under the authority of the Father of mercy? Yes, if in the Spirit of Christ I pursue the true good for myself and others.

Father gracious beyond all telling, make me ever more pleasing to you by causing the Spirit of your Word made flesh to permeate my every action.

The Vineyard of the World

J. David Franks

Then [Jesus] proceeded to tell the people this parable. "[A] man planted a vineyard, leased it to tenant farmers, and then went on a journey for a long time. At harvest time he sent a servant to the tenant farmers to receive some of the produce of the vineyard. But they beat the servant and sent him away empty-handed. So he proceeded to send another servant, but him also they beat and insulted and sent away empty-handed. Then he proceeded to send a third, but this one too they wounded and threw out." (Lk 20:9-12)

The vineyard is God's garden. It is the garden of the world, summed up in the land of Israel. In the beginning, God had given into the hands of man, male and female, dominion over the world. We were to love, be fruitful, and bear the Father's authority in advancing the process of cosmic development through culture. The Father wants us to be regents of his providence in the drama of world history—but our first parents said no. Every time we sin, we replay Adam and Eve's same prideful-fearful rejection of the Father's authority, rejecting thereby his plan to make us his royal representatives on earth.

Man's failure doesn't block God's plan. God moves people to raise up culture's monuments of spirit: from the first cities of Mesopotamia to Shakespeare and Austen, from loving homes to Borromini and Rothko and the U.S. Constitution, from Bruckner's symphonies to the Large Hadron Collider. But these triumphs are admixed with grave assaults on human dignity, from Moloch to Hiroshima.

Because God wills *only* our good, after the Fall he creates a new people from Abraham, who trusts. Israel is to produce fruit: show the world what it means to be a kingdom of priests administering the graciousness of God in the deepest rhythms of the world—family, economics, politics. But the Jews, an epitome of mankind, replay man's lack of trust, following after strange gods.

Why were Jews streaming into the wilderness to be baptized by John in the Jordan? As the Scripture scholar N. T. Wright elaborates, the people of God suspected that the Exile had never really ended. The Second Temple, grandly rebuilt by Herod, didn't even contain the ark of the covenant. The glory of God should emanate from Jerusalem to all the world, but prophets perish there instead.

So Jesus has come to the temple, and the salvation of human creativity begins.

Provident Father, energize the powers of our souls by your Creator Spirit, so that we might offer to you fruits that manifest the glory of your wisdom and love, for the rejuvenation of the world.

A Prison of Our Own Devising

J. David Franks

"The owner of the vineyard said, 'What shall I do? I shall send my beloved son; maybe they will respect him.' But when the tenant farmers saw him they said to one another, 'This is the heir. Let us kill him that the inheritance may become ours.' So they threw him out of the vineyard and killed him." (Lk 20:13-15a)

It was only with our fourth child that we really experienced the terrible twos. The boy is cute—but so obstinate.

One night he locked himself in the bedroom. At first, you could tell from the impish laughter from beyond the door that he was quite proud of himself, despite my vocal expression of pique. The laughter continued as the minutes went by, my burgling skills failing me, credit cards and bobby pins cast aside in defeat. Eventually, though, he began to realize that he was not in a good place. Finally, he was crying.

It struck me that this was a living parable of what our self-assertive cleverness looks like before God. I was working to get him out of a situation that was in fact contrary to his happiness, and he didn't want to be liberated—until very late.

God the Father sends his Son to liberate his people. The glory of God returns to the temple in the Person of Jesus, so that Jerusalem may become the source from which flows the salvation of all peoples.

The leaders of Jerusalem do not want to acknowledge a new order of things. But the advent of the kingdom of God must by definition mean that a higher authority is asserting itself. When God comes to town, the arrangements we've grown comfortable with get upended—not because God wants to discomfit us, but because he wants to lead us into a life beyond our ability to arrange, that is, a life beyond our finest dreams.

Jesus is the true vine. God repeatedly comes into our minds and hearts; in baptism, he sets up the grace of the Spirit of Christ as the deepest principle of our life, so that we might bear the fruits of true, and divine, love. Do we spurn God's self-offering, to seize heaven's fruit on our own terms—only to find our true happiness evaporate in the vanity of self-assertion?

Father of infinite love, who have given everything for our sake in giving us your Son, please outwit our strategies of evasion. Do not let us escape the divine happiness you want to give us. Grant that I follow your plan for me with trusting obedience.

297

Hewn from Living Rock
J. David Franks

*"What will the owner of the vineyard do to [the tenant farmers]?
He will come and put those tenant farmers to death and turn
over the vineyard to others." When the people heard this, they
exclaimed, "Let it not be so!" But [Jesus] looked at them and
asked, "What then does this scripture passage mean: 'The stone
which the builders rejected/ has become the cornerstone'?
Everyone who falls on that stone will be dashed to pieces;
and it will crush anyone on whom it falls." (Lk 20:15b-18)*

Love is a hard thing, adamant and unyielding. To love someone means being broken time and again. Fact is, we grow
accustomed to the little empire of self over which we reign
supreme. Loving another means surrendering this kingdom of
"me," and being drawn into the far country of another heart. Why
are we tempted to run when true love draws near? Because we
rightly sense that it's going to "cost not less than everything," as
T. S. Eliot puts it.

The prophet Daniel interpreted a dream in which a statue
symbolizing the succession of mighty Near Eastern empires is
shattered by a stone that "became a great mountain and filled the
whole earth" (Dn 2:35). Hewn from Israel, Jesus is that stone cast
by God to break the empires of our imagining. The Father wills
one thing: to make us divinely happy in a life of infinitely fruitful love. Because love alone brings happiness, when we retreat
into our imperial cocoons, making the transcendence of love
impossible, we discover how serious God is about loving us. He
hammers the prison house of our apparent self-sufficiency until
not one stone is left upon another.

The house of one's life can only stand on the rock of love. "No
one can lay a foundation other than the one that is there" (1 Cor
3:11), which is the love of Jesus, faithful to the end: "We proclaim
Christ crucified, a stumbling block to Jews and foolishness to
Gentiles" (1 Cor 1:23). Upon this is built the new temple that is
the Church.

"Come to him, a living stone, rejected by human beings but
chosen and precious in the sight of God, and, like living stones, let
yourselves be built into a spiritual house to be a holy priesthood to
offer spiritual sacrifices acceptable to God through Jesus Christ"
(1 Pt 2:4-5). In the Spirit of Christ, our love grows crystalline, ra-
diating the glory of divine love, in everyday life.

*Father of truest love, break open my self-enclosure. Cause me to
trust you as you lead me on the way of life, the way of spiritual
intimacy—uniting with others in truth and love, within the vast
breadth of your Trinitarian life.*

A Golden Line of Receptivity

J. David Franks

The scribes and chief priests sought to lay their hands on [Jesus] at that very hour, but they feared the people, for they knew that he had addressed this parable to them. They watched him closely and sent agents pretending to be righteous who were to trap him in speech, in order to hand him over to the authority and power of the governor. (Lk 20:19-20)

Jesus challenges us: it is not only the temple elite who vainly seek to be in control of their destiny. We resent the revelation of true love. We join the scribes and chief priests in plotting to hand Jesus over to be crucified by worldly power.

This "handing over" is the betrayal of love, but enveloping this is a movement beginning in the heart of God, before the foundation of the world. The Father, for our salvation, resolves to give his beloved Son into our sinful hands. Assuming a human nature, the Son of God becomes utterly vulnerable.

Saint Peter preaches this at Pentecost: "This man [Jesus], delivered up by the set plan and foreknowledge of God, you killed using lawless men to crucify him" (Acts 2:23). This is *God's plan*, as Jesus tells Pilate: "You would have no power over me if it had not been given to you from above" (Jn 19:11).

To give us his Son, the Father prepares an arc of loving receptivity, traceable in the joyful and luminous mysteries of the rosary.

The Blessed Virgin Mary receives the Son with her *Fiat*: "Be it done unto me according to thy Word." The fetal Baptist welcomes Jesus with joy. John later receives Jesus with wonder at the Jordan, hearing the Father's attestation that this man is the Agent of his loving plan.

At Cana, Mary tells us, "Do whatever he tells you." Jesus preaches the coming kingdom, showing that it must involve our praying that the Father's "will be done, on earth [in my heart] as in heaven."

The Transfiguration draws the conclusion of the baptism. If Jesus fulfills the Father's plan of love, he bears the authority of love: "Listen to him." Christ transforms the bread and wine of the Last Supper into the living presence of himself in his total self-gift on the cross. He thus enables us to love as he loves: "Do this in memory of me."

Heavenly Father, make me to receive your Son Jesus as he is, as your very Word spoken to my heart. By the intercession of the Mother of your Son, may Mary's Fiat sound from my heart more readily and absolutely, so that the Spirit of your Son may increase in me.

Image Is Everything

J. David Franks

[The scribes and chief priests] posed this question to [Jesus], "Teacher, we know that what you say and teach is correct, and you show no partiality, but teach the way of God in accordance with the truth. Is it lawful for us to pay tribute to Caesar or not?" Recognizing their craftiness he said to them, "Show me a denarius; whose image and name does it bear?" They replied, "Caesar's." (Lk 20:21-24)

Jesus "is the image of the invisible God" (Col 1:15). Jesus is the Word of the Father, who is in his Person, and in the flesh, the expression of everything divine. Though the scribes and chief priests are being ironic in praising the trustworthiness of Jesus' teaching, their words are correct. When Jesus teaches, it is the Father's mind and heart that is being revealed.

And by revealing the Father's love for us, Jesus reveals man fully to himself (*Gaudium et spes* 22). In the beginning, God creates man, male and female, in his image, that is, to know and love. Our imaging of God is perfected in Christ alone, in Christ crucified. And Jesus, the New Adam, has a helpmate in his Mother Mary, the New Eve, as he causes his self-giving love to grow in us. Mary is Holy Mother Church in person; our love is perfected within her life.

We thus bear the exalted name of Christian, engaged in worldly necessities as royal emissaries of Christ. Paying tribute to Caesar doesn't raise a question about whether taxes as such should be paid. (A citizen should recognize that government, as an instrument of the people in securing the common good, has a limited but real claim on his property.) The question is whether this act of recognition of Roman rule betrays the kingship of God over Israel. If so, it would be an act of idolatry.

We live in a culture saturated with images. Images, indeed any created thing, become idols when they no longer express the glory of God's sovereignty, when they are wrenched out of the immense sweep of divine providence. Amidst all the sensory signals of the digital age, we are to shine as images of the invisible God—by living out his sovereignty in our lives. God claims everything, by inherent right. This is the claim of holiness. God's kingdom is made visible in the splendor of the saints.

Almighty Father, from whom all authority derives, send the Spirit of your Son in power upon our minds and hearts so that we may shine as beacons of true love in a darkening world, for the sake of all those in need of your mercy.

One Vast Divine Blessing

J. David Franks

So [Jesus] said to [the scribes and chief priests], "Then repay to Caesar what belongs to Caesar and to God what belongs to God." They were unable to trap him by something he might say before the people, and so amazed were they at his reply that they fell silent. (Lk 20:25-26)

Money, power, pleasure, fame: claimants for our ultimate loyalty. A plugged-in hook-up world inflames consumerist desire. How often do I defer happiness! "When I get that new gadget, then I'll be happy." "I need to look at just one more image." Another drink, another woman,…

The solution is not to close one's eyes to the beauty of the world's pageant; God created it after all. "From the beginning until the end of time, the whole of God's work is a *blessing*. From the liturgical poem of the first creation to the canticles of the heavenly Jerusalem, the inspired authors proclaim the plan of salvation as one vast divine blessing" (*Catechism of the Catholic Church* 1079).

Luke's Gospel is one of song, highlighting the artistry of God's plan of loving goodness—an arrangement of all things for the good of man. Money, power, pleasure, fame: each has a proper place in our lives. But whenever I place finite goods above their infinitely Good Source, I frustrate their ability to express the glory of God's providential ordering. Commandeered into our little empires of self-generated desire, these fine flowers in the garden of the world wither away.

What should we repay to God? Everything. Then all else works out: "But seek first the kingdom [of God] and his righteousness, and all these things will be given you besides" (Mt 6:33). Earthly power has its place in God's plan, as do pleasure and money and fame. They are means by which God blesses us—but only *within* his wise ordering.

It comes down to trust. In the face of God's wise, though incomprehensible, initiative, do I trust that his plan for me is the only way to true happiness? If we surrender ourselves into the slipstream of divine providence, which draws all things sweetly upward, we will find ourselves within happiness so adamantine, even suffering won't be able to break it.

Father, every good and perfect gift descends upon us from you. Thank you for your infinite artistry. Thank you for the extravagant care you have lavished on us, making us witnesses to so many wonders of love in our everyday lives.

Wisdom Orders All Things Sweetly

J. David Franks

Some Sadducees, those who deny that there is a resurrection, came forward and put this question to [Jesus], saying, "Teacher, Moses wrote for us, 'If someone's brother dies leaving a wife but no child, his brother must take the wife and raise up descendants for his brother.' Now there were seven brothers; the first married a woman but died childless. Then the second and the third married her, and likewise all the seven died childless. Finally the woman also died. Now at the resurrection whose wife will that woman be?" (Lk 20:27-33a)

Too often, ethical reflection begins with outlandish problems, such as the "lifeboat scenario" in which we are asked to consider which person should be tossed off a raft that can't support everyone on board. (Usually the weakest are cast aside, contrary to the preferential option for the poor.)

This is not a promising way to begin grappling with the hard cases that actually occur in life. If I don't understand the ordered pattern of the world (the intelligible natures of things in their intelligible relations to each other, all caught up in a divine process aimed at human happiness), I'll end up inventing my morals as I go along, to suit myself. Having scared myself into thinking I'm stranded in a world of radical scarcity, I calculate ways to exploit others before being exploited. I become the strongman making emergency decisions in my little kingdom.

One needs to seek wisdom from teachers only if reality is in fact wisely ordered. I do not need to listen to an authority other than myself if cosmic process and history are random affairs.

Jesus' teaching authority is being challenged in the name of Moses. The aristocratic Sadducees present their own outlandish scenario. They do not recognize the resurrection of the body, based on a secularizing interpretation of Moses. In Saint Matthew's account, Jesus notes their failure to recognize the sweep of the ancient divine plan: "You are misled because you do not know the scriptures or the power of God" (Mt 22:29).

God's plan transcends and embraces history, transfiguring it in its futility and suffering. We are promised *eternal* life, and this *in the body*. Saint Paul describes the yearning of cosmic process as it finds voice in us, "We also groan within ourselves as we wait for adoption, the redemption of our bodies" (Rom 8:23). All we must do is trust God's love for us.

Father, who open over us hands full of blessing, free me from the habits of hanging back from love, habits formed in a fallen world. Open my eyes to see the golden reality of sacrificial love your Son and Spirit are building amidst the darkness.

Intimacy without Limit

J. David Franks

Jesus said to [the Sadducees], "The children of this age marry and remarry; but those who are deemed worthy to attain to the coming age and to the resurrection of the dead neither marry nor are given in marriage. They can no longer die, for they are like angels; and they are the children of God because they are the ones who will rise." (Lk 20:34-36)

What is life after death like? Jesus here lifts the veil on the consummation of God's plan of love. At first, we might be disconcerted because, yes, Jesus is saying that sex will be a thing of the past. (And, no, this wouldn't make a good advertising slogan for Christianity.) But this is in fact very good news.

Because sex is bad? Of course not. God invented it: "Be fruitful and multiply." No, because sex will be superseded—on two counts.

First, evolutionary biology tells us that sexual differentiation (and thus sex), an adaptation inchoate in plants and fully emergent in animals, serves successful reproduction. The billions and billions of human persons, each of whom God directly wills into existence at his or her conception, arise from male and female. Saint Gregory of Nyssa personalizes the span of world history by noting that it will last as long as it takes for God to create all the humans he intends. Then a new, heavenly, order will interrupt and fulfill cosmic process and history.

Second, in this New Jerusalem (the kingdom of God come definitively)—peopled with those who have allowed themselves to be drawn into the life of Christ—all are saints enjoying the face-to-face vision of God, in their resurrected bodies. By that beatific vision, we will also know and love each other in a way that has left behind the tentativeness and fear and meanness characterizing too many even of our cherished relationships now. In the New Jerusalem, the intimacy will be so total that sex would be superfluous.

What every human heart ultimately yearns for is not pleasure but intimacy—to know and be known, to love and be loved. Prone to big mistakes such as seeking sexual pleasure outside of marriage and apart from openness to life, we nevertheless really sigh for love without limit, which Jesus prepares for us in his Father's house.

Our Father in heaven, may your will be done in my life. Through the intercession of the Blessed Virgin Mary, bestow upon me the grace of purity so that I might know and love those whom you place in my life according to divine charity fully ablaze in my heart.

The Word of Life, Extravagant

J. David Franks

"That the dead will rise even Moses made known in the passage about the bush, when he called 'Lord' the God of Abraham, the God of Isaac, and the God of Jacob; and he is not God of the dead, but of the living, for to him all are alive." Some of the scribes said in reply, "Teacher, you have answered well." And they no longer dared to ask [Jesus] anything. (Lk 20:37-40)

A theologian (!) once said, "If Jesus were alive today, he would not agree with the Church's teachings on sexual morality." Indeed. If I don't believe that Jesus is alive today, then I can't believe that he teaches through the Church.

The past tense does not apply to Jesus. He *is* the Resurrected One, seated at the Father's right hand, who gives us life *today*, especially through the preaching and sacraments of the Church. The liturgy lives in Christ's present tense with apocalyptic urgency: "Oh, that today you would hear his voice:/ Do not harden your hearts" (Ps 95:7b-8a).

As the new life we receive in baptism is fed by the Eucharist and Scripture meditation (including the rosary), the mysteries of Christ's life transfigure our everyday lives. These mysteries are consummated in the exodus from suffering to death to indestructible life that Jesus comes to Jerusalem to accomplish.

Often, like the Sadducees, we would prefer a dead and gone god, one who spoke platitudes a long time ago. That god would be safe, pliable, undemanding. He could not interrupt the futile pageant of human melodrama or the comfortable life I tell myself I control. But only a living God can "answer well" to all our deepest questions and longings.

And only a living God can give us a share in his life. The kingdom of God is the kingdom of life. Saint Irenaeus said, "The glory of God is man fully alive." For a person to be fully alive is to know and love God and all others in God. The Father does not want us living in a subhuman state, passive and awash in media-delivered stimuli. He does not want us living in isolation, cut off from others by resentment or pettiness. He wants us to glorify him by living as the intelligent, loving persons he created us to be.

Jesus is the living God who makes us fully alive.

Father of truth and love, empower me by your Spirit, the Lord and Giver of life, to give glory to you today by living a fully human life—creative, loving, holy. Make me abide in your Word of life.

Alpha and Omega

J. David Franks

Then [Jesus] said to [the scribes], "How do they claim that the Messiah is the Son of David? For David himself in the Book of Psalms says: 'The Lord said to my lord,/ "Sit at my right hand/ till I make your enemies your footstool."' Now if David calls him 'lord,' how can he be his son?" (Lk 20:41-44)

Many Jews looked for a Davidic Messiah who would cast off the yoke of the Roman Empire. Jesus, the long-awaited Messiah, *is* the Son of David, as Gabriel tells Mary: "the Lord God will give him the throne of David his father" (Lk 1:32b). That is, Jesus' whole life is the following of a script: his Father's ancient plan of loving goodness, recorded in the Scriptures of Israel. Born to die for us, "when [Christ] came into the world, he said, 'Sacrifice and offering you [Father] did not desire,/ but a body you prepared for me'" (Heb 10:5). Jesus is a Jew, born of a Jewish mother, of the house of David, embedded in Israel's history.

Here's the paradox. No mere man could play this role invented by the Father for our beatification. Jesus challenges the scribes to see this. A son should show deference to a father, not the other way around, yet David in Psalm 110 speaks of the Messiah as his Lord. Somehow this descendant of David has precedence over his forefather. In fact, this man Jesus teaching in the temple is the Word who prophesied through David. Christians confess that Jesus is the LORD, the eternal I AM, the living God who revealed himself to Moses.

Jesus Christ enters history from the bosom of eternity: "In times past, God [the Father] spoke in partial and various ways to our ancestors through the prophets; in these last days, he spoke to us through a Son, whom he made heir of all things and through whom he created the universe" (Heb 1:1-2). Jesus is both Alpha and Omega, the source of history and its consummation. Jesus can be the Son of David only because he is the eternal Son of the Father.

For our lives to be brought to fulfillment, let us continue to be astonished at the authority of this Teacher who is God's eternal Word, resounding through all times—and Scripture.

Father of time and space, integrate by your Spirit the history of my life and of the world in the Body of your Son broken open for every one of us. Make eternity wax strong in the way I love here and now.

The Radiation of Paternal Love
J. David Franks

Then, within the hearing of all the people, [Jesus] said to [his] disciples, "Be on guard against the scribes, who like to go around in long robes and love greetings in marketplaces, seats of honor in synagogues, and places of honor at banquets. They devour the houses of widows and, as a pretext, recite lengthy prayers. They will receive a very severe condemnation." (Lk 20:45-47)

A novice mistress once asked a young nun what virtues she was working on. "Well, I've pretty much mastered humility, so I'm moving on to something else." The older sister said, "Not so fast."

The Christian emphasis on humility is scandalous. Worldly people consider us weak (see Nietzsche) when we drop out of social-dominance games whereby status is gained by undercutting neighbor.

But true Christian humility is the only path to nobility. To be magnanimous requires humility, because humility is intrinsic to love, and there is no greatness without love. Love surrenders itself into the power of the beloved. Love becomes small. The mystery of the incarnation is "God's infinity dwindled to infancy," in the words of poet Gerard Manley Hopkins, s.j.

All that Jesus says and does, unto the godforsakenness of the cross, derives from his infinite love for suffering humanity, for each and every one of us. The Son of Man comes to serve, not to be served. This expresses what is in the Father's heart.

Humility is especially necessary for those in authority, who must always serve love, serve the full development of the persons in their care. Authority must first take care of the weak because that is every person's first responsibility. How urgent it is that we image the Father in the culture of death, with its sexual regime, which devours women and children. Abortion, euthanasia, the sexualization of children: primary violations of the preferential option for the poor.

The Father risks everything (his very Son) according to his loving plan, for no other reason than to bring those in his care (every suffering human) to greatness, to happiness, to a love that never ends. Such a King we have! Whoever bears authority on earth (parent, teacher, cleric, politician, boss) should be an icon of this radiant, infinitely beneficent Paternity.

Almighty, wise, and loving Father—who are the infinitely luminous Source of all truth, goodness, and beauty—give me a heart for the weakest among us, especially for the victims of the culture of death. Dear God, send your Son in the fullness of your kingdom.

Giving All You've Got

Father Romanus Cessario, O.P.

When [Jesus] looked up he saw some wealthy people putting their offerings into the treasury and he noticed a poor widow putting in two small coins. He said, "I tell you truly, this poor widow put in more than all the rest; for those others have all made offerings from their surplus wealth, but she, from her poverty, has offered her whole livelihood." (Lk 21:1-4)

God changes the rules of life's game. Ordinarily, people in the workaday world judge others on their achievements. Merit rating is built into the way we think about free enterprise. Folk wisdom urges people toward industriousness. We've all heard how, "The early bird catches the worm." These outlooks and sayings can contribute to character development and even, eventually, lead to success. However, they do not prepare us well for reading the Gospel.

Christ sees in the poor widow someone worthy of merit, although she contributed to the treasury only two small coins. No big donor she! Our Lord goes on to explain why the poor widow merits commendation whereas the wealthy do not. They enjoy a surplus; she, only the two coins, "her whole livelihood." It would be easy to conclude that this parable affords comfort only for the poor person with a streak of generosity. We, on the other hand, know that whatever Christ teaches in the Gospel serves everyone. Behind the poor widow's generosity stands her charity. Her love for God and for neighbor. Were her condition in life to allow such munificence, the poor widow—so Christ assures us—possesses a disposition of soul that prepares her to give more than the two coins.

This spiritual preparation of soul works not only for almsgiving. Charity disposes the one who receives this divine gift to do many things that one's circumstances in life may not allow. For example, we should recall that spiritual authors hold that someone who has suffered the loss of physical virginity still can observe, by drawing upon a disposition in the soul that loving God creates, the virtue of virginal chastity. The poor widow provides a patron saint for everybody who would like to do more for God but who find themselves impeded by circumstances whether of their own making or not.

Heavenly Father, increase in me the virtue of charity. Make me love you more and more each day. Give me eyes to see the good works of others as your Son teaches us.

A New and Better Temple

Father Romanus Cessario, O.P.

While some people were speaking about how the temple was adorned with costly stones and votive offerings, [Jesus] said, "All that you see here—the days will come when there will not be left a stone upon another stone that will not be thrown down." Then they asked him, "Teacher, when will this happen? And what sign will there be when all these things are about to happen?"

(Lk 21:5-7)

For today's pilgrim in Jerusalem, little remains of the temple that Jesus points out. In the year 70, the Romans ordered its destruction. This leveling took place within forty years of Christ's death on Calvary. So it happened that Christ's prophecy comes to fulfillment. The old temple, which once served as a place of worship and sacrifice, points to Jesus. Our blessed Savior introduces into the world the perfect form of divine worship.

Many people, however, are persuaded to think that the choice to practice religion ultimately lies with the individual. Nothing falls further from the truth about the human being created in the image of God. All people need a new and better Temple. Our status as a creature imposes on each member of our race the obligation to worship God. So each Sunday, the Church invites us to confess: "I believe in one God, the Father almighty, maker of heaven and earth, of all things visible and invisible." This confession commits people to recognize that they both come forth from God and depend on God for their personal continuance in existence. Worship represents the first response of a creature to the One on whose Being all depends.

Christ alerts us to recognize that the disappearance of the temple in Jerusalem coincides with the emergence of a new form of worship. Each time a Catholic priest celebrates the Holy Sacrifice of the Mass, Jesus' perfect worship finds its reenactment. Today every Catholic church establishes a place where this perfect worship continues. The Church assumes the obligation of ensuring that this sacrifice of worship and praise never cease until Christ comes again to welcome those whose participation in his perfect worship has made them friends of God. In order for this mystery of the new Temple to flourish, eligible Catholic men must present themselves for the priesthood.

Lord of heaven, I give you the full expression of my worship by joining myself to the Sacrifice that happens each day on the altars of the Catholic Church.

How to Stop Worrying

Father Romanus Cessario, O.P.

[Jesus] answered, "See that you not be deceived, for many will come in my name, saying, 'I am he,' and 'The time has come.' Do not follow them! When you hear of wars and insurrections, do not be terrified; for such things must happen first, but it will not immediately be the end." (Lk 21:8-9)

Christians are taught to live their lives with one eye set keenly on the four last things: death, judgment, heaven, hell. The first, death, stands, as it were, in the public domain. Nobody can miss it. The other last things are best discovered within the context of God's revelation. True enough, it is possible for persons who do not confess the Catholic faith to glimpse that a free person's inescapable destiny involves some form of judgment and, afterwards, either reward or punishment. If not, what would give our freedom its ultimate personal meaning? Without a divine context for human freedom, our choices would serve only the pursuit of time-bound possibilities. No wonder that Jesus warns us to avoid speculating about the time when the end will arrive. Whether he refers to our mortal death or to the final end makes no difference. Again, death stands in the public domain.

Should the plain inevitability of death cause perpetual anxiety? No. Heaven welcomes those who depart this world in God's friendship. How can I be sure that I am ready? The answer is simple: live today with Christian hope. The virtue of hope disposes us to look upon God as both omnipotent and merciful. God can save us. He shows us mercy for our sins. One cannot wait until tomorrow to start making an act of hope. If we do, then we risk not being prepared for death today. Hope unites us to God as the highest Good for me. Hope also sustains the expectation that God can overcome the obstacles that intervene between me and a happy end. At the same time, the virtue of hope encourages us to trust that God will forgive our sins no matter how tedious they become or heinous they seem. While Catholics bear in mind the ultimate realities of life, they do not think only about the future. They sanctify the present moment. They always cherish the divine friendship.

Eternal Father, grant me the grace to live today and every day as if it were my last on earth. Strengthen my confidence in your mercy and power. Bring me safely home to heaven.

Strengths in Temptation

Father Romanus Cessario, O.P.

Then [Jesus] said to [the people], "Nation will rise against nation, and kingdom against kingdom. There will be powerful earthquakes, famines, and plagues from place to place; and awesome sights and mighty signs will come from the sky. Before all this happens, however, they will seize and persecute you, they will hand you over to the synagogues and to prisons, and they will have you led before kings and governors because of my name. It will lead to your giving testimony." (Lk 21:10-13)

Jesus never said that everybody would like you. On the contrary, the one who follows the Lord may expect some tough sledding. Why would someone take inspiration from the thought that his religious convictions would invite persecution? Have we not become accustomed to think about religion as an instrument of peace? Jesus clearly foretells a series of unpleasant experiences: earthquakes, famines, plagues, persecution, and betrayal. The bouncy and optimistic songs that we sometimes hear in our churches hardly prepare one for this passage from Saint Luke. Therapeutic spirituality and well-being retreats must block out this bracing announcement. Cheap grace and civic religion offer little to prepare one for prison terms and social ostracization. Only the complete body of Catholic instruction readies a person to face the challenges Jesus promises will emerge.

At the heart of this holy teaching stands martyrdom. "Martyr" means witness, which implies speaking the truth. This does not describe someone who dies on behalf of a falsehood. True martyrs die for divine truth. The Christian stands out in the world as the privileged recipient and bearer of this divine truth. Christ himself promises this gift to those who follow him. Thousands of men, women, and children have died for the truth that Christ introduces into the world. It is estimated that in Korea alone more than ten thousand Catholics were killed through hatred of the faith. This witnessing took place over roughly half a century before missionary and native priests became active in the country. These saints and many others who heard this Gospel came to understand all too well what Jesus promises. As we know from the liturgical calendar, the martyrs occupy a central place in the Church's life and worship. They strengthen every Catholic for the battles that Truth eventually engages.

Merciful Father, give me the fortitude of the martyrs. Make me grow each day in love of your Truth so that I may stand ready to bear witness to your Son and his Church.

The Best Deal Possible

Father Romanus Cessario, O.P.

*"Remember, you are not to prepare your defense beforehand,
for I myself shall give you a wisdom in speaking that all your
adversaries will be powerless to resist or refute."*
(Lk 21:14-15)

Have you every worried about what you would say to someone? Perhaps the occasion was a joyful one. How should I propose to the woman whom I want to marry? Or, it may have been a momentous one. How should I tell my parents that the most expensive college has accorded me early admission? Oftentimes, we find ourselves lost for words when it comes to announcing sorrowful news. How can I tell a wife that her husband has died? How can I tell a father that one of his children has been killed in a tragic accident?

Besides these very recognizable situations that arise in the life of just about every person on earth, there exists another set of circumstances that causes us to wonder, "What should I say?" How do I evangelize? How do I help someone return to the practice of the Catholic faith? How do I warn a person, especially one for whom I have some responsibility, about the dangers that sinful behavior produces? Each Christian believer should find great comfort in the knowledge that Jesus anticipates the dilemma that addressing difficult circumstances occasions. Jesus not only anticipates our distress. He also provides the comforting reassurance that the right word will be given to us. "I myself shall give you a wisdom," says the Lord. Bishops sometimes warn preachers not to use this Gospel passage as an excuse for delivering off-the-cuff homilies. Seminary teachers remind their students that the Lord's promise does not excuse them from assiduous study.

What must we do, then, to benefit from the Lord's promise? Each Christian must cultivate the virtue of prudence. Prudence requires that one remain well-informed about divine truth taught in the Church. Marriage. Careers. Deaths. We can learn a lot from the Church on these topics. When we do, then we find ourselves well-disposed to say the right things when required.

Provident Father, you guide the course of human events. Give me the wisdom to see your holy will manifest in the things that happen one by one.

Hangin' in There

Father Romanus Cessario, O.P.

"You will even be handed over by parents, brothers, relatives, and friends, and they will put some of you to death. You will be hated by all because of my name, but not a hair on your head will be destroyed. By your perseverance you will secure your lives." (Lk 21:16-19)

Who among us has not faced the temptation to give up on pursuing something we hold dear? When faced with difficult challenges, people tend to consider capitulation. Foolhardiness admittedly characterizes the swaggering soldier-of-fortune. However, more people opt to slip away from difficult situations rather than run headlong into them. In fact, we honor those men and women who risk their own lives to save others. There are countless examples of public servants and private citizens who display heroic fortitude in the face of what places them in harm's way. The brave person faces life-threatening situations with a steeled poise. Such encounters require a strong expression of the virtue of fortitude.

The stark prediction that Jesus announces in this passage alerts the Christian believer to the central place that fortitude holds in the Christian life. Fortitude braces a person to withstand bravely the challenges that fearful future events bring. Betrayal. Hatred. Death. These possibilities call forth fortitude. Our blessed Lord also puts the call for fortitude into a context. Even if these frightful circumstances befall you, "not a hair on your head will be destroyed." In other words, the Lord of Life overcomes all the evils that the world can throw up against the person who bravely clings to him. The words that Jesus speaks shape the way we face extraordinary and everyday challenges alike.

We are also told that "by your perseverance you will secure your lives." Another translation speaks about saving one's soul. For generations pious Christians prayed for the gift of final perseverance. They have set for us a good example. We should remain persevering until our last breath. Why? Elsewhere the Lord promises that they who hunger and thirst after righteousness will be satisfied.

Heavenly Father, grant me the grace of final perseverance. Keep me strong in the practice of the Catholic faith, and strong against the temptations that would keep me from you.

Jerusalem, Jerusalem!

Father Romanus Cessario, O.P.

"When you see Jerusalem surrounded by armies, know that its desolation is at hand. Then those in Judea must flee to the mountains. Let those within the city escape from it, and let those in the countryside not enter the city, for these days are the time of punishment when all the scriptures are fulfilled. Woe to pregnant women and nursing mothers in those days."
(Lk 21:20-23a)

The city of Jerusalem holds a central place in salvation history. In an odd way, the political turbulence that today erupts around Jerusalem suggests that it also holds a special place in world history. There is something about Jerusalem that makes it different from other national and religious places of importance. The Christian claim to enjoy unimpeded access to and freedom of worship in Jerusalem stems from the historical events that link Jesus to the city. Still, the Lord announces a time of punishment for the city that King David made his home and where his son, King Solomon, built his temple.

How are we to interpret this prediction of vengeance that will affect even the presumably innocent population of pregnant women and nursing mothers? The Lord interprets the destruction that will befall Jerusalem, presumably in the year 70, as a manifestation of divine retribution for the sins of the people. Jerusalem pays the price for the sins of the human race. These sins nail Jesus to his cross set up outside Jerusalem. Christ's death happens in Jerusalem through the agency of various nations and peoples who lived and worked there—Roman civil authorities, religious leaders who pressed for Jesus' death, Gentile soldiers under Roman rule. Saint Thomas Aquinas likes to point out that Jesus dies at the hands of both Jews and Gentiles in order to show that his death in Jerusalem effects the salvation of the whole world, that is, of Jew and Gentile alike.

So we can find comfort from the international status that Jerusalem enjoys. It signals the promise of universal reconciliation. While we wait for this grace to flood the planet, each Catholic should regard Jerusalem as a spiritual home. Even if one cannot go there on pilgrimage, we can place ourselves in those places that have been made holy by the death of the Redeemer.

Merciful Father, keep me a spiritual pilgrim on the way to the New Jerusalem. Guide my steps, every day.

Frightful Events

Father Romanus Cessario, O.P.

"A terrible calamity will come upon the earth and a wrathful judgment upon this people. They will fall by the edge of the sword and be taken as captives to all the Gentiles; and Jerusalem will be trampled underfoot by the Gentiles until the times of the Gentiles are fulfilled. There will be signs in the sun, the moon, and the stars, and on earth nations will be in dismay, perplexed by the roaring of the sea and the waves." (Lk 21:23b-25)

Woeful events occur throughout the world. Automobile wrecks, train collisions, and airplane crashes familiarize us with the disastrous. Rebellions and revolutions accustom us to expecting the violent. The aftermaths of earthquakes, hurricanes, and floods train us to think of nature as a potential enemy instead of a pleasant mother. Many other grotesque happenings erupt one after another. We still find it surprising that the New Testament would predict a "terrible calamity" for Jerusalem. The problem of evil remains an unsolvable riddle that confronts human beings everywhere. No one escapes this *mysterium iniquitatis*. The mystery, as we say, of evil.

Catholic teaching excludes making the good God the simple cause of evil. The calamities that Jesus foretells in this passage arise, then, as the result of human sinfulness. Why would Jesus call our attention to these impending calamities? He warns us about the turbulence of nature and the uprising of men to prepare us for the final resolution of all disorder. In a word, in the end, God's goodness overcomes all disaster, violence, and upheaval. God's goodness trumps whatever sin introduces into the world. True enough, the final manifestation of this triumph waits the last day. Catholic teaching insists, however, that this triumph already permeates the fragile world of men and nature.

We discover this divine intrusion into our lives first of all in the Eucharist. Each time that the Catholic priest celebrates the holy sacrifice of the Mass, in which he commits a certain violence against the bread and wine, Jesus Christ becomes really, truly, and substantially present in the Sacrament of the Altar. In the Eucharist we discover God's answer to the problem of evil. It too abides as a mystery. In this mystery, however, we pray that God deliver us from all evil.

Heavenly Father, steady me against the day of temptation and trial. Make me love the Eucharist!

Oh! Happy Day

Father Romanus Cessario, O.P.

"People will die of fright in anticipation of what is coming upon the world, for the powers of the heavens will be shaken. And then they will see the Son of Man coming in a cloud with power and great glory. But when these signs begin to happen, stand erect and raise your heads because your redemption is at hand."
(Lk 21:26-28)

Throughout our lives we look forward to happy events. Young people look forward to their professional accomplishments and to their vocations in the Church. Husbands and wives anticipate the arrival of their children, and then their grandchildren, and then, even, their great-grandchildren. Consecrated persons look forward to their lives of prayer and contemplation, to the works of mercy to which they will dedicate themselves, and to the happy fulfillment of their vows. Seminarians await the day of their priestly ordinations. Priests expect years of fruitful priestly ministry in the Church. We not only anticipate the happy completion of our lives, we also find ourselves guided by these happy outcomes. Herein of course lies the challenge of life. While there are several vocations open to members of the Church, there remains one final end for every baptized person. Happy communion with the happy God.

So Jesus instructs us to stand erect and raise our heads. For those who fulfill what their vocations require of them, the final days—whether at death or at the end of the world—bring redemption. What is redemption? Redemption means that we have been rescued—literally, bought back—from all that would work against our well-being and happiness. Saint Luke further reveals that we are not bought back to remain in ourselves. We are rescued from sin and death so that we can meet the Lord when he comes. Jesus comforts us with the words: "Your redemption is at hand." Redemption delivers us over to Someone whom we love.

How do we prepare for this moment of personal encounter? Let our happy end dominate the beginning of everything we do. Whatever we undertake, whether we are married, consecrated, or a cleric, we should undertake in the name of Jesus. He is the "Son of Man" who will come on the day of our redemption.

Provident Father, guide me along the way of redemption. Steady my faltering steps. Point me toward your Son, the Lord Jesus Christ.

Getting It Straight

Father Romanus Cessario, O.P.

[Jesus] taught [the people] a lesson. "Consider the fig tree and all the other trees. When their buds burst open, you see for yourselves and know that summer is now near; in the same way, when you see these things happening, know that the kingdom of God is near. Amen, I say to you, this generation will not pass away until all these things have taken place. Heaven and earth will pass away, but my words will not pass away." (Lk 21:29-33)

Most people who today read this Gospel passage have never seen a fig tree. Still, it does not require a degree in horticultural science to figure out the meaning of the instruction that Jesus gives us. Who does not understand that buds signal the arrival of the full-grown fruit? Again, who does not know that fruits ripen best during the summer period—at least in those climates where summers differ from winters? The analogy is simple to make: just as nature gives signs that signal the maturation of living things, so God gives signs that signal the end for a living person. It makes little sense to wonder about the signs that will precede the end of the world. The final word on that great day of judgment remains that we know not the day nor the hour.

It does make a great deal of sense, however, to prepare ourselves for the end of our lives on earth. Age, illness, high-risk occupations, such as armed combat, offer the Christian the salutary sign of the fig tree. These and other possible indications are like "buds burst open." They tell us that mortality remains as much part of human life as does vitality. Summer comes, and so also does winter. Christian faith assures us that death marks a transition in life's pilgrimage, not an end of it. Still we need some support to face the reality of our own death. Jesus gives us this comfort: "My words will not pass away."

Where do we find these words? We hear them in the sacraments of healing, reconciliation, and holy anointing. Each time that we confess our sins to a priest, we hear the consoling words, "I absolve you." When the priest comes to anoint a gravely sick or dying person, the sacrament promises healing unto eternal life. With these generous provisions of the divine mercy, we need not fear the signs that the end may be approaching.

Merciful Father, grant me the grace to prepare for a happy death. Make me attentive to the signs that your love provides, and keep me close to the sacraments of the Church.

No Time for Snoozin'

Father Romanus Cessario, O.P.

"Beware that your hearts do not become drowsy from carousing and drunkenness and the anxieties of daily life, and that day catch you by surprise like a trap. For that day will assault everyone who lives on the face of the earth. Be vigilant at all times and pray that you have the strength to escape the tribulations that are imminent and to stand before the Son of Man." (Lk 21:34-36)

People adopt all kinds of attitudes toward life and death. Sometimes they say, "Eat, drink, and be merry, for tomorrow we die!" Or, "Live life to the full; you never know." Christians, however, cannot live as if there is no tomorrow. Tomorrow always comes. One tomorrow will find each of us facing the Lord. No person escapes judgment and the eternal tomorrow it begins. We must keep a lookout for the moment when we will meet the Lord. Jesus counsels vigilance. Given what is at stake, one may inquire what it means to remain "vigilant at all times." If a devil-may-care attitude does not suit the Christian calling, then what does the alternative look like?

The Lord gives the answer to this question: "pray," he tells us. No one can pray constantly. Some monks in the early days of the Church tried to pray all the time, and they became discouraged and stopped. Saint Benedict wisely ordained a life of prayer and work (*ora et labora*) for his monks. Typically, the monks spend eight hours at prayer, eight at work, and eight in repose. For the person who must dwell outside of a monastery, this is impossible. In order to remain vigilant, what does the everyday Catholic do? Develop the prayer of the heart. Keeping a watchful heart means remaining sufficiently vigilant while going about our business. When we maintain a prayerful vigilance, we will recognize when our spirits have begun to lose their strength. At that moment, the vigilant person will renew an act of confidence in Jesus. The watchful person will ask for the strength to remain upright and awake. Then the temptation to seek comfort in carousing or drunkenness or to escape into the anxieties of life diminishes.

Restoring our spiritual energies does not require stepping away from our daily work for long periods of time. We need only pronounce the Holy Name of Jesus.

Father of all, come to my rescue. Keep me vigilant. Make me always ready to turn to your Son, Jesus. Let me find my salvation in his name.

Waiting for Jesus

Father Romanus Cessario, O.P.

During the day, Jesus was teaching in the temple area, but at night he would leave and stay at the place called the Mount of Olives. And all the people would get up early each morning to listen to him in the temple area. (Lk 21:37-38)

There are many times in life when we find ourselves waiting for something to happen. When we wait for good things, we experience a heightened sense of joyful anticipation. The anticipation of bad things leads to fright, not joy. To hear a friend speak falls among the good things that causes us to wait in joy. The millions of people around the world who wait to hear the pope speak afford the best example. The triennial World Youth Day celebrations illustrate joyful waiting. Millions of young persons from every continent wait for hours to hear the Holy Father speak the Truth. In order to witness the pope celebrate Mass and to hear his words, his preaching, they even spend the night on the ground in open fields.

What draws these millions of young people to see and to hear one man? It would be difficult to argue that World Youth Day attendees anticipate the religious equivalent of a rock concert or that they seek the prestige of socializing with their peers. These millions of young people find themselves drawn to the very person of the pope. So we should not be surprised that the "people would get up early each morning to listen to" Jesus. One might say to onself, "Were Jesus preaching somewhere, I would also go to listen to him." In his infinite goodness, God has provided for this aspiration. Of course it is not possible to listen to Jesus speak in the same way that the people of first-century Palestine did. We can, however, hear Jesus speak through the Church that he established as an instrument of our salvation. The pope stands at the center of this worldwide communion. He sends bishops to each place in the world. Their job is to teach and to govern and to sanctify. Bishops appoint priest pastors to help them. Priests also teach and preach. The Christian people may still anticipate hearing what Jesus teaches.

Gracious Father, make me an enthusiastic hearer of your Word. Draw me close to your Son, our Lord Jesus Christ. For ever.

Final Victory

Father Romanus Cessario, O.P.

*Now the feast of Unleavened Bread, called the Passover, was
drawing near, and the chief priests and the scribes were seeking
a way to put [Jesus] to death, for they were afraid of the people.
Then Satan entered into Judas, the one surnamed Iscariot,
who was counted among the Twelve. (Lk 22:1-3)*

Passover commemorates the miraculous events that accompanied the departure of the Hebrew people from Egypt.
God delivered his people from oppression. They left in such
haste that there was no time to leaven their bread, and so the Hebrews baked an unleavened bread. The festival whereby the Jewish
people annually recalled God's deliverance forms the background
for Jesus' death. The Passover drama achieves a new height when
we discover that the Evangelist identifies Satan as the one who
instigates the series of events that will lead to the crucifixion. We
discover that the divisions, which Jesus became the occasion of
creating, now reach directly into the chosen men whom he had
gathered around him. There emerges the figure of "Judas, the one
surnamed Iscariot, who was counted among the Twelve." Deliverance remains an essential feature of Christian life. How many
times have we experienced the temptation to think, "If only things
would go well all the time, then I'd feel close to God"? The truth
of human experience leaves no room for doubt: human life entails
suffering. These sufferings also enveloped the one whom God sent
into the world to save us.

Sometimes Catholics dream of easier ways to follow Christ than
the one that the Church teaches. In fact, Pope Benedict XVI has
spoken about the dangers of creating a "Dream Church," a church
of one's own making. As the chief priests and scribes began to plot
against Jesus, the Evangelist alerts us to a non-negotiable premise
for the practice of the Christian religion. Those who follow Christ
must also brace themselves for the hardships that his followers
must endure in this world. Hardships come in unexpected forms
for different people. One hardship, however, faces everybody.
Death. For this suffering, only the Passover of the Lord provides
a remedy.

*Heavenly Father, give me the grace to welcome the cross in my
life. Preserve me in love. Sustain me in suffering.*

Blood Money

Father Romanus Cessario, O.P.

[Judas] went to the chief priests and temple guards to discuss a plan for handing [Jesus] over to them. They were pleased and agreed to pay him money. He accepted their offer and sought a favorable opportunity to hand him over to them in the absence of a crowd. (Lk 22:4-6)

One need not profess Christian faith to recognize that Judas commits a gravely dishonorable action. How else would one characterize betrayal of an innocent in exchange for money? Only caddish people might wink an eye at such reprehensible skullduggery. Right thinking people, however, will rightly judge Judas' actions as worthy of the highest condemnation. They will gladly allow Dante's intuition that places Judas in the lowest pit of hell. Judas not only betrays an innocent man. Judas betrays his master. Judas betrays his friend. Judas then reverses the order of human priorities. He puts something before someone. Efforts to psychoanalyze Judas always fail. We don't know what caused Judas to betray Christ. We don't know what the "something" is that motivated him to strike a deal with the chief priests and temple guards. All one knows for sure is what the Gospel tells us. Judas accepted the offer, and he looked for "a favorable opportunity" to put Jesus into the hands of his enemies.

Catholics are familiar with Judas' iniquity. It is easy for each of us to measure our own sins against his, and to conclude that we have never gone as far as Judas went. We have never betrayed God's only Son. There is no room for complacency. Judas warns Christian believers. First, Judas shows that expediency dominates our everyday actions more than we like to admit. When it comes to choosing between what is excellent and what is easy, we often opt for the easy. The ease with which we choose expediency feeds the subliminal relativism that dominates contemporary culture. Second, Judas sadly shows the danger of despair. The practice of too much relativism leads one to a point where we become forgetful of the divine mercy. Then we find ourselves in the same place as Judas.

Merciful Father, grant me the grace to live in the Truth. Keep me confident in your mercy. When my sins cause me to tremble, raise me up.

Chance Occurrences

Father Romanus Cessario, O.P.

When the day of the Feast of Unleavened Bread arrived, the day for sacrificing the Passover lamb, [Jesus] sent out Peter and John, instructing them, "Go and make preparations for us to eat the Passover." They asked him, "Where do you want us to make the preparations?" And he answered them, "When you go into the city, a man will meet you carrying a jar of water. Follow him into the house that he enters." (Lk 22:7-10)

Life is full of chance occurrences. One never knows whom one will meet in the street. Where one may discover unexpected income. When an old friend will call. Those who have never heard of the providence of God consider such random happenings as, well, random. Truth to be told, for the Christian believer, there are no chance occurrences. All falls under the providence of God. Even when bad things happen, God allows them. Otherwise nothing would happen. People seldom complain when the chance occurrences bring them good fortune. When we meet someone who will help us to achieve a personal goal. When the unexpected income helps us to meet heavy financial obligations. When the old friend who calls is someone from whom we had hoped to hear. Chance occurrences challenge us when they introduce unwelcome circumstances into our lives. When bad things happen, then people wonder about a divine and loving providence.

In order to understand how chance occurrences work in our lives, we should consider the example of Peter and John. Jesus sends them out on an important errand. They must prepare a room for the Last Supper. Because he is God, there are no chances for Jesus. So he tells Peter and John, go out into the city and you will meet a man carrying water. What otherwise may have seemed a merely chance occurrence in fact forms part of the divine plan to give us the Eucharist. We know the rest of the story. From this same room, Judas will depart to betray Jesus. From this upper room, Jesus will leave to meet those who will kill him. Only the Resurrection of the Lord provides the context for us to evaluate chance occurrences. When we believe in the glory that Christ introduces into the world by his cross and Resurrection, then we "know that all things work for good for those who love God" (Rom 8:28). Even chance occurrences.

Almighty Father, grant me a loving trust in your providence for me. Keep me always in your care.

Eating Together

Father Romanus Cessario, O.P.

"Say to the master of the house, 'The teacher says to you, "Where is the guest room where I may eat the Passover with my disciples?"' He will show you a large upper room that is furnished. Make the preparations there." Then [Peter and John] went off and found everything exactly as he had told them, and there they prepared the Passover. When the hour came, he took his place at table with the apostles. (Lk 22:11-14)

These verses from Saint Luke point to the human context within which Jesus institutes the sacrament of his love. Because of our sinful condition, we know that the full effects of the Eucharist are realized only once blood and water flow from the pierced heart of Christ. The cross leaves the imprint of a sacrifice on the Eucharist. Each Mass reenacts without repeating this sacrifice. Still, we cannot overlook that Jesus makes eating together the sacramental sign of the Eucharist. Even when a priest celebrates alone, as happens in monasteries of priest-hermits, the celebration of the Mass unites him with the whole Church. People of our generation find themselves more accustomed to eating alone than did people of earlier periods. One reason is simple. The preparation of food envisaged many hungry persons. For example, steaming bowls of rice or heaping portions of pasta. Individual servings belong to the modern period. Eating alone weakens the sacramental sign of eating together. The family meal should form the center of the family's day. Friends make dinner plans in order to share each other's company. Even the hermit belongs to a fraternity of hermits. They eat separately but not alone. So Peter and John, the Apostles who will first discover the Resurrection, set about to make arrangements for a common meal.

When Jesus takes his place at table, he raises the human good of eating with friends to a new level. Now the eating together becomes a sign of the unity that Jesus brings to the world. In order to benefit fully from our participation in the Eucharist, we should cultivate the habit of eating with friends or family. When circumstances make it impossible for someone to eat with another, we may also think of arranging the occasional common meal. Then we follow the example of two great Apostles.

Omnipotent Father, you give us the Eucharist of your Son as food and drink. Make me grateful for the gift of love and unity that this sacrament brings to the world.

The Wine of Salvation

Father Romanus Cessario, O.P.

[Jesus] said to [the apostles], "I have eagerly desired to eat this Passover with you before I suffer, for, I tell you, I shall not eat it [again] until there is fulfillment in the kingdom of God." Then he took a cup, gave thanks, and said, "Take this and share it among yourselves; for I tell you [that] from this time on I shall not drink of the fruit of the vine until the kingdom of God comes."
(Lk 22:15-18)

Everyone anticipates enjoying a meal at a favorite restaurant. Some people become so attached to an eating place that they regret when it goes out of business. There is a Chinese restaurant in Boston where a certain priest I know regularly dines with friends and students. After nearly two decades of his patronage, many of his guests, who have dined on pork strips and egg rolls while discussing theology, entertain happy memories of their learning experiences. They anticipate returning to the Chinese restaurant, even though they have established themselves in their own careers and vocations in life. Food and friendship go together.

So we can understand the emotion that the Apostles experienced when they heard the Lord announce that he was celebrating a final Passover meal with them. The Lord happily announces a fulfillment, not a termination. The wine of the Passover meal now becomes the wine of salvation. What Jesus does with his Apostles, he confides to them and to their successors. Each time that we partake of Holy Communion, we receive a promise of fulfillment. So the Last Supper becomes for Catholics not a moment for lament. Rather the Last Supper establishes a festival.

Each year on Holy Thursday, priests reenact what Jesus did on the night before he died. The daily Eucharist establishes a pattern of expectation in the Church. We return again and again to the Mass in order to dispose ourselves for the final fulfillment that accompanies the return of Christ in glory. The continuity of the Eucharist that the Church assures through the ministry of priests brings great consolation to the world. No one need fear that this meal will come to an end. When the kingdom of God comes, then all will recognize the wine of salvation as God's special gift to a world that fears its own instability in the good.

Gracious Father, grant me the grace to love the Eucharist. Keep me faithful to its celebration. Forgive my sins so that I may always approach this sacrament with reverence and love.

Bells Are Ringing

Father Romanus Cessario, O.P.

Then [Jesus] took the bread, said the blessing, broke it, and gave it to [the apostles], saying, "This is my body, which will be given for you; do this in memory of me." And likewise the cup after they had eaten, saying, "This cup is the new covenant in my blood, which will be shed for you." (Lk 22:19-20)

Some churches preserve the practice of ringing bells at important moments during the Mass. The origin of the practice arises from purely practical considerations. In an age when not everyone understood Latin, and when in any case the priest celebrated the Mass in a soft voice with his back to the people, it was necessary to find a way to announce the progress of the Mass. People then would know when to kneel or when to come forward for Holy Communion. Above all, people would know when the priest was about to speak the words that Jesus speaks at the Last Supper, the words of consecration. Then the bells would ring in two sets of three bells each. One set of three for the consecration of the bread and one set for the consecration of the wine.

Today these consecratory words are fairly well known to those who attend the Catholic Mass. The intuition that prompted altar servers to ring the most bells during the consecration of the Eucharistic bread and wine remains a sound one. When the priest repeats the words that Jesus speaks in this passage from Saint Luke's Gospel, he enacts the mystery of faith. So important are the words of consecration that the Church holds priests accountable for pronouncing them exactly as they are set down in the liturgical books. They are to be recited with reverence, attention, and devotion.

Priest and laity alike recognize that the words of consecration spoken over the bread and wine establish a model for other sacred words. For instance, those the priest speaks over us in the other sacraments or the words that bridegroom and bride speak to each other during the celebration of marriage. Each sacrament effects a change in the one who receives it worthily. So wondrously abounds the grace that bells are ringing all of the time. Listen for them.

Father in heaven, grant me the grace to love the Mass. Unite me each day to your Son's sacrifice. Then I shall be free from my sins.

Whatever You Do, Don't Despair

Father Romanus Cessario, O.P.

"And yet behold, the hand of the one who is to betray me is with me on the table; for the Son of Man indeed goes as it has been determined; but woe to that man by whom he is betrayed." And [the apostles] began to debate among themselves who among them would do such a deed. (Lk 22:21-23)

One easily encounters bad news. Newspapers blast the tragedies that befall people around the world. Social networking shoots bad news rapidly to the four corners of the globe. Barber shops, beauty parlors, and just about every place where ordinary folks gather serve as exchange posts for the latest news about the woes of our neighbors. What's wrong with a preoccupation with the bad and blameworthy? Too much bad news leads people to develop dark thoughts about the world and about the God who rules it. Dark thoughts then foster despair. We conclude that in the end, evil will befall us. Nothing stands further from the promise of salvation that Christ brings. Christians commit themselves to hope for their salvation. This means that they trust that God will deliver them from all evil.

The sad case of Judas, the one who betrays Jesus, illustrates what happens when we make the mistaken judgment that some sins find no forgiveness before God. Of course, what Judas did merits the harshest condemnation. Judas betrays his Master. The other Apostles find it difficult to believe that one of their number "would do such a thing." We know that Judas unleashes a chain of events that he himself would live to regret. This regret pushed Judas to despair. He takes his own life. When Jesus utters his "woe" against Judas, the Lord indicates that he foresees how Judas will react. How could things have been different? Judas could have recalled the many times that Jesus forgave sinners. Judas could have turned back in repentance. The lesson for us is clear: despair never fits the logic of Christian living.

Whatever our condition, there always remains the chance to turn back to the Lord. To make sure that we maintain this disposition within ourselves, we should avoid dwelling more than our station in life requires on the bad things that happen.

Father of life, grant me an unfailing hope in the power of your goodness. Keep me safe from all evil. Let Jesus guide my steps.

Kingdom and Banquet

Father Joseph T. Lienhard, s.j.

Then an argument broke out among [the apostles] about which of them should be regarded as the greatest. [Jesus] said to them, "The kings of the Gentiles lord it over them and those in authority over them are addressed as 'Benefactors'; but among you it shall not be so. Rather, let the greatest among you be as the youngest, and the leader as the servant. For who is greater: the one seated at table or the one who serves? Is it not the one seated at table? I am among you as the one who serves." (Lk 22:24-27)

The people of Great Britain refer to themselves as "subjects" of the queen; they are governed by a House of Lords and a House of Commons; they address judges as "my lord." In the United States, such distinctions of class do not exist; we have no hereditary titles, and we name ourselves "citizens," not subjects. But we are the exception; for much of human history, people lived under rulers: kings, emperors, czars. Such rulers might be benevolent, but often they were not.

Jesus draws on the resentment that Gentiles felt toward their rulers, who "lorded it over" their subjects and, ironically, were hailed as "benefactors," when they were probably oppressors. Jesus does not teach a political lesson here; he does not recommend democracy. He proposes a more radical model for Christian society: it is to be based, not on equality or even strict justice, but on humility and service. Jesus does not deny that there will be, or may be, a "greatest" among Christians, and a "leader." But these leaders are to act in a most unlikely way: the greatest like the youngest in the group, and the leader like a servant.

Jesus then makes a notable transition, from a kingdom to a meal. He seldom spoke about political structures; far more often, he spoke about meals and table fellowship. His image for the kingdom was not a state, a political entity; it was a meal, a dinner. In the kingdom, some will sit at table, and some will serve. Jesus is the model to be imitated; he is as the one who serves, even though he is truly Lord. Jesus' frequent references to table and meals and supper are surely echoes of the unique role of the Eucharist in the origin of Christianity: Christians are most at home before the altar, not in the voting booth.

God our Father, increase in us, we ask you, deep love for the Eucharistic meal; may our reception of Holy Communion bring us to the fullness of life.

God's Faithful Love

Father Joseph T. Lienhard, s.j.

"It is you who have stood by me in my trials; and I confer a kingdom on you, just as my Father has conferred one on me, that you may eat and drink at my table in my kingdom; and you will sit on thrones judging the twelve tribes of Israel."
(Lk 22:28-30)

When Jesus says that he confers a kingdom on his disciples, we encounter an unusual and surprising element in the Gospels. He proposes a kind of succession: the Father conferred a kingdom on Jesus, and Jesus now confers a kingdom on his disciples. Yet the two kingdoms are somehow one, for the disciples will eat and drink at the table in Jesus' kingdom. The condition for these mysterious rewards is fidelity: the disciples have stood by Jesus in his trials.

And perhaps fidelity is the central point here, fidelity and table fellowship. One of the most important Hebrew words in the Old Testament is *hesed*, a word not easy to translate in a single concept. The word is often rendered "fidelity," or "faithful love," or "loving fidelity." It describes a beautiful quality attributed to God: when God makes a covenant and commits himself to his people, he can be trusted to abide by it. He does not break the covenant, even if his people fail to live up to it. God is utterly trustworthy, trustworthy in a way that human beings could never be. But they might approximate that divine quality. A child trusts his or her mother to provide food, protection, and love. Husband and wife trust each other to be faithful to their marriage vows. The passage from the Gospel suggests how highly Jesus regarded this fidelity in his disciples: he would make them kings as a reward.

There is a further dimension to these words. Jesus invites us to imitate God's most characteristic quality, his fidelity; he invites us to participate in God's own nature. The Greek Fathers of the Church spoke readily of "deification," our taking on God's qualities. Latin writers spoke more often of sanctifying grace, receiving a share in God's life. In either case, though, the effect is the same: Jesus promises to take us up into the divine life.

Eternal Father and Lord, you are faithful to your promises, even when we turn our backs on you; strengthen us by your grace, we implore you, and keep us always true to you.

Cockcrow and a New Dawn

Father Joseph T. Lienhard, S.J.

"Simon, Simon, behold Satan has demanded to sift all of you like wheat, but I have prayed that your own faith may not fail; and once you have turned back, you must strengthen your brothers." [Simon] said to [Jesus], "Lord, I am prepared to go to prison and to die with you." But he replied, "I tell you, Peter, before the cock crows this day, you will deny three times that you know me." (Lk 22:31-34)

Long before alarm clocks, cockcrow was the sign of the end of night and the beginning of day: the rooster in the barnyard was, symbolically, the first one awake. For Peter, too, the cock's crowing was the end of the darkness of his sin and the beginning of the light of repentance and forgiveness.

Even as he foretells that Simon will betray his Lord, Jesus tells Simon, "You must strengthen your brothers." Simon Peter's fiery temperament is a familiar theme to every Catholic: the man of faith, who says to Jesus, "You are the Messiah, the Son of the living God" (Mt 16:16); the man wholly committed, who first would not let Jesus wash his feet but then wanted his whole body washed; the cowardly man, as we read here, the one who will deny that he knows Jesus to avoid being implicated; and the deeply repentant sinner, who went out and wept bitterly. Even before his sin, Jesus commissioned Simon Peter with a unique office: "You must strengthen your brothers."

Recent popes have used this phrase to define the papal office, and rightly so. Peter and his successors are a source of strength and encouragement. In Peter's case, the man who was to commit an abominable sin, the man who was to betray Jesus' trust, was also the man who would experience the fullness of forgiveness. Jesus had told him, "I have prayed that your own faith may not fail." Peter had faith in Jesus; Judas did not. Both sinned grievously. Judas despaired and hanged himself. Peter repented and was made the head of the Church. Peter, the repentant sinner, is surely the ideal of every confessor. If a Catholic has a difficult confession to make, who better to think of as a confessor than Peter? Who more than Peter experienced the full meaning of forgiveness? Who more than Peter knew the love of Christ's Sacred Heart?

Almighty God and Father, Christ your Son gave us the sacrament of reconciliation as his Easter gift; may we celebrate this sacrament often and well.

Faith and Works
Father Joseph T. Lienhard, s.j.

[Jesus] said to [the apostles], "When I sent you forth without a money bag or a sack or sandals, were you in need of anything?" "No, nothing," they replied. He said to them, "But now one who has a money bag should take it, and likewise a sack, and one who does not have a sword should sell his cloak and buy one."
(Lk 22:35-36)

We often hear statements like, "Pray as if everything depended on God; work as if everything depended on you." Such statements are not especially profound, and they can even be misleading. But they point in the right direction. Saint John Chrysostom writes that if everything depended on grace, everyone would be saved; if everything depended on works, no one would be saved. Hence, our salvation must depend on some combination of faith and works. This is not the place to resolve any great theological question, a question that has been discussed almost from the first days of Christianity. (One need only read Saint Paul's Epistle to the Galatians and compare it with the Epistle of Saint James to see the contrast.)

At the end of the Last Supper, Jesus suggests that the Apostles had depended on grace in the past, but now the time for works had come. The one who has a money bag or a sack should take it, and the one who does not have a sword should sell his cloak and buy one. These are mysterious words. Is Jesus advocating self-reliance? Independence from him? Violence? Is he preparing the Apostles for the next three days? Or for the centuries and millennia to come, the time throughout which the Church will perdure, until he returns to take his Bride home to himself?

We live in the age of the Church, that "little while" between the first Pentecost and the Second Coming. It is the time when each of us needs to ponder what the money bag, the sack, or the sword means for us—that is, what sort of works we are called to. But it is also the time to recall that Jesus does not leave us in need. As he said to Saint Paul, "My grace is sufficient for you" (2 Cor 12:9). But Paul still needed to struggle; and we do, too.

Almighty, ever-living God, open my heart to know your will for me and to carry it out with joy and peace.

Christ Is the Key

Father Joseph T. Lienhard, S.J.

*"For I tell you that this scripture must be fulfilled in me, namely,
'He was counted among the wicked'; and indeed what is written
about me is coming to fulfillment." Then [the apostles] said,
"Lord, look, there are two swords here." But he replied,
"It is enough!" (Lk 22:37-38)*

"What is written about me is coming to fulfillment." We should not miss the profound implications of our Lord's statement. Jesus lived seventeen centuries after Abraham, twelve centuries after Moses, a thousand years after David. The Hebrew people had recorded their history, their prophecy, their wisdom, and their songs in a great body of writing that we call the Old Testament.

Jesus, and those who wrote about him in the earliest decades after the first Easter, read the Old Testament in an entirely new light. Suddenly, the Old Testament was not just a record of the past, but a prophecy of the future. Read rightly, it foreshadowed the coming of Christ and even details of his earthly life. Christ's person became the key that unlocked the final meaning of the Old Testament. On the first Easter Sunday, in the evening, Jesus met two of his disciples on the road to Emmaus. And, as they walked, he explained to them the meaning of the Scriptures, beginning with Moses and the prophets. In one sense, we might long to know which prophecies Jesus quoted to his two disciples. In another sense, though, it is better not to know, for then our interest will remain with the whole Old Testament.

Each Sunday at Mass, and on other days, too, we hear or read a passage from the Old Testament. We ought to hear or read those passages in the way that those two disciples did, so that our eyes are opened. "What is written about me is coming to fulfillment," Jesus says, and thereby gives us the key to searching the Scriptures. We have the key, but the door is not yet fully open; only a lifetime of meditation on the Scriptures, all the Scriptures, will open the door for us. The biblical word is one of God's greatest gifts to us; we ought to become loving and devoted readers of the Bible.

Almighty and eternal God, you revealed yourself to us in the biblical word; make us, we ask you, attentive listeners and devoted followers of your Word.

The One Christ

Father Joseph T. Lienhard, S.J.

Then going out [Jesus] went, as was his custom, to the Mount of Olives, and the disciples followed him. When he arrived at the place he said to them, "Pray that you may not undergo the test." After withdrawing about a stone's throw from them and kneeling, he prayed, saying, "Father, if you are willing, take this cup away from me; still, not my will but yours be done." (Lk 22:39-42)

"Father, if you are willing, take this cup away from me; still, not my will but yours be done." Christians down the centuries have pondered the mysterious person of Jesus Christ. Some have fallen into error, saying that he was only a man who acted in a divine way, or that he was God who only took on the appearance of a man. The Council of Chalcedon taught the truth: as Son of God, Jesus Christ is God just as the Father is; as son of Mary, Jesus Christ is man just as we are: true God and true man, one Person.

The confrontation between two wills in Jesus' agony in the garden helps us to ponder the meaning of his Person. And Pope Benedict XVI, in his book *Jesus of Nazareth: Holy Week*, provides excellent insights. The man Jesus has a natural will, which resists the fearful destructiveness of what is happening and wants the chalice of suffering to pass from him. But he also had a filial will, which wants to abandon itself wholly to the Father. Jesus really and truly prays for deliverance from this hour, but he also submerges that prayer into his awareness of his mission; he subordinates his person to his mission. He accepts the horror of the cross, its utter indignity, and the suffering it involves, for the glory of God's name.

Jesus' prayer, and his action, manifest God as he truly is: in the unfathomable depth of his self-giving love, the power of good triumphs over all the powers of evil, and, in this action, Jesus' two natures are merged perfectly into his one Person. Thus the infinite difference between God and man is preserved; humanity remains humanity and divinity remains divinity. But the radical unity of the two in Christ's one Person is the unfailing hope of our own salvation, and of our ultimate union with God. The sacrifice of obedience makes all the difference.

Eternal God and Father, deepen our faith in your Son Jesus Christ, true God and true man; through him and through his cross, may we come to the fullness of life in you.

Jesus' Sweat of Blood

Father Joseph T. Lienhard, s.j.

[And to strengthen (Jesus) an angel from heaven appeared to him. He was in such agony and he prayed so fervently that his sweat became like drops of blood falling on the ground.] When he rose from prayer and returned to his disciples, he found them sleeping from grief. He said to them, "Why are you sleeping? Get up and pray that you may not undergo the test."
(Lk 22:43-46)

Beginning with Saint Paul, Christians have used the contrast between Adam and Christ to understand Christ. Paul spoke about Christ as the last Adam, and wrote that "just as through one person sin entered the world…" (Rom 5:12).

A great Syrian writer of the fourth century, Saint Ephrem, notes an intriguing detail of the comparison of Christ with Adam. As one of the punishments for his sin, God said to Adam, "by the sweat of your face/ shall you get bread to eat" (Gn 3:19). Now, the sweat of Jesus is so intense that it becomes like blood. Adam was to sweat, like every laborer, like everyone who plows a field, builds a house, or paves a road. Christ takes on himself, not the burden of manual labor, but the burden of all the world's sin. Under this burden, he breaks out into a sweat of blood. No human being could carry this burden; it would break the strongest back. So the Son of God made man carries it for us. All the sins of the world are heaped on his back, and he bears them; he bears them and carries them away; we are freed of them. The words we say at each Mass should remind us of this moment in Saint Luke's Gospel, and of what Christ has done for us: "Lamb of God, you take away the sins of the world; have mercy on us."

Perhaps we should pause to consider the real experience of forgiveness. This does not mean saying "pardon me" if we bump into someone. What if we deeply offend someone—a spouse, a parent, a friend? What if we do someone damage that can never be repaired? Can we expect forgiveness? What would it be like, if that person somehow convinced us that our relationship was now just as it had been before? Is such a thing even thinkable? Yet we know that God forgives.

God our Father, your Son Jesus Christ took upon himself the burden of the world's sin; by his suffering and death, we implore you, deliver us from the bondage of sin and evil and give us the gift of true life.

Judas' Kiss

Father Joseph T. Lienhard, S.J.

While [Jesus] was still speaking, a crowd approached and in front was one of the Twelve, a man named Judas. He went up to Jesus to kiss him. Jesus said to him, "Judas, are you betraying the Son of Man with a kiss?"
(Lk 22:47-48)

"In front was one of the Twelve, a man named Judas." Perhaps it would have been less painful, less ironic, less contemptuous, if Judas had hung back, if he had stayed in the shadows, if he had covered his face. But no; he was in front; he was leading the mob to Jesus. What was going through his mind when he did that? Was it the money he had gotten? Was it a way out of a commitment he no longer wanted to maintain? Was it jealousy of others of the Twelve, maybe Peter, James, and John, who were always the inner circle, while he, Judas, was never invited in? Is there some trace of Judas in each of us?

The irony only deepens when Judas kisses Jesus. He could simply have pointed him out. He could even have laid hands on Jesus. But instead, he kisses him. In its clearest sense, a kiss is a sign of love. The word "love" has been overused and trivialized, but its true meaning is not lost; its true meaning can never be lost. One way to ponder the meaning of true love is to hold Judas up to a mirror. As Jesus himself would say, the greatest love there is is this: to lay down one's life for one's friends. The opposite is clear: the greatest betrayal of love there is is to make one's friend die for one's own selfish reasons. The meaning of friendship is reversed, turned on its head; trust is poisoned by treachery.

Once again, Judas' betrayal of Jesus should be an opportunity for us to ask questions of ourselves. It is never right to speak contemptuously of another's sin without asking ourselves whether there is not something of the same sinner in us. The kiss of Judas is the kiss that the sinful world gave to Christ.

Almighty God and Father, give us, we beg you, the gift of true fidelity; may we always remain true to you and to all who love us.

Malchus' Ear

Father Joseph T. Lienhard, s.j.

[Jesus'] disciples realized what was about to happen, and they asked, "Lord, shall we strike with a sword?" And one of them struck the high priest's servant and cut off his right ear. But Jesus said in reply, "Stop, no more of this!" Then he touched the servant's ear and healed him. (Lk 22:49-51)

The Gospel narrative of our Lord's Passion obviously deals with the single most important event in the history of the world: the crucifixion and death of the Son of God incarnate to deliver the world from sin, and his Resurrection from the dead as our hope. But these narratives also contain small vignettes, which are based, perhaps, on the living memories of people who were present, at one moment or another, at Jesus' Passion.

One such moment is the young man, reported in Saint Mark's Gospel, who was spending the night outdoors, near the garden where Jesus prayed. He had covered himself only with a sheet. When the soldiers tried to lay hold of him, he left the sheet and ran away naked. (I've always wondered whether that young man was Saint Mark; did he enjoy telling this embarrassing story about himself?)

Another is Simon of Cyrene. We know that the Roman soldiers forced him to carry Jesus' cross. But Saint Mark also reports that he was the father of Alexander and Rufus. Why add this detail, unless the Christian community knew Alexander and Rufus?

Still another such detail is the disciple's rather inept swordsmanship. Jesus had wanted his disciples to be armed, perhaps so that they could offer at least symbolic resistance to the Romans; they could never really fight off trained soldiers. Saint Luke tells us that one of the disciples swung his sword and cut an ear off the high priest's servant, and Jesus touched it to heal it. Saint John adds that it was Peter who did this, and he also tells us that the servant's name was Malchus. Did this young Jewish man later join the Christian community? As the years went by, did other members of the community say, "Tell us again what happened that night in the garden. And show us your ear; which one was it?" Perhaps Jesus' small miracle brought Malchus to faith.

Eternal God and Father, open our eyes to the wonders of your creation; deepen our faith in you, we humbly ask, and give us the gift of trust in your providence.

The Power of Darkness

Father Joseph T. Lienhard, s.j.

And Jesus said to the chief priests and temple guards and elders who had come for him, "Have you come out as against a robber, with swords and clubs? Day after day I was with you in the temple area, and you did not seize me; but this is your hour, the time for the power of darkness." (Lk 22:52-53)

"The power of darkness" is a fearsome phrase. We all know what physical darkness is. Children are afraid of the dark because they imagine that monsters, figures they've seen in movies or cartoons, are hiding somewhere. Adults can be afraid of darkness, too, but usually because they fear for their safety. If you've ever been caught in an inside stairwell when the power fails, you understand fear of the darkness. We feel along with our hands and feet, afraid of missing a step, afraid of falling. To lock a prisoner in a cell without the least ray of light is a terrifying punishment.

But still, we haven't come to the "power of darkness." The darkness that makes us fearful is a passive thing, an absence of light. But, of itself, it has no power. What Jesus speaks of is something active, something that threatens to upset the whole right order of things. Some ancient religions, like Manicheism, proposed that the world is a battleground between two equal and opposing forces—Light and Darkness, Good and Evil, Matter and Spirit.

Christians surely do not think that way. The Book of Genesis teaches us that the one God created the whole world out of nothing. God is all good, and everything he made necessarily participates in his goodness. Evil comes, not from God, but from the abuse of free choice of the will. Such is Catholic teaching, stated in a few short sentences. But the experience of evil goes far beyond those sentences. The experience of sickness, disease, loneliness, betrayal, desertion—all of these can suggest an evil that has a power of its own. The hour of Jesus' Passion represents his encounter with the power of evil, the power of darkness. We should never lightly dismiss the power of darkness, the power of evil. Jesus did not. He faced it and—thanks be to God—conquered it.

God our Father, you are all good and the font of all goodness; deliver us, we pray, from the power of darkness and evil, and bring us to the fullness of your light.

Following at a Distance

Father Joseph T. Lienhard, S.J.

After arresting [Jesus] [the chief priests, temple guards, and elders] led him away and took him into the house of the high priest; Peter was following at a distance. They lit a fire in the middle of the courtyard and sat around it, and Peter sat down with them. (Lk 22:54-55)

Peter's triple denial of Jesus is one of the most moving vignettes in the narrative of Jesus' Passion. The contrast between Jesus and Peter is striking. Jesus knows what is happening to him, and, after the lonely agony in the garden, he accepts it willingly and without hesitation. For the Savior of the world, the hour had come. Peter's situation is different. He does not know what is about to happen, and he has not accepted it. Two phrases in the Gospel passage stand out: "Peter was following at a distance," and "Peter sat down with them." Perhaps he didn't mean it that way, but Peter's commitment to Jesus was less than complete. The night before, he had said, "Even though I should have to die with you, I will not deny you" (Mt 26:35). Now, he is not so sure.

Before we condemn Peter and say, "I would never act like that," perhaps we should ask ourselves, isn't Peter's behavior the behavior of everyone who is tempted? Our behavior, so often? We think of something that is wrong, and picture ourselves doing it. That's only the beginning of a temptation; it is not a sin. We don't commit the sin; we just follow along at a distance, thinking, I won't do it, but it won't hurt to think about it. Then the temptation becomes stronger. Peter sat down with the party that had arrested Jesus. Perhaps Peter is thinking: It won't do any harm, just to sit here. If Jesus is attacked, I can run over and defend him. Besides, nobody here knows who I am. I can always leave, whenever I want.

It's a sad story, isn't it? But it's also our story. We each have our own temptations. And each of us is Peter: we follow at a distance, we sit down where we don't belong. Sometimes, like Peter, we sin; like him, too, we can pray for the Lord's forgiveness.

Almighty God and Father, each day we pray, "lead us not into temptation, but deliver us from evil"; confirm our hearts, we pray, and strengthen our wills, by the power of this prayer.

Seated in the Light

Father Joseph T. Lienhard, S.J.

When a maid saw [Peter] seated in the light, she looked intently at him and said, "This man too was with him." But he denied it saying, "Woman, I do not know him." A short while later someone else saw him and said, "You too are one of them"; but Peter answered, "My friend, I am not."
(Lk 22:56-58)

The narrative of Peter's triple denial of Jesus is surely familiar to all of us. But each detail of the denial is significant. For example, Saint Luke writes that Peter was "seated in the light." Perhaps the phrase means only that the maid could make out Peter's face. But perhaps it means more, too.

Light is the most powerful metaphor for knowledge that we have. "I see," we say, and mean, "I understand." We speak of an insight into the truth as an illumination. Even in children's cartoons, a light bulb over a character's head means knowledge, insight, a new idea. Far more profoundly, Saint Augustine of Hippo proposed a theory of knowledge that is called the illumination theory. Just as the eye cannot see an object without light from the sun, so the mind cannot perceive an eternal and necessary truth without the divine light, without God who is eternal and necessary. To go even further: perhaps the most neglected phrase in the whole Creed is "Light from Light." We say, "God from God, Light from Light, true God from true God," and glide over the middle phrase. Each of the pairs means that the Son is from the Father, and the two are equal in divinity. The Son is Light, from the Father, who is Light. In the world of the Creed, light means life, and darkness is death.

So when we read that Peter was seated in the light, the phrase may mean much more than simply that the maid could see him. He was seated in the light that is the second Person of the Blessed Trinity; his mind could perceive the fullness of truth. Once again, before we blame Peter or reprehend him, we ought to remember that we, too, by our Catholic faith, are seated in the Light. Do we see?

God our Father, ever living and omnipotent, hear our prayer, we implore you, and enlighten our hearts with your saving truth.

Interrogation—Denial—Mockery

Father Joseph T. Lienhard, s.j.

About an hour later, still another insisted, "Assuredly, this man too was with him, for he also is a Galilean." But Peter said, "My friend, I do not know what you are talking about." Just as he was saying this, the cock crowed, and the Lord turned and looked at Peter; and Peter remembered the word of the Lord, how he had said to him, "Before the cock crows today, you will deny me three times." He went out and began to weep bitterly.

(Lk 22:59-62)

Pope Benedict XVI, in his beautiful book *Jesus of Nazareth: Holy Week*, meditates on the key moments of the Passion, with extensive chapters on the Last Supper, the crucifixion and burial of Jesus, and Jesus' Resurrection from the dead. The pope does not treat Peter's denial at length, but in a few sentences he focuses attention on one significant aspect of the denial, namely, a triple simultaneity.

To paraphrase the pope, at the decisive moment in the history of the world, three levels intersect. And all three levels must be considered together, if the event is to be grasped in all it complexity. One level is Caiaphas' interrogation of Jesus, which culminates in the high priest's question about Jesus' identity as the Messiah. The second level is Peter, who sits in the forecourt of the palace and denies that he knows Jesus. The third level is the mockery to which Jesus is subjected: first by the palace guards and then by the Roman soldiers. In one of the Gospel accounts, the high priest uses precisely the title for Jesus that Peter had confessed at Caesarea Philippi: "the Messiah, the Son of the living God" (Mt 16:16). So the bitter irony: Peter, who had confessed that Jesus was the Christ, and the Son of the living God, now denies him; and, in his place, the high priest takes up Peter's words—but not his faith. And further: Jesus could have avoided a verdict of guilty by denying that he was the Messiah, but he didn't; Peter did deny Jesus and merely avoided an embarrassment.

Following upon Jesus' answer to the high priest, the guards mock him. A few days before, they had feared Jesus; now they make him feel their contempt. But mockery is the tactic of cowards. They did not remember Jesus' words, "you will see 'the Son of Man' seated at the right hand of the Power'" (Mt 26:64).

Almighty, eternal God, we humbly pray: give us the strength never to deny you, but to profess our faith with courage before all the world.

True and False Prophecy
Father Joseph T. Lienhard, s.j.

*The men who held Jesus in custody were ridiculing and beating
him. They blindfolded him and questioned him, saying,
"Prophesy! Who is it that struck you?" And they reviled
him in saying many other things against him.*
(Lk 22:63-65)

The men who held Jesus in custody ridiculed him and beat
him. They blindfolded him and shouted, "Prophesy!" It is
worth our while to stop and ponder the role of Jesus as a
prophet. Prophecy is one of the great categories of the Old Testament writings. We read and hear the great prophets, like Isaiah,
Jeremiah, and Ezekiel; and the minor prophets, like Amos and
Joel and Micah. Verses from each of them are familiar to us, often
because the New Testament writers quoted them. Isaiah, in particular, is read at Mass during the strong seasons of the liturgical
year: Advent, and the last days of Lent.

The Old Testament prophets—a varied lot—spoke out against
the sins of the people: idolatry, injustice, neglect of widows and
orphans, religious formalism. But there is one characteristic that
all the prophets share: they spoke God's words, not their own.
Consider Micaiah, son Imlah, in the Book of Kings (1 Kgs 22:6-33).
Four hundred prophets told the king that he would be victorious.
But the king did not trust them. He summoned Micaiah. Micaiah
first lied to him, but then told the truth: by sunset the dogs would
lick up the king's blood. He had to speak God's Word, because he
was a true prophet.

How does Jesus fit into this picture? How do his tormentors fit
in? The tormentors have a false idea of prophecy: they think it is a
kind of clairvoyance, seeing through a blindfold. The true prophet
sees the difference between right and wrong, truth and falsehood.
And so, Jesus is the truest prophet of all. The irony of the Passion becomes almost unbearable. Jesus' captors could not be more
wrong, more misguided. Yet unbeknownst to them, their words
can be taken in a true sense. As so often, we need to ask ourselves,
"Do I say 'Prophesy!' to Jesus? Do I mistake him for what he is
not?"

*Almighty and eternal God, hear our prayer, we ask you: let your
Word live in our hearts and fill us with your Truth.*

Jesus Is the Messiah

Father Joseph T. Lienhard, S.J.

When day came the council of elders of the people met, both chief priests and scribes, and they brought [Jesus] before their Sanhedrin. They said, "If you are the Messiah, tell us," but he replied to them, "If I tell you, you will not believe, and if I question, you will not respond. But from this time on the Son of Man will be seated at the right hand of the power of God." (Lk 22:66-69)

One can say, and say rightly, that all of Christian theology is the answer to one question: "Who do you say that I?" (Mk 8:29). The identity of Jesus Christ, the meaning of his person—and therefore of his mission—is a question that will never receive a single, definitive answer. When he is questioned before the Sanhedrin, and later before Pontius Pilate and Herod, Jesus' answers to questions about his identity are complex, showing that there is no simple answer to these questions.

Pope Benedict XVI, in his book *Jesus of Nazareth: Holy Week*, reflects at some length on Jesus' answers to these interrogators. Following Pope Benedict, we can see the complexity of the moment. Jesus did accept the title "Messiah" for himself. But he excluded any political or military interpretation of that title. He was not going to be an earthly king; he was not going to lead a rebellion against the Romans. Before the Sanhedrin, he accepted the title "Messiah" but qualified it in such a way that it could only lead to a verdict of guilty. He could have avoided that verdict; he could have cut down the meaning of "Messiah" until it was some bland, sentimental term that anyone could accept; he might have said, "After all, every one of us is anointed, in some personal way or other." But he did not. If anything, he upped the ante by appealing to Psalm 110 and to chapter 7 of the Book of Daniel. He is the Son of God, and the Son of Man. As Son of God, he participates in God's own nature. As Son of Man, he will come on the clouds of heaven.

We might close by meditating on those two verses: "before the daystar,/ like the dew, I begot you" (Ps 110:3); and, "I saw one like a son of man coming,/ on the clouds of heaven" (Dn 7:13).

God our Father, hear us as we pray to you, and give us true knowledge of Christ our Lord; may he be the center of our lives and the goal of all our hopes, now and for ever.

Jesus, Son of God

Father Joseph T. Lienhard, S.J.

[The assembly] all asked, "Are you then the Son of God?" [Jesus] replied to them, "You say that I am." Then they said, "What further need have we for testimony? We have heard it from his own mouth." (Lk 22:70-71)

The assembled Sanhedrin reduce Jesus' trial to a single question: "Are you then the Son of God?" Jesus answers enigmatically, "You say that I am." The question arises, which word in Jesus' answer should be stressed? "You"? In that case, it would mean, "I might phrase it differently." But if "say" is stressed, then Jesus is saying, "What you say is clear and true; I have nothing to add to your words."

Whatever the case, the assembled Sanhedrin had a remarkable insight into what would later be called Catholic and Christian doctrine: the title "Son of God" is not some bland synonym for "caring person" or "good and holy man." The title specifies an ontological state, and for Jesus to claim it makes him deserving of a death sentence, on grounds of blasphemy.

How does Catholic theology understand the title "Son of God"? The sense of the term is far from obvious. Clearly, we do not believe in a God who has a family. "Son" is, in that sense, metaphorical. We believe in one God, whom Jesus habitually addressed as "Father." We also believe that the Father begot another divine Person, eternally, immutably, and without passion. That Person is called Son; he is also called Word, Power, Wisdom, and Image. From the mutual love of Father and Son there proceeds a third Person, the Holy Spirit. The five titles, which are all privileged titles from the New Testament, help us to understand who the second Person is: Son—a person, not a thing; Word—the way God speaks to us; Power—how God governs the world; Wisdom—the depths of God's unbounded knowledge and prudence made present; Image—God, no less than the Father.

Surely the assembled Sanhedrin were not professing faith in the Blessed Trinity; but they saw some of the great implications of the title "Son of God."

Eternal God and Father, in Christ your Son you reveal to us the fullness of your life; help us always to worship you in spirit and in truth.

Fail-Safe

Father Lawrence Donohoo

Then the whole assembly of them arose and brought [Jesus] before Pilate. They brought charges against him, saying, "We found this man misleading our people; he opposes the payment of taxes to Caesar and maintains that he is the Messiah, a king." Pilate asked him, "Are you the king of the Jews?" He said to him in reply, "You say so." (Lk 23:1-3)

Soon to be condemned as an insurrectionist and crucified, Jesus of Nazareth appears in court as a complete failure. The evidence appears not only in his present condition and impending crucifixion, but the previous failures of his mission and the dispersion of his followers. In a few moments he will be the loser who will set Barabbas free. Any other king in such a hopeless situation would conceal his regal identity, but Jesus succeeds in making these failures his own.

And why did he fail? He never said no to the Father. The frightening truth is that the Father's will leads to failure—at least in the short run. Ultimate success only comes through transient failure with a numbing and reliable cruelty.

Jesus failed because he obeyed, because he was sinless, because he was human. People who have no regrets are either sinless or liars. Jesus had no regrets, but he did have failures. Not to fail in some sense is not to be human, as even his sinless life shows.

But we see a difference between Jesus' failure and ours. Most of our failures are due to sin, ignorance, and stupidity on our part or that of others. A few are traced back to the booby traps of life. But the failures of Christ were all of one stripe. As the Messiah who came to establish a kingdom of truth and life, holiness and grace, justice and peace, he failed because he loved. For to love another is to chance failure if another refuses my love.

Have I not failed in love? Has not my heart been broken by another—and to be honest, have I not broken another's heart? Haven't I broken Christ's? When my love fails, Jesus is a failure. Only when I am subject to his rule of love will he succeed, for his task is to turn my failure into his success and my defeats into his victory of love.

Loving Father, may my only failures be due to my unconditional obedience to your will. May my only successes be due to your love manifested in the sacrifice of your Son.

Your Move

Father Lawrence Donohoo

Pilate then addressed the chief priests and the crowds, "I find this man not guilty." But they were adamant and said, "He is inciting the people with his teaching throughout all Judea, from Galilee where he began even to here." On hearing this Pilate asked if the man was a Galilean; and upon learning that he was under Herod's jurisdiction, he sent him to Herod who was in Jerusalem at that time. (Lk 23:4-7)

Aristotle observes that the weak person is prone to deliberate too fast and execute too slowly. It's exactly the opposite for the virtuous person, who deliberates slowly and executes fast. But Aristotle also teaches that good deliberation ends in decision, and decision resolves in action.

Pilate becomes a participant in extreme injustice because he cannot make up his mind. He consorts with evil by second-guessing a decision already made after a thorough examination of the facts. This is not evidence of reflection, but vacillation. And we are right to assume that his prior examination of Jesus was thorough because it would have been easier from the start to please the crowd by condemning the man. There is no new evidence now to consider, just the same old charges. Had they been true, the prefect of the Roman province of Judea would have known them long before now. The only difference is that the charges are now made in a louder crescendo of hate and a shriller key of anger.

How different in the life of Christ. It is on the mountain at night that we find him in intimate union with the Father, whose will is the lodestar of his deliberations and the guidepost of his decisions. It is on the roads at day that we see him in fast-paced action, executing with dexterous love and sensitive efficiency. This seamless weave of deliberation and action assures a perfect execution of the Father's plan in every phase of Jesus' life.

It should be no different in mine. All day long I must deliberate, decide, act. Have I reflected on how I'm doing and how I'm doing it? Are my deliberations thorough, my decisions rational, my actions productive? Most importantly, is the Holy Spirit guiding the process with his gifts of wisdom, understanding, knowledge, counsel, piety, fear of the Lord, and— with Pilate in mind— fortitude? He'd love to help.

Almighty Father, please send your Holy Spirit to kindle in me the light of divine deliberation. Send forth your Spirit, and I shall be more reasonable and obedient.

Song and Dance

Father Lawrence Donohoo

Herod was very glad to see Jesus; he had been wanting to see him for a long time, for he had heard about him and had been hoping to see him perform some sign. He questioned him at length, but he gave him no answer. (Lk 23:8-9)

Herod is fascinated by supernatural phenomena and holy men. After imprisoning John, Herod liked listening to him. We can only imagine what he heard. And after murdering John, holy man Jesus comes to his attention, so he keeps trying to see him as well. Herod's schizophrenic behavior, swaying between vicious immorality and supernatural fascination, manifests an attitude toward religion best described as a lust for frightening amusement. We know this from his birthday party. Religion here is the art of being supernaturally entertained, of being frenziedly amused.

Now Herod's long-standing wish is fulfilled: Jesus is standing before him, and he wants a one-man show. But no results. He plays the flute, but no dancing; he sings a dirge, but no weeping. Instead, the silent treatment. You want action, Herod? You perform. Let's see you dance and sing.

Herod has his followers who, if in a less perverted fashion, also approach the divine mysteries as a source of frightening fun. Their pew for the religious program is the armchair: just please sit down, call up God, and enjoy the show. On this view, religion represents a parallel universe you access when you need a break from the aches and pains of the universe you live and work in.

Jesus' religion looks quite different. There are real breaks and pains and aches in it, as he will soon experience in full fury. The truly supernatural mysteries do not negate or bypass this world, but enter into it more deeply than it can itself by transforming it from within. In this sense, the true Christian is more worldly than his or her pagan counterpart. So was the incarnate One who was a real carpenter, real preacher, real victim. He worked with wood and it worked on him. He lived in one universe where the yeast mixes with the wheat flour and everything is still no longer the same.

Heavenly Father, your Son took our world and our salvation seriously by entering fully into it. Help me to do likewise, for true joy requires my real presence in your real world.

Pictures at an Exhibition

Father Lawrence Donohoo

The chief priests and scribes, meanwhile, stood by accusing [Jesus] harshly. [Even] Herod and his soldiers treated him contemptuously and mocked him, and after clothing him in resplendent garb, he sent him back to Pilate. Herod and Pilate became friends that very day, even though they had been enemies formerly. (Lk 23:10-12)

Well, Herod didn't get the show he wanted, so he produces one himself. His soldiers perform exactly as they're told, and Pilate's soldiers later will continue the fun and games of mocking Jesus. The chief priests and scribes are doing what they always do best. Everyone in the chorus is on key and in step: the herd is having a field day. All the world is a stage, and nearly everyone in it is a willing or unwilling pawn of the script.

In his most famous allegory, Plato describes human beings who are chained from childhood in a cave. They think the shadows on the wall are real, and do not know that they are victims of an elaborate deception. They see only shadows of man-made images of real animals outside the cave. We learn from this not only that members of the herd act alike, but that they first think alike and interpret the world far removed from truth. "Pilate said to him, 'What is truth?'" (Jn 18:38). How we see guides our actions. Each person receives the world through the marred lens of the ignorant and wicked who are themselves victims of others like them, and so each becomes a faithful member of the herd.

I cannot be a genuine follower of Christ if I am a dues-paying member of the herd, wherever it may be found. I can only discern the deep things of the Spirit and the genuine will of the Father if I cut through the shadows, artifacts, and unified ignorance of the various herds in my world. Nor may I ignore them, for to imagine that I can live in blissful ignorance of their caves is to risk falling into them unwittingly. I need to be alert to the dues paid, the perks enjoyed, and the compromises made in the attempts to destroy truth and feast on its corpse. I need to learn why Herod and Pilate are friends.

Eternal Father, your Son's unwavering commitment to truth made him a bright star on a darkened horizon. Give me the courage to face Truth in the eyes and face down his detractors.

Not Thoughts, but Belonging

Father Vincent Nagle, F.S.C.B.

Pilate then summoned the chief priest, the rulers, and the people and said to them, "You brought this man to me and accused him of inciting the people to revolt. I have conducted my investigation in your presence and have not found this man guilty of the charges you have brought against him, nor did Herod, for he sent him back to us. So no capital crime has been committed by him. Therefore I shall have him flogged and then release him." (Lk 23:13-16)

Why did Pilate act against his convictions and have this man flogged whom he himself had judged to be innocent? It was convenient. Something is convenient if it helps us protect what we are attached to. It is inconvenient if it challenges what we are attached to. Pilate was attached to something that did not uphold his sense of justice or truth.

I can recall a period when after several years of discussion, prayer, and reading I had come to be convinced that the Church was indeed who she claimed to be and that Jesus is Lord. But I noticed that certain areas of my life were not changing. I was not living according to my convictions. Like Pilate, my convictions about right and truth were in one place, but my actions in another.

What introduced real change in my life was when I met a group of friends attached to one another through a beautiful experience of communion in Christ, and they gratuitously invited me to join them on their journey. The name of Jesus Christ began to take on their faces, and belonging to Christ implicated belonging to this human experience, and vice versa. My convictions were now rooted in an affective belonging. Little by little, my convictions stopped being simply thoughts, and became a force that was shaping my life. Life in Christ is not first of all what we think, but who we are attached to.

What shaped Pilate's life? Was it not his attachment to power? What is it then that we are attached to? As Jesus warns us, "Where your treasure is, there also will your heart be" (Mt 6:21). Love and truth are inextricable. Ultimately we will find convenient whatever protects our attachments. Only a loving, affective belonging allows us to live the truth.

Heavenly Father, let me be always reborn within the body of your Son, the company of saints, and so live in your Spirit for ever.

What I Saw through the Window

Father Vincent Nagle, F.S.C.B.

But all together [the chief priests, the rulers, and the people]
shouted out, "Away with this man! Release Barabbas to us."
(Now Barabbas had been imprisoned for a rebellion that had
taken place in the city and for murder.) Again Pilate addressed
them, still wishing to release Jesus, but they continued their
shouting, "Crucify him! Crucify him!" (Lk 23:18-21)

I was riding an inter-city mini-bus in a foreign country, when soldiers came on and made all the young men get off. I watched from a window. One soldier came to a young man, spoke loudly, and repeatedly poked him in the chest with his fingers. After several pokes the young man slapped away the soldier's fingers, which brought a storm of soldiers upon him to handcuff him. The young man did not let them put his hands together for the handcuffs, which brought on a shower of blows to various parts of the body, including the private parts. Even after they did put the cuffs on, one soldier, a woman, continued physically to abuse him.

When asked why I had not done anything to intervene, many things came to mind: "It all happened so fast; the soldiers represented the legal power; I was a foreigner; what difference could I make?" But the fact is that I passively sat and observed an act that I took to be an injustice. I did nothing because I was afraid.

Fear makes us the slaves of power. As the Letter to the Hebrews says, it is through "fear of death [that we were] subject to slavery [to the devil]" (2:15). It is not for nothing that the phrase of Christ most often recorded in the Gospels is "Be not afraid." He has come to liberate us from fear, the source of sin.

Fear is also what makes the crowd instruments of Satan's rage. How easily they were maneuvered into their shrill cry, "Crucify him!" When we lose sight of the one who has conquered death, we are filled with fear and end up standing (or sitting) with them, as I did that day on the bus. Let us ask always for the grace for our hearts to be fixed on him, and so to be witnesses of his kingdom.

Merciful Father, my fear of death reduces me to enslavement
within Satan's manipulations. Let the victory of your Son in my
life liberate me to be your loving child and servant.

Healing the Splintered Soul

Father Vincent Nagle, F.S.C.B.

Pilate addressed [the chief priests, the rulers, and the people] a third time, "What evil has this man done? I found him guilty of no capital crime. Therefore I shall have him flogged and then release him." With loud shouts, however, they persisted in calling for his crucifixion, and their voices prevailed. The verdict of Pilate was that their demand should be granted.

(Lk 23:22-24)

Jesus was offering to Pilate the opportunity to live as a true man, whole and of one piece. Pilate was following the well-known logic of power, by which no matter what your ideals are—justice, equality, or human dignity—you have to have a separate sphere of thinking that works on a different level in order to achieve and maintain power: the level of intimidation and the raw exercise of force divorced from justice. This divides our minds and destroys the unity of our persons. Jesus wants the presence of his person to be the new focus and healing of this inner splintering.

I lived this splintering for some time. It was the example of Blessed John Paul II that obliged me finally to face it head-on. He had repeatedly called upon the international community to intervene in an ongoing ethnic conflict. But when planes finally began to drop bombs, the Holy Father condemned the recourse to violence. I was confused. Had not he called for an intervention? How did he think that would happen? Did he think that it was possible for powerful people to care enough that they would actually show up in person and confront the leaders involved face to face? Wasn't he being unrealistic?

But he had spent a lifetime facing down the raw exercise of power, and had won. He was not unrealistic. John Paul had discovered the true power, which resides in the love of Christ Jesus. His actions obliged me to ask that my faith in Christ become my only face, even in questions of power. Christ's trust in the Father and infinite regard for human dignity not only unifies our lives by setting our hearts upon one hope only, but is also the only path that is finally able to reach the goal of politics: justice.

Unlike Pilate, let us allow Christ's gaze upon us to unify our persons and redeem our identity in front of the Father and the world.

Loving Father, let the attraction and grace of your Son unify my heart and mind in the truth and hope of his presence.

Thanking God for the Cross

Father Vincent Nagle, f.s.c.b.

So [Pilate] released [Barabbas] who had been imprisoned for rebellion and murder, for whom they asked, and he handed Jesus over to them to deal with as they wished. As they led him away they took hold of a certain Simon, a Cyrenian, who was coming in from the country; and after laying the cross on him, they made him carry it behind Jesus. (Lk 23:25-26)

Along the Way of the Cross, in the Old City of Jerusalem, I always feel anxious to get to the fifth station so I can spend some time meditating on Simon's experience, which tells us so much about our own.

Sometimes the things that were imposed upon me with violence have led me to some of my deepest experiences of conversion. For example, when the girl that I had been with for five years and whom I had been planning to marry suddenly abandoned me for someone else, it led to several years of tormented prayer and the discovery of God.

I think of Simon. A terrible injustice was imposed upon him. Innocent, he was forced to bear the shame and torment of carrying the cross of a stranger. And what did it lead to? The Gospel gives a big hint. First of all, we know Simon's name, and where he came from. Second, in the Gospel of Mark, we read that he was just coming in from the country and that he was the father of Alexander and Rufus. How do the Evangelists have all of this information? Because the Christian community knew him, and especially knew his sons. It means that Simon never forgot the bloody and struggling man he met under the weight of the wood, and he became his follower. In what was violently imposed, his freedom opened to receive the face of God. Who knows how many times he thanked God for that act of injustice, even as I, after many years, thanked God for what I had suffered.

The injustice of this world is not an obstacle to our freedom in Christ. If we ask, God can move our freedom to find him, even in those dark occasions. Let us ask for Simon's prayers, so that we might not fear the violence of this world, but be certain that Jesus makes all things new.

Just and loving Father, how I am tempted to think that you are not there in the darkness. Let me discover your Son as the cross is set upon my shoulder!

Nothing Is All Right

Father Vincent Nagle, F.S.C.B.

A large crowd of people followed Jesus, including many women who mourned and lamented him. Jesus turned to them and said, "Daughters of Jerusalem, do not weep for me; weep instead for yourselves and for your children, for indeed, the days are coming when people will say, 'Blessed are the barren, the wombs that never bore and the breasts that never nursed.'"

(Lk 23:27-29)

Even on this extreme journey, it is a volcanic passion for the redemption of everyone he meets that moves our Lord. Jesus reproaches the wailing women, seeking to awaken them to the true drama overtaking them. They weep and beat their breasts because of his unjust suffering, but his suffering is not the issue. Salvation is the issue. His suffering, like everything, is a sign. He challenges them, and us, to read it.

I too remember words that penetrated my thinking and helped to awaken me. I had been given a tape of a famous American preacher giving a retreat for priests. At one point—and I can still remember the little car, the cloudy weather, and the New England road, so great was the impression it made upon me—he said loudly, "You think that despite a few problems, things in your life are basically all right. Nothing is all right! Our lives are crying out for salvation." These words brought new clarity to my life, and opened my ears to hear Jesus speaking more powerfully. Without him we remain afraid and cannot bear to face the real drama of our lives.

This is what Jesus is telling the wailing women. "Let my unjust suffering be a sign to you. Do you think that it is only my affliction you have to weep over? Don't you understand that this crime is only a sign of the age-old, soul-deep, dramatic need for salvation? Don't you see that things are coming to a head? A decision must be made. You have to beg for salvation, now. I am in front of you now."

Jesus never stops gazing at others with all the intensity of the Father's eternal mercy. No circumstances can change it. Let his passion make our souls melt and tremble, and lift our eyes to heaven, seeking salvation.

Merciful Father, please send your grace to me so that I do not miss what is really happening—my need for salvation and your Son's offer of redemption.

Truth and Mercy

Father Vincent Nagle, F.S.C.B.

"At that time people will say to the mountains, 'Fall upon us!'
and to the hills, 'Cover us!' for if these things are done when
the wood is green what will happen when it is dry?"
(Lk 23:30-31)

I was once visiting a woman in the hospital who was very bitter toward priests. She listed at great length the sins of priests she had known. They had, she said, slighted her in favor of those who had more money and could offer more comforts. I answered her saying, "It is true that we priests have sinned and deserve punishment and even death. Will you pray with me for the salvation of us priests?" She did not answer, but I hope she thought about what I said.

The fact is that the most useless thing in the world is to spend energy on a pretense or protestation of innocence. Life is too short for that. We want to live our lives, and the truth of our lives is that we have need of forgiveness. The only useful position is to admit our need, our beggaring need for salvation. In fact, when I find myself at the first station of the Way of the Cross, what comes over me is this sense of his having been exposed, rejected, and punished. But I am no innocent one.

Jesus' words to the women are more than just a shattering prophecy that will become horrifyingly realized with the fall of Jerusalem in the year AD 70. They also deliver a stunning shock to our system, placing us in a position that we could never endure without his intervention of grace and hope. He is innocent, the only innocent man. And, if this is his fate, what will be ours, we who are far from innocent? In front of these words, we can feel the abyss open up that we have suspected lies beneath us. What fire is prepared there to consume us? Let us not flee from this truth, from our lives, but follow him upon this journey, throwing ourselves upon his mercy, the only place where truth and hope thrive side by side.

Loving Father, don't let me keep running away from the truth;
that is, my need for the mercy you have granted us in your Son,
our Savior.

The Loss of Compassion

Father Vincent Nagle, F.S.C.B.

Now two others, both criminals, were led away with [Jesus] to be executed. When they came to the place called the Skull, they crucified him and the criminals there, one on his right, the other on his left. [Then Jesus said, "Father, forgive them, they know not what they do."] They divided his garments by casting lots.
(Lk 23:32-34)

I n the midst of the barbarity and the blood, how can our Lord step back to have pity on the foolishness of these blind people torturing him to death? How moved he is by the darkness in these lost sheep tearing his body to pieces! Where does this penetration come from? This clarity on the part of the Lord in his extreme prostration can come only because of his freedom, the expression of his complete consignment to his heavenly Father. He is not afraid.

By ourselves we cannot afford to have compassion on those who make us feel threatened. It does not work that way. Trust alone, the opposite of fear, is what allows us to open our hearts in compassion, to stand as moral beings in front of the deadly events of this world.

I am no stranger to moral blindness due to fear. Like many, I was profoundly shaken by the events of September 11, 2001. I had a background in living in Muslim countries, and had studied Islam in depth. I recognized the ideological power behind those attacks, and I was afraid. From that time on, I did not bother to question or withhold my support for things that were done in the name of security. I never opened my heart to those caught in the web of violence. Since then I have come to live in a place where I witness many unjustifiable acts committed in the name of security. And I see others on the other side who cannot question or withhold their support for these acts, due to fear. I see myself in them. Our lack of trust destroys our morality.

Who will restore to us our humanity, our morality, our ability to judge clearly and have compassion? Only the one who liberates us, only the one who has conquered, only the one who said, "Father, forgive them, for they know not what they do."

Heavenly Father, you wanted your Son to suffer all things so he could be our road to heaven. Let me not fail to hear him pray for us sinners, and to desire to join him in that prayer without fear.

Sticks and Stones

Father Vincent Nagle, F.S.C.B.

*The people stood by and watched; the rulers, meanwhile,
sneered at [Jesus] and said, "He saved others, let him
save himself if he is the chosen one, the Messiah of God."
Even the soldiers jeered at him. (Lk 23:35-36a)*

In the Arab world, the spoken word is still considered a very powerful force in life. No one says, "Sticks and stones may break my bones but words will never hurt me." Here words certainly can and do hurt. They are well known to be weapons, and they are feared and respected as such. In the past, poets would be placed on the front lines of tribal clashes, sometimes even achieving victory simply through their evidently superior put-downs and boasts. Such weapons were being massively unleashed against our Lord. Why do they do this now that he is helpless?

A hint as to why their violence mounts occurred to me after I recently had a bad fall, breaking some bones. Other complications set in to make it all rather unsightly. People are often put off by any accidental direct exposure to my now misshapen limbs. There is something about what happened to me that is distinctly threatening. For them it is a very small but real sign of the enemy, of death.

Naked, bloodied, and fixed to the wood, the more wretched Jesus' appearance, the greater threat he seems to be to those around him. They "sneer" and "jeer" at him. Why is this? Egged on by the Prince of Darkness, the onlookers find his powerlessness more threatening than his evident power had been.

Even as my ugly limbs do on a tiny scale, his lacerated and humiliated body acts as a terrible provocation. The onlookers see in his condition the tenuousness of their own existence and the enemy, death, waiting at the gates. And so they throw spear-tipped words, spewing out the rage erupting from their terror.

The irony in this is that by his obedience to the Father, in subjecting himself to their violence, our Lord is bringing to fruition what their frenzy cannot—the defeat of death and the opening of the door to everlasting life.

All-powerful Father, do not let the terror of pain and death overtake me, but rather let your Son's loving presence keep me on the path of love.

Part of the Plan

Father Vincent Nagle, F.S.C.B.

As [the soldiers] approached to offer [Jesus] wine they called out, "If you are King of the Jews, save yourself." Above him there was an inscription that read, "This is the King of the Jews."
(Lk 23:36b-38)

"We know that all things work for good" (Rom 8:28). Saint Paul's words help explain the mysteriously and yet comfortingly appropriate message set above Christ on the cross, *The King of the Jews*. In the midst of all the rejection and degradation, how does this fitting title come to be placed on the scene by Jesus' very persecutors? It is because, even in our lust for evil, we cannot help but pave the way for the good intended by our Father, the glory of our Lord Jesus Christ.

This occurred to me after seeing Mel Gibson's movie *The Passion of the Christ*. Ever since, I have been haunted by the mesmerizing figure of Satan as he drifts through the crowd, stoking their hate, kindling their lust for blood, urging on the greatest crime of mankind: putting to death the only innocent man. But ever since, I have also been in awe of the fact that Satan must have known how this would end, with the defeat of the very weapon by which he held men and women in thralldom, the defeat of death. Yet knowing that it would end in his own defeat, he couldn't help himself. He was powerless to resist this opportunity. It makes us see how Satan himself, for all his fearsomeness, is almost pitiable in front of the majesty of our Lord shining forth in his magnificent patience and compassion. Even Satan's scheming works for the good.

Pilate, in ironically ordering the placard, may have thought that he was above all of the drama. But his amoral detachment, too, works for the good. Thus, in his jab at the pride of the Jewish leaders, he leaves behind for us, preserved today in the Basilica of the Holy Cross in Rome, this written witness to the man executed that day, the king of God's chosen people. May this small sign give us confidence in God's providence.

Merciful Father, in the midst of the chaotic events of life, do not let me forget to look for signs of your grace at work, so that I may walk with your Son and live with you for ever.

Rage and Curiosity

Father Vincent Nagle, F.S.C.B.

*Now one of the criminals hanging there reviled Jesus, saying,
"Are you not the Messiah? Save yourself and us." The other,
however, rebuking him, said in reply, "Have you no fear of God,
for you are subject to the same condemnation? And indeed,
we have been condemned justly, for the sentence we received
corresponds to our crimes, but this man has done
nothing criminal." (Lk 23:39-41)*

The words of the two men crucified with Jesus reveal two fundamental positions of our humanity: one results in a rage against our fate; the other is a more realistic position kept alive only by that spark of hope born of a humility that says, "Could this be the one?"

Rage is NOT unknown to me even in my later years. In my youth it was more like a way of life. As a university student, one of my teachers accused me of trying to kill him by launching into furious arguments when he was sick. My rage was born of fear masked by a sense of righteousness and a need to remake the world in my image. It felt intoxicating, liberating, and empowering. Thus the first thief seeks to strengthen himself through attacking. But it is a position that is unable to bring life.

The other position is more realistic, and began to dawn on me one day when, during a prolonged period of pain and prayer, I started to wonder where love and truth came from, and to look around me to see if I could find where the grace I needed might be appearing. In our envious and thieving hearts we desire and we need. Yet we desire and need something that we ourselves cannot name or imagine. This opens a wound within us, and also a gaze that asks, "Is it you I have been waiting for?" The appearance of unexpected goodness arouses us, makes us curious.

While the first man was trapped within himself, Dismas, as the Church names him, even in his extremity, cannot help but acknowledge the goodness of his co-sufferer. He is attracted precisely because of the contrast with his own state. May our own desire for goodness arouse a curiosity in our lives so that we may also be looking for "the one"!

All-seeing Father, never let me stop looking for the face of the one my heart was made for, your Son our Savior.

Hidden Heroes of Faith

Father Vincent Nagle, F.S.C.B.

Then [the criminal] said, "Jesus, remember me when you come into your kingdom." [Jesus] replied to him, "Amen, I say to you, today you will be with me in Paradise."
(Lk 23:42-43)

A single mother I knew had a daughter who had lost her way. She had dropped out of college and moved in with disreputable companions in another city. With no visible means of support, she was completely out of contact with her mother, her parish, and former friends. The mother suffered and prayed.

One day we were with some other people, and talk turned to a second girl of the same age making good steps in her life, and was being praised. Seeing the pain in the mother of the missing girl, I drew her aside and said, "We speak well of what we see in the other girl, but no one knows what is going on inside the mind and heart of your daughter. No one knows what entreaties she may be making to God. No one knows what mighty, even heroic struggle she might be waging for her soul, her yearning for virtue and begging for redemption. God sees, and he may well be looking at her as a hero of faith. Let us be with her in this struggle through prayer." This girl did finally come to trust God's love in some people of faith, and to walk in a new direction.

But I think of her, and many like her, and even myself, when meditating upon the "good" thief, Dismas. We may correctly judge the sins of others' lives, but how can we know of an inner struggle seen only by God? Perhaps only in the last moment, as with this man, will an answer to these unseen prayers appear in the face of someone unexpected, whose good presence shows them the face of God and allows them to beg, however weakly, "Don't abandon me! Let me share the true life I see in you!" May God grant that the hope we have in his Son will make our faces the ones that are an unexpected answer to an unsuspected plea.

Loving Father, let my weak but sincere prayers for change come before you, and today let me recognize the One who saves.

We Die as We Live

Father Vincent Nagle, F.S.C.B.

It was now about noon and darkness came over the whole land until three in the afternoon because of an eclipse of the sun. Then the veil of the temple was torn down the middle. Jesus cried out in a loud voice, "Father, into your hands I commend my spirit"; and when he had said this he breathed his last.
(Lk 23:44-46)

As our Lord lived so he died, consigning himself into the hands of his heavenly Father. We cannot but die as we lived. In the weakness and agony of sickness and death, what one has lived, the position of one's heart, comes out no matter how well hid this might have been previously.

A great grace came to me when as a young man I went to Sunday Mass in a new town. After Mass, announcements were made for volunteer work. Later I went into the lobby, saw the table for sign-ups for visiting the local rest homes, and put my name down. It turned out that I enjoyed this work a lot. I also learned the necessity of facing our demons and conquering them now, while there is still the will and energy. I saw again and again how people's anger, suspicions, bitterness, and obsessions, though perhaps "managed" during their more healthy and active years, would come out, becoming very visible when their habitual modes of defense were diminished. I took note of this, and said to myself, "It is no good simply covering up. Somehow I have got to face my demons now. The true nature of our hearts is sooner or later exposed, if only in front of God."

Easier said than done. One does not simply expel one's goblins and clean one's inner house with a sweep of the hand. But it did teach me to expose myself often to God in confession and to ask Jesus to help me join him in handing myself over to the Father. And even if I never distance myself from my sins, at least the habit of begging forgiveness and rejoicing in its presence will be with me too. And as my sinful heart is unveiled in the light of day, may I also be able to say in the grace of Christ, "Into your hands, I commend my spirit."

O just and loving God, let me not delay, but give myself over to your Son today, so that when I come before you, you may recognize your Son in me.

Beyond Doubt

Father Vincent Nagle, F.S.C.B.

The centurion who witnessed what had happened glorified God and said, "This man was innocent beyond doubt."
(Lk 23:47)

What did that centurion see, hear, or notice to spark within him such a statement? What could it have been that made him affirm the innocence of Christ with such boldness?

I think that it is analogous to films for me. If I walk into a room and a film is on television, it usually does not take me more than ten or fifteen seconds to recognize what film it is. This happens often when I have not even seen the film before, but recognize it from a review. I know from the texture of the image, the kind of color and sound, from the pacing and music, immediately how to place the film. When it comes to film, I know what I am looking at and when I see something extraordinary, I am not in doubt. I can point it out and say, "Look at that!"

The centurion knew about men on the cross. He knew what it was to watch them die in pain and defeat. He was more than an expert. He was a master. And what he saw filled him with wonder. Why? What particular word, gesture, or look told him that he was in front of something, someone extraordinary? Perhaps it was many things, all of it, and perhaps he himself could not have articulated it. But he knew about how men died, and he had never seen anything like this.

This can be our experience today. It can happen in the life of the Church today, in the saints, known and unknown, in the beautiful gestures of truth, charity, and faith that we can observe as we share in his mystical Body. What comes into play is our own expertise in humanity; our ability to recognize what is ordinary and extraordinary. The Church is reborn when we can say, "Here is the Son of God, beyond doubt."

Almighty Father, let me recognize with certainty the exceptional presence of your Son, so today I may confess him as Lord and God.

It Cannot End

Father Vincent Nagle, F.S.C.B.

*When all the people who had gathered for this spectacle saw
what had happened, they returned home beating their breasts;
but all [Jesus'] acquaintances stood at a distance, including
the women who had followed him from Galilee and saw
these events. (Lk 23:48-49)*

What keeps these followers of Christ rooted in that spot? Are they just too sad, wounded, and lost to move on? All of that had to play a part. But it was more than that. They were certain that they had not seen the last act. Something more was coming. It had to be. They'd have to be crazy to think that this was all there was.

I remember when I first applied to enter the seminary of my home diocese. Years before I had been active in my diocese teaching CCD, counseling in the summer camps, helping to guide youth retreats, and even starting a large Catholic college student group. After my interview I went away and waited to hear from them. I waited months. And when I finally did get the letter and opened it, I was informed that they had not accepted me. I had not been expecting that. I kept taking the envelope in my hand, examining the return address, taking out the letter, looking to see if it was really addressed to me or not, rereading the letter itself to see whether I had understood correctly or not. It went on for hours.

I kept thinking: "There is some mistake. After all the graces, events, miracles, and encounters that led to this step, this cannot be what comes out of it. It just cannot be." And so I could not stop looking over and over at what lay before me.

Christ's disciples are in a similar position, but in a much greater way. They are certain of what they have lived with this man, and they are certain that this cannot be the end. And so they stand there looking, waiting, and anticipating something that they cannot predict. In front of even the violent contradictions of this world, may we stand with them, anticipating with certainty the good end that God is bringing to our story with Jesus.

Heavenly Father, help me to grow in my certainty of your Son's exceptional presence, so that the evils of this world may not bring me despair.

Not a Prison, but a Launching Pad

Father Vincent Nagle, F.S.C.B.

Now there was a virtuous and righteous man named Joseph who, though he was a member of the council, had not consented to their plan of action. He came from the Jewish town of Arimathea and was awaiting the kingdom of God. He went to Pilate and asked for the body of Jesus. After he had taken the body down, he wrapped it in a linen cloth and laid him in a rock-hewn tomb in which no one had yet been buried.
(Lk 23:50-53)

Inexplicably, there was a period of my life when I kept on meeting and befriending young people from very wealthy families. The encounters were usually positive, and, on my part, accompanied by admiration and affection. At the same time, I noticed a dynamic that was more or less common among them. They were faced with the temptation to view their lives not in view of the fulfillment that they were waiting for, like Joseph of Arimathea, who "was awaiting the kingdom of God," but in view of being good managers of what they had been given.

Our hearts live upon promises. This is not paradise, and evil exists around us and in us. Yet a loving God has placed us here because there is a promise that he intends to keep. On our part, a *risk* is called for. We have to be ready to invest everything in our hands in something greater. This is the human adventure. All of the gifts that are handed to us or which we acquire—cultural, spiritual, and material—must either serve to launch us toward a fulfillment that they themselves cannot communicate, or they become prisons for our minds and souls.

This was the argument between our Lord and the Pharisees. This is a drama that we are immersed in ourselves: we have to decide whether it is better to risk everything for the promise of a relationship with something exceptional that promises us the infinite, or to try to let the things we already have satisfy us.

Joseph of Arimathea, a rich man (Mt 27:57), made his decision. Though he waited until after our Lord's death to do so, Joseph came forward publicly and risked everything for a relationship with that exceptional man, Jesus. Thus he remains a model for us of true humanity to this day.

Gracious Father, your providence has filled my life with good things. May these propel me to throw myself into the arms of your Son, our Lord.

Rest and Hope

Father Vincent Nagle, F.S.C.B.

It was the day of preparation, and the sabbath was about to begin. The women who had come from Galilee with [Jesus] followed behind, and when they had seen the tomb and the way in which his body was laid in it, they returned and prepared spices and perfumed oils. Then they rested on the sabbath according to the commandment. (Lk 23:54-56)

Somehow they rest. It takes nothing less than a commandment of God. It is only by following this commandment that these women will find it possible to adjust their vision to recognize what it is that is about to happen. Without this rest, they might succumb to the temptation of thinking only of how they need to react to these overwhelming events and not of what the Father is doing. If we do not see that he is the One at work, our imaginations and our sense of the possibilities of life will be very limited. It can lead to a loss of hope. They needed hope.

I know all about the temptation to activism. At seventeen years of age, I was suddenly the provider for my mother and my two little brothers, so I started to work at night and go to school during the day. Sleeping was for weekends. It started a pattern of working myself way, way beyond the safety markers. In the years leading up to my ordination, I started to drive myself again, prompted by a combination of enthusiasm for the faith and terror of my vocation. This led to a complete breakdown that kept me basically bedridden for years.

I learned to put great value in those few experiences that help me listen and watch with trust. Rest opens our hearts to something beyond our immediate concerns, and allows our minds to gaze upon things that are more than just possible solutions to present problems. It allows us to hope for something we cannot easily name.

This is what the sabbath did for these women. Their obedience to the commandment to rest prepares them for something they could not name, but to which they will be the first witnesses. If we wish to be his witnesses, let us ask for obedience to this commandment to rest, and let him turn our hearts to hope.

Merciful Father, I am so tempted to think only of what I am doing, and forget to look for what you are doing. Let me take the time to open my heart to you today.

The Fertile Garden Tomb

Father Anthony Giambrone, O.P.

But at daybreak on the first day of the week [the women] took the spices they had prepared and went to the tomb. They found the stone rolled away from the tomb; but when they entered, they did not find the body of the Lord Jesus. (Lk 24:1-3)

Those who venture into the later verses of familiar Christmas carols often reap theological rewards. I recall my puzzled amusement as a child whenever I heard our scratchy Mario Lanza record singing deep into "We Three Kings": "Myrrh is mine/ its bitter perfume breathes a life of gathering gloom/ sorrowing sighing, breathing, dying/ sealed in the stone cold tomb." What Christmas cheer! I always imagined the other two kings as being slightly embarrassed, reckoning Balthasar (to whom the album's melodramatic voiceover attributed this verse) a bit like a morbid neighbor of ours who had a legendary capacity for turning every conversation to funerals.

In fact, the myrrh carried by both Magi and mourners does reveal a real link between the mysteries of the Nativity and Jesus' burial. Saint Jerome saw the connection in the detail that Jesus was laid in a tomb "in which no one had yet been buried" (Lk 23:53). Joseph of Arimathea's tomb is a virgin tomb, calling to mind the virgin womb from which a new life of divine Sonship was miraculously born. Christ is laid not in earth, but sterile stone; yet the cold grave flowers fertile as the Virgin. This is the final fulfillment of Isaiah 11:"A shoot shall sprout from the stump of Jesse..." for "unto us a child is born" (Is 9:6, KJV); for the prophet ultimately foresees that "his sepulcher shall be glorious" (Vulgate).

By this association, the tomb oddly becomes an image of the Church, the virgin Mother of Christians. If Nicodemus was right that a man "cannot reenter his mother's womb and be born again" (Jn 3:4), with the women we *can* enter this rejuvenating tomb. In baptism we mystically do this: "We were indeed buried with him through baptism" (Rom 6:4). May we also learn from the women that to follow the fate of our crucified Lord to its very end will always disable our morbid expectation of embalming.

Father in heaven, usher me into the tomb of your Son that I might be rejuvenated. Put to death all in me that still serves sin, so that born anew in the Spirit I might blossom as you will.

"He is not here"

Father Anthony Giambrone, O.P.

While [the women] were puzzling over this, behold, two men in
dazzling garments appeared to them. They were terrified and
bowed their faces to the ground. They said to them, "Why do
you seek the living one among the dead? He is not here,
but he has been raised." (Lk 24:4-6a)

Wearing a religious habit tends to make you look official. As a consequence, wherever I go in the world, people seem to come up and ask me stupid questions. I remember once being smack in the middle of Saint Peter's Square and having a pair of tourists, busily bumbling with their maps, approach me and ask in a slow, loud American accent where the "churcho Santo Pietro" was. My favorite, however, was in Jerusalem. I was standing by the Holy Sepulcher, when a man approached and asked what "that thing" was. I said it was the tomb of Jesus, to which he replied in genuine awe, "Wow. So he's *in there*!" Garbed in (semi-)dazzling white, I played the angel and said "No, he's risen."

Pious as the dutiful women in the Gospel are, we must admit that the angels' words make the mourners look a little lost. "Why do you seek the living one among the dead?" It is an excellent and embarrassing question. It is a graced question meant to turn our world right-side-up and give us back our bearings in a flash. Why do we instinctively seek the Lord in gloomy graveyards? Do we think Christ haunts the desolate corners of our lives, the lonely spots untouched by vitality or happiness? Too often, we are drawn to the tomb only to mourn ourselves and the painful mortification of our vices. Our thoughts rise early like the women and race to the monuments we have raised over old wounds, there to lament our fortune and to preserve and prolong its bitter memory with the arts of our unguents and spices. We suppose we are serving God by our trappings of devotion. But *he* is not there; for he is not God of the dead, but of the living. And if we would find him, we should start our search by searching for the deepest life alive within us.

Father, show me where to find your Son. Help me to leave behind
the dark shadows of death and abandon my rituals of mourning,
so I may seek him out and find him alive in the light of life.

Remembrance of Things Past

Father Anthony Giambrone, O.P.

"Remember what [Jesus] said to you while he was still in Galilee, that the Son of Man must be handed over to sinners and be crucified, and rise on the third day." And [the women] remembered his words. Then they returned from the tomb and announced all these things to the eleven and to all the others.
(Lk 24:6b-9)

The white light of the Lord's Resurrection hits his disciples like a lightning flash of memory. "And the women remembered his words." It is supremely interesting that the stunning surprise of Easter should penetrate the memory first. Of all the fallen parts of our broken nature, healing touches neither our weak wills nor our ignorant understanding. Rather, the grace of the Resurrection first seeks out that place in our soul where we have failed to register God's words spoken to us in the past. In illuminating our memory, the Lord rewrites our history, a history distorted by the forgetful darkness which has settled on our soporific minds.

This strange forgetfulness is a most curious thing. As a general rule, prophecies of resurrection are worthy of mental note. What explains such memory loss? How does one gracefully recover from the gentle angelic reminder? "Well shucks! I do faintly recall him mentioning something about rising from the dead. It didn't seem important." The point is not to find excuses, of course. It is to let the Lord's long-established plan, announced in advance, emerge fully into the light.

Our lives require this gracious flash of recollection. To know what the Lord *is doing* we must allow him to remind us what he *has already done*. We must let him awaken our sluggish memories to re-envision our misunderstood past. No matter who we are or what we have experienced, the plan God has for our lives has been announced time and again. But chances are it has still not yet registered, whatever our excuses might be. Our memories are filled with many things, but not yet filled with God's Word. May the clutter of trivialities, misperceptions, and grudges, which clog our soul's preoccupied remembrance, fade into blissful amnesia to let the clarity of Jesus' prophecies resound.

Father in heaven, purify my memory. Clear out every useless and destructive thought so I can see myself more clearly in the light of your plan for my eternal happiness.

Left Behind

Father Anthony Giambrone, O.P.

The women were Mary Magdalene, Joanna, and Mary the mother of James; the others who accompanied them also told this to the apostles, but their story seemed like nonsense and they did not believe them. But Peter got up and ran to the tomb, bent down, and saw the burial cloths alone; then he went home amazed at what had happened. (Lk 24:10-12)

When I was in college I had a friend who owned the entire collection of *Left Behind* movies. He was not Protestant and didn't believe in the rapture; he simply loved watching Kirk Cameron, Mr. T, and other born-again has-beens fight the end-time villainy of the Anti-Christ. Ridiculous as the films were, I confess sharing his delight in the thought of an eschatological A-Team, and I recall one time trying to convince my pal that *he* had been left behind. Taking my cue from the movies, I neatly folded a set of my clothes and conspicuously laid them out on my chair… the unmistakable sign that I had gone to meet Jesus in the clouds. My friend's only response was to pity the fool (me) who would rather be raptured than shoot bazookas at Armageddon.

When Peter sees Jesus' empty burial cloths we are not told what conclusion he draws. He is amazed, but this only reflects his puzzled wonder. Sure faith still eludes him. This is clear in the fourth Gospel, where the immediate understanding of the Beloved Disciple upon seeing the shroud stands in stark contrast with Peter's uncertain response. Peter's slowness to believe only highlights his eagerness to verify the women's report. Though it seems like nonsense to the others, he runs to the tomb in hope of finding some confirmation. Later Luke will allude to an appearance of the Lord to Peter, when every shadow of doubt will flee. At this point, however, Peter still lives in the pre-dawn of anticipation.

Our own encounter with the Lord is often characterized by this same playful tease. As Jesus leads us to belief in greater wonders, he begins with hints and tokens. In this way, he means to elicit from us an ever more ardent desire to find him in faith. He wants us to run after him and leave behind those who reckon his power as nonsense.

Father, lead me to deeper faith. Help me to understand the clues you leave in a ready response of belief. May my heart run after you in awe at the wonder of your power.

Evangelical Eavesdropping

Father Anthony Giambrone, O.P.

*Now that very day two of [the disciples] were going to a village
seven miles from Jerusalem called Emmaus, and they were
conversing about all the things that had occurred. And it
happened that while they were conversing and debating,
Jesus himself drew near and walked with them, but their eyes
were prevented from recognizing him.* (Lk 24:13-16)

Tom Sawyer famously attended his own funeral; and it is
hard to blame his interest in knowing what people would
say. There is a touch of the same mischievous playfulness
here on Easter morning, as Jesus saunters along with his disciples,
eavesdropping incognito. For Tom, Huck, and Joe, of course, the
attraction in playing dead was having their legacy as delinquents
rewritten in more flattering terms. Jesus' aim is less puerile. His
hope is not a truant's plot to see sad faces and manipulate a more
welcome reception; it is the divine physician's need to see *unguarded hearts*, to reach the core of his disciples' disbelief with the
grace of his living presence.

The Lord consciously catches the disciples in animated discussion. Their failure to recognize him reveals the mysterious quality
of his resurrected body, but this strange blindness is not uncon-
nected to the turmoil and misunderstanding that still clouds their
debating minds. They cannot yet recognize him because they *cannot yet understand* "all the things that had occurred." The eyes of
the body and the eyes of the spirit are not yet one in the purity of
faith; and it is this discrepancy of double vision that the light of the
Lord's Resurrection comes to cure.

Our own vision of the world is too often crippled by this same
malady of heart and mind, so that, like these two on the road to
Emmaus, we are prevented from seeing the living, abiding presence of the risen Christ beside us. As the Letter to the Hebrews
says, though, all things are naked before him—starting with our
confused and clouded hearts. For this reason, the living and effective Word of God comes himself to converse with us, to penetrate
the thoughts of our minds, and, as a surgeon's scalpel, remove all
the inner doubts which prevent our eyes from seeing.

*Loving Father, lower my guard and reveal what I'm really think-
ing. Listen to the doubts of my heart. Send your Word into my
mind that you might direct it. Guide my thoughts until I see you
face to face.*

Living under a Rock

Father Anthony Giambrone, O.P.

[Jesus] asked [the two disciples], "What are you discussing as you walk along?" They stopped, looking downcast. One of them, named Cleopas, said to him in reply, "Are you the only visitor to Jerusalem who does not know of the things that have taken place there in these days?" And he replied to them, "What sort of things?" (Lk 24:17-19a)

One of the peculiar joys of religious life is being unplugged from the twenty-four hour news cycle. The effect is a sense of serene freedom and the occasional experience of being taken for an unfortunate imbecile. I recall recently confessing my utter ignorance about some raging news story and being stared at with undisguised wonderment and horror.

The whole, unfolding story of Jesus' death has for days so fixated and consumed the energies of Cleopas (most likely Clopas, husband of Mary, brother of Joseph, uncle of the Lord) and his companion that they are unable to imagine someone unaffected (hence unperturbed) by this latest news. So preoccupied are these two disciples with the events of the Passion that they cannot so much as conceive of people even *discussing* another topic. Their answer to Jesus' initial question supposes that no one could be talking about anything else. There is only one subject of discussion.

In this context, Jesus confronts the two as an outsider, someone somehow *undisturbed* by the horrible tragedy "everyone" has been watching. The serenity of his demeanor is not a show, however; he never says he does not know the things that have transpired. Instead, the Lord's calm comes from his perfect familiarity and profound understanding of the events—an understanding of God's plan that he will soon disclose, transforming their agitation to adoration.

Often enough, especially in these times, our hearts are troubled by wave after wave of distressing news—personal or in the world. The risen Lord wants to teach us that he is our rock of refuge, with whom we can be serene. Our anxious doubt and confusion will begin to melt away if only we let the Lord wean us from our own efforts at news analysis. But first we must let his questions guide and startle us with their sovereign unconcern.

Father, take control of my preoccupations. Save me from being prematurely disturbed. Shatter my unhealthy fixations, and steady me with the rock of your presence.

Resurrecting Hope

Father Anthony Giambrone, O.P.

*[The two disciples] said to [Jesus], "The things that happened
to Jesus the Nazarene, who was a prophet mighty in deed and
word before God and all the people, how our chief priests and
rulers both handed him over to a sentence of death and crucified
him. But we were hoping that he would be the one to redeem
Israel; and besides all this, it is now the third day
since this took place." (Lk 24:19b-21)*

"O disciples, you 'were hoping,' therefore you do not now hope. Behold *Christ lives*, but *your hope within you is dead*." So does Saint Augustine chide the two disciples and show the irony of this scene. The sentence of death passed on Jesus has done greater damage to their trusting spirits than it has harmed the crucified Lord. In a real sense, the verdict handed down by the chief priests and rulers convicts the disciples more than Jesus.

The one these two call a mighty prophet has met the fate of all the prophets: a fate that in Israel's history betokened exile and slavery for the people. The pair of pilgrims do not comprehend that rejecting this particular prophet has finally poured forth the redeeming blood of the prophesied new covenant. This is where their despair signals a deadly lack of Christian imagination. This prophet is not like the others, for he is truly the Son of God.

If all seems lost, however, a spark of hope still smolders. Jesus' word of prophecy still sounds weakly in their hearts. "It is now the third day." It is the day foretold, the day of limitless expectation and promise of rising from the dead. True, the news the two have heard this morning should have fanned their hope to flame, but it is enough. The word of the Lord abides in their hearts like a tiny seed, a faint echo, a glimmer of light. "They will kill him, but on the third day he will rise" (Lk 18:33). From the death of black despair their hope will come rolling back to life like Lazarus from the tomb.

The voice of Christ can call forth hope, breathing Spirit on the embers of our dying trust. One scrap of faith suffices to fuel a burning heart. May the sure promises of Christ never be extinguished within us. In our moments of despair may we think to say, "It is now the third day."

Father in heaven, let the words of your Son resound in my heart in those moments when I am dying of despair. Help me to recognize today as the time of your rising and open my heart to the grace of new hope.

When Jesus Goes AWOL

Father Anthony Giambrone, o.p.

"Some women from our group, however, have astounded us: they were at the tomb early in the morning and did not find his body; they came back and reported that they had indeed seen a vision of angels who announced that he was alive. Then some of those with us went to the tomb and found things just as the women had described, but him they did not see."
(Lk 24:22-24)

If Jesus is risen, where is he? Why is he not there at the grave? It is an interesting conundrum posed by Cleopas' story. Christ is risen, but no one has seen him. Death has no writ of *habeas corpus*. The Lord's crucified body is not lawfully held in the tomb. But now everyone is helplessly hunting. "They have taken my Lord, and I don't know where they laid him" (Jn 20:13). Is he off in a booth changing into gardener's clothes? Is he consulting maps to Emmaus? What would be the first priority of the risen Lord?

Cleopas never names names, but his summary underscores another big question. Where is Mary? Why was the Mother of Jesus not among these "women from our group"? Why doesn't Mary rush to the grave with John and Simon Peter? The Third Joyful Mystery, found only in Luke's Gospel, would seem to hold the key. What Mary pondered in her heart bore fruit on Easter morning. In contemplating Jesus' question, "Why were you looking for me?" Mary began to understand. The Mother of Christ knows that her Son must be about his Father's affairs. Once before he was lost for three days. Her Son has taught not only the doctors, but also his Mother. Mary alone has learned that she need not worry, anxiously looking for him.

Where were Jesus and Mary? Catholic devotion has traditionally understood that on Easter Sunday morning Jesus appeared first to his Mother. Though it is often dismissed as pure pious invention, it is a beautiful and (to my mind) perfectly sound theological impulse. The lesson for our lives is simple. The Lord is never lost. He is only separated from us for some purpose for a time. If we do not see him or cannot find him, if he is absent from our prayer, we must learn with Mary to ponder the pointed question of the Christ child: "Why were you looking for me?"

Father, when I experience the loss of your Son's comforting and joyful presence confirm me in the knowledge that he is still in control. Make my heart wise like Mary's to await him peacefully.

Improving Our Spiritual Heart Rate

Father Anthony Giambrone, O.P.

And [Jesus] said to [the two disciples], "Oh, how foolish you are! How slow of heart to believe all that the prophets spoke! Was it not necessary that the Messiah should suffer these things and enter into his glory?" Then beginning with Moses and all the prophets, he interpreted to them what referred to him in all the scriptures. (Lk 24:25-27)

Hard-heartedness is a common symptom in the Gospels. It is more unusual to hear of *slow-heartedness*. Both maladies come in for a kind of shock therapy ("How foolish you are!"); but there is greater hope of defibrillating a sluggish heart than resuscitating a spirit hard as stone.

The cardiac condition of Cleopas and his companion is a problem cured by Scripture. Jesus offers a remedial course in prophecy to revive the pulse of their lagging faith. It is interesting to see the diagnosis implied in this precise prescription. The Lord does not say, "How slow you are to believe what those women said!" Instead he speaks of the prophets. We might recall the parable of Lazarus and the rich man: "If they will not listen to Moses and the prophets, neither will they be persuaded if someone should rise from the dead" (Lk 16:31). The fundamental illness afflicting the hearts of these pilgrims is not an excessive suspicion of personal testimony. Rather, at a basic level they are not attuned to revelation. They are slow to see what God is doing *now* because they haven't yet seen what he has done. They are unequipped to judge what is true religious witness, because they lack a trained eye to recognize God's authentic signature.

Often enough, we find ourselves in the shoes of these disciples. We are hesitant and uncertain about believing. Events happen in our lives, and we do not know how to piece them all together. "Is God behind this? Is there some other explanation? Would I be gullible to take this as a sign? Perhaps I should wait to see a bit more evidence." The prudent desire to discern well is good—no disease at all. The illness comes when our slowness reveals unfamiliarity with God. But for this, Jesus shows the certain remedy. We must meditate on the glorious plan revealed in all the Scriptures.

Father, quicken my spirit. Enliven my sluggish heart to recognize what you are doing in my life. When you lead me into suffering, give me the grace to be prompt to see in it your plan for my glory.

Going Farther

Father Anthony Giambrone, O.P.

As [the two disciples] approached the village to which they were going, [Jesus] gave the impression that he was going on farther. But they urged him, "Stay with us, for it is nearly evening and the day is almost over." So he went in to stay with them.

(Lk 24:28-29)

Why does Jesus feign to go farther? Perhaps the better question is why the disciples stop so soon? Physically, of course, they have come to their destination. On the other hand, their spiritual journey with the Lord is far from complete. They have experienced the illumination of his words, but Jesus still wishes to bring them along to a place of deeper initiation and more profound intimacy. He wants them to reach that place where the Messiah is not merely spoken of, but seen in his full glory.

This place where the Lord conducts them is obviously not a locale in the neighborhood of Emmaus. Jesus brings them to a spiritual state. His pretense effects charity. He elicits from his traveling companions the offer of hospitality. "Stay with us." It makes little difference that their invitation is self-interested. Their offer of welcome is eased by the deep curiosity this stranger's speech aroused; but this only means that *they truly desire to be with Jesus*. They are hungry to hear more. It is thus Jesus who takes the lead by walking on farther. Although he accepts their invitation, they in fact follow his indication and go on with him finally to reach the reality of the things he spoke of in the Scriptures.

The invitation to host Jesus is the gift and moment of grace that bridges two distinct paths, two different ways of advancing toward God. The disciples have reached the end of the illuminative way; they are now on the brink of divine union. Holy Communion with the risen Lord will soon surpass all their desires of gracious charity. When we likewise desire to cling to Jesus and plumb the mysteries more profoundly, it is happening again that Jesus wants to go on farther. It is the sign that he is ready to take us deeper and pass into a new stage of union.

Father, lead me deeper into the life of your Son. Inspire within me the charity to stay with him. Help me follow him as he leads me farther on the path that leads to you.

"Their eyes were opened"

Father Anthony Giambrone, O.P.

And it happened that, while [Jesus] was with [the two disciples] at table, he took bread, said the blessing, broke it, and gave it to them. With that their eyes were opened and they recognized him, but he vanished from their sight. Then they said to each other, "Were not our hearts burning [within us] while he spoke to us on the way and opened the scriptures to us?" (Lk 24:30-32)

The phrase "their eyes were opened" rings with a major biblical echo. The phrase appears in one other place (Gn 3:7) where (we might recall) the eyes of two other companions partaking of a meal are suddenly and mysteriously opened. Unlike Adam and Eve, however, Cleopas and his friend are not treated to the shameful vision of their own nakedness. Instead, they behold for a moment the very face of God. They suddenly understand, as evening sets, that they have walked with the one who walked in Eden in the cool part of the day. Where our first parents were made to realize that they were certainly *not* "like gods," but were mortal things now "surely doomed to die," a different wisdom here fills those who taste this blessed bread. They gaze upon a glorified humanity—still doomed to die, but risen from the grave. They see the mortal, naked thing, dust to dust, changed and now remade imperishable; they look upon what Saint Paul calls, not the man of earth, but of Spirit.

It seems to be no accident that the Lord answers the prayer "Stay with us" by immediately vanishing. The lesson is important. Bodily vision is too weak to take in all this vision. The resurrected Lord is transformed; his presence is not ruled by a local lump of clay. This is why the promise to be "with you always, until the end of the age" (Mt 28:20) is fulfilled in a way beyond the physical senses in the miracle of the Eucharist. *Visus, tactus, gustus in te fallitur*: "vision, touch, and taste fail in grasping you." It is only the believing heart, the burning heart within us, which can pierce through the veil of appearances and penetrate to the truth.

At every Mass, our eyes are blinded from perceiving the one whose real presence we enjoy. May they be opened in the Spirit each time we taste of the fruit of the Tree of Life.

Father, open my eyes to see, not my shame, but your forgiveness. Remove the scales that blind me, so that each time I taste the Body and Blood of your Son my heart might burn with living faith.

The Joy of (Re-)Discovery

Father Anthony Giambrone, O.P.

So [the two disciples] set out at once and returned to Jerusalem where they found gathered together the eleven and those with them who were saying, "The Lord has truly been raised and has appeared to Simon!" Then the two recounted what had taken place on the way and how he was made known to them in the breaking of the bread. (Lk 24:33-35)

Those of a certain age will recall an animated spot that used to run during Saturday morning cartoons. It was a long-limbed, globular cheese man who lived in the refrigerator and gave diet advice to kids. Misled by this fellow as a little boy, I eventually figured out one night that the fridge light was not in fact operated by an inhabitant of our dairy drawer. Flooded with enthusiasm, I ran down to the basement and breathlessly disclosed my discovery to my dad—and to the gang of men present at his poker party. It seems they already knew.

Experiences in our life of faith often fill us with enthusiasm. Like many Christians—though in an extraordinary fashion—the two disciples in Emmaus have an enormously powerful experience of the risen Lord's presence, and their responsive instinct is instructive. They rush straightaway to the assembly of believers. What do they find? They find that they have not in fact made a new discovery, but wondrously confirmed something already firmly known. They find a rule of faith, an ecclesial confession not bound to the speakers' own experience, but based on the rock of Peter. "The Lord has truly been raised!" This anticipation by the apostolic Church validates in advance the disciples' own story.

The risen Lord does marvelous, individual things with all of us. He shows himself to be living and the source of true enlightenment. He does this by walking with us on our personal paths, accompanying us, to confirm for us in our own experience the deposit of faith handed down once for all. For our part, we are meant to wear out a path from our homes to Jerusalem, connecting the experiences of our personal lives with the Church's common faith, sharing our joy for the edification of other believers, and testing our experience by the judgment of the apostles and saints before us.

Father, grant me the joy to discover in my life the Church's faith in your risen Son. Flood my mind with your light and make the cup of my heart run over with the experience of Jesus' real presence.

Expect Not Less

Father Anthony Giambrone, O.P.

While [the disciples] were still speaking about this, [Jesus] stood in their midst and said to them, "Peace be with you." But they were startled and terrified and thought that they were seeing a ghost. Then he said to them, "Why are you troubled? And why do questions arise in your hearts?" (Lk 24:36-38)

A childhood friend of mine, of the "spiritual but not religious" variety, confesses an un-dogmatic belief that we are "powerful spiritual beings," immortal in some realm of cosmic energy. Ultimately, I think she thinks we'll be ghosts. Post-mortem existence is for her a kind of wraith-like being, living on as a version of our former self, stripped of all bodily substance. It all seems to me just a happy New Age face on the depressing ancient view that we'll groan on as half-human shades. True, we die into light and not into darkness (there is no such thing as judgment for these people); yet still we live on in a spooky world, alien to everything we know. For her, a good half of human life will experience no salvation and not survive. We may be rational animals in this life, but in the world to come we'll drop the messy animal half of our nature. Interestingly enough, she herself feels the *thinness* of her hope and so keeps asking about the Christian afterlife.

As Christians, of course, we believe not simply in the immortality of the soul, but in the resurrection of the *body*. As the disciples here reveal, confronting this truth can be difficult and troubling. They have just confessed that Jesus is alive, yet somehow they are taken unprepared. The transformed body of the risen Lord appears to them as something so spiritual and light that they mistake it for a shadow. Jesus embodies before them the *paradox and mystery of abundant endless life*, the "spiritual body" (*soma pneumatikon*) spoken of by Paul (1 Cor 15:44). This mode of existence is so foreign yet familiar that it leaves the disciples quite startled. What is clear, though, is that *Jesus bears the substantial weight of a better hope*. In confessing our belief that the body tastes eternity, we await something more beyond this life—not less.

Father, put to rest the questions which trouble my heart. Settle me in the hope of abundant life. Let your peace assure me that the way of the cross leads to something greater and not to something less.

Reverent Disbelief

Father Anthony Giambrone, O.P.

"Look at my hands and my feet, that it is I myself. Touch me and see, because a ghost does not have flesh and bones as you can see I have." And as [Jesus] said this, he showed [the disciples] his hands and his feet. While they were still incredulous for joy and were amazed, he asked them, "Have you anything here to eat?" They gave him a piece of baked fish; he took it and ate it in front of them. (Lk 24:39-43)

This is the Sunday doubting Thomas had the bad luck to be away. If his absence has earned him a dubious reputation, it helps his case that Jesus goes through the same drill with all the others. "Look at my hands and my feet… Touch me and see." The risen Lord even goes so far as to prove himself by eating. At least Thomas never required the baked fish test.

Luke is very interested in this probing of Christ's risen body. At the beginning of Acts, in fact, he says that during the forty days before his Ascension, Jesus "presented himself alive to them by many proofs." We can only wonder what else he did to confirm he was really real. What is interesting, however, is the *initiative* that the Lord takes in offering the disciples these many signs. In John's account, for instance, we have the embarrassing sense that Jesus is condescending to Thomas' words of incredulity when he offers him the nail prints in his hands. Luke, by contrast, lets us see a less stubborn type of skepticism ("incredulous for joy"), as well as a more generous readiness on Jesus' part to supply for the weakness of our dumbfounded faith. There is no sense of reproach, and we even get the feeling Jesus has some fun alternately eating fish and walking through walls.

The mystery of the forty days, which begins this Easter evening, is that space of time when the glorified body of the Lord rests awhile with the disciples to let them absorb the Resurrection. In our Christian lives—we who have not seen and yet believe—the mystery of the "proofs" of Christ's bodily Resurrection come (as all the mysteries do) in sacramental signs. We know Jesus' body is real, because we touch him in the Eucharist—and yet like the disciples on Easter night we experience innocent incredulity. Amazed we wonder, "Is it truly he?" confessing, "My Lord and my God."

Father, give me the grace to balance wonder and belief. Help me to stand amazed before the Body and Blood of your Son, ready to bow my mind in worship, accepting the signs he offers to know him with my senses.

"He opened their minds"

Father Anthony Giambrone, o.p.

[Jesus] said to [the disciples], "These are my words that I spoke to you while I was still with you, that everything written about me in the law of Moses and in the prophets and psalms must be fulfilled." Then he opened their minds to understand the scriptures. (Lk 24:44-45)

G.K. Chesterton once said that an open mind is like an open mouth—it is meant to close on something. This is shrewd wisdom for an age of mental mouth-breathers, but it also helps us see what Jesus is doing when he opens the disciples' minds. He prepares them to be *satisfied*. He readies them to feed on the fulfilling Word of God. They have fed his risen body, now he feeds their open minds: "Open wide your mouth that I may fill it." (Ps 81:11).

Of all the authors of Scripture, Luke focuses most clearly on this special grace of opening. Just as the bodily senses of the two on the road had to be suddenly freed, so too the minds of the disciples must now be unlocked by an intervention of the risen Christ. It is clear that we cannot do this for ourselves; it is an action of Jesus, and the simple reason is because of what we are opened to receive. "We have the mind of Christ," Paul tells us (1 Cor 2:16). This is what fills our opened minds: "The fullness of the one who fills all things" (Eph 1:23). To understand the Scriptures is to understand God's plan, hidden from the foundation of the world; it is to have in our tiny head the Wisdom which orders all things sweetly. This is why our meager minds must be pried open by God's grace. They must be made supernaturally capacious, "to comprehend... what is the breadth and length and height and depth, and to know the love of Christ that surpasses knowledge" (Eph 3:18-19).

How can we experience this tremendous grace of openness? Saint Augustine speaks about stretching wide our vessels by stretching our desires. Love alone expands us and swells us with the Spirit. It is charity that teaches us to understand the Scriptures, for the Bible can be plumbed only by the Spirit which first inspired it.

Father, open my understanding. Let me not be conformed to this age, but transformed by the renewal of my mind. Expand me in charity, and sate me with the pages of Scripture, that I may understand the fullness of your plan.

Beginning in Jerusalem

Father Anthony Giambrone, O.P.

And [Jesus] said to [the disciples], "Thus it is written that the Messiah would suffer and rise from the dead on the third day and that repentance, for the forgiveness of sins, would be preached in his name to all the nations, beginning from Jerusalem. You are witnesses of these things." (Lk 24:46-48)

With imperceptible subtlety, Luke has fast-forwarded to the Acts of the Apostles. To put it another way, Luke binds his two volumes together with overlapping material; and we find compressed here what there we find expanded. Forty days of teaching are compacted into the barest mention of opening the disciples' minds (Lk 24:45). With this instruction in place, Jesus now commissions his witnesses, and in the Gospel's last verses we will hear of the promise of the Spirit and finally of the Lord's Ascension (cf. Acts 1:4-9).

"You are witnesses of these things." The disciples have been officially subpoenaed. They not only can testify; *they must*. In Acts it is clear that the disciples themselves will carry the message to the very ends of the earth. "You will be my witnesses in Jerusalem, throughout Judea and Samaria, and to the ends of the earth" (Acts 1:8). This worldwide spread of testimony is not the focus here, however. Rather, the accent is on the mandate to witness *beginning right here in Jerusalem*.

For our faith lives, this has an important implication. Our first commission is to witness *exactly where we are*. Jerusalem for us means our immediate circle of contacts—and we should begin by thinking as small as possible. With whom do we have the most direct contact? That is the place where we must be cautious not to quench the Spirit with excuses, but let the promised gift impel us to give our witness. Jesus does not tell us how. It is enough to know that forgiveness in his name is our message. Such a commission might rightly leave us uneasy and even a little afraid. We can guess in advance where this is going: "No prophet is accepted in his own native place" (Lk 4:24). But Jesus began with his own, and his own received him not—and the disciple is not above his master.

Father, move me by your Spirit. Inspire me with the courage and creativity to preach your Son to all those who are most near to me. Let me never decline the call to serve you as your witness.

Clothed with Christ

Father Anthony Giambrone, O.P.

"And [behold] I am sending the promise of my Father upon you; but stay in the city until you are clothed with power from on high." Then [Jesus] led [the disciples] [out] as far as Bethany, raised his hands, and blessed them. (Lk 24:49-50)

The beginning of religious life is the ritual of vestition. It is a strange (and inefficient) experience to be dressed by another person. When I was clothed in the habit of Saint Dominic, I remember how my lordly sense of dignity was soon deflated when I saw myself in a mirror. My capuche was crooked, my scapular bunched up, and my belt fastened eight inches above my navel. Having subsequently tried on occasion to dress my little nieces and nephew—usually with the result that my sister has to intervene, put the shoes on the right feet, turn the underwear around, and otherwise redo everything—I have learned just how difficult it can be to invest another person.

As we see with little children, the trick is when we squirm, when (for whatever unclear reason) we forcibly resolve not to let ourselves be dressed. How often must parents tell their half-clothed children, "Hold still"? This is precisely the instruction Jesus gives his disciples as he is about to clothe them: "Don't move. Stay in the city until you are clothed." He commands a posture of motionlessness, a passive and pliable attitude, yielding all direction to the Lord, spiritually ready to be outfitted. It is admittedly difficult to maintain this patience. How long might it take? We would rather run around semi-naked.

The idiom of being "clothed with power" is not obvious. It does not mean that the disciples are given conservative, red neckties. It implies nothing so uncomfortable. Rather, to be invested with the Spirit is to have our mortal body slowly put on Jesus' glory (Phil 3:21); and being clothed with Christ is something worth the wait. "In this tent we groan, longing to be further clothed with our heavenly habitation… We do not wish to be unclothed, but further clothed, so that what is mortal may be swallowed up by life" (2 Cor 5:2, 4).

Father, clothe me in Christ. Cover the shame of my sin with the glory of conversion. Adorn me with your Spirit, and always give me the grace to be still and supple to your direction.

Blessing from Zion

Father Anthony Giambrone, O.P.

As [Jesus] blessed [the disciples] he parted from them and was taken up to heaven. They did him homage and then returned to Jerusalem with great joy, and they were continually in the temple praising God. (Lk 24:51-53)

I t happens on occasion that a person's departure fills us with great joy. This is not, however, generally a compliment to the person. Why then do the disciples rejoice after Jesus is taken up to heaven?

In a word, the joy that swells in their hearts is the first fruit of Jesus' blessing. In the Old Testament, the climax of all good things sought in the Psalms is to enjoy the Lord's blessing from Zion: "May the LORD who made heaven and earth/ bless you from Zion." (Ps 134:3). This blessing now given by the Lord comes from the place of God's dwelling, not the temple made by man, but the heavenly Jerusalem. The significance of the Ascension lies precisely in this. Jesus' resurrected humanity has entered the true Holy of Holies to live for ever making intercession for us (Heb 7:25).

Saint Thérèse famously promised to spend her heaven doing good on earth and to let a "shower of roses" fall. She has kept her word, as many faithful know from the favors they have had from her prayers. It is the same for all the saints. We now honor Blessed John Paul II because we have experienced the blessing of his heavenly intercession. Saint Dominic told his brothers, "I will be more use to you after my death." What we see hinted at through the favors bestowed by all the saints is only a shadow of the blessings that come to us through Christ. His divine humanity has now taken its seat at the Father's right hand—plunged into the heart of the Triune God—to become the channel of "every spiritual blessing in the heavens" (Eph 1:3). Thus from the high priestly hands of Jesus falls to us not a shower of roses, but a downpour of divine grace. The joy of this knowledge leads us to worship, to praise God in his temple, the earthly image of the place where Christ is seated now on high.

Father in heaven, you have given us every blessing in the gift of your only Son. May we rejoice to receive through him the promise of your Spirit that we might worship you in fitting and ceaseless praise.

Brief Biographies of Contributors

- **Father Timothy Bellamah, O.P.**, teaches systematic theology at the Pontifical Faculty of the Immaculate Conception in Washington, DC. He is also editor of the *The Thomist* and a member of the Leonine Commission, editors of the works of Saint Thomas Aquinas.

- **Douglas Bushman** is director of the Institute for Pastoral Theology at Ave Maria University. He received his S.T.L. degree from the University of Fribourg, Switzerland.

- **Father Peter John Cameron, O.P.**, is editor-in-chief of MAGNIFICAT and author of *Blessing Prayers: Devotions for Growing In Faith*.

- **Father Gary C. Caster**, a priest of the Diocese of Peoria, IL, currently serves as the Catholic chaplain of Williams College in Massachusetts. He is the author of *Mary, in Her Own Words: The Mother of God in Scripture* and *The Little Way of Lent: Meditations in the Spirit of St. Thérèse of Lisieux*.

- **Father Romanus Cessario, O.P.**, serves as senior editor for MAGNIFICAT and teaches theology at Saint John's Seminary in Boston, MA.

- **Father John Dominic Corbett, O.P.**, teaches fundamental moral theology at the Dominican House of Studies in Washington, DC. He also preaches retreats and gives spiritual direction.

- **Father Lawrence Donohoo** is associate professor of systematic theology at Mount Saint Mary's Seminary in Emmitsburg, MD, and assigned priest for Saint Anthony Shrine/Our Lady of Mount Carmel Parishes.

- **Anthony Esolen** is professor of English at Providence College, a senior editor of *Touchstone Magazine*, and a regular contributor to MAGNIFICAT. He is the translator and editor of Dante's *Divine Comedy* and author of *Ironies of Faith*.

- **J. David Franks** teaches systematic and moral theology at Saint John's Seminary, Boston, MA, and serves as the vice president for mission of the Seminary's Theological Institute for the New Evangelization (TINE).

- **Father Michael Gaudoin-Parker**, a British priest, has been living near Assisi, Italy, for over twenty years. A contemplative lifestyle has permitted him to write articles and books on the Eucharist.

- **Father Anthony Giambrone, O.P.**, is a Dominican priest of the Province of Saint Joseph and a doctoral student in Scripture at the University of Notre Dame.

- **Frances Hogan** is an Irish lay missionary, educator, and author of many books.

- **Father William M. Joensen**, a priest of the Archdiocese of Dubuque, IA, is dean of Campus Spiritual Life at Loras College, where he also teaches philosophy and is spiritual director for seminarians.

■ **Heather King** is a contemplative laywoman and convert who lives in Los Angeles, CA. She is the author of three memoirs and blogs at shirtofflame.blogspot.com.

■ **Father Joseph T. Lienhard, s.j.**, teaches patristic theology at Fordham University and Saint Joseph's Seminary, Yonkers, NY. He is currently translating Saint Augustine's commentaries on the Old Testament.

■ **Monsignor Gregory E. S. Malovetz** is a priest of the Diocese of Metuchen, NJ, and serves as pastor of Saint Charles Borromeo Church in Montgomery Township, NJ.

■ **Father Francis Martin** currently hosts a web site designed to aid priests in their sermon preparation and lay people in acquiring a deeper knowledge of Sacred Scripture (www.frfrancismartin.com).

■ **Regis Martin** is professor of theology at Franciscan University in Steubenville, OH, and the author of half a dozen books, including most recently *Still Point: Loss, Longing, and the Desire for God.*

■ **Andrew Matt** is a member of the MAGNIFICAT editorial team and holds a doctorate in comparative literature. He lives with his wife and two sons in Chester, CT.

■ **Father Fidelis Moscinski, C.F.R.**, is a member of the Franciscan Friars of the Renewal. He currently resides in the Bronx, NY.

■ **Father Vincent Nagle, F.S.C.B.**, is a member of the Missionaries of Saint Charles Borromeo and currently serves in Immaculate Conception Parish in Bir Zeit, Palestinian Authority.

■ **Father George William Rutler** is pastor of the Church of Our Saviour in New York City. His latest book is *Cloud of Witnesses.*

■ **Father Richard G. Smith**, a priest of the Archdiocese of New York, currently serves as pastor of Saint Joachim/Saint John the Evangelist Parish in Beacon, NY.

■ **Father James M. Sullivan, O.P.**, serves as novice master for the Dominican Province of Saint Joseph at Saint Gertrude Priory in Cincinnati, OH.

■ **Father Albert Trudel, O.P.**, is a Dominican friar of the Province of Saint Joseph. He serves at Saint Gertrude Parish as an associate pastor and in the Dominican novitiate as assistant novice master.

■ **Father Richard Veras** is pastor of the Church of Saint Rita in Staten Island, NY, and a regular contributor to MAGNIFICAT. He is author of *Jesus of Israel: Finding Christ in the Old Testament* and *Wisdom for Everyday from the Book of Revelation.*

■ **Father Emmerich Vogt, O.P.**, is a priest of the Western Dominican Province. A former provincial, pastor, and teacher, he currently serves as chaplain to Dominican nuns.

MAGNIFICAT®